Cultures and Organizations

Software of the Mind

GEERT HOFSTEDE AND GERT JAN HOFSTEDE

McGraw·Hill

New York   Chicago   San Francisco   Lisbon   London   Madrid   Mexico City
Milan   New Delhi   San Juan   Seoul   Singapore   Sydney   Toronto

The McGraw-Hill Companies

Library of Congress Cataloging-in-Publication Data

Hofstede, Geert H.
　　Cultures and organizations : software of the mind / Geert Hofstede and Gert Jan Hofstede.
　　　　p.　　cm.
　　Includes index.
　　ISBN 0-07-143959-5
　　　1. Intercultural communication.　　2. Pluralism (Social sciences)　　I. Hofstede, Gert Jan.
　　II. Title.

　　HM1211.H574　　2005
　　306—dc22
　　　　　　　　　　　　　　　　　　　　　　　　　　　　　　2004063164

3 4 5 6 7 8 9 10 11　　DOC/DOC　　0 9 8 7 6 5

ISBN 0-07-143959-5

McGraw-Hill books are available at special quantity discounts to use as premiums and sales promotions, or for use in corporate training programs. For more information, please write to the Director of Special Sales, Professional Publishing, McGraw-Hill, Two Penn Plaza, New York, NY 10121-2298. Or contact your local bookstore.

This book is printed on acid-free paper.

Contents

PART I

Dimensions of National Cultures

Attribute (handwritten annotation)

Ompetencies

PART II

Cultures in Organizations

PART III

Implications

Preface

In the late 1960s Geert accidentally became interested in national cultural differences—and got access to rich data for studying them. His research resulted in the publication in 1980 of a book titled *Culture's Consequences*. It was written for a scholarly readership; it had to be, because it cast doubts on the universal validity of established theories in psychology, organization sociology, and management theory, and it presented the theoretical reasoning, base data, and statistical treatments used to arrive at the conclusions. A 1984 paperback edition of the book left out the base data and the statistics but was otherwise identical to the 1980 hardcover version.

Culture's Consequences appeared at a time when the interest in cultural differences, both between nations and between organizations, was sharply rising, and there was a dearth of empirically supported information on the subject. The book provided such information, but maybe too much of it at once. Many readers evidently only read parts of the message. For example, Geert lost count of the number of people who claimed that he studied the values of IBM (or "Hermes") *managers*. The data used actually were from IBM *employees*, and that, as the book itself showed, makes quite a difference.

In 1991, after having taught the subject to many different audiences and tested his text on various helpful readers, Geert published another book, this time for an intelligent lay readership—the first edition of *Cultures and Organizations: Software of the Mind*. The theme of cultural differences is, of course, not only nor even primarily of interest to social scientists or international business students. It pertains to anyone who meets people from outside his or her own narrow circle, and in the modern world this means virtually everybody. The new book addressed itself to any interested reader. It avoided social scientific jargon where possible and explained it where necessary; a Glossary was added for this purpose. Slightly updated paperback editions appeared in 1994 and 1997.

Since 1991 the worlds of politics, of business, and of ideas have been changing rapidly. At the academic level, Geert's 1980 book has been followed by a large amount of research by others. In 2001 he published a rewritten and updated version of *Culture's Consequences*. Anybody whose purpose is research or academic scrutiny is referred to this source.

The present book updates Geert's message for the intelligent lay reader. It has also been completely rewritten. Geert has asked his son Gert Jan to join him as a coauthor. Gert Jan has current hands-on experience teaching the subject to students and practitioners; in 2002 he published the book *Exploring Culture: Exercises, Stories and Synthetic Cultures*, together with Paul B. Pedersen and Geert.

On a trip around the world several years ago, Geert bought three world maps. All three are the flat kind, projecting the surface of the globe on a plane. The first shows Europe and Africa in the middle, the Americas to the west, and Asia to the east. The terms *the West* and *the East* were products of a Euro-centered worldview. The second map, bought in Hawaii, shows the Pacific Ocean in the center, Asia and Africa on the left (and Europe, tiny, in the far upper left-hand corner), and the Americas to the right. From Hawaii, the East lies west and the West lies east! The third map, bought in New Zealand, was like the second but upside down: south on top and north at the bottom. Now Europe is in the far lower right-hand corner. Which of these maps is right? All three, of course—the Earth is round and any place on the surface is as much the center as any other. All peoples have considered their country the center of the world. The Chinese call China the "Middle Kingdom" (*zhongguo*), and the ancient Scandinavians called their country by a similar name (*midgaard*). We believe that even today most citizens, politicians, and academics in any country in their heart feel that their country is the middle one—and they act correspondingly.

These feelings are so powerful that it is almost always possible, when reading a book, to determine the nationality of the author, even if it has not been mentioned. The same, of course, applies to our work. We are from the Netherlands, and even when we write in English, the Dutch software of our minds will remain evident to the careful reader. This makes reading the book by others than our compatriots a cross-cultural experience in itself, maybe even a culture shock. That is OK. Studying culture without experiencing culture shock is like practicing swimming without water. In *Asterix*, a famous French cartoon, the oldest villager expresses his dislike of visiting foreigners as follows: "I don't have anything against foreigners. Some of my best friends are foreigners. But *these* foreigners are not from here!"

In the booming market for cross-cultural training, there are courses and books that show only the sunny side: cultural synergy, no cultural conflict. Maybe that is the message some business-minded people like to hear, but it is false. Studying culture without culture shock is like listening to only the foreigners who are from here.

In Geert's research the Netherlands scored clearly individualist. In individualist societies, sons are less likely to follow in their fathers' footsteps than in collectivist societies. People from collectivist societies tend to praise Gert Jan for carrying on his father's work. People from individualist societies sometimes speak of the "son of" in a rather derogatory way, indicating the son might not have any ideas of his own. Gert Jan does not worry, for he was an independent academic of forty when he started collaborating with his father when his discipline, information systems, was swept toward intercultural communication by the rise of the World Wide Web. Meanwhile it is true that in this book Gert Jan's contribution is modest. "If it ain't broke, don't fix it." Gert Jan contributed an evolutionary perspective to Chapter 1, some graphics, many discussions, and numerous minor changes.

Geert in 1991 dedicated the first edition to his first grandchildren, the generation to whom the future belongs. In the meantime they have grown up, and we thank Liesbeth Hofstede, Gert Jan's eldest daughter, for contributing to this new edition as our documentation assistant, typing among other things the bibliography.

The first edition appeared in seventeen languages (English with translations into Bulgarian, Chinese, Czech, Danish, Dutch, Finnish, French, German, Japanese, Korean, Norwegian, Polish, Portuguese, Romanian, Spanish, and Swedish). We hope the message of this new version will be distributed as widely.

Introduction: The Rules of the Social Game

11th juror: *(rising)* "I beg pardon, in discussing . . ."

10th juror: *(interrupting and mimicking)* "I beg pardon. What are you so goddam polite about?"

11th juror: *(looking straight at the 10th juror)* "For the same reason you're not. It's the way I was brought up."

—REGINALD ROSE, *Twelve Angry Men*, 1955

welve Angry Men is an American theater piece that became a famous motion picture, starring Henry Fonda. The play was published in 1955. The scene consists of the jury room of a New York court of law. Twelve jury members who had never met before have to decide unanimously on the guilt or innocence of a boy from a slum area who has been accused of murder. The quote just given is from the second and final act when emotions have reached the boiling point. It is a confrontation between the tenth juror, a garage owner, and the eleventh juror, a European-born, probably Austrian, watchmaker. The tenth juror is irritated by what he sees as the excessively polite manners of the other man. But the watchmaker cannot behave otherwise. After many years in his new home country, he still behaves the way he was raised. He carries within himself an indelible pattern of behavior.

Different Minds but Common Problems

The world is full of confrontations between people, groups, and nations who think, feel, and act differently. At the same time, these people, groups, and nations, just like our twelve angry men, are exposed to common problems that demand cooperation for their solution. Ecological, economic, political, military, hygienic, and meteorologic developments do not stop at national or regional borders. Coping with the threats of nuclear warfare, global warming, organized crime, poverty, terrorism, ocean pollution, extinction of animals, AIDS, or a worldwide recession demands cooperation of opinion leaders from many countries. They in turn need the support of broad groups of followers in order to implement the decisions taken.

Understanding the differences in the ways these leaders and their followers think, feel, and act is a condition for bringing about worldwide solutions that work. Questions of economic, technological, medical, or biological cooperation have too often been considered as merely technical. One of the reasons why so many solutions do not work or cannot be implemented is because differences in thinking among the partners have been ignored.

The objective of this book is to help in dealing with the differences in thinking, feeling, and acting of people around the globe. It will show that although the variety in people's minds is enormous, there is a structure in this variety that can serve as a basis for mutual understanding.

Culture as Mental Programming

Every person carries within him- or herself patterns of thinking, feeling, and potential acting that were learned throughout their lifetime. Much of it has been acquired in early childhood, because at that time a person is most susceptible to learning and assimilating. As soon as certain patterns of thinking, feeling, and acting have established themselves within a person's mind, he or she must unlearn these before being able to learn something different, and unlearning is more difficult than learning for the first time.

Using the analogy of the way computers are programmed, this book will call such patterns of thinking, feeling, and acting *mental programs*, or, as per this book's subtitle, *software of the mind*. This does not mean, of course, that people are programmed the way computers are. A person's behavior is only partially predetermined by her or his mental programs: she or he has a basic ability to deviate from them and to react in ways that are new, creative, destructive, or unexpected. The software of the mind that this book is about only indicates what reactions are likely and understandable, given one's past.

The sources of one's mental programs lie within the social environments in which one grew up and collected one's life experiences. The programming starts within the family; it continues within the neighborhood, at school, in youth groups, at the workplace, and in the living community. The European watchmaker from the quote at the beginning of this chapter came from a country and a social class in which polite behavior is still at a premium today. Most people in that environment would have reacted as he did. The American garage owner, who worked his way up from the slums, acquired quite different mental programs. Mental programs vary as much as the social environments in which they were acquired.

A customary term for such mental software is *culture*. This word has several meanings, all derived from its Latin source, which refers to the tilling of the soil. In most Western languages *culture* commonly means "civilization" or "refinement of the mind" and, in particular, the results of such refinement, including education, art, and literature. This is culture in the narrow sense. Culture as mental software, however, corresponds to a much broader use of the word that is common among sociologists and, especially, anthropologists;[1] it is this meaning that will be used throughout this book.

Social (or cultural) anthropology is the science of human societies—in particular (although not only), traditional or "primitive" ones. In social anthropology, *culture* is a catchword for all those patterns of thinking, feeling, and acting referred to in the previous paragraphs. Not only activities supposed to refine the mind are included, but also the ordinary and menial things in life—for example, greeting, eating, showing or not showing feelings, keeping a certain physical distance from others, making love, or maintaining body hygiene.

Culture is always a collective phenomenon, because it is at least partly shared with people who live or lived within the same social environment, which is where it was learned. Culture consists of the unwritten rules of the social game. It is *the collective programming of the mind that distinguishes the members of one group or category[2] of people from others.*[3]

Culture is learned, not innate. It derives from one's social environment rather than from one's genes. Culture should be distinguished from human nature on one side and from an individual's personality on the other (see Figure 1.1), although exactly where the borders lie between nature and culture, and between culture and personality, is a matter of discussion among social scientists.[4]

Human nature is what all human beings, from the Russian professor to the Australian Aborigine, have in common: it represents the universal level in one's mental software. It is inherited within one's genes; again using the computer analogy, it is the "operating system" that determines one's phys-

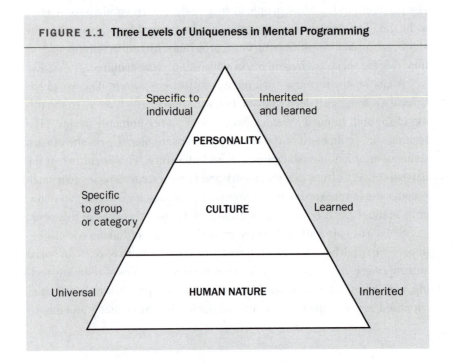

FIGURE 1.1 Three Levels of Uniqueness in Mental Programming

ical and basic psychological functioning. The human ability to feel fear, anger, love, joy, sadness, shame; the need to associate with others and to play and exercise oneself; and the facility to observe the environment and to talk about it with other humans all belong to this level of mental programming. However, what one does with these feelings, how one expresses fear, joy, observations, and so on, is modified by culture.

The *personality* of an individual, on the other hand, is her or his unique personal set of mental programs that needn't be shared with any other human being. It is based on traits that are partly inherited within the individual's unique set of genes and partly learned. *Learned* means modified by the influence of collective programming (culture) as well as by unique personal experiences.

Cultural traits have often been attributed to heredity, because philosophers and other scholars in the past did not know how to otherwise explain the remarkable stability of differences in culture patterns among human groups. They underestimated the impact of learning from previous generations and of teaching to a future generation what one has learned oneself. The role of heredity is exaggerated in pseudotheories of race, which have been responsible for, among other things, the Holocaust organized by the Nazis during World War II. Ethnic strife is often justified by unfounded arguments of cultural superiority and inferiority.

In the United States there have been periodic scientific discussions on whether certain ethnic groups (in particular, blacks) could be genetically less intelligent than others (in particular, whites).[5] The arguments used for genetic differences, by the way, make Asians in the United States on average *more* intelligent than whites. It is extremely difficult if not impossible, however, to find tests of intelligence that are culture free. Such tests should reflect only innate abilities and be insensitive to differences in the social environment. In the United States a larger share of blacks than of whites has grown up in socially disadvantaged circumstances, which is a cultural influence no test known to us can circumvent. The same logic applies to differences in intelligence between ethnic groups in other countries.

Cultural Relativism

In daily conversations, in political discourse, and in the media that feed them, alien cultures are often pictured in moral terms, as better or worse.

Yet there are no scientific standards for considering the ways of thinking, feeling, and acting of one group as intrinsically superior or inferior to those of another.

Studying differences in culture among groups and societies presupposes a neutral vantage point, a position of cultural relativism. A great French anthropologist, Claude Lévi-Strauss (born 1908), has expressed it as follows:

> *Cultural relativism affirms that one culture has no absolute criteria for judging the activities of another culture as "low" or "noble." However, every culture can and should apply such judgment to its own activities, because its members are actors as well as observers.*[6]

Cultural relativism does not imply normlessness for oneself, nor for one's society. It does call for suspending judgment when dealing with groups or societies different from one's own. One should think twice before applying the norms of one person, group, or society to another. Information about the nature of the cultural differences between societies, their roots, and their consequences should precede judgment and action.

Even after having been informed, the foreign observer is still likely to deplore certain ways of the other society. If professionally involved in the other society—for example, as an expatriate manager or development cooperation expert—she or he may very well want to induce changes. In colonial days foreigners often wielded absolute power in other societies, and they could impose their rules on it. In these postcolonial days foreigners who want to change something in another society will have to negotiate their interventions. Negotiation again is more likely to succeed when the parties concerned understand the reasons for the differences in viewpoints.

Symbols, Heroes, Rituals, and Values

Cultural differences manifest themselves in several ways. From the many terms used to describe manifestations of culture, the following four together cover the total concept rather neatly: symbols, heroes, rituals, and values. Figure 1.2 depicts these terms as the skins of an onion: symbols represent the most superficial and values the deepest manifestations of culture, with heroes and rituals in between.

FIGURE 1.2 The "Onion": Manifestations of Culture at Different Levels of Depth

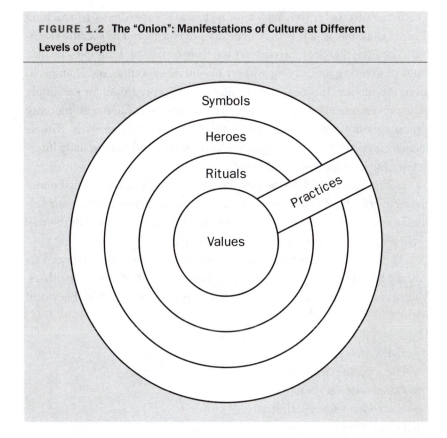

Symbols are words, gestures, pictures, or objects that carry a particular meaning only recognized as such by those who share the culture. The words in a language or jargon belong to this category, as do dress, hairstyles, flags, and status symbols. New symbols are easily developed and old ones disappear; symbols from one cultural group are regularly copied by others. This is why symbols have been put into the outermost (superficial) layer of Figure 1.2.

Heroes are persons, alive or dead, real or imaginary, who possess characteristics that are highly prized in a culture and thus serve as models for behavior. Even Barbie, Batman, or, as a contrast, Snoopy in the United States, Asterix in France, or Ollie B. Bommel (Mr. Bumble) in the Netherlands have served as cultural heroes. In this age of television, outward appearances have become more important than they were before in the choice of heroes.

Rituals are collective activities, technically superfluous to reaching desired ends, but which within a culture are considered as socially essential. They are therefore carried out for their own sake. Examples include ways of greeting and paying respect to others, as well as social and religious ceremonies. Business and political meetings organized for seemingly rational reasons often serve mainly ritual purposes, such as reinforcing group cohesion or allowing the leaders to assert themselves. Rituals include *discourse*, the way language is used in text and talk, in daily interaction, and in communicating beliefs.[7]

In Figure 1.2 symbols, heroes, and rituals have been subsumed under the term *practices*. As such they are visible to an outside observer; their cultural meaning, however, is invisible and lies precisely and only in the way these practices are interpreted by the insiders.

The core of culture according to Figure 1.2 is formed by *values*. Values are broad tendencies to prefer certain states of affairs over others. Values are feelings with an arrow to it: a plus and a minus side. They deal with:

- Evil versus good
- Dirty versus clean
- Dangerous versus safe
- Forbidden versus permitted
- Decent versus indecent
- Moral versus immoral
- Ugly versus beautiful
- Unnatural versus natural
- Abnormal versus normal
- Paradoxical versus logical
- Irrational versus rational

Values are acquired early in our lives. Contrary to most animals, humans at birth are incompletely equipped for life. Fortunately our human physiology provides us with a receptive period of some ten to twelve years, a period in which we can quickly and largely unconsciously absorb necessary information from our environment. This includes symbols (such as language), heroes (such as our parents), and rituals (such as toilet training), and most importantly it includes our basic values. At the end of this period, we gradually switch to a different, conscious way of learning, focusing primarily on new practices. The process is pictured in Figure 1.3.

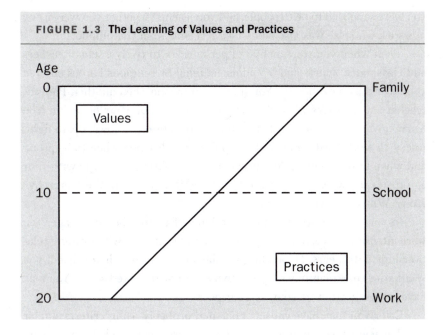

FIGURE 1.3 The Learning of Values and Practices

Culture Reproduces Itself

Remember being a small child. How did you acquire your values? The first years are gone from your memory, but they are influential. Did you move about on your mother's hip or on her back all day? Did you sleep with her or with your siblings? Or were you kept in your own cot, pram, or crib? Did both your parents handle you, or only your mother, or other persons? Was there noise or silence around you? Did you see taciturn people, laughing ones, playing ones, working ones, tender or violent ones? What happened when you cried?

Then, memories begin. Who were your models, and what was your aim in life? Quite probably, your parents or elder siblings were your heroes and you tried to imitate them. You learned which things were dirty and bad and how to be clean and good. For instance, you learned rules about what is clean and dirty about bodily functions including spitting, eating with your left hand, blowing your nose, defecating, or belching in public and about gestures such as touching various parts of your body or exposing them while sitting or standing. You learned how bad it was to break rules. You learned how much initiative you were supposed to take and how close you were supposed to be to people, and you learned whether you were a boy or a girl, who else was also a boy or a girl, and what that implied.

Then when you were a child of perhaps six to twelve, schoolteachers and classmates, sports and TV idols, national or religious heroes entered your world as new models. You imitated now one, then another. Parents, teachers, and others rewarded or punished you for your behavior. You learned whether it was good or bad to ask questions, to speak up, to fight, to cry, to work hard, to lie, to be impolite. You learned when to be proud and when to be ashamed. You also exercised politics, especially with your age-mates: How to make friends? Is it possible to rise in the hierarchy? How? Who owes what to whom?

In your teenage years, your attention shifted to others your age. You were intensely concerned with your gender identity and with forming relationships with peers. Depending on the society in which you lived, you spent your time mainly with your own sex or with mixed sexes. You may have intensely admired some of your peers.

Later you may have chosen a partner, probably using criteria similar to other young people in your country. You may have had children—and then the cycle starts again.

There is a powerful stabilizing force in this cycle that biologists call *homeostasis*. Parents tend to reproduce the education that they received, whether they want to or not. And there is only a modest role for technology. The most salient learning in your tender years is all about the body and about relationships with people. Not coincidentally, these are also sources of intense taboos.

Because they were acquired so early in our lives, many values remain unconscious to those who hold them. Therefore they cannot be discussed, nor can they be directly observed by outsiders. They can only be inferred from the way people act under various circumstances. If one asks why they act as they do, people may say they just "know" or "feel" how to do the right thing. Their heart or their conscience tells them.

Layers of Culture

Every group or category of people carries a set of common mental programs that constitutes its culture. As almost everyone belongs to a number of different groups and categories at the same time, we unavoidably carry several layers of mental programming within ourselves, corresponding to different levels of culture. In particular:

- A national level, according to one's country (or countries for people who migrated during their lifetime)
- A regional and/or ethnic and/or religious and/or linguistic affiliation level, as most nations are composed of culturally different regional and/or ethnic and/or religious and/or language groups
- A gender level, according to whether a person was born as a girl or as a boy
- A generation level, separating grandparents from parents from children
- A social class level, associated with educational opportunities and with a person's occupation or profession
- For those who are employed, organizational, departmental, and/or corporate levels, according to the way employees have been socialized by their work organization

The mental programs from these various levels are not necessarily in harmony. In modern society they are often partly conflicting; for example, religious values may conflict with generation values or gender values with organizational practices. Conflicting mental programs within people make it difficult to anticipate their behavior in a new situation.

Culture Change: Changing Practices, Stable Values

If you could step into a time machine and travel back fifty years to the time of your parents or grandparents, you would find the world much changed. There would be no computers and television would be quite new. The cities would appear small and provincial, with only the occasional car and few big retail chain outlets. Travel back another fifty years and cars disappear from the streets, as do telephones, washing machines, and vacuum cleaners from our houses and airplanes from the air.

Our world is changing. Technology invented by people surrounds us. The World Wide Web has made our world appear smaller, so that the notion of a "global village" seems appropriate. Business companies operate worldwide. They innovate rapidly; many do not know today what products they will manufacture and sell next year or what new job types they will need in five years. Mergers and stock market fluctuations shake the business landscape.

So on the surface, change is all-powerful. But how deep are these changes? Can human societies be likened to ships that are rocked about aimlessly on turbulent seas of change? Or to shores, covered and then bared again by new waves washing in, altered ever so slowly with each successive tide?

A book by a Frenchman about his visit to the United States contains the following text:

> The American ministers of the Gospel do not attempt to draw or to fix all the thoughts of man upon the life to come; they are willing to surrender a portion of his heart to the cares of the present. . . . If they take no part themselves in productive labor, they are at least interested in its progress, and they applaud its results. . . .

The author, we might think, is referring to U.S. TV evangelists. In fact, he was Alexis de Tocqueville and his book appeared in 1835.[8]

Recorded comments by visitors from one country to another are a rich source of information on how national culture differences were perceived in the past, and they often look strikingly modern, even if they date from centuries ago.

There are many things in societies that technology and its products do not change. If young Turks drink Coca-Cola, this does not necessarily affect their attitudes toward authority. In some respects young Turks differ from old Turks, just as young Americans differ from old Americans. In the "onion" model of Figure 1.2, such differences mostly involve the relatively superficial spheres of symbols and heroes, of fashion and consumption. In the sphere of values—that is, fundamental feelings about life and about other people—young Turks differ from young Americans just as much as old Turks differ from old Americans. There is no evidence that the values of present-day generations from different countries are converging.

Culture change can be fast for the outer layers of the onion diagram, labeled *practices*. Practices are the visible part of cultures. New practices can be learned throughout our lifetime; people older than seventy happily learn to surf the Web on their first personal computer, acquiring new symbols, meeting new heroes, and communicating through new rituals. Culture change is slow for the onion's core, labeled *values*. As already argued, these were learned when we were children, from parents who acquired them when *they* were children. This makes for considerable stability in the basic values of a society, in spite of sweeping changes in practices.

These basic values affect primarily the gender, the national, and maybe the regional layer of culture. Never believe politicians, religious leaders, or business chiefs who claim they will reform national values. These should be considered given facts, as hard as a country's geographic position or its weather. Layers of culture acquired later in life tend to be more changeable. This is the case, in particular, for organizational cultures that the organization's members joined as adults. It doesn't mean that changing organizational cultures is easy—as will be shown in Chapter 8—but at least it is feasible.

There is no doubt that dazzling technological changes are taking place that affect all but the poorest or remotest of people. But people put these new technologies to familiar uses. Many of them are used to doing much the same things as our grandparents did, to make money, to impress other people, to make life easier, to coerce others, or to seduce potential partners. All these activities are part of the social game. We are attentive to how other people use technology, what clothes they wear, what jokes they make, what food they eat, how they spend their vacations. And we have a fine antenna that tells us what choices to make ourselves if we wish to belong to a particular social circle.

The social game itself is not deeply changed by the changes in today's society. The unwritten rules for success, failure, belonging, and other key attributes of our lives remain similar. We need to fit in, to behave in ways that are acceptable to the groups we belong to. Most changes concern the toys we use in playing the game.

Prehistory of Culture

How old is the social game itself? Millions of years. Modern humans (*Homo sapiens*) have existed for more than 100,000 years. It is estimated that by the end of the next-to-last ice age (c. 130,000 B.C.), some ten thousand to fifty thousand of them existed worldwide—that is, in Africa.

Around five million years earlier, their ancestors separated from those of today's chimpanzees and bonobos, our closest relatives. Students of animal behavior have convincingly demonstrated that these apes possess all the important characteristics of culture, notably notions of "good" and "bad" behavior that we call values.[9] Each social group has its own version of important social rituals, such as grooming or food sharing. Group members spend amazing amounts of time together performing these rituals, and closer studies reveal that stable relations exist between individuals. Each group possesses its own forms of technological expertise (for example, using stones to crack palm nuts or sticks to collect termites). These rituals and capabilities are passed on through social learning or, if you will, aping. Chimpanzees also have finely calibrated mental models of who owes what to whom when it comes to food sharing.

There is a remarkable difference between the societies of chimpanzees and bonobos. The two species have a common ancestry. They are so similar in appearance that bonobos have long been taken for another subspecies of chimpanzee. But whereas chimpanzees are hunter-gatherer societies dominated by political coalitions of males with a good deal of endemic violence, bonobos are vegetarian groups with female bonding in which the male leaders are much less dominant and social tensions are resolved not through violence but through erotic activity. Chimps are from Mars, while bonobos are from Venus.

These primates, immensely less intelligent than we are, possess social units with distinctive cultures. Why? Population exchanges occur all the time. In the case of chimpanzees, adolescent females switch social groups, ensuring that genetic diversity is maintained. But usually these migrants do not take their practices with them. Instead, they adapt to the culture of the receiving group in order to fit in. So while the females' transfer guarantees genetic crossover, it does not do so for cultural crossover. The rituals and practices of each group effectively serve as a way to maintain group identity.

At the same time, chimpanzee and bonobo cultures do change—how else could the two species have grown so widely apart, or how could each chimpanzee colony have its own practices? But cultural change among them has been slow. There are social forces that inhibit cultural change in favor of the status quo. Group cultures can perpetuate themselves.

Early humans also lived as hunter-gatherers, in analogy to chimpanzees and bonobos. Only they were much quicker of wit. They mastered fire and developed elaborate hunting tools. They also developed an intricate information society with complex symbolic language. This enabled them to communicate about the movements of animals and the properties of plants and to discuss hunting stratagems. Around 100,000 B.C. they started to migrate across the globe. Modern DNA research has enabled geneticists to trace the various moves, from Africa to central Asia and from there to Europe, Australia, and finally the Americas.[10] By the end of the last ice age, around 10,000 B.C., humans were present on all continents. From about this time, archaeological findings afford a much clearer picture of our prehistory. Burial sites of hunter-gatherers, as well as cave paintings, show a remarkable variety in styles and arrangements. There were obviously many different cultures in the ice-age world.

In the centuries from 10,000 until 5000 B.C., with a milder climate, population sizes increased, leading to depletion of wild resources. In various parts of the world, people responded by starting to manipulate the environment through resowing wild grains (for example, wheat and barley in Asia Minor, rice along the Yangtze River) and herding wild animals (for example, sheep and goats in the Mediterranean, cattle in Europe, horses in central Asia). Thus agriculture was invented. It led to a social revolution. Social units were no longer restricted to small bands of hunter-gatherers with limited hierarchy and flexible division of labor. Much higher concentrations of people could now live together. Stores of food could be made. Specialization of labor and concentration of knowledge and power became possible, as did large-scale wars. All the main attributes of today's human societies were present by that time.[11]

From about 3000 B.C., prehistory starts to change into history as written accounts have come down to us. In fertile areas of the world large empires were built, usually because the rulers of one part succeeded in conquering other parts. The oldest empire in existence within living memory is China. Although it has not always been unified, the Chinese Empire possesses a continuous history of about four thousand years. Other empires disintegrated. In the eastern Mediterranean and southwestern part of Asia, empires grew, flourished, and fell, only to be succeeded by others: the Sumerian, Babylonian, Assyrian, Egyptian, Persian, Greek, Roman, and Turkish empires, to mention only a few. The South Asian subcontinent and the Indonesian archipelago had their empires, for instance, the Maurya, the Gupta, and later the Mughal in India and the Majapahit on Java. In Central and South America the Aztec, Maya, and Inca empires have left their monuments. And in Africa, Ethiopia and Benin are examples of ancient states.

Next to and often within the territory of these larger empires, smaller units survived in the form of independent small "kingdoms" or tribes. Even now, in New Guinea most of the population lives in small and relatively isolated tribes, each with its own language and hardly integrated into the larger society.

In social life, including economic processes, few things are invented from scratch. Multinational companies existed as early as 2000 B.C.; the Assyrians, Phoenicians, Greeks, and Romans all had their own versions of globalized business.[12]

The cultural diversity among our ancestors has been inherited by the present generation. National and regional culture differences today still partly reflect the borders of the former empires. In the coming chapters it will be shown how Latin cultures still hold common traits derived from the Roman Empire and how Chinese cultures reflect the inheritance of the Chinese Empire.

From this brief sweep through history we can conclude that the intricate social game that makes us cultural beings is very, very ancient indeed.

Sources of Cultural Diversity and Change

The present world shows an amazing variety of cultures, both in terms of values and in terms of practices. If all humankind descends from common ancestors, and if cultures seek continuity, what forces were responsible for diversifying our ancestors' cultures so much? Recognizing these will also help us predict future changes.

Culture changes have been brought about, and will continue to be brought about, by major impacts of forces of nature and forces of humans.

The first reason for cultural diversity has been adaptation to new natural environments. As humankind gradually populated almost the entire world, the very need for survival led to different cultural solutions. For example, Chapter 2 will show that societies in cooler climates tended to develop greater equality among their members than did societies in tropical climates.

Collective migrations to different environments were often forced by famines, owing to climate changes (like desertification), to overpopulation, or to political mismanagement (as by the British rulers of Ireland in the nineteenth century). Natural disasters, such as earthquakes and floods, have sometimes wiped out entire societies and created new opportunities for others.

Archaeological finds have proven that trade between different cultures has existed as long as the cultures themselves. Traders transferred not only foreign goods but also new habits and technologies.

Military conquest has drastically changed cultures by killing, moving, and mixing populations and imposing new lords and new rules. Chapters 2 through 6 will show repeated evidence of the lengthening cultural shadows of the Roman and Chinese Empires.

Missionary zeal converting people to new religions has also changed cultures. If we trace the religious history of countries, however, what religion a population has embraced and which version of that religion seem to have been a *result* of previously existing cultural value patterns as much as, or more than, a *cause* of cultural differences. The great religions of the world, at some time in their history, have all undergone profound schisms: between Roman Catholics, Eastern Orthodox, and various Protestant groups in Christianity; between Sunni and Shia in Islam; between liberals and various fundamentalist groups in Jewry; between Hinayana and Mahayana in Buddhism. Preexisting cultural differences among groups of believers played a major role in these schisms. For example, the Reformation movement within the Roman Catholic Church in the sixteenth century initially affected all of Europe. However, in countries that more than a thousand years earlier had belonged to the Roman Empire, a Counter-Reformation reinstated the authority of the Roman church. In the end the Reformation only succeeded in countries without a Roman tradition. Although today most of northern Europe is Protestant and most of southern Europe Roman Catholic, what is at the origin of the cultural differences is not this religious split but the inheritance of the Roman Empire. Religious affiliation by itself is therefore less culturally relevant than is often assumed.[13] This does not exclude that once a religion has settled, it does reinforce the culture patterns on the basis of which it was adopted, by making these into core elements in its teachings.

Scientific discoveries and innovations, whether native or imported from outside, as previously argued, tend to affect the practices more than the social games. Some, like the invention of agriculture, were so fundamental that they did change entire cultures, including their values.

Nearly all of these changes affect more than one society; some are truly global. When cultures change together because of a common cause, the differences between them often remain intact. This is why observations by de Tocqueville and other travelers of past centuries can still sound so modern.

National Culture Differences

The invention of *nations*, political units into which the entire world is divided and to one of which every human being is supposed to belong—as manifested by her or his passport—is a recent phenomenon in human history. Earlier there were states, but not everybody belonged to or identified with one of these. The nation system was only introduced worldwide in the mid-twentieth century. It followed the colonial system that had developed during the preceding three centuries. In this colonial period the technologically advanced countries of western Europe divided among themselves virtually all territories of the globe that were not held by another strong political power. The borders between the former colonial nations still reflect the colonial legacy. In Africa in particular, most national borders correspond to the logic of the colonial powers rather than to the cultural dividing lines of the local populations.

Nations, therefore, should not be equated with *societies*, which are historically, organically developed forms of social organization. Strictly speaking, the concept of a common culture applies to societies, not to nations. Nevertheless, many nations do form historically developed wholes even if they consist of clearly different groups and even if they contain less integrated minorities.

Within nations that have existed for some time there are strong forces toward further integration: (usually) one dominant national language, common mass media, a national education system, a national army, a national political system, national representation in sports events with a strong symbolic and emotional appeal, a national market for certain skills, products, and services. Today's nations do not attain the degree of internal homogeneity of the isolated, usually nonliterate societies studied by field anthropologists, but they are the source of a considerable amount of common mental programming of their citizens.[14]

On the other hand, there remains a tendency for ethnic, linguistic, and religious groups to fight for recognition of their own identity, if not for national independence; this tendency has been increasing rather than decreasing since the 1960s. Examples are the Ulster Roman Catholics; the Belgian Flemish; the Basques in Spain and France; the Kurds in Iran, Iraq, Syria, and Turkey; the ethnic groups of the former Yugoslavia; the Hutu and Tutsi tribes in Rwanda; and the Chechens in Russia.

In research on cultural differences, nationality—the passport one holds—should therefore be used with care. Yet it is often the only feasible criterion for classification. Rightly or wrongly, collective properties are ascribed to the citizens of certain countries: people refer to "typically American," "typically German," "typically Japanese" behavior. Using nationality as a criterion is a matter of expediency, because it is immensely easier to obtain data for nations than for organic homogeneous societies. Nations as political bodies supply all kinds of statistics about their populations. Survey data (that is, the answers people give on paper-and-pencil questionnaires related to their culture) are also mostly collected through national networks. Where it *is* possible to separate results by region, ethnic, or linguistic group, this should be done.

A strong reason for collecting data at the level of nations is that one of the purposes of cross-cultural research is to promote cooperation among nations. As argued at the beginning of this chapter, the (more than two hundred) nations that exist today populate one single world, and we either survive or perish together. So it makes practical sense to focus on cultural factors separating or uniting nations.

National Cultures or National Institutions?

Different countries have different institutions: governments, laws and legal systems, associations, enterprises, religious communities, school systems, family structures. Some people, including quite a few sociologists and economists, believe these are the true reasons for differences in thinking, feeling, and acting between countries. If we can explain such differences by institutions that are clearly visible, do we really need to speculate about cultures as invisible mental programs?

The answer to this question was given more than two centuries ago by a French nobleman, Charles-Louis de Montesquieu (1689–1755), in *De l'esprit des lois (The Spirit of the Laws)*.

Montesquieu argued that there is such a thing as "the general spirit of a nation" (what we now would call its culture) and that "[t]he legislator should follow the spirit of the nation . . . for we do nothing better than what we do freely and by following our natural genius."[15] Thus institutions follow mental programs, and in the way they function they adapt to local culture. Similar laws work out differently in different countries, as the

European Union has experienced on many occasions. In their turn institutions that have grown within a culture perpetuate the mental programming on which they were founded. Institutions cannot be understood without considering culture, and understanding culture presumes insight into institutions. Reducing explanations to either one or the other is sterile.

An important consequence of this is that we cannot change the way people in a country think, feel, and act by simply importing foreign institutions. After the demise of communism in the former Soviet Union and other parts of Eastern Europe, some economists thought that all the former communist countries needed was capitalist institutions, U.S. style, in order to find the road to wealth. Things did not work out that way. Each country has to struggle through its own type of reforms, adapted to the software of the minds of its people. Globalization by multinational corporations and supranational institutions such as the World Bank meets fierce local resistance because economic systems are not culture free.

What About National *Management* Cultures?

The business and business school literature often refers to national "management" or "leadership" cultures. Management and leadership, however, cannot be isolated from other parts of society. U.S. anthropologist Marvin Harris has warned that "one point anthropologists have always made is that aspects of social life which do not seem to be related to another, actually are related."[16]

Managers and leaders, as well as the people they work with, are part of national societies. If we want to understand their behavior, we have to understand their societies—for example, what types of personalities are common in their country, how families function and what this means for the way children are brought up, how the school system works and who goes to what type of school, how the government and the political system affect the life of the citizens, and what historical events their generation has experienced. We may also need to know something about their behavior as consumers and their beliefs about health and sickness, crime and punishment, and religious matters. We may learn a lot from their countries' literature, arts, and sciences. The following chapters will at times pay attention to all of these fields, and most of them will prove relevant for understanding a country's *management* as well. In culture there is no shortcut to the business world.

Measuring Values

As values, more than practices, are the stable element in culture, comparative research on culture presumes the measurement of values. Inferring values from people's actions only is cumbersome and ambiguous. Various paper-and-pencil questionnaires have been developed that ask for people's preferences among alternatives. The answers should not be taken too literally: in reality people will not always act as they have scored on the questionnaire. Still, questionnaires provide useful information, because they show differences in answers between groups or categories of respondents. For example, suppose a question asks for one's preference for time off from work versus more pay. An individual employee who states that he or she prefers time off may in fact choose the money if presented with the actual choice, but if in group A more people claim preferring time off than in group B, this indicates a cultural difference between these groups in the relative value of free time versus money.

In interpreting people's statements about their values, it is important to distinguish between the *desirable* and the *desired*: how people think the world ought to be versus what people want for themselves. Questions about the desirable refer to people in general and are worded in terms of right/ wrong, agree/disagree, important/unimportant, or something similar. In the abstract everybody is in favor of virtue and opposed to sin, and answers about the desirable express people's views about what represents virtue and what corresponds to sin. The desired, on the contrary, is worded in terms of you or me and what we want for ourselves, including our less virtuous desires. The desirable bears only a faint resemblance to actual behavior. But even statements about the desired, although closer to actual behavior, do not necessarily correspond to the way people really behave when they have to choose.

The desirable differs from the desired in the nature of the norms involved. *Norms* are standards for behavior that exist within a group or category of people.[17] In the case of the desirable, the norm is absolute, pertaining to what is ethically right. In the case of the desired, the norm is statistical: it indicates the choices made by the majority. The desirable relates more to ideology, the desired to practical matters.

Interpretations of value studies that neglect the difference between the desirable and the desired may lead to paradoxical results. A case in which the two produced diametrically opposed answers was found in the IBM studies described later in this chapter. Employees in different countries were asked for their agreement or disagreement with the statement "Employees in industry should participate more in the decisions made by management." This is a statement about the desirable. In another question people were asked whether they personally preferred a manager who "usually consults with subordinates before reaching a decision." This is a statement about the desired. A comparison between the answers to these two questions revealed that in countries in which the consulting manager was less popular, people agreed more with the general statement that employees should participate in decisions, and vice versa; the ideology was the mirror image of the day-to-day relationship with the boss.[18]

Dimensions of National Cultures

In the first half of the twentieth century, social anthropology developed the conviction that all societies, modern or traditional, face the same basic problems—only the answers differ. American anthropologists, in particular Ruth Benedict (1887–1948) and Margaret Mead (1901–78), played an important role in popularizing this message for a wide audience.

The logical next step was that social scientists attempted to identify *what* problems were common to all societies, through conceptual reasoning and reflection on field experiences as well as through statistical studies. In 1954 two Americans, the sociologist Alex Inkeles and the psychologist Daniel Levinson, published a broad survey of the English-language literature on national culture. They suggested that the following issues qualify as common basic problems worldwide, with consequences for the functioning of societies, of groups within those societies, and of individuals within those groups:

1. Relation to authority
2. Conception of self—in particular, the relationship between individual and society—and the individual's concept of masculinity and femininity
3. Ways of dealing with conflicts, including the control of aggression and the expression of feelings[19]

Twenty years later Geert was given the opportunity to study a large body of survey data about the values of people in more than fifty countries around the world. These people worked in the local subsidiaries of one large multinational corporation: IBM. At first sight it may look surprising that employees of a multinational—a very specific kind of people—could serve for identifying differences in *national* value systems. From one country to another, however, they represented almost perfectly matched samples: they were similar in all respects except nationality, which made the effect of nationality differences in their answers stand out unusually clearly.

A statistical analysis of the country averages of the answers to questions about the values of similar IBM employees in different countries[20] revealed common problems, but with solutions differing from country to country, in the following areas:

1. Social inequality, including the relationship with authority
2. The relationship between the individual and the group
3. Concepts of masculinity and femininity: the social and emotional implications of having been born as a boy or a girl
4. Ways of dealing with uncertainty and ambiguity, which turned out to be related to the control of aggression and the expression of emotions

These empirical results covered amazingly well the areas predicted by Inkeles and Levinson twenty years before. Discovering their prediction provided strong support for the theoretical importance of the empirical findings. Problems that are basic to all human societies should be reflected in different studies regardless of the approaches followed. The Inkeles and Levinson study is not the only one whose conclusions overlap with ours, but it is the one that most strikingly predicts what Geert found.

The four basic problem areas defined by Inkeles and Levinson and empirically found in the IBM data represent dimensions of cultures. A *dimension* is an aspect of a culture that can be measured relative to other cultures. The basic problem areas correspond to four dimensions that will be described in Chapters 2 through 5 of this book. They have been named *power distance* (from small to large), *collectivism versus individualism, femininity versus masculinity*, and *uncertainty avoidance* (from weak to strong). Each of these terms existed already in some part of the social sciences, and they seemed to apply reasonably well to the basic problem area each dimension stands for. Together they form a four-dimensional model of differences between national cultures. Each country in the model is characterized by a score on each of the four dimensions.

A dimension groups together a number of phenomena in a society that were empirically found to occur in combination, regardless of whether there seems to be a logical necessity for their going together. The logic of societies is not the same as the logic of individuals looking at them. The grouping of the different aspects of a dimension is always based on statistical relationships—that is, on trends for these phenomena to occur in combination, not on iron links. Some aspects in some societies may go against a general trend found across most other societies. Because they are found with the help of statistical methods, dimensions can only be detected on the basis of comparative information from a number of countries—say, at least ten. In the case of the IBM research, Geert was fortunate to obtain comparable data about culturally determined values from fifty countries and three multicountry regions, which made the dimensions within their differences stand out quite clearly.

The scores for each country on one dimension can be pictured as points along a line. For two dimensions at a time, they become points in a diagram. For three dimensions, they could, with some imagination, be seen as points in space. For four or more dimensions, they become difficult to imagine. This is a disadvantage of dimensional models. Another way of picturing differences between countries (or other social systems) is through typologies. A *typology* describes a set of ideal types, each of them easy to imagine. A common typology of countries in the second half of the twentieth century was dividing them into a First, Second, and Third World (a capitalist, communist, and former colonial bloc).

Whereas typologies are easier to grasp than dimensions, they are problematic in empirical research. Real cases seldom fully correspond to one single ideal type. Most cases are hybrids, and arbitrary rules have to be made for classifying them as belonging to one type or another. With a dimensional model, on the contrary, cases can always be scored unambiguously. On the basis of their dimension scores, cases can *afterward* empirically be sorted into clusters with similar scores. These clusters then form an empirical typology. More than fifty countries in the IBM study could, on the basis of their four-dimensional scores, be sorted into twelve such clusters.[21]

In practice typologies and dimensional models are complementary. Dimensional models are preferable for research, and typologies are useful for teaching purposes. This book will use a kind of typology approach for explaining each of the dimensions. For every separate dimension, it describes the two opposite extremes as pure types. Later on the four dimensions are plotted two by two, every plot creating four types. The country scores on the dimensions will show that most real cases are somewhere in between the extremes.

Replications of the IBM Research

While IBM survey data still continued to come in, Geert administered some of the same questions to an international population of non-IBM managers. These people, who came from different companies in fifteen different countries, attended courses at a business school in Switzerland where Geert was a visiting lecturer.[22] At that time he did not yet have a clear concept of dimensions in the data, but the replication showed that on a key question about power (later part of the *power distance* dimension), the countries ranked almost exactly the same as in IBM. Other questions indicated country differences in what we now call individualism versus collectivism, again very similar to those in IBM. This was the first proof that the country differences found inside IBM existed elsewhere as well.

In later years many people administered the IBM questionnaire—or parts of it, or its later, improved versions called Values Survey Modules (VSMs)—to other groups of respondents. The usefulness of replications increases with the number of countries included. The more countries, the easier it becomes to use statistical tests for verifying the degree of similarity in the results. Until the end of 2002, next to many smaller studies, we count six major replication studies, each covering fourteen or more countries from the IBM database. They are listed in Table 1.1.

Four of the six replications in Table 1.1 confirm only three out of the four dimensions—and each time the one missing is different. For example, data obtained from consumers did not replicate the power distance dimension. We assume this is because the respondents included people in different jobs with different relationships to power or people without paid jobs at all, like students and housewives.

Most smaller studies compared two or three countries at a time. It would be too good to expect confirmation of the IBM results in all of these cases, but a review of nineteen small replications by the Danish researcher Mikael Søndergaard found that together they statistically confirmed all four dimensions.[23] The strongest confirmation was for individualism. Most small replications start from the United States, which in the IBM studies

TABLE 1.1 Six Major Replications of the IBM Research

Author	Year Publ	Sample	No. of Ctrs	DIMENSIONS REPLICATED			
				Power	Indiv	Mascu	Uncer
Hoppe	1990	Elites[1]	18	x	x	x	x
Shane	1995	Employees[2]	28	x	x		x
Merritt	1998	Pilots[3]	19	x	x	x	x
de Mooij	2001	Consumers[4]	15		x	x	x
Mouritzen	2002	Municipal[5]	14	x		x	x
van Nimwegen	2002	Bank empl[6]	19	x	x	x	

1 Members of government, parliamentarians, labor and employers' leaders, academics, and artists. These people were surveyed in 1984 via the Salzburg Seminar in American Studies. On the basis of the formulas in the VSM 82, their answers confirmed power distance, uncertainty avoidance, and individualism (Hoppe, 1990); using the VSM 94 they also confirmed masculinity (Hoppe, 1998).

2 Employees of six international corporations (but not IBM) from between 28 and 32 countries: Shane (1995); Shane & Venkataraman (1996). This study confirmed power distance, uncertainty avoidance, and individualism. It did not include questions about masculinity, which was judged politically incorrect(!).

3 Commercial airline pilots from 19 countries: Helmreich & Merritt (1998). Using the VSM 82 this study confirmed power distance and individualism; including other IBM questions judged more relevant to the pilot's situation, it confirmed all four dimensions (Merritt, 2000).

4 Consumers from 15 European countries: de Mooij (2004); Culture's Consequences (2001), pp. 187, 262, 336. Using the VSM 94 this study confirmed uncertainty avoidance, individualism, and masculinity. It did not confirm power distance, probably because the consumers were not selected on the basis of the jobs they did (or whether they had a paid job at all).

5 Top municipal civil servants from 14 countries: Søndergaard (2002); Mouritzen & Svara (2002). Using the VSM 94 they confirmed power distance, uncertainty avoidance, and masculinity and related the first two to the forms of local government in the countries.

6 Employees of an international bank in 19 countries: van Nimwegen (2002). This study confirmed power distance and individualism and also, but with a somewhat lesser fit, masculinity and long-term orientation, but not uncertainty avoidance.

was the highest scorer on individualism, and any comparison with the United States is likely to show a clear individualism difference.

Table 1.2 lists in alphabetical order seventy-four countries or regions for which the IBM research and its replications produced usable dimension scores. The scores in question will be shown in Chapters 2 through 6.

TABLE 1.2 **Countries and Regions for Which Dimension Scores Are Available**

Arabic-speaking	Ecuador	Panama
countries (Egypt,	Estonia	Peru
Iraq, Kuwait,	Finland	Philippines
Lebanon, Libya,	France	Poland
Saudi Arabia,	Germany	Portugal
United Arab	Great Britain	Romania
Emirates)	Greece	Russia
Argentina	Guatemala	Salvador
Australia	Hong Kong	Serbia
Austria	(China)	Singapore
Bangladesh	Hungary	Slovakia
Belgium Flemish	India	Slovenia
(Dutch speaking)	Indonesia	South Africa[1]
Belgium Walloon	Iran	Spain
(French speaking)	Ireland	Suriname
Brazil	Israel	Sweden
Bulgaria	Italy	Switzerland French
Canada Quebec	Jamaica	Switzerland German
Canada total	Japan	Taiwan
Chile	Korea (South)	Thailand
China	Luxembourg	Trinidad
Colombia	Malaysia	Turkey
Costa Rica	Malta	United States
Croatia	Mexico	Uruguay
Czech Republic	Morocco	Venezuela
Denmark	Netherlands	Vietnam
East Africa	New Zealand	West Africa
(Ethiopia, Kenya,	Norway	(Ghana, Nigeria,
Tanzania, Zambia)	Pakistan	Sierra Leone)

1 The data were from whites only.

The success of the replications does not necessarily mean that the countries' cultures did not change since the IBM research, but that if they changed, they changed together, so that their relative positions remained intact.

Using Correlations

The comparisons between the replications and the original IBM scores used a statistical method, *correlation.*

For those unfamiliar with the statistical term *correlation* and the meaning of correlation coefficients, a brief explanation follows. Two measures are said to be correlated if they vary together. For example, if we were to measure the height and weight of a hundred people randomly picked from the street, we would find the height and weight measures to be correlated; taller people would also usually be heavier, and shorter ones would also tend to be lighter. Because some people are tall and skinny and some are short and fat, the correlation would not be perfect.

The coefficient of correlation[24] expresses the strength of the relationship. If the correlation is perfect, so that one measure follows entirely from the other, the coefficient takes the value 1.00. If the correlation is nonexistent—the two measures are completely unrelated—the coefficient is 0.00. The coefficient can become negative if the two measures are each other's opposite—for example, a person's height and the number of times she or he would meet someone who is still taller. The lowest possible value is −1.00; in this case the two measures are again perfectly correlated, only the one is positive when the other is negative, and vice versa. In the example of the height and weight of people, one could expect a coefficient of about 0.80 if the sample included only adults and even higher if both children and adults were included in the sample, because children are extremely small and light compared to adults.

A correlation coefficient is said to be (statistically) significant if it is sufficiently different from 0 (to the positive or to the negative side) to rule out the possibility that the similarity between the two measures could be due to pure chance. The *significance level,* usually 0.05, 0.01, or 0.001, is the remaining risk that the similarity could still be accidental. If the significance level is 0.05, the odds against an association by chance are 19 to 1; if it is 0.001, the odds are 999 to 1.[25]

If the correlation coefficient between two measures is 1.00 or −1.00, we can obviously completely predict one if we know the other. If their correlation coefficient is ±0.90, we can predict 81 percent of the differences in one if we know the other; if it is ±0.80, we can predict 64 percent, and so on. The predictive power decreases with the square of the correlation coefficient. If we have a lot of data, a correlation coefficient of 0.40 may still be significant, although the first measure predicts only 0.40 × 0.40 = 16 percent of the second. The reason we are interested in such relatively weak correlations is that often phenomena in the social world are the result of many factors working at the same time: they are multicausal. Correlation analysis helps us to isolate possible causes, one by one.

Adding a Fifth Dimension

In late 1980, just after *Culture's Consequences* had been published, Geert met Michael Harris Bond from the Chinese University of Hong Kong. Bond and a number of his colleagues from the Asia-Pacific region had just finished a comparison of the values of female and male psychology students from each of ten national or ethnic groups in their region.[26] They had used an adapted version of the Rokeach Value Survey (RVS), developed by U.S. psychologist Milton Rokeach on the basis of an inventory of values in U.S. society around 1970. When Bond analyzed the RVS data in the same way that Geert had analyzed the IBM data, he also found four meaningful dimensions. Across the six countries that were part of both studies, each RVS dimension was significantly correlated with one of the IBM dimensions.[27]

The discovery of similar dimensions in completely different material represented strong support for the basic nature of what was found. With another questionnaire, using other respondents (students instead of IBM employees) at another point in time (data collected around 1979 instead of 1970) and in a restricted group of countries, four similar dimensions emerged. Yet both Bond and Geert were not just pleased but also puzzled. The survey results themselves demonstrated that people's ways of thinking are culturally constrained. As the researchers were human, they, too, were children of their culture. Both the IBM questionnaire and the RVS were products of Western minds. In both cases respondents in non-Western countries had answered Western questions. To what extent had this been responsible for the correlation between the results of the two studies? To what extent had irrelevant questions been asked and relevant questions been omitted?

The standard solution suggested in order to avoid cultural bias in research is *decentering*: involving researchers from different cultures. In this respect the IBM questionnaire was better than the RVS: it had been developed by a five-nationality team and pretested in ten countries. The RVS was a purely American product, although the Asian-Pacific research team had adapted it somewhat by adding four values they felt to be relevant in their countries but missing on the Rokeach list.[28]

The problem about decentered research is the dynamics in the research team. All members are equal, but some are more equal than others. There is usually a senior researcher, the one who took the initiative, and he (rarely she) is usually from a Western background. Researchers from countries where respect for the senior guru and harmony within the team prevail will often be almost too eager to follow the magic of the prestigious team leader. This means that the project team will maintain its Western bias even with a predominantly non-Western membership. When the chief researcher comes from a non-Western country, he or she has often studied in the West and sometimes overadopts Western value positions, becoming "more Catholic than the pope."

Bond, himself a Canadian but having lived and worked in the Far East since 1971, found a creative solution to the Western bias problem. He had a new questionnaire designed with a deliberate non-Western bias, in this case a Chinese culture bias, which he used in the same way as Western questionnaires had been used, so that the results could be compared. Bond asked a number of Chinese social scientists from Hong Kong and Taiwan to prepare in Chinese a list of at least ten basic values for Chinese people. Through the elimination of overlap and, on the other side, adding some values that from his reading of Chinese philosophers and social scientists seemed to be similarly important, he arrived at a questionnaire of forty items—the same number as in the previously used RVS. The new questionnaire was called the Chinese Value Survey (CVS).

Subsequently the CVS was administered to one hundred students—fifty men and fifty women, like in the RVS study—in each of twenty-three countries around the world. The students used the Chinese version, the English version, or one of eight other language versions, translated, where possible, directly from the Chinese. A statistical analysis of the CVS results yielded again four dimensions. Across twenty overlapping countries, three dimensions of the CVS replicated dimensions earlier found in the IBM surveys, but the fourth CVS dimension was not correlated with the fourth IBM dimension: uncertainty avoidance had no equivalent in the CVS. The fourth CVS dimension instead combined values opposing an orientation on the future to an orientation on the past and present.[29] Geert labeled it *long-term versus short-term orientation,* and we treat it as a fifth universal dimension. Chapter 6 will analyze it in depth.

Validation of the Country Culture Scores Against Other Measures

The next step was showing the practical implications of the dimension scores for the countries concerned. This was done quantitatively by correlating the dimension scores with other measures that could be logically expected to reflect the same culture differences. These quantitative checks were supplemented with qualitative, descriptive information about the countries. This entire process is called *validation.*

Examples, which will be elaborated on in Chapters 2 through 6, are that power distance was correlated with the use of violence in domestic politics and with income inequality in a country. Individualism was correlated with national wealth (GNP per capita) and with mobility between social classes from one generation to the next. Masculinity was correlated negatively with the share of GNP that governments of wealthy countries spent on development assistance to the Third World. Uncertainty avoidance was associated with Roman Catholicism and with the legal obligation in developed countries for citizens to carry identity cards. Long-term orientation was correlated with national savings rates.

Altogether, the 2001 edition of *Culture's Consequences* lists more than four hundred significant correlations of the IBM dimension scores with other measures.[30] A striking fact of the various validations is that correlations do not tend to become weaker over time. The IBM national dimension scores (or at least their relative positions) have remained as valid in the year 2000 as they were around 1970, indicating that they describe relatively enduring aspects of these countries' societies.

Other Classifications of National Cultures

The basic innovation of *Culture's Consequences,* when it appeared in 1980, was classifying national cultures along a number of dimensions. In the study of culture this represented a new *paradigm*—that is, a radically new approach. A paradigm is not a theory, but rather one step before a theory: a way of thinking that leads to developing theories. New paradigms invariably lead to controversy, as they reverse cherished truths but also open new perspectives.[31] Since *Culture's Consequences*, several other theories of national cultures have used the same paradigm, each suggesting its own way of classifying them.

The most elaborate and best researched classification was developed by the Israeli psychologist Shalom H. Schwartz. From a survey of the literature, he composed a list of fifty-six values. Through a network of colleagues, he collected scores from samples of college students in fifty-four countries and elementary school teachers in fifty-six countries.[32] They scored the importance of each value "as a guiding principle in my life." Schwartz at first looked at differences between individuals, but his next step was comparing countries. On the basis of his data, he distinguished seven dimensions: conservatism, hierarchy, mastery, affective autonomy, intellectual autonomy, egalitarian commitment, and harmony. Based on country data published by Schwartz in 1994, there are significant correlations between his country scores and the IBM scores.[33] His is a different way of cutting the same pie.

A classification well known in the business world is used in the publications by Dutch business consultant Fons Trompenaars. He distinguishes universalism versus particularism, individualism versus collectivism, affectivity versus neutrality, specificity versus diffuseness, achievement versus ascription, time orientation, and relation to nature.[34] These dimensions derive from sociological theories of the 1950s and '60s[35] that Trompenaars applied to countries. He administered a questionnaire (with seventy-nine items) to samples of employees and managers from various organizations in various countries. In his 1993 book *Riding the Waves of Culture*, Trompenaars showed answer scores for thirty-nine countries on seventeen questions from the questionnaire, but these were not combined into country scores for his dimensions. The book shows no validation of Trompenaars's seven dimensions, which without country scores would have been impossible anyway. Trompenaars's database was analyzed by British psychologist Peter Smith and his colleague Shaun Dugan, who found only two independent dimensions in the data, one correlated with our individualism-collectivism dimension and the other primarily with our power distance dimensions, but also again with individualism-collectivism.[36] Trompenaars's questionnaire did not cover other aspects of national cultures.

Individualism-collectivism is the least controversial of our five dimensions, which may explain the popularity of Trompenaars's message among managers who dislike conflicts.

An application of the dimensions-of-culture paradigm for which, as this was written, the main results had not yet appeared, is the Global Leadership and Organizational Behavior Effectiveness (GLOBE) Research Project, originally conceived by U.S. management professor Robert J. House in 1991. It focuses on the relationships between societal culture, organizational culture, and leadership. House has built an extensive network of some 150 coinvestigators who collected data from about nine thousand managers in five hundred different organizations in sixty-one countries. The project aims at measuring nine dimensions derived from the literature, including *Culture's Consequences*: power distance, uncertainty avoidance, social collectivism, in-group collectivism, gender egalitarianism, assertiveness, future orientation, performance orientation, and humane orientation.[37] These are hypothetical dimensions; the results should show to what extent the empirical dimensions in the data correspond with the theories.[38]

Originally not based on the dimensions-of-culture paradigm but still with direct consequences for classifying national cultures is the World Values Survey (WVS), led by U.S. political scientist Ronald Inglehart. A study of values via public opinion surveys was started in the early 1980s as the European Values Survey. In 1990 a second round was started, renamed the World Values Survey. Eventually covering some sixty thousand respondents across forty-three societies, representing about 70 percent of the world's population, this questionnaire included more than 360 forced-choice questions. Areas covered were ecology, economy, education, emotions, family, gender and sexuality, government and politics, happiness, health, leisure and friends, morality, religion, society and nation, and work.[39] In an overall statistical analysis, Inglehart found two key cultural dimensions, which he called *well-being versus survival* and *secular-rational versus traditional authority*.[40] These were significantly correlated with the IBM dimensions. Well-being versus survival correlated with individualism and masculinity; secular-rational versus traditional authority negatively correlated with power distance. Again, a different way of cutting the same pie. We expect that further analysis of the enormous WVS survey data bank may produce additional dimensions. In the meantime a third WVS round has been started.[41]

Cultural Differences According to Region, Ethnicity, Religion, Gender, Generation, and Class

Regional, ethnic, and religious cultures account for differences within countries; ethnic and religious groups often transcend political country borders. Such groups form minorities at the crossroads between the dominant culture of the nation and their own traditional group culture. Some assimilate into the mainstream, although this may take a generation or more; others continue to stick to their own ways. The United States, as the world's most prominent example of a people composed of immigrants, shows examples of both assimilation (the melting pot) and of retention of group identities over generations (for example, the Pennsylvania Dutch). Discrimination according to ethnic origin delays assimilation and represents a problem in many countries. Regional, ethnic, and religious cultures, insofar as they are learned from birth onward, can be described in the same terms as national cultures: basically the same dimensions that were found to differentiate among national cultures apply to these differences within countries.

Gender differences are not usually described in terms of cultures. It can be revealing to do so. If we recognize that within each society there is a men's culture that differs from a women's culture, this helps to explain why it is so difficult to change traditional gender roles. Women are not considered suitable for jobs traditionally filled by men, not because they are technically unable to perform these jobs, but because women do not carry the symbols, do not correspond to the hero images, do not participate in the rituals, or are not supposed to hold the values dominant in the men's culture, and vice versa. Feelings and fears about behaviors by the opposite sex can be of the same order of intensity as reactions of people exposed to foreign cultures. The subject of gender cultures will return in Chapter 4.

Generation differences in symbols, heroes, rituals, and values are evident to most people. They are often overestimated. Complaints about youth having lost respect for the values of their elders have been found on Egyptian papyrus scrolls dating from 2000 B.C. and in the writings of Hesiod, a Greek author from the end of the eighth century B.C. Many differences in practices and values between generations are normal attributes of age that repeat themselves for each successive pair of generations. Historical events, however, do affect some generations in a special way. The Chinese who were of student age during the 1966–76 Cultural Revolution stand witness to this. Chinese who in this period would normally have become students were sent to the countryside as laborers and missed their education. The Chinese speak of "the lost generation." The development of technology may also lead to a difference between generations. An example is the spread of television, which showed people life in other parts of the world previously outside their perspective.

Social classes carry different class cultures. Social class is associated with educational opportunities and with a person's occupation or profession. Education and occupation are in themselves powerful sources of cultural learning. There is no standard definition of social class that applies across all countries, and people in different countries distinguish different types and numbers of classes. The criteria for allocating a person to a class are often cultural: symbols, such as manners, accents in speaking the national language, and the use and nonuse of certain words, play an important role. The confrontation between the two jurors in *Twelve Angry Men* clearly contains a class component.

Gender, generation, and class cultures can only partly be classified by the dimensions found for national cultures. This is because they are categories of people within social systems, not integrated social systems such as countries or ethnic groups. Gender, generation, and class cultures should be described in their own terms, based on special studies of such cultures.

Organizational Cultures

Organizational, or corporate, cultures have been a fashionable topic in the management literature since the early 1980s. At that time, authors began to popularize the claim that the "excellence" of an organization is contained in the common ways by which its members have learned to think, feel, and act. *Corporate culture* is a soft, holistic concept with, however, presumed hard consequences.

Organization sociologists have stressed the role of the soft factor in organizations for more than half a century. Using the label *culture* for the shared mental software of the people in an organization is a convenient way of repopularizing these sociological views. Yet organizational cultures are a phenomenon by themselves, different in many respects from national cultures. An organization is a social system of a different nature than a nation, if only because the organization's members usually did not grow up in it. On the contrary, they had a certain influence in their decision to join the organization, are only involved in it during working hours, and will one day leave it.

Research results about national cultures and their dimensions proved to be only partly useful for the understanding of organizational cultures. The part of this book that deals with organizational culture differences (Chapter 8) is not based on the IBM studies but rather on a special research project carried out in the 1980s within twenty organizational units in Denmark and the Netherlands.

Summing Up: Culture as a Phoenix

During a person's life, new body cells continually replace old ones. The twenty-year-old does not retain a single cell of the newborn. In a restricted physical sense, therefore, one could say we have no identity but we are a sequence of cell assemblies. Yet a person has a clear identity, as we all know from firsthand experience. This is because all these cells share the same genes.

At the level of societies, an analogous phenomenon occurs. Our societies have a remarkable capacity for conserving their identity through generations of successive members and despite varied and numerous forces of change. While change sweeps the surface, the deeper layers remain stable, and the culture rises from its ashes like the phoenix.

But what do these deeper layers consist of? There are no genes to carry culture. Culture is the unwritten book with rules of the social game that is passed on to newcomers by its members, nesting itself in their minds. In this book we describe the main themes that these unwritten rules cover. They deal with the basic issues of human social life.

DIMENSIONS OF NATIONAL CULTURES

More Equal Than Others

In a peaceful revolution, the last revolution in Swedish history, the nobles of Sweden in 1809 deposed King Gustav IV, whom they considered incompetent, and surprisingly invited Jean-Baptiste Bernadotte, a French general who served under their enemy Napoleon, to become king of Sweden. Bernadotte accepted and he became King Charles XIV John; his descendants have occupied the Swedish throne to this day. When the new king was installed, he addressed the Swedish parliament in their language. His broken Swedish amused the Swedes, and they roared with laughter. The Frenchman who had become king was so upset that he never tried to speak Swedish again.

In this incident Bernadotte was a victim of culture shock: never in his French upbringing and military career had he experienced subordinates who laughed at the mistakes of their superior. Historians tell us he had more problems adapting to the egalitarian Swedish and Norwegian mentality (he became king of Norway as well) and to his subordinates' constitutional rights. He was a good learner (except for language), however, and he ruled the country as a highly respected constitutional monarch until 1844.

Inequality in Society

One of the aspects in which Sweden differs from France is the way society handles *inequality*. There is inequality in any society. Even in the most simple hunter-gatherer band, some people are bigger, stronger, or smarter than others. The next thing is that some people have more power than others: they are more able to determine the behavior of others than vice versa. Some people acquire more wealth than others. Some people are given more status and respect than others.

Physical and intellectual capacities, power, wealth, and status may or may not go together. Successful athletes, artists, or scientists usually enjoy status but only in some societies do they enjoy wealth as well, and rarely do they have political power. Politicians in some countries can enjoy status and power without wealth; businesspeople, wealth and power without status. Such inconsistencies between the various areas of inequality are often felt to be problematic. In some societies people try to resolve them by making the areas more consistent. Sportsmen become professionals to become wealthy; politicians exploit their power in order to do the same; successful businesspeople enter public office in order to acquire status. This trend obviously increases the overall inequalities in these societies.

In other societies the dominant feeling is that it is a good thing, rather than a problem, if a person's rank in one area does not match his or her rank in another. A high rank in one area should partly be offset by a low rank in another. This process increases the size of the middle class in between those who come on top in all respects and those who lack any kind of opportunity. The laws in many countries have been conceived to serve this ideal of equality by treating everybody as equal regardless of status, wealth, or power, but there are few societies in which reality matches the ideal. The praise of poverty in the Christian Bible can be seen as a manifestation of a desire for equality; the same is true for Karl Marx's plea for a "dictatorship of the proletariat."

Measuring the Degree of Inequality in Society: The Power Distance Index

Not only Sweden and France, but other nations as well can be distinguished by the way they tend to deal with inequalities. The research among IBM employees in similar positions but different countries has allowed us to assign to each of these countries a score indicating its level of power distance. Power distance is one of the dimensions of national cultures suggested in Chapter 1. It reflects the range of answers found in the various countries to the basic question of how to handle the fact that people are unequal. It derives its name from research by a Dutch experimental social psychologist, Mauk Mulder, into the emotional distance that separates subordinates from their bosses.[1]

Scores on power distance for fifty countries and three multicountry regions have been calculated from the answers by IBM employees in the same kind of positions on the same survey questions. All questions were of the precoded answer type so that answers could be represented by a score number: usually 1, 2, 3, 4, or 5. A mean score was computed for the answers of an equally composed sample of people from each country (say, 2.53 as the mean score for the sample from country X and 3.43 for country Y), or the percentage was computed of people choosing particular answers (say, 45 percent of the sample choosing answer 1 or 2 in country X and 33 percent in country Y). Thus a table was composed of mean scores or percentages for each question and for all countries.

A statistical procedure (*factor analysis*) was used to sort the survey questions into groups, called *factors* or *clusters*, for which the mean scores or percentages varied together.[2] This meant that if a country scored high on one of the questions from the cluster, it also could be expected to score high on the others, or not high but low for questions carrying the opposite meaning. If, on the other hand, a country scored low on one question from the cluster, it also would most likely score low on the others, or high on questions formulated the other way around. If a country scored average on one question from the cluster, it probably would score average on all of them.

One of the clusters found was composed of questions that all seemed to have something to do with power and (in)equality. From the questions in this cluster we selected the three that were most strongly related.[3] From the mean scores of the standard sample of IBM employees in a country on these three questions a *power distance index* (PDI) for the country was calculated. The formula developed for this purpose uses simple mathematics (adding or subtracting the three scores after multiplying each with a fixed number, and finally adding another fixed number). The purpose of the formula was (1) to ensure that each of the three questions would carry equal weight in arriving at the final index and (2) to get index values ranging from about 0 for a small-power-distance country to about 100 for a large-power-distance country. Two countries, added later, score above 100.

The three survey items used for composing the power distance index were:

1. Answers by nonmanagerial employees on the question "How frequently, in your experience, does the following problem occur: employees being afraid to express disagreement with their managers?" (mean score on a 1 to 5 scale from "very frequently" to "very seldom")
2. Subordinates' *perception* of their boss's actual decision-making style (percentage choosing the description of either an autocratic or a paternalistic style, out of four possible styles plus a "none of these" alternative)
3. Subordinates' *preference* for their boss's decision-making style (percentage preferring an autocratic or a paternalistic style or, on the contrary, a style based on majority vote, but *not* a consultative style)

Country PDI scores can be read from Table 2.1. For fifty-seven of the countries or regions (printed in bold) the scores were calculated directly from the IBM database. The remaining cases were calculated from replications or based on informed estimates.[4] Because of the way they were calculated, the scores represent *relative*, not absolute, positions of countries: they are measures of differences only. The scores that were based on answers by IBM employees paradoxically contain no information about the corporate culture of IBM: they only show to what extent people from the subsidiary in country X answered the same questions differently from similar people in country Y. We found more or less the same differences in populations outside IBM, which proves that they reflect the different national cultures in which people grew up.

TABLE 2.1 Power Distance Index (PDI) Values for 74 Countries and Regions

COUNTRY/REGION	SCORE	RANK	COUNTRY/REGION	SCORE	RANK
Malaysia	104	1–2	Colombia	67	30–31
Slovakia	104	1–2	Salvador	66	32–33
Guatemala	95	3–4	Turkey	66	32–33
Panama	95	3–4	East Africa	64	34–36
Philippines	94	5	Peru	64	34–36
Russia	93	6	Thailand	64	34–36
Romania	90	7	Chile	63	37–38
Serbia	86	8	Portugal	63	37–38
Suriname	85	9	Belgium Flemish	61	39–40
Mexico	81	10–11	Uruguay	61	39–40
Venezuela	81	10–11	Greece	60	41–42
Arab countries	80	12–14	Korea (South)	60	41–42
Bangladesh	80	12–14	Iran	58	43–44
China	80	12–14	Taiwan	58	43–44
Ecuador	78	15–16	Czech Republic	57	45–46
Indonesia	78	15–16	Spain	57	45–46
India	77	17–18	Malta	56	47
West Africa	77	17–18	Pakistan	55	48
Singapore	74	19	Canada Québec	54	49–50
Croatia	73	20	Japan	54	49–50
Slovenia	71	21	Italy	50	51
Bulgaria	70	22–25	Argentina	49	52–53
Morocco	70	22–25	South Africa[1]	49	52–53
Switzerland			Trinidad	47	54
French	70	22–25	Hungary	46	55
Vietnam	70	22–25	Jamaica	45	56
Brazil	69	26	Estonia	40	57–59
France	68	27–29	Luxembourg	40	57–59
Hong Kong	68	27–29	United States	40	57–59
Poland	68	27–29	Canada total	39	60
Belgium Walloon	67	30–31	Netherlands	38	61

continued

continued

TABLE 2.1 Power Distance Index (PDI) Values for 74 Countries and Regions

COUNTRY/REGION	SCORE	RANK	COUNTRY/REGION	SCORE	RANK
Australia	36	62	Ireland	28	69
Costa Rica	35	63–65	Switzerland		
Germany	35	63–65	German	26	70
Great Britain	35	63–65	New Zealand	22	71
Finland	33	66	Denmark	18	72
Norway	31	67–68	Israel	13	73
Sweden	31	67–68	Austria	11	74

Scores for countries or regions given in **bold type** were calculated from the IBM database. Scores for other countries were based on replications or estimates.

1 The data were from whites only.

For the multilingual countries Belgium and Switzerland, Table 2.1 gives the scores by the two largest language areas. For Canada there is an IBM score for the whole country and a replication-based score for the French-speaking part (Quebec). The IBM sample for what was once Yugoslavia has been split into Croatia, Serbia, and Slovenia. The other countries in Table 2.1 all have a single score. This does not mean that they are necessarily culturally homogeneous, only that the available data did not allow a splitting up into subcultures.

Table 2.1 shows high power distance values for most Asian countries (such as Malaysia and the Philippines), for eastern European countries (such as Slovakia and Russia), for Latin countries (Latin America, such as Panama and Mexico, and to a somewhat lesser extent Latin Europe, such as France and Wallonia, the French-speaking part of Belgium), for Arab-speaking countries, and for African countries. The table shows low values for German-speaking countries, such as Austria, the German-speaking part of Switzerland, and Germany; for Israel; for the Nordic countries (Denmark, Finland, Norway, and Sweden); for the United States, Great Britain and the white part of its former empire (New Zealand, Ireland, Australia, Canada), and the Netherlands (but not for Flanders, the Dutch-speaking part of Belgium, which scored quite similar to Wallonia). Sweden scored 31 and France 68. If such a difference existed already two hundred years ago—for which there is a good case, as will be argued in the following—this explains Bernadotte's culture shock. The third column in Table 2.1 lists the rank numbers of the countries and regions from high to low (1 for the largest power distance, 74 for the smallest): France is ranked 27 to 29 and Sweden 67 to 68, which accentuates their difference even more.

Power Distance Defined

Looking at the three questions used to compose the PDI, you may notice something surprising: questions 1 (employees afraid) and 2 (boss autocratic or paternalistic) indicate the way the respondents perceive their daily work environment. Question 3, however, indicates what the respondents express as their *preference*: how they would like their work environment to be.

The fact that the three questions are part of the same cluster shows that from one country to another there is a close relationship between the reality one perceives and the reality one desires.[5] In countries in which employees are not seen as very afraid and bosses as not often autocratic or paternalistic, employees express a preference for a *consultative* style of decision making: a boss who, as the questionnaire expressed it, "[u]sually consults with his/her subordinates before reaching a decision."

In countries on the opposite side of the power distance scale, where employees are seen as frequently afraid of disagreeing with their bosses and bosses as autocratic or paternalistic, employees in similar jobs are less likely to prefer a consultative boss. Instead, many among them express a preference for a boss who decides autocratically or paternalistically; but some switch to the other extreme—that is, preferring a boss who governs by majority vote, which means that he or she does not actually make the decision at all. In the practice of the life of most organizations, majority vote is difficult to handle, and few people actually perceived their boss as using this style (bosses who pretend doing it are often accused of manipulation).

In summary, PDI scores inform us about *dependence* relationships in a country. In small-power-distance countries, there is limited dependence of subordinates on bosses, and there is a preference for consultation (that is, *interdependence* between boss and subordinate). The emotional distance between them is relatively small: subordinates will rather easily approach and contradict their bosses. In large-power-distance countries, there is considerable dependence of subordinates on bosses. Subordinates respond by either preferring such dependence (in the form of an autocratic or paternalistic boss) or rejecting it entirely, which in psychology is known as *counterdependence*—that is, dependence but with a negative sign. Large-power-distance countries thus show a pattern of polarization between dependence and counterdependence. In these cases the emotional distance between subordinates and their bosses is large: subordinates are unlikely to approach and contradict their bosses directly.

Power distance can therefore be defined as *the extent to which the less powerful members of institutions and organizations within a country expect and accept that power is distributed unequally. Institutions* are the basic elements of society, such as the family, the school, and the community; *organizations* are the places where people work.

Power distance is thus described based on the value system of the *less* powerful members. The way power is distributed is usually explained from the behavior of the *more* powerful members, the leaders rather than those led. The popular management literature on leadership often forgets that leadership can only exist as a complement to subordinateship. Authority survives only where it is matched by obedience. Bernadotte's problem was not a lack of leadership on his side; the Swedes had another conception of the deference due to a ruler than the French had—and Bernadotte was a Frenchman.

Comparative research projects on leadership values from one country to another show that the differences observed exist in the minds of both the leaders *and* those led, but often the statements obtained from those who are led are a better reflection of the differences than those obtained from the leaders. This is because we are all better observers of the leadership behavior of our bosses than we are of ourselves. Besides the questions on perceived and preferred leadership style of the boss—questions 2 and 3 in the PDI—the IBM surveys also asked managers to rate their *own* style. It appeared that self-ratings by managers resembled closely the styles these managers preferred in their own boss—but not at all the styles their subordinates perceived them to have. In fact, the subordinates saw their managers in just about the same way as the managers saw *their* bosses. The moral for managers is, if you want to know how your subordinates see you, don't try to look in the mirror—that just produces wishful thinking. Turn around 180 degrees and face your own boss.[6]

Power Distance in Replication Studies

In Table 1.1 six studies were listed, published between 1990 and 2002, which used the IBM questions or later versions of them with other cross-national populations. Five of these, covering between fourteen and twenty-eight countries from the IBM set, produced PDI scores highly significantly correlated with the original IBM scores.[7] The sixth study got its data from consumers who were not selected on the basis of their relationships to power, who were in very different jobs or, such as students and housewives, who did not have paid jobs at all. We have investigated whether the new scores would justify correcting some of the original IBM scores, but the new scores were not consistent enough for this purpose.[8] None of the new populations covered as many countries or used such well-matched samples as found in the original IBM set. Also, correlations of the original IBM scores with other data, such as consumer purchases, have not become weaker over time.[9] One should remember that the scores measured *differences between* country cultures, not cultures in an absolute sense. The cultures may have shifted, but as long as they shifted together under the influence of the same global forces, the scores remain valid.

Bond's Chinese Value Survey study among students in twenty-three countries, described in Chapter 1, produced a *moral discipline* dimension on which the countries positioned themselves largely in the same way as they had done in the IBM studies on power distance (in statistical terms, moral discipline was significantly correlated with PDI).[10] Students in countries scoring high on power distance answered that the following were particularly important:

- Having few desires
- Moderation, following the middle way
- Keeping oneself disinterested and pure

In unequal societies, ordinary people like students felt they should not have aspirations beyond their rank.

Students in countries scoring low on power distance, on the other hand, answered that the following were particularly important:

- Adaptability
- Prudence (carefulness)

In more egalitarian societies, where problems cannot be resolved by someone's show of power, students stressed the importance of being flexible in order to get somewhere.

Power Distance Differences Within Countries: Social Class, Education Level, and Occupation

Inequality within a society is visible in the existence of different social classes: upper, middle, and lower, or however one wants to divide them—this varies by country. Classes differ in their access to and their opportunities for benefiting from the advantages of society, one of them being education. A higher education automatically makes one at least middle class. Education, in turn, is one of the main determinants of the occupations one can aspire to, so that in practice in most societies, social class, education level, and occupation are closely linked. In Chapter 1 all three have been listed as sources of our mental software: there are class, education, and occupation levels in our culture, but they are mutually dependent.

The data used for the computation of the PDI in Table 2.1 were from IBM employees in various occupations and, therefore, from different education levels and social classes. The mix of occupations studied, however, was kept constant for all countries. Comparisons of countries or regions should always be based on people in the same set of occupations. One should not compare Spanish engineers to Swedish secretaries. The mix of occupations to be compared across all the subsidiaries was taken from the sales and service offices: these were the only activities that could be found in *all* countries. IBM's product development laboratories were located in only ten of the larger subsidiaries, and its manufacturing plants in thirteen.

The sales and service people had all completed secondary or higher education and could be considered largely middle class. The PDI scores in Table 2.1, therefore, are really expressing differences among *middle-class* persons in these countries. Middle-class values affect the institutions of a country, such as governments and education systems, more than do lower-class values. This is because the people who control the institutions usually belong to the middle class. Even representatives of lower-class groups, such as union leaders, tend to be better educated or self-educated, and by this fact alone they have adopted some middle-class values. Lower-class parents often have middle-class ambitions for their children.

For three large countries (France, Germany, and Great Britain), in which the IBM subsidiaries contained the fullest possible range of industrial activities, PDI scores were computed for all the different occupations in the corporation, including those demanding only a lower level of education and therefore usually taken by lower- or "working"-class persons.[11] Altogether, thirty-eight different occupations within these three countries could be compared.

It was possible to calculate PDI scores by occupation, because the answers to the three questions used for calculating the PDI across the fifty-three countries and regions were also correlated across the thirty-eight occupations. The way survey questions cluster together depends on the way respondents are grouped. Questions that form a cluster for countries need not do so for occupations. Exceptionally, the three PDI questions, as it appeared, could form an index at the occupation level as well as at the country level. The reason is that the PDI measures social inequality across countries. Differences in social status leading to inequality are also the prime criterion by which occupations can be distinguished. Among the other three dimensions derived from the IBM data, only for masculinity-femininity could the country index also be used for occupations.

The result of the comparison across thirty-eight occupations is summarized in Table 2.2. It demonstrates that the occupations with the lowest status and education level (unskilled and semiskilled workers) showed the highest PDI values, and those with the highest status and education level (managers of professional workers, such as engineers and scientists) produced the lowest PDI values. Between the extremes in terms of occupation, the range of PDI scores was about 100 score points—which is of the same order of magnitude as across seventy-four countries and regions (see Table 2.1; but the country differences were based on samples of people with equal jobs and equal levels of education!).

The next question is whether the differences in power distance between occupations were equally strong within all countries. In order to test this, a comparison was done of four occupations of widely different status, from each of eleven country subsidiaries of widely different power distance levels. A table crossing the four occupations against the eleven countries, thus producing forty-four (4 × 11) PDI values, showed that the occupation differences were largest in the countries with the lowest PDI scores and were relatively small in the countries with high PDI scores.[12]

**TABLE 2.2 PDI Values for Six Categories of Occupations
(Based on IBM Data from Great Britain, France, and Germany)**

| | NUMBER OF OCCUPATIONS IN THIS | PDI RANGE | | |
CATEGORY OF OCCUPATIONS	CATEGORY	FROM	TO	MEAN
Unskilled and semiskilled workers	3	85	97	90
Clerical workers and nonprofessional salespeople	8	57	84	71
Skilled workers and technicians	6	33	90	65
Managers of the previous categories	8	22	62	42
Professional workers	8	−22[1]	36	22
Managers of professional workers	5	−19[1]	21	8
Total	38	−22[1]	97	47

1 Negative values exceed the 0 to 100 range established for countries.

In other words, if the country as a whole scored larger power distance in Table 2.1, this applied to all employees, those in high-status as well as those in low-status occupations. If the country scored smaller power distance, this applied most to the employees of middle or higher status: the lower-status, lower-educated employees produced power distance scores nearly as high as their colleagues in the large PDI countries. The values of high-status employees with regard to inequality seem to depend strongly on nationality; those of low-status employees much less.[13]

The fact that less educated, low-status employees in various Western countries hold more "authoritarian" values than their higher-status compatriots had already been described by quite a few sociologists. These authoritarian values not only are manifested at work but also are found in their home situation. A study in the United States and Italy in the 1960s showed that working-class parents demanded more obedience from their children than did middle-class parents, but that the difference was larger in the United States than in Italy.[14]

Measures Associated with Power Distance: The Structure in This and Following Chapters

In the next part of this chapter, the differences in power distance scores for countries will be associated with differences in family, school, workplace, state, and ideas prevailing within the countries. Chapters 3 through 6, which deal with the other dimensions, will also be structured similarly. The associations described are mostly based on the results of statistical analyses, in which the IBM dimension scores have been correlated with the results of other quantitative studies, in the way described in Chapter 1. In addition, use has been made of qualitative information about families, schools, workplaces, and so on, in various countries. In this book the statistical proof will be omitted; interested readers are referred to *Culture's Consequences*.

Power Distance Difference Between Countries: Roots in the Family

Most people in the world are born into a family. All people started acquiring their mental software immediately after birth, from the elders in whose presence they grew up, modeling themselves after the examples set by these elders.

In the large-power-distance situation, children are expected to be obedient toward their parents. Sometimes there is even an order of authority among the children themselves, younger children being expected to yield to older children. Independent behavior on the part of a child is not encouraged. *Respect* for parents and other elders is seen as a basic virtue; children see others showing such respect and soon acquire it themselves. There is often considerable warmth and care in the way parents and older children treat younger ones, especially those who are very young. They are looked after and not expected to experiment for themselves. Respect for parents and older relatives lasts through adulthood: parental authority continues to play a role in a person's life as long as the parents are alive. Parents and grandparents are treated with formal deference even after their children have actually taken control of their own lives. There is a pattern of dependence on seniors that pervades all human contacts, and the mental software that people carry contains a strong *need* for such dependence. In parents' old age or if they become otherwise infirm, children are expected to support them financially and practically; grandparents often live with their children's families.

In the small-power-distance situation, children are more or less treated as equals as soon as they are able to act, and this may already be visible in the way a baby is handled in its bath.[15] The goal of parental education is to let children take control of their own affairs as soon as they can. Active experimentation by the child is encouraged; being allowed to contradict their parents, children learn to say "no" very early. Behavior toward others is not dependent on the other's age or status; formal respect and deference are seldom shown. Family relations in such societies often strike people from other societies as lacking intensity. When children grow up they start relating to their parents as friends, or at least as equals, and there is no question of a grown-up person's asking his or her parents' permission or even advice for an important decision. In the ideal family, adult members are mutually independent. A need for *independence* is supposed to be a major component of the mental software of adults. Parents should make their own provisions for when they become old or infirm; they cannot count on their children to support them, nor can they expect to live with their children.

The pictures in the two previous paragraphs have deliberately been polarized. Reality in a given situation will most likely be in between the opposite ends of the power distance continuum: countries score somewhere along the continuum. We saw that the social class and education levels of the parents, especially in the small-power-distance countries, play an important role. Families develop their own family cultures that may be at variance with the norms of their society, and the personalities of individual parents and children can lead to nontypical behavior. Nevertheless, the two pictures indicate the ends of the line along which solutions to the human inequality dilemma in the family vary.

As the family is the source of our very first social mental programming, its impact is extremely strong, and programs set at this stage are difficult to change. Psychiatrists and psychoanalysts are aware of this importance of one's family history, but not always of its cultural context. Psychiatry tries to help individuals whose behavior deviates from societal norms. This book describes how the norms themselves vary from one society to another. Different norms mean that psychiatric help to a person from another society or even from a different sector of the same society is a risky affair. It demands that the helper is aware of his or her own cultural differences with and biases toward the client.[16]

Power Distance at School

In most societies today, children go to school for at least some years. In the more affluent societies, the school period may cover more than twenty years of a young person's life. In school the child further develops his or her mental programming. Teachers and classmates inculcate additional values, being part of a culture that honors these values. It is an unanswered question to what extent an education system can contribute to changing a society. Can a school create values that were not yet there, or will it unwittingly only be able to reinforce what already exists in a given society? In a comparison of schools across societies, the same patterns of differences resurge that were already found within families. The role pair parent-child is replaced by the role pair teacher-student, but basic values and behaviors are carried forward from one sphere into the other. And of course, most schoolchildren continue to spend most of their time within their families.

In the large-power-distance situation, the parent-child inequality is perpetuated by a teacher-student inequality that caters to the need for dependence well established in the student's mind. Teachers are treated with respect (and older teachers even more so than younger ones); students may have to stand up when teachers enter a classroom. The educational process is teacher centered; teachers outline the intellectual paths to be followed. In the classroom there is supposed to be strict order, with the teacher initiating all communication. Students in class speak up only when invited to; teachers are never publicly contradicted or criticized and are treated with deference even outside school. When a child misbehaves, teachers involve the child's parents and expect them to help put the child in order. The educational process is highly personalized: especially in more advanced subjects at universities, what is transferred is not seen as an impersonal "truth," but as the personal wisdom of the teacher. The teacher is a *guru*, a term derived from the Sanskrit word for "weighty" or "honorable," which in India and Indonesia is, in fact, what a teacher is called. The French term is a *maître à penser*, a "teacher for thinking." In such a system the quality of one's learning is highly dependent on the excellence of one's teachers.

In the small-power-distance situation, teachers are supposed to treat the students as basic equals and expect to be treated as equals by the students. Younger teachers are more equal and are therefore usually more liked than older ones. The educational process is student centered, with a premium on student initiative; students are expected to find their own intellectual paths. Students make uninvited interventions in class; they are supposed to ask questions when they do not understand something. They argue with teachers, express disagreement and criticisms in front of the teachers, and show no particular respect to teachers outside school. When a child misbehaves, parents often side with the child against the teacher. The educational process is rather impersonal; what is transferred are "truths" or "facts" that exist independently of this particular teacher. Effective learning in such a system depends very much on whether the supposed two-way communication between students and teacher is, indeed, established. The entire system is based on the students' well-developed need for independence; the quality of learning is to a considerable extent determined by the excellence of the students.

Earlier in this chapter it was shown that power distance scores are lower for occupations needing a higher education, at least in countries that as a whole score relatively low on power distance. This means that in the latter countries, students will become more independent from teachers as they proceed in their studies: their need for dependence decreases. In large-power-distance countries, however, students remain dependent on teachers even after reaching high education levels.

Small-power-distance countries spend a relatively larger part of their education budget on secondary schools for everybody, contributing to the development of middle strata in society. Large-power-distance countries spend relatively more on university-level education and less on secondary schools, maintaining a polarization between the elites and the uneducated.

Corporal punishment at school, at least for children of prepuberty age, is much more acceptable in a large-power-distance culture than in its opposite. It accentuates and symbolizes the inequality between teacher and student and is often considered good for the development of the child's character. In a small-power-distance society, it will readily be classified as child abuse and may be a reason for parents to complain to the police. There are exceptions, which relate to the dimension of masculinity (versus femininity) to be described in Chapter 4: in some masculine, small-power-distance cultures, such as Great Britain, corporal punishment at school is not considered objectionable by everybody.

As in the case of the family discussed in the previous section, reality is somewhere in between these extremes. An important conditioning factor is the ability of the students: less gifted or handicapped children in small-power-distance situations will not develop the culturally expected sense of independence and will be handled more in the large-power-distance way. Able children from working-class families in small-power-distance societies are at a disadvantage in educational institutions such as universities that assume a small-power-distance norm: as shown in the previous section, working-class families often have a large-power-distance subculture.

Table 2.3 summarizes the key differences between small- and large-power-distance societies discussed so far.

Power Distance in the Workplace

Most people start their working lives as young adults, after having gone through learning experiences in the family and at school. The role pairs parent-child and teacher-student are now complemented with the role pair boss-subordinate, and it should not surprise anybody when attitudes toward parents, especially fathers, and toward teachers, which are part of our mental programming, are transferred toward bosses.

In the large-power-distance situation, superiors and subordinates consider each other as existentially unequal; the hierarchical system is based on this existential inequality. Organizations centralize power as much as possible in a few hands. Subordinates expect to be told what to do. There is a lot of supervisory personnel, structured into tall hierarchies of people reporting to each other. Salary systems show wide gaps between top and bottom in the organization. Workers are relatively uneducated, and manual work has a much lower status than office work. Superiors are entitled to privileges (literally, "private laws"), and contacts between superiors and subordinates are supposed to be initiated by the superiors only. The ideal boss in the subordinates' eyes, the one they feel most comfortable with and whom they respect most, is a benevolent autocrat, or "good father." After some experiences with "bad fathers," they may ideologically reject the boss's authority completely, while complying in practice.

Relationships between subordinates and superiors in a large-power-distance organization are frequently loaded with emotions. Philippe d'Iribarne heads up a French public research center on international management. Through extensive interviews his research team compared manufacturing plants from the same French multinational in France (PDI

68), the United States (PDI 40), and the Netherlands (PDI 38). In his book on this project, d'Iribarne comments:

> *The often strongly emotional character of hierarchical relationships in France is intriguing. There is an extreme diversity of feelings towards superiors: they may be either adored or despised with equal intensity. This situation is not at all universal: we found it neither in the Netherlands nor in the USA.*[17]

This quote confirms the polarization in France between dependence and counterdependence versus authority persons, which we found to be characteristic of large-power-distance countries in general.

Visible signs of status in large-power-distance countries contribute to the authority of bosses; it is quite possible that a subordinate feels proud if he can tell his neighbor that *his* boss drives a bigger car than the neighbor's boss. Older superiors are generally more respected than younger ones. Being a victim of power abuse by one's boss is just bad luck; there is no assumption that there should be ways of redress against such a situation. If it gets too bad, people may join forces for a violent revolt. Packaged leadership methods invented in the United States, such as Management by Objectives (MBO),[18] will not work, because they presuppose some form of negotiation between subordinate and superior that neither party will feel comfortable with.

In the small-power-distance situation, subordinates and superiors consider each other as existentially equal; the hierarchical system is just an inequality of roles, established for convenience; and roles may be changed, so that someone who today is my subordinate may tomorrow be my boss. Organizations are fairly decentralized, with flat hierarchical pyramids and limited numbers of supervisory personnel. Salary ranges between top and bottom jobs are relatively small; workers are highly qualified, and high-skill manual work has a higher status than low-skill office work. Privileges for higher-ups are basically undesirable, and all should use the same parking lot, toilets, and cafeteria. Superiors should be accessible for subordinates, and the ideal boss is a resourceful (and therefore respected) democrat. Subordinates expect to be consulted before a decision is made that affects their work, but they accept that the boss is the one who finally decides.

Status symbols are suspect, and subordinates will most likely comment negatively to their neighbors if their boss spends company money on an excessive car, for example. Younger bosses are generally more appreciated

TABLE 2.3 Key Differences Between Small- and Large-Power-Distance Societies: General Norm, Family, and School

SMALL POWER DISTANCE	LARGE POWER DISTANCE
Inequalities among people should be minimized.	Inequalities among people are expected and desired.
Social relationships should be handled with care.	Status should be balanced with restraint.
There should be, and there is to some extent, interdependence between less and more powerful people.	Less powerful people should be dependent; they are polarized between dependence and counterdependence.
Parents treat children as equals.	Parents teach children obedience.
Children treat parents and older relatives as equals.	Respect for parents and older relatives is a basic and lifelong virtue.
Children play no role in old-age security of parents.	Children are a source of old-age security to parents.
Students treat teachers as equals.	Students give teachers respect, even outside of class.
Teachers expect initiative from students in class.	Teachers should take all initiative in class.
Teachers are experts who transfer impersonal truths.	Teachers are gurus who transfer personal wisdom.
Quality of learning depends on two-way communication and excellence of students.	Quality of learning depends on excellence of teacher.
Less educated persons hold more authoritarian values than more educated persons.	Both more and less educated persons show equally authoritarian values.
Educational policy focuses on secondary schools.	Educational policy focuses on universities.

than older ones. Organizations are supposed to have structured ways of dealing with employee complaints about alleged power abuse. Some packaged leadership methods, such as MBO, may work if given sufficient management attention.

Peter Smith of the University of Sussex in the United Kingdom, through a network of colleagues, collected statements in the 1990s from more than seven thousand department managers in forty-seven countries on how they handled each of eight common work "events" that normally occur in any work organization (for example, "when some of the equipment or machinery in your department seems to need replacement"). For each event, eight possible sources of guidance were listed, for which the managers had to indicate to what extent they relied on each of these (for example, "formal rules and procedures"). For each of the forty-seven countries, Smith computed a *verticality index*, combining reliance on one's superior and on formal rules, *not* on one's own experience and *not* on one's subordinates. Verticality index scores were strongly correlated with PDI: in large-power-distance countries, the managers in the sample reported relying more on their superior and on formal rules and less on their own experience and on their subordinates.[19]

There is no research evidence of a systematic difference in effectiveness between organizations in large-power-distance versus small-power-distance countries. They may be good at different tasks: small-power-distance cultures at tasks demanding subordinate initiative, and large-power-distance cultures at tasks demanding discipline. The important thing is for management to utilize the strengths of the local culture.

This section has again described the extremes; most work situations will be in between and contain some elements of both large and small power distance. Management theories have rarely recognized that these different models exist and that their occurrence is culturally determined. Chapter 7 will return to this issue and show how different theories of management and organization reflect the different nationalities of their authors.

Table 2.4 summarizes key differences in the workplace between small- and large-power-distance societies.

Power Distance and the State

The previous sections have looked at the implications of power distance differences between countries for the role pairs of parent-child, teacher-student, and boss-subordinate; one that is obviously equally affected is authority-citizen. It must be immediately evident to anyone who reads any world news at all that in some countries power differences between authorities and citizens are handled very differently than in others. What is not so evident, yet is essential for understanding, is that ways of handling

TABLE 2.4 **Key Differences Between Small- and Large-Power-Distance Societies: The Workplace**

SMALL POWER DISTANCE	LARGE POWER DISTANCE
Hierarchy in organizations means an inequality of roles, established for convenience.	Hierarchy in organizations reflects existential inequality between higher and lower levels.
Decentralization is popular.	Centralization is popular.
There are fewer supervisory personnel.	There are more supervisory personnel.
There is a narrow salary range between the top and bottom of the organization.	There is a wide salary range between the top and bottom of the organization.
Managers rely on their own experience and on subordinates.	Managers rely on superiors and on formal rules.
Subordinates expect to be consulted.	Subordinates expect to be told what to do.
The ideal boss is a resourceful democrat.	The ideal boss is a benevolent autocrat, or "good father."
Subordinate-superior relations are pragmatic.	Subordinate-superior relations are emotional.
Privileges and status symbols are frowned upon.	Privileges and status symbols are normal and popular.
Manual work has the same status as office work.	White-collar jobs are valued more than blue-collar jobs.

power in a country tend to be rooted in the beliefs held by large sectors of the population regarding the proper ways for authorities to behave.

In his analysis of data from forty-three societies, collected through the World Values Survey (see Chapter 1), U.S. political scientist Ronald Inglehart found he could order countries on a *secular-rational versus traditional authority* dimension. Correlation analysis showed that this dimension corresponds closely to what we call power distance. In a society in which power distances are large, authority tends to be traditional, sometimes even rooted in religion. Power is seen as a basic fact of society that precedes the choice between good and evil. Its legitimacy is irrelevant. Might prevails over right. This is a strong statement that may rarely be presented in this form but is reflected in the behavior of those in power *and* of ordinary people. There is an unspoken consensus that there should be an order of inequality in this world in which everybody has his or her place. Such an order satisfies people's need for dependence, and it gives a sense of security both to those in power and to those lower down.

At the beginning of this chapter, reference was made to the tendency in some societies to achieve consistency in people's positions with regard to power, wealth, and status. A desire for status consistency is typical for large-power-distance cultures. In such cultures the powerful are entitled to privileges and are expected to use their power to increase their wealth. Their status is enhanced by symbolic behavior that makes them look as powerful as possible. The main sources of power are one's family and friends, charisma, and/or the ability to use force; the latter explains the frequency of military dictatorships in countries on this side of the power distance scale. Scandals involving persons in power are expected, and so is the fact that these scandals will be covered up. If something goes wrong, the blame goes to people lower down the hierarchy. If it gets too bad, the way to change the system is by replacing those in power through a revolution. Most such revolutions fail even if they succeed, because the newly powerful, after some time, repeat the behaviors of their predecessors, in which they are supported by the prevailing values regarding inequality.

In large-power-distance countries people read relatively few newspapers (but they express confidence in those they read), and they rarely discuss politics: political disagreements soon deteriorate into violence. The system often admits only one political party; where more parties are allowed, the same party usually always wins elections. The political spectrum, if it is allowed to be visible, is characterized by strong right and left wings with a weak center, a political reflection of the polarization between dependence and counterdependence described earlier in this chapter. Incomes in these countries are unequally distributed, with a few very rich and many very poor people. Moreover, taxation protects the wealthy, so that incomes after taxes can be even more unequal than before taxes. Labor unions tend to be government controlled; where they are not, they are ideologically based and involved in politics.

Authority in small-power-distance societies was qualified by Inglehart as secular-rational: based on practical considerations rather than on tradition. In these societies the feeling dominates that politics and religion should be separated. The use of power should be subject to laws and to the judgment between good and evil. Inequality is considered basically unde-sirable; although unavoidable, it should be minimized by political means. The law should guarantee that everybody, regardless of status, has equal rights. Power, wealth, and status need not go together—it is even consid-ered a good thing if they do not. Status symbols for powerful people are suspect, and leaders may enhance their informal status by renouncing for-mal symbols (for example, the minister taking the streetcar to work). Most countries in this category are relatively wealthy, with a large middle class. The main sources of power are one's formal position, one's assumed exper-tise, and one's ability to give rewards. Scandals usually mean the end of a political career. Revolutions are unpopular; the system is changed in evo-lutionary ways, without necessarily deposing those in power. Newspapers are read regularly by many, although confidence in them is not high. Polit-ical issues are often discussed, and violence in domestic politics is rare. Countries with small-power-distance value systems usually have pluralist governments that can shift peacefully from one party or coalition to another on the basis of election results. The political spectrum in such countries shows a powerful center and weaker right and left wings. Incomes are less unequally distributed than in large-power-distance coun-tries. Taxation serves to redistribute income, making incomes after taxes less unequal than before. Labor unions are independent and less oriented to ideology and politics than to pragmatic issues on behalf of their members.

The reader will easily recognize that some elements of both extremes can be found in many countries. A country such as Spain, ruled dictatori-ally until the 1970s, has shifted to a pluralist government system.[20] The countries of the former Soviet Union struggle with a similar transition, with varying success. Authorities in old democracies occasionally show dictatorial behaviors—for example, in trying to prevent the publication of unwanted revelations by whistle-blowers.

Institutions from small-power-distance countries are sometimes copied in large-power-distance countries, because political ideas travel. Political leaders who studied in other countries may try to emulate these countries' political systems. Governments of smaller-power-distance countries often eagerly try to export their institutional arrangements in the context of development cooperation. Just going through the moves of an election, however, will not change the political mores of a country, if these are deeply rooted in the mental software of a large part of the population. In partic-ular, underfed and uneducated masses make poor democrats, and ways of government customary in more well-off countries are unlikely to function in poor ones. Actions by foreign governments intended to lead other countries toward democratic ways and respect for human rights are clearly inspired by the mental programming of the foreign helpers, and they are usually more effective in dealing with the opinions of the foreign electorate than with the problems in the countries supposed to be helped. In Chapter 9 we will come back to this dilemma and possible ways out of it.

Power Distance and Corruption

A phenomenon that affects the functioning of the state, and sometimes also of private organizations, is corruption. Official and unofficial side payments occur in many situations throughout the world. What is called *corruption* is partly a matter of definition. We speak of corruption when people use the power of their position to illegally enrich themselves or when citizens buy the collaboration of authorities for their private purposes. But what to say about excessive levels of chief executive compensation in some companies and of large amounts spent in some countries on lobbying, which, although formally legal, rest on similar motives? In Japan, China, and many other cultures, the giving of gifts is an important ritual, and the borderline between gift giving and bribing is diffuse. To a purist even tipping can be considered a form of bribing.

Since 1995 Transparency International (a nongovernmental organization located in Berlin, Germany) has been issuing, for a large number of countries, a yearly Corruption Perceptions Index (CPI) on the Internet. The CPI combines information from up to twelve different sources in business, the press, and the foreign services. The index ranges from 10, for a perfectly "clean" country, to 1, for an extremely corrupt country. Our analysis of the 2002 CPI scores showed that worldwide, they depended primarily on wealth: for the sixty-seven countries for which we had all the necessary data, 74 percent of the differences in CPI could be predicted from a country's wealth (GNP [gross national product] per capita), or rather from its poverty, and another 5 percent from power distance index (PDI). Under conditions of poverty, acquiring money in unofficial ways is not just a matter of greed; it may be a matter of survival. Officials, police, and teachers in poor countries are often so ill paid that without side payments they cannot feed their families, and the habit of collecting such payments pervades the entire system. On top of the influence of poverty, power distance adds to the frequency of corruption, as larger power distances stand for fewer checks and balances against power abuse.

The explanation of corruption by poverty cannot apply to wealthy countries. For explaining differences in the CPI of wealthier countries, GNP per capita was irrelevant, but power distance played a much stronger role. The strongest correlations were found with the self-scored PDI values of country elites surveyed in 1984 by a German-U.S. researcher, Michael Hoppe. Hoppe collected IBM-type value scores from parliamentarians, members of government, labor and employers' leaders, academics, and artists in eighteen developed countries (see Table 1.1). Seventy-six percent of the differences in CPI in the year 2002 could be predicted from their elites' PDI in 1984. The elites had described their own values; the CPI, on the other hand, measured how their country was perceived by others. So the power-related values of the elites back in 1984 allowed predicting the perceived corruption in their countries, eighteen years later, with astonishing accuracy.

Corruption, of course, presumes corruptors. Some of these are international trade partners. Next to the CPI, Transparency International publishes periodically a Bribe Payers Index (BPI). The 2002 scores on this index, across twenty-one countries, were also significantly correlated with PDI. Forty-five percent of the differences in BPI could be predicted from the exporting countries' PDI values in Table 2.1. Exporting countries with larger-power-distance cultures are more likely to use side payments to their customers abroad than exporting countries with smaller power distances at home.[21]

To Lord Acton, a nineteenth-century British politician turned Cambridge professor, we owe a famous aphorism: "Power tends to corrupt, and absolute power corrupts absolutely."

Power Distance and Ideas

Parents, teachers, managers, and rulers are all children of their cultures; in a way they are the followers of their followers, and their behavior can only be understood if one also understands the mental software of their children, students, subordinates, and subjects. However, not only the doers in this world but also the thinkers are children of a culture. The authors of management books and the founders of political ideologies generate their ideas from the background of what they learned when they were growing up.

Thus differences between countries along value dimensions such as power distance help not only in understanding differences in thinking, feeling, and behaving by the leaders and those led but also in appreciating the theories produced or adopted in these countries to explain or prescribe thought, feeling, and behavior.

In world history philosophers and founders of religions have dealt explicitly with questions of power and inequality. In China around 500 B.C., Kong Ze, whom the Jesuit missionaries two thousand years later latinized as Confucius (from the older name Kong Fu Ze), maintained that the stability of society is based on unequal relationships between people. He distinguished the *wu lun*, the five basic relationships: ruler-subject, father-son, older brother–younger brother, husband-wife, and senior friend–junior friend. These relationships contain mutual and complementary obligations: for example, the junior partner owes the senior respect and obedience, and the senior owes the junior partner protection and consideration. Confucius's ideas have survived as guidelines for proper behavior for Chinese people to this day. In the People's Republic of China, Mao Zedong tried to wipe out Confucianism, but in the meantime his own rule contained strong Confucian elements.[22] Countries in the IBM study with a Chinese majority or that have undergone Chinese cultural influences are, in the order in which they appear in Table 2.1, China, Singapore, Hong Kong, South Korea, Taiwan, and Japan; they occupy the upper-medium and medium PDI zones. People in these countries accept and appreciate inequality but feel that the use of power should be moderated by a sense of obligation.

In ancient Greece around 350 B.C., Plato recognized a basic need for equality among people, but at the same time, he defended a society in which an elite class, the guardians, would exercise leadership. He tried to resolve the conflict between these diverging tendencies by playing on two meanings of the word *equality*, a quantitative and a qualitative one, but to us his arguments resemble the famous quote from George Orwell's *Animal Farm*: "All animals are equal but some are more equal than others." Present-day Greece in Table 2.1 is found about halfway on power distance (rank 41–42, score 60).

The Christian New Testament, composed in the first centuries A.D., preaches the virtue of poverty.[23] Pursuing this virtue will lead to equality in society, but its practice has been reserved to members of religious orders. It has not been popular with Christian leaders, neither of states, nor of businesses, nor of the Church itself. The Roman Catholic Church has maintained the hierarchical order of the Roman Empire; the same holds for

Eastern Orthodox churches; Protestant denominations to various degrees are nonhierarchical. Traditionally Protestant nations tend to score lower on PDI than Catholic or Orthodox nations.

The Italian Niccolò Machiavelli (1469–1527) is one of world literature's greatest authorities on the use of political power. He distinguished two models: the model of the fox and the model of the lion. The prudent ruler, Machiavelli writes, uses both models each at the proper time: the cunning of the fox will avoid the snares, and the strength of the lion will scare the wolves.[24] Relating Machiavelli's thoughts to national power distance differences, one finds small-power-distance countries to be accustomed to the fox model and large-power-distance countries to the lion model. Italy, in the twentieth-century IBM research data, scores in the middle zone on power distance (rank 51, score 50). It is likely that, were one to study Italy by region, the North would be more foxy and the South more lionlike. What Machiavelli did not write but what the association between political systems and citizens' mental software suggests is that which animal the ruler should impersonate depends strongly on what animals the followers are.

Karl Marx (1818–83) also dealt with power, but he wanted to give it to the powerless; he never really dealt with the question of whether the revolution he preached would create a new powerless class or not. In fact, he seemed to assume that the exercise of power can be transferred from persons to a system, a philosophy in which we can recognize the mental software of the small-power-distance societies to which Marx's mother country, Germany, today belongs. It was a tragedy for the modern world that Marx's ideas have been mainly exported to countries at the large-power-distance side of the continuum in which, as was argued earlier in this chapter, the assumption that power should yield to law is absent. This absence of a check to power has enabled government systems claiming Marx's inheritance to survive even where these systems would make Marx himself turn in his grave. In Marx's concept of the "dictatorship of the proletariat," the *dictatorship* has appealed to rulers in some large-power-distance countries, but the *proletariat* has been forgotten. In fact, the concept is naive: in view of what we know of the human tendency toward inequality, a dictatorship by a proletariat is a logical contradiction.

The exportation of ideas to people in other countries without regard for the values context in which these ideas were developed—and the importation of such ideas by gullible believers in those other countries—is not limited to politics but can also be observed in the domains of education and, in particular, management and organization. The economic success of the United States in the decades before and after World War II has made people in other countries believe that U.S. ideas about management must be superior and therefore should be copied. They forgot to ask about the kind of society in which these ideas were developed and applied—*if* they were really applied as the books claimed. Since the late 1960s the same has happened with Japanese ideas.

The United States in Table 2.1 scores on the low side, but not extremely low, on power distance (rank 57–59 out of 74). U.S. leadership theories tend to be based on subordinates with medium-level dependence needs: not too high, not too low. A key idea is *participative management*— that is, a situation in which subordinates are involved by managers in decisions at the discretion and initiative of these managers. Comparing U.S. theories of leadership to "industrial democracy" experiments in countries such as Sweden or Denmark (which scored extremely low on PDI), one finds that in these Scandinavian countries, subordinates often take the initiative to participate, something U.S. managers find difficult to digest because it represents an infringement on their "management prerogatives." Management prerogatives, however, are less sacred in Scandinavia. On the other hand, U.S. theories of participative management are also unlikely to apply in countries higher on the power distance scale. One study reports the embarrassment of a Greek subordinate when his expatriate U.S. boss asked his opinion on how much time a job should take: "He is the boss. Why doesn't he tell me?"[25]

Table 2.5 summarizes key differences between small- and large-power-distance societies from the last three sections; together with Tables 2.3 and 2.4, it provides an overview of the essence of power distance differences across all spheres of life discussed in this chapter.

Origins of Power Distance Differences

Countries in which the native language is Romance (French, Italian, Portuguese, Romanian, Spanish) scored medium to high on the power distance scale (in Table 2.1, from 50 for Italy to 90 for Romania). Countries in which the native language is Germanic (Danish, Dutch, English, German, Norwegian, Swedish) scored low (from 11 in Austria to 40 in Luxembourg). There seems to be a relationship between language area and present-day mental software regarding power distance. The fact that a country belongs to a language area is rooted in history: Romance languages all derive from

TABLE 2.5 **Key Differences Between Small- and Large-Power-Distance Societies: The State**

SMALL POWER DISTANCE	LARGE POWER DISTANCE
The use of power should be legitimate and follow criteria of good and evil.	Might prevails over right: whoever holds the power is right and good.
Skills, wealth, power, and status need not go together.	Skills, wealth, power, and status should go together.
Mostly wealthier countries with a large middle class.	Mostly poorer countries with a small middle class.
All should have equal rights.	The powerful should have privileges.
Power is based on formal position, expertise, and ability to give rewards.	Power is based on tradition or family, charisma, and the ability to use force.
The way to change a political system is by changing the rules (evolution).	The way to change a political system is by changing the people at the top (revolution).
There is more dialogue and less violence in domestic politics.	There is less dialogue and more violence in domestic politics.
Pluralist governments based on outcome of majority votes.	Autocratic or oligarchic governments based on cooptation.
The political spectrum shows a strong center and weak right and left wings.	The political spectrum, if allowed to exist, has a weak center and strong right and left wings.
There are small income differentials in society, further reduced by the tax system.	There are large income differentials in society, further increased by the tax system.
There is less perceived corruption; scandals end political careers.	There is more perceived corruption; scandals are usually covered up.

Low Latin and were adopted in countries once part of the Roman Empire or, in the case of Latin America, in countries colonized by Spain and Portugal, which themselves were former colonies of Rome. Germanic languages are spoken either in countries that remained "barbaric" in Roman days or in areas once under Roman rule but reconquered by barbarians (such as England). Thus some roots of the mental program called power distance go back at least to Roman times, two thousand years ago. Countries with a Chinese (Confucian) cultural inheritance also cluster on the medium to high side of the power distance scale—and they carry a culture at least four thousand years old.

None of us was present when culture patterns started to diverge between peoples: the attribution of causes for these differences is a matter of educated speculation on the basis of historical and prehistorical sources. Both the Roman and the Chinese Empires were ruled from a single power center, which presupposes a population prepared to take orders from the center. The Germanic part of Europe, on the other hand, was divided into small tribal groups under local lords that were not inclined to accept directives from anybody else. It seems a reasonable assumption that early statehood experiences helped to develop in these peoples the common mental programs necessary for the survival of their political and social system.

The question remains, of course, why these early statehood experiences deviated. One way of supporting the guesswork for causes is to look for quantitative data about countries that might be correlated with the power distance scores. A number of such quantitative variables were available. A statistical tool called *stepwise multiple regression* allowed us to select from these variables the ones that successively contributed most to explaining the differences in PDI scores in Table 2.1. The result is that a country's PDI score can be fairly accurately predicted from the following:

1. The country's geographic latitude (higher latitudes associated with lower PDI)
2. Its population size (larger size associated with higher PDI)
3. Its wealth (richer countries associated with lower PDI)[26]

Geographic latitude (the distance from the equator of a country's capital city) alone allows us to predict 43 percent of the differences (the variance) in PDI values among the fifty countries in the original IBM set. Latitude and population size together predicted 51 percent of the variance, and latitude, population size, plus national wealth (per capita GNP in 1970, the middle year of the survey period) predicted 58 percent. If one knew nothing else about these countries than those three hard to fairly hard data, one would be able to make a list of predicted PDI scores that pretty closely resembled Table 2.1. On average, the predicted values deviate 11 scale points from those found in the IBM surveys. The worst fit is for Israel, where the prediction is 47 and the actual value is 13, a difference of 34 points.

Geographic latitude, the first predictor, is an extremely interesting measure to relate with power distance. It is a rough indication of a country's climate: countries with low latitudes are tropical, with medium latitudes subtropical to moderate, with high latitudes cold. Philosophers and popular wisdom have for centuries ventured climate differences as an explanation for differences in the character of inhabitants. Warm climates, for example, would make people lazy; cold ones would make them industrious. Such assertions are impossible to prove, and it is not difficult to come up with examples that do not fit, such as the industrious Singaporeans, who live almost right on the equator. However, the relationship with PDI is solid and statistically highly significant. For the reader who has not been trained in probability calculus: the relationship found does not mean that geographic latitude *determines* power distance, but rather that higher latitude *contributes to* smaller power distances, along with other elements.

Statistical relationships do not indicate the direction of causality: they do not tell which is cause and which is effect or whether the related elements are maybe both the effects of a common third cause. But in the unique case of a country's geographic position, it is difficult to consider it as anything other than a cause, even an archicause, unless we assume that in prehistoric times peoples have migrated to climates that fit their concepts of power distance, which is rather far-fetched.

The logic of the relationship, supported by various research studies,[27] could be about as follows: First of all, the societies involved have all developed to the level of sedentary agriculture and urban industry. The more primitive hunter-gatherer societies for which a different logic may apply are not included. At lower latitudes (that is, more tropical climates), agricultural societies generally meet a more abundant nature. Survival and population growth in these climates demands a relatively limited intervention of humans with nature: everything grows. In this situation the major threat to a society is the competition of other human groups for the same territory and resources. The better chances for survival exist for those societies that have organized themselves hierarchically and in dependence on one central authority that keeps order and balance.

At higher latitudes (that is, moderate and colder climates), nature is less abundant. There is more of a need for people's intervention with nature in order to carve out an existence. These conditions support the creation of industry next to agriculture. Nature, rather than other humans, is the first enemy to be resisted. Societies in which people have learned to fend for themselves without being too dependent on more powerful others have a better chance of survival under these circumstances than societies that educate their children toward obedience.

Size of population, the second predictor of power distance, fosters dependence on authority because people in a populous country will have to accept a political power that is more distant and less accessible than people from a small nation. On the other hand, a case can be made for a reversal of causality here because less dependently minded peoples will fight harder to avoid being integrated into a larger nation.

National wealth, the third predictor, in itself stands for many other factors, each of which could be both an effect and a cause of smaller power distances. In fact, we are dealing with phenomena for which causality is almost always spiral, such as the causality of the chicken and the egg. Factors associated with more national wealth *and* less dependence on powerful others are:

- Less traditional agriculture
- More modern technology
- More urban living
- More social mobility
- A better educational system
- A larger middle class

More former colonies than former colonizing nations show large power distances, but having been either a colony or a colonizer at some time during the past two centuries is also strongly related to present wealth. The data do not allow establishing a one-way causal path between the three factors of poverty, colonization, and large power differences. Assumptions about causality in this respect usually depend on what one likes to prove.

The Future of Power Distance Differences

So far the picture of differences between countries with regard to power distance has been static. The previous section claimed that some of the differences have historical roots of up to four thousand years or more. So much for the past. But what about the future? We live in an era of unprecedented intensification of international communication: shouldn't this eradicate the differences and help us to grow toward a world standard? And if so, will this be one of large, small, or medium power distances?

Impressionistically at least it seems that dependence on the power of others in a large part of our world has been reduced over the past few generations. Many of us feel less dependent than we assume our parents and grandparents to have been. Moreover, independence is a politically attractive topic. Liberation and emancipation movements abound. Educational opportunities have been improved in many countries, and we have seen that power distance scores within countries decrease with increased education level. This does not mean, however, that the *differences* between countries described in this chapter should necessarily have changed. Countries can all have moved to lower power distance levels without changes in their mutual ranking as shown in Table 2.1.

The IBM research project allowed a comparison between data for 1968 and 1972.[28] During this four-year term, the *desire* for independence among IBM employees increased worldwide, no doubt under the influence of the international communication of ideas. But this desire was only matched by a shift in the direction of more equality in *perceived* power in countries in which power distances had already been small. In fact, countries at opposite ends of the scale grew wider apart.

Using data from the European and World Values Surveys, we compared answers around 1980, 1990, and 2000 on a set of questions on "qualities children can be encouraged to learn at home" for matched samples of the populations of ten developed European countries. Country PDI scores in 2000 were positively correlated with children being encouraged to learn hard work and thrift, and negatively with independence and imagination. From these, the importance of hard work and of thrift had decreased from 1980 via 1990 to 2000, and the importance of imagination had increased. The importance of independence did not change. So the importance of three out of four qualities had changed toward smaller power distances, which suggests a mild overall reduction.[29]

One may try to develop a prediction about longer-term changes in power distance by looking at the underlying forces identified in the preceding section ("Origins of Power Distance Differences"). Of the factors shown to be most closely associated with power distance (latitude, population size, and wealth), the first is immutable. As to the second, size of population, one could argue that in a globalizing world, small and even large countries will be less and less able to make decisions at their own level, and that all will be more and more dependent on decisions made internationally. This should lead to a global *increase* in power distances.

The third factor, wealth, increases for some countries but not for others. Wealth increases may reduce power distances, but only if and where they benefit an entire population. In the last decade of the twentieth century, income distribution in some wealthy countries, led by the United States, has become more uneven rather than more even: wealth increases have benefited disproportionately those who were quite wealthy already. This has the opposite effect: it increases inequality in society, not only in economic but also in legal terms, as the superrich can lobby with legislators and pay lawyers who earn a multiple of the salaries of judges. This kind of wealth increase therefore also *increases* power distances. In countries where the economy stagnates or deteriorates (that is, mainly in countries that are already poor), no reduction or even a further increase in power distance is to be expected anyway.

Nobody, as far as we know, has offered evidence of a convergence of countries toward smaller *differences* in power distance. We believe that the picture of national variety presented in this chapter, with its old historical roots, is likely to survive for a long time, at least for some centuries. A worldwide homogenization of mental programs about power and dependence, independence, and interdependence under the influence of a presumed cultural melting-pot process is still far away, if it will ever happen.

In December 1988 the following news item appeared in the press:

> *Stockholm, December 23. The Swedish King Carl Gustav this week experienced considerable delay while shopping for Christmas presents for his children, when he wanted to pay by check but could not show his check card. The salesperson refused to accept the check without legitimation. Only when helpful bystanders dug in their pockets for one-crown pieces showing the face of the king did the salesperson decide to accept this for legitimation— but not, however, without testing the check thoroughly for authenticity and noting name and address of the holder.*[30]

This Bernadotte (a direct descendant of the French general) still met with the same equality norm as his ancestor. How much time will have to pass before the citizens of the United States, Russia, or Zimbabwe treat their presidents in this way? Or before Swedes start to venerate their king in the same way as Thais do theirs?

I, We, and They

A medium-size Swedish high-technology corporation was approached by a compatriot, a businessman with good contacts in Saudi Arabia. The corporation sent one of its engineers—let us call him Johannesson—to Riyadh, where he was introduced to a small Saudi engineering firm run by two brothers in their mid-thirties, both with British university degrees. The brothers were looking for someone to assist in a development project on behalf of the Saudi government. However, after six visits over a period of two years, nothing seemed to happen. Johannesson's meetings with the brothers were always held in the presence of the Swedish businessman who had established the first contact. This annoyed him and his superiors because they were not at all sure that this businessman did not have contacts with their competitors as well— but the Saudis wanted the intermediary to be there. Discussions often dwelt on issues having little to do with the business—for instance, Shakespeare, of whom both brothers were fans.

Just when Johannesson's superiors started to doubt the wisdom of the corporation's investment in these expensive trips, a fax arrived from Riyadh inviting him for an urgent visit. A contract worth several millions of dollars was ready to be signed. From one day to the next, the Saudis' attitude changed: the presence of the businessman-intermediary was no longer necessary, and Johannesson for the first time saw the Saudis smile and even make jokes.

So far, so good—but the story goes on. The remarkable order acquired contributed to Johannesson's being promoted to a management position in a different division. Thus he was no longer in charge of the Saudi account. A successor was nominated, another engineer with considerable international experience, whom Johannesson personally introduced to the Saudi brothers. A few weeks later another fax arrived from Riyadh in which the Saudis threatened to cancel the contract over a detail in the delivery conditions. Johannesson's help was requested. When he went to Riyadh, it appeared that the conflict was over a minor issue and could easily be resolved—but only, the Saudis felt, with Johannesson as the corporation's representative. So the corporation twisted its structure to allow Johannesson to handle the Saudi account although his main responsibilities were now in a completely different field.

The Individual and the Collective in Society

The Swedes and the Saudis in this true story have different concepts of the role of personal relationships in business. For the Swedes, business is done with a company; for the Saudis, with a person whom one has learned to know and trust. When one does not know the other person well enough, it is best that contact take place in the presence of an intermediary or go-between, someone who knows and is trusted by both parties. At the root of the difference between these cultures is a fundamental issue in human societies: the role of the individual versus the role of the group.

The vast majority of people in our world live in societies in which the interest of the group prevails over the interest of the individual. We will call these societies *collectivist*, a word that to some readers may have political connotations, although the word is not being used in any political sense here. It does not refer to the power of the state over the individual but to the *power of the group*. The first group in our lives is always the family into which we are born. Family structures, however, differ between societies.

In most collectivist societies, the "family" within which the child grows up consists of a number of people living closely together: not just the parents and other children, but, for example, grandparents, uncles, aunts, servants, or other housemates. This is known in cultural anthropology as the *extended family*. When children grow up, they learn to think of themselves as part of a "we" group, a relationship that is not voluntary but is given by nature. The "we" group is distinct from other people in society who belong to "they" groups, of which there are many. The "we" group (or *in-group*) is the major source of one's identity and the only secure protection one has against the hardships of life. Therefore one owes lifelong loyalty to one's in-group, and breaking this loyalty is one of the worst things a person can do. Between the person and the in-group a mutual dependence relationship develops that is both practical and psychological.

A minority of people in our world live in societies in which the interests of the individual prevail over the interests of the group, societies that we will call *individualist*. In these, most children are born into families consisting of two parents and, possibly, other children; in some societies there is an increasing share of one-parent families. Other relatives live elsewhere and are rarely seen. This type is the *nuclear family* (from the Latin *nucleus*, meaning "core"). Children from such families, as they grow up, soon learn to think of themselves as "I." This "I," their personal identity, is distinct from other people's "I"s, and these others are classified not to their group membership but according to individual characteristics. Playmates, for example, are chosen on the basis of personal preferences. The purpose of education is to enable children to stand on their own feet. Children are expected to leave the parental home as soon as this has been achieved. Not infrequently, children, after having left home, reduce relationships with their parents to a minimum or break them off altogether. Neither practically nor psychologically is the healthy person in this type of society supposed to be dependent on a group.

Measuring the Degree of Individualism in Society

Extreme collectivism and extreme individualism can be considered the opposite poles of a second global dimension of national cultures, after power distance (which was described in Chapter 2). All countries in the IBM studies could be given an individualism index score that was low for collectivist and high for individualist societies.

The new dimension is defined as follows. *Individualism* pertains to *societies in which the ties between individuals are loose: everyone is expected to look after himself or herself and his or her immediate family.* Collectivism as its opposite pertains to *societies in which people from birth onward are integrated into strong, cohesive in-groups, which throughout people's lifetimes continue to protect them in exchange for unquestioning loyalty.*

Degrees of individualism obviously vary within countries as well as between them, so it is again important to base the country scores on comparable samples from one country to another. The IBM samples offered this comparability.

The survey questions on which the individualism index is based belong to a set of fourteen *work goals*. People were asked, "Try to think of those factors which would be important to you in an ideal job; disregard the extent to which they are contained in your present job. How important is it to you to . . . " followed by fourteen items, each to be scored on a scale from 1 (of utmost importance) to 5 (of very little or no importance). When the answer patterns for the respondents from forty countries on the fourteen items were analyzed, they reflected two underlying dimensions. One was *individualism versus collectivism.* The other came to be labeled *masculinity versus femininity* (see Chapter 4).

The dimension to be identified with individualism versus collectivism was most strongly associated with the relative importance attached to the following work goal items:

For the individualist pole
1. **Personal time:** have a job that leaves sufficient time for your personal or family life.
2. **Freedom:** have considerable freedom to adopt your own approach to the job.
3. **Challenge:** have challenging work to do—work from which you can get a personal sense of accomplishment.

For the opposite, collectivist, pole
4. **Training:** have training opportunities (to improve your skills or learn new skills).
5. **Physical conditions:** have good physical working conditions (good ventilation and lighting, adequate work space, etc.).
6. **Use of skills:** fully use your skills and abilities on the job.

If the IBM employees in a country scored work goal 1 as relatively important, they generally also scored 2 and 3 as important, but 4, 5, and 6 as
unimportant. Such a country was considered individualist. If work goal 1
was scored as relatively unimportant, the same generally held for 2 and 3,
but 4, 5, and 6 would be scored as relatively more important. Such a country was considered collectivist.

Obviously these items from the IBM questionnaire do not totally cover
the distinction between individualism and collectivism in a society. They
only represent the issues in the IBM research that relate to this distinction.
The correlations of the IBM individualism country scores with non-IBM
data about other characteristics of societies confirm (validate) the claim
that this dimension from the IBM data does indeed measure individualism.

It is not difficult to identify the importance of personal time, freedom,
and (personal) challenge with individualism: they all stress the employee's
independence from the organization. The work goals at the opposite pole—
training, physical conditions, and skills being used on the job—refer to
things the organization does for the employee and in this way stress the
employee's dependence on the organization that fits with collectivism.
Another link in the relationship is that, as will be shown, individualist countries tend to be rich and collectivist countries poor. In rich countries training, physical conditions, and the use of skills may be taken for granted,
which makes them relatively unimportant as work goals. In poor countries
these things cannot at all be taken for granted: they are essential in distinguishing a good job from a bad one, which makes them quite important
among one's work goals.

The actual calculation of the individualism index is not, as in the case
of power distance, based on simply adding or subtracting question scores
after multiplying them with a fixed number. The statistical procedure used
to identify the individualism and, in Chapter 4, the masculinity dimension
(a *factor analysis* of the country scores for the fourteen work goals) produced a *factor score* for either dimension for each country. These factor
scores are a more accurate measure of that country's position on the dimension than could be obtained by adding or subtracting question scores. The
factor scores for the individualism dimension were multiplied by 25 and a
constant number of 50 points was added. This puts the scores in a range
from close to 0 for the most collectivist country to close to 100 for the
most individualist one. This method of calculation was used for the countries of the IBM database. For the various follow-up studies, approximation

formulas were used in which the individualism index value could be directly computed by simple mathematics from the mean scores of four of the work goals.[1]

The individualism index (IDV) scores can be read from Table 3.1. As in the case of the power distance index in Chapter 2, the scores represent *relative* positions of countries. Table 3.1 confirms that nearly all wealthy countries score high on IDV while nearly all poor countries score low. There is a strong relationship between a country's national wealth and the degree of individualism in its culture; we will come back to this later in the chapter.

TABLE 3.1 Individualism Index (IDV) Values for 74 Countries and Regions

COUNTRY/REGION	SCORE	RANK	COUNTRY/REGION	SCORE	RANK
United States	91	1	Finland	63	21
Australia	90	2	Estonia	60	22–24
Great Britain	89	3	Luxembourg	60	22–24
Canada total	80	4–6	Poland	60	22–24
Hungary	80	4–6	Malta	59	25
Netherlands	80	4–6	Czech Republic	58	26
New Zealand	79	7	Austria	55	27
Belgium Flemish	78	8	Israel	54	28
Italy	76	9	Slovakia	52	29
Denmark	74	10	Spain	51	30
Canada Quebec	73	11	India	48	31
Belgium Walloon	72	12	Suriname	47	32
France	71	13–14	Argentina	46	33–35
Sweden	71	13–14	Japan	46	33–35
Ireland	70	15	Morocco	46	33–35
Norway	69	16–17	Iran	41	36
Switzerland German	69	16–17	Jamaica	39	37–38
Germany	67	18	Russia	39	37–38
South Africa[1]	65	19	Arab countries	38	39–40
Switzerland French	64	20	Brazil	38	39–40

continued

COUNTRY/REGION	SCORE	RANK	COUNTRY/REGION	SCORE	RANK
Turkey	37	41	Singapore	20	56–61
Uruguay	36	42	Thailand	20	56–61
Greece	35	43	Vietnam	20	56–61
Croatia	33	44	West Africa	20	56–61
Philippines	32	45	Salvador	19	62
Bulgaria	30	46–48	Korea (South)	18	63
Mexico	30	46–48	Taiwan	17	64
Romania	30	46–48	Peru	16	65–66
East Africa	27	49–51	Trinidad	16	65–66
Portugal	27	49–51	Costa Rica	15	67
Slovenia	27	49–51	Indonesia	14	68–69
Malaysia	26	52	Pakistan	14	68–69
Hong Kong	25	53–54	Colombia	13	70
Serbia	25	53–54	Venezuela	12	71
Chile	23	55	Panama	11	72
Bangladesh	20	56–61	Ecuador	8	73
China	20	56–61	Guatemala	6	74

Scores for countries or regions in **bold type** were calculated from the IBM database. Scores for other countries or regions were based on replications or estimates.

1 The data were from whites only.

Sweden scored 71 on IDV, and the group of Arab-speaking countries to which Saudi Arabia belongs scored an average of 38, which demonstrates the cultural roots of Johannesson's dilemma. Of course, the Arab countries differ among themselves, and impressionistically the Saudis within this region are even more collectivist than some other Arabs, such as the Lebanese or the Egyptians. In the IBM sample, the latter were more strongly represented than the Saudis. Sweden's rank among seventy-four countries and regions is 13–14, and the Arab countries rank 39–40, so there are still a lot of countries scoring more collectivist than the Arab average. As stated earlier, collectivism is the rule in our world, and individualism the exception.

Individualism and Collectivism in Other Cross-National Studies

Table 1.1 listed six major replications of the IBM research, published between 1990 and 2002. Five of these, covering between fifteen and twenty-eight countries from the IBM set, produced IDV scores significantly correlated with the original IBM scores.[2] As in the case of PDI (Chapter 2), the various replications did not sufficiently agree to justify changing the score of any of the countries. The original IBM set still served as the best common denominator for the various studies.

Bond's Chinese Value Survey study among students in twenty-three countries, described in Chapter 1, produced an *integration* dimension, on which the countries positioned themselves largely in the same way as they had done on individualism-collectivism in the IBM studies (in statistical terms, integration was significantly correlated with IDV).[3] Students from countries scoring "individualist" answered that the following values were particularly important:

- Tolerance of others
- Harmony with others
- Noncompetitiveness
- A close, intimate friend
- Trustworthiness
- Contentedness with one's position in life
- Solidarity with others
- Being conservative

This was the largest cluster of CVS values associated with any single IBM dimension pole. In the individualist society, relationships with others are not obvious and prearranged, but rather they are voluntary and have to be carefully fostered. The values at the individualist pole of the integration dimension describe conditions for the ideal voluntary relationship.

Students in collectivist societies answered that the following values were particularly important:

- Filial piety (obedience to parents, respect for parents, honoring of ancestors, financial support of parents)

- Chastity in women
- Patriotism

In the collectivist society, there is no need to make specific friendships: who one's friends are is predetermined by one's family or group membership. The family relationship is maintained by filial piety and chastity in women and is associated with patriotism. In some versions of the IBM questionnaire, a work goal "serve your country" was included. This, too, was found to be strongly associated with collectivism.

Chapter 1 mentioned four other cross-national values databases: by Schwartz, Trompenaars, GLOBE, and the World Values Survey. All four produced dimensions or categories strongly correlated with IDV. Schwartz identified seven categories of values from which no fewer than five were significantly correlated with IDV.[4]

Smith's analysis of the Trompenaars database produced two major dimensions, one primarily correlated with IDV and one with PDI.[5]

The GLOBE project defined two categories of collectivism: social and in-group. As this is written, their correlations with IDV have not yet been published. We expect both to be significant.

Inglehart's overall analysis of the huge database of the World Values Survey produced two statistical factors. One of these, *secular-rational versus traditional authority*, was associated with small versus large power distance, and we met it in the previous chapter. The other, *well-being versus survival*, was strongly correlated with individualism versus collectivism.[6]

An ingenious study by British psychologist Peter Smith compared not the results of the various international studies but rather the degree of acquiescence in their answers. *Acquiescence*, which occurs in all paper-and-pencil surveys, is the tendency among respondents to give positive answers regardless of the content of the questions. Smith compared six studies that each covered thirty-four or more countries, including studies by Geert, Schwartz, and GLOBE. For sections of the questionnaires dealing with values, all six studies demonstrated similar acquiescence patterns. Smith showed that the common tendency to give positive answers in the six studies was stronger in countries that, according to our measures, were collectivist and large power distance. Smith's study has supplied us with a nonobtrusive measure of the degree to which respondents in a culture want to maintain formal harmony and respect toward the researchers.[7]

Are Individualism and Collectivism One or Two Dimensions?

A frequently asked question is whether it is correct to treat individualism and collectivism as opposite poles of the same dimension. Shouldn't they be seen as two separate dimensions? The answer is that it depends on whether we compare entire societies (which is what our book is about) or individuals within societies. This is known as the *level of analysis* issue.

Societies are composed of a wide variety of individual members, holding a variety of personal values. Tests have shown that a person can score high on both individualist and collectivist values, high on one kind and low on the other, or low on both. So when we compare the values of individuals, individualism and collectivism should be treated as two separate dimensions.[8]

When we study societies, we compare two types of data: average value scores of the individuals within each society, plus characteristics of the societies as wholes, including their institutions. Research by us and by others has shown that in societies where people on average hold more individualist values, they also on average hold less collectivist values. Individual persons may differ from this pattern, but those who differ are fewer than those who conform to it. The institutions of such societies reflect the fact that they evolved or were designed primarily for catering to individualists. In societies where people on average hold more collectivist values, they also on average hold less individualist values. The institutions of such societies assume that people are primarily collectivist. Therefore at the society (or country) level, individualism and collectivism appear as opposite poles of one dimension. The position of a country on this dimension shows the society's solution for a universal dilemma: the desirable strength of the relationships of an adult person with the group or groups with which she or he identifies.

Collectivism Versus Power Distance

Many countries that score high on the power distance index (Table 2.1) score low on the individualism index (Table 3.1), and vice versa. In other words, the two dimensions tend to be negatively correlated: large-power-distance countries are also likely to be more collectivist, and small-power-distance countries to be more individualist. The relationship between the two indices is plotted in Figure 3.1.

FIGURE 3.1 Power Distance Versus Individualism

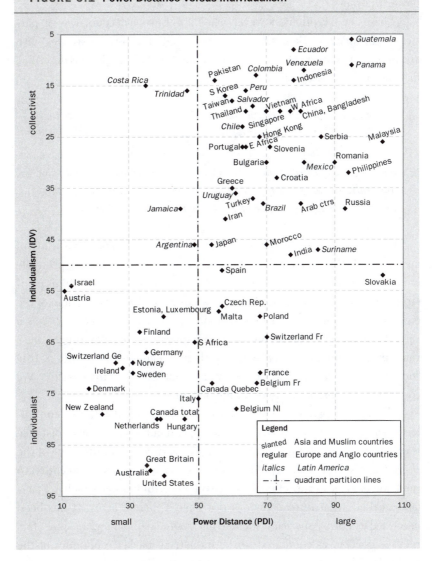

In the plot of Figure 3.1, the countries are grouped around a diagonal from lower left to upper right, reflecting the correlation between power distance and collectivism.[9] In cultures in which people are dependent on ingroups, these people are *usually* also dependent on power figures. Most extended families have patriarchal structures with the head of the family exercising strong moral authority. In cultures in which people are relatively independent from in-groups, they are *usually* also less dependent on powerful others.

There are exceptions, however. The Latin European countries—in particular, France and Belgium—combined medium power distances with strong individualism. The French sociologist Michel Crozier has described his country's culture as follows:

> *Face-to-face dependence relationships are . . . perceived as difficult to bear in the French cultural setting. Yet the prevailing view of authority is still that of . . . absolutism. . . . The two attitudes are contradictory. However, they can be reconciled within a bureaucratic system since impersonal rules and centralization make it possible to reconcile an absolutist conception of authority and the elimination of most direct dependence relationships.*[10]

Crozier's compatriot Philippe d'Iribarne, in his comparative study of a French, a U.S., and a Dutch organization, describes the French principle of organizing as "the rationale of honor" (*la logique de l'honneur*). This principle, which d'Iribarne finds already present in the French kingdom of the eighteenth century A.D., prior to Napoleon, means that everybody has a rank (large power distance) but that the implications of belonging to one's rank are less imposed by one's group than determined by tradition. It is "not so much what one owes to others as what one owes to oneself."[11] We could call it a *stratified* form of individualism.

The reverse pattern, small power distance combined with medium collectivism, was found in Austria and Israel, and fairly small power distance is combined with strong collectivism in Costa Rica. Costa Rica, one of the seven Central American republics, is widely recognized as an exception to the Latin American rule of dependence on powerful leaders, which in Spanish is called *personalismo*. It does not have a formal army. It has been described as Latin America's "most firmly rooted democracy," in spite of its relative poverty as compared to the industrial market economies of the world. In a comparison between Costa Rica and its larger but much poorer neighbor Nicaragua, U.S. development expert Lawrence E. Harrison has written:

> *[T]here is ample evidence that Costa Ricans have felt a stronger bond to their countrymen than have Nicaraguans. That bond is reflected in Costa Rica's long-standing emphasis on public education and public health; in its*

more vigorous cooperative movement; in a judicial system notable by Latin American standards for its impartiality and adherence to fundamental concepts of due process; and above all in the resilience of its politics, its capacity to find peaceful solutions, its appreciation of the need for compromise.[12]

Cases like France and Costa Rica justify treating power distance and collectivism as two separate dimensions, in spite of the fact that for most countries they go together. One reason for the correlation between these dimensions is that both are associated with a third factor: economic development. If economic development is held constant (that is, if rich countries are compared to rich ones only and poor to poor ones), the relationship almost disappears.[13]

Comparisons between the results of the IBM and other studies support the distinction between power distance and collectivism. Studies dealing with inequality show results that are more correlated with power distance than with individualism-collectivism, and studies dealing with the integration of individuals into groups show results more correlated with collectivism than with power distance.[14]

Individualism and Collectivism According to Occupation

One more argument in favor of distinguishing power distance from collectivism is that while, as Chapter 2 showed, power distance indices could be computed not only for countries but also for occupations, individualism indices can only be calculated for countries, not for occupations. In a comparison of how people in different *occupations* answered the fourteen work goal questions from which the IDV was computed, their answers could not be classified in terms of individualist or collectivist. In distinguishing occupations, for example, the importance of challenge and of use of skills go together, while in distinguishing countries they are opposites. Across occupations, when personal time is rated more important, challenge tends to be less important, while across countries the two reinforce each other.[15]

A pair of terms that can be used to distinguish occupations is *intrinsic* versus *extrinsic*. These words refer to what motivates people in a job: the work itself (intrinsically motivating jobs) or the conditions and material rewards provided (extrinsically motivating jobs). This distinction was popularized in the late 1950s through the research on work motivation by the

U.S. psychologist Frederick Herzberg and his team, who argued that the intrinsic factors are the real "motivators" while the extrinsic ones represent the psychological "hygiene" of the job.[16] People in occupations demanding more education tend to score intrinsic elements as more important, while people in lower-status, lower-education occupations prefer extrinsic elements. The intrinsic-extrinsic distinction, while useful for distinguishing occupation cultures, in its turn is not suitable for comparing countries.

Individualism and Collectivism in the Family

In the beginning of this chapter, individualism was associated with a nuclear family structure and collectivism with an extended family structure, the latter leading to the distinction between in-groups and out-groups. The relationship between the individual and the group, like other basic elements of human culture, is first learned in the family setting. The fact that Japan scores about halfway in Table 3.1 (with a rank of 33–35 and an IDV of 46) can at least be partly understood from the fact that in the traditional Japanese family, only the oldest son continued to live with his parents, thus creating a lineal structure somewhere in between nuclear and extended.

The child who grows up among a number of elders, peers, and juniors learns naturally to conceive of him- or herself as part of a "we," much more so than does the nuclear family child. A child of an extended family is seldom alone, whether during the day or at night. An African student who came to Belgium for a university study told us that this was the first time in her life she had ever been alone in a room for any sizable length of time. Conversely, northern European students returning from internships in Peru or Malaysia complained that they were never left alone by their hosts.

In a situation of intense and continuous social contact, the maintenance of harmony with one's social environment becomes a key virtue that extends to other spheres beyond the family. In most collectivist cultures, direct confrontation of another person is considered rude and undesirable. The word *no* is seldom used, because saying "no" *is* a confrontation; "you may be right" or "we will think about it" are examples of polite ways of turning down a request. In the same vein, the word *yes* should not necessarily be seen as an approval, but as maintenance of the line of communication; "yes, I heard you" is the meaning it has in Japan.

In individualist cultures, on the other hand, speaking one's mind is a virtue. Telling the truth about how one feels is a characteristic of a sincere and honest person. Confrontation can be salutary; a clash of opinions is believed to lead to a higher truth. The effect of communications on other people should be taken into account, but it does not, as a rule, justify changing the facts. Adult individuals should be able to take direct feedback constructively. In the family, children are told one should always tell the truth, even if it hurts. Coping with conflict is a normal part of living together as a family.

A former Dutch missionary in Indonesia (a country with an IDV of 14 and a rank of 68–69) told about his parishioners' unexpected exegesis of the following parable from the Bible: "A man had two sons. He went to the first and said 'Son, go and work in the vineyard today'; he replied 'I will go, sir,' but he did not go. The man went to the second and said the same to him. He replied 'I will not,' but afterwards he changed his mind and did go. Which of the two did the will of the father?"[17] The biblical answer is that the last did, but the missionary's Indonesian parishioners chose the first, for this son observed the formal harmony and did not contradict his father. Whether he actually went was of secondary importance.

In the collectivist family, children learn to take their bearings from others when it comes to opinions. Personal opinions do not exist—they are predetermined by the group. If a new issue comes up on which there is no established group opinion, some kind of family conference is necessary before an opinion can be given. A child who repeatedly voices opinions deviating from what is collectively felt is considered to have a bad character. In the individualist family, on the contrary, children are expected and encouraged to develop opinions of their own, and a child who always only reflects the opinions of others is considered to have a weak character. The behavior corresponding with a desirable character depends on the cultural environment.

The loyalty to the group that is an essential element of the collectivist family also means that resources are shared. If one member of an extended family of twenty persons has a paid job and the others do not, the earning member is supposed to share his or her income in order to help feed the entire family. On the basis of this principle, a family may collectively cover the expenses for sending one member to get a higher education, expecting that when this member subsequently gets a well-paid job, the income will also be shared.

In individualist cultures parents will be proud if children at an early age take small jobs in order to earn pocket money of their own, which they alone can decide how to spend. In the Netherlands, as in many other indi-

vidualist western European countries, the government contributes substantially to the living expenses of students. In the 1980s the system was
changed from an allowance to the parents to an allowance directly to the
students themselves, which stressed their independence. Boys and girls
were now treated as independent economic actors from age eighteen
onward. In the United States it is quite normal for students to pay for their
own studies by getting temporary jobs and personal loans; without government support they, too, are less dependent on their parents and not at
all on more distant relatives.

Obligations to the family in a collectivist society are not only financial
but also ritual. Family celebrations like baptisms, marriages, and, especially,
funerals are extremely important and should not be missed. Expatriate
managers from individualist societies are often surprised by the family reasons given by employees from a collectivist host society who apply for a
special leave; the expatriates think they are being fooled, but most likely the
reasons are authentic.

In an individualist culture when people meet they feel a need to communicate verbally. Silence is considered abnormal. Social conversations can
be depressingly banal, but they are compulsory. In a collectivist culture
the fact of being together is emotionally sufficient; there is no compulsion
to talk unless there is information to be transferred. Raden Mas Hadjiwibowo, an Indonesian businessman from a Javanese noble family, recalled
the family visits from his youth in the 1930s as follows:

> *Visits among Javanese family members needed no previous appointment.*
> *Actually that could easily be done, for although the telephone had not come*
> *into common use yet, one could always send a servant with a letter asking*
> *for an appointment. But it was not done, it never occurred to one that a*
> *visit would not suit the other party. It was always convenient. Unexpected*
> *visitors did not exist. The door was (and still is) always open.*
>
> *The visitors were welcomed with joyful courtesy and would be asked*
> *to take a seat. The host and hostess hurriedly withdrew to change into more*
> *suitable attire than their workaday clothes. Without asking, a servant*
> *brought in coffee or tea. Cookies were offered, while in the meantime the*
> *host and hostess had joined the party.*
>
> *There we sat, but nobody spoke. We were not embarrassed by this*
> *silence; nobody felt nervous about it. Every now and then, thoughts and*
> *news were exchanged. But this was not really necessary. We enjoyed being*

together, seeing each other again. After the first exchange of news, any other communication was utterly redundant. If one did not have anything to say, there was no need to recite platitudes. After an hour or so, the guests would ask permission to leave. With mutual feelings of satisfaction, we parted. In smaller towns on the island of Java life is still like this.[18]

U.S. anthropologist and popular author Edward T. Hall distinguished cultures on the basis of their way of communicating along a dimension from high-context to low-context.[19] A *high-context* communication is one in which little has to be said or written because most of the information is either in the physical environment or supposed to be known by the persons involved, while very little is in the coded, explicit part of the message. This type of communication is frequent in collectivist cultures; Hadjiwibowo's family visit is a case example. A *low-context* communication is one in which the mass of information is vested in the explicit code, which is typical for individualist cultures. Many things that in collectivist cultures are self-evident must be said explicitly in individualist cultures. American business contracts are much longer than Japanese business contracts.

Next to harmony another important concept in connection with the collectivist family is *shame*. Individualist societies have been described as *guilt* cultures: persons who infringe upon the rules of society will often feel guilty, ridden by an individually developed conscience that functions as a private inner pilot. Collectivist societies, on the contrary, are shame cultures: persons belonging to a group from which a member has infringed upon the rules of society will feel ashamed, based on a sense of collective obligation. Shame is social in nature, guilt individual; whether shame is felt depends on if the infringement has become known by others. This becoming known is more of a source of shame than the infringement itself. Such is not the case for guilt, which is felt whether or not the misdeed is known by others.

One more concept bred in the collectivist family is *face*. "Losing face," in the sense of being humiliated, is an expression that penetrated into the English language from the Chinese; the English had no equivalent for it. David Yau-Fai Ho, a Hong Kong social scientist, defined it as follows: "Face is lost when the individual, either through his action or that of people closely related to him, fails to meet essential requirements placed upon him by virtue of the social position he occupies."[20] The Chinese also speak of "giving someone face," in the sense of honor or prestige. Basically, *face* describes the proper relationship with one's social environment, which is as essential to a person (and that person's family) as the front part of his or her head. The importance of face is the consequence of living in a society very conscious of social contexts. The languages of other collectivist cultures have words with more or less similar meanings. In Greece, for example, there is a word *philotimo*; Harry Triandis, a Greek-American psychologist, has written:

> *A person is* philotimos *to the extent in which he conforms to the norms and values of his in-group. These include a variety of sacrifices that are appropriate for members of one's family, friends, and others who are "concerned with one's welfare"; for example, for a man to delay marriage until his sisters have married and have been provided with a proper dowry is part of the normative expectations of traditional rural Greeks as well as rural Indians (and many of the people in between).*[21]

In the individualist society the counterpart characteristic is self-respect, but this again is defined from the point of view of the individual, whereas face and *philotimo* are defined from the point of view of the social environment.

Collectivist societies usually have ways of creating family-like ties with persons who are not biological relatives but who are socially integrated into one's in-group. In Latin America, for example, this can be done via the institution of *compadres* and *comadres* who are treated as relatives even if they are not. In Japan younger sons in past times became apprentices to crafts masters through a form of adoption. Similar customs existed in medieval central Europe.

Because families are so important in a collectivist society, selection of marriage partners is a crucial event, not only for the partners but also for both their families. U.S. psychologist David Buss coordinated a survey study of criteria for selecting a potential marriage partner.[22] His respondents were almost ten thousand young women and men, with an average age of twenty-three, from thirty-seven countries. Universally desired characteristics for both future brides and future grooms were mutual love, kindness, emotional stability, intelligence, and health. Other characteristics varied between brides and grooms and across countries. Country differences were primarily related to individualism. In collectivist countries, men preferred future brides to be younger, and they put more stress on brides being wealthy, industrious, and chaste. Women in collectivist countries wanted their future grooms to be older and wealthier, but the groom's industriousness to them played a smaller role, and the groom's chastity none at all.

The men's desire for chastity in brides, however, depended even more on the countries' poverty than on their collectivism. This can be explained as follows: increasing affluence provides women with more educational opportunities (in any society, when education becomes first available, parents give priority to boys who are not needed around the house). With affluence, girls start to move around more freely and get more opportunities for meeting boys. It also gives people more living space and more privacy. Medical care and information improve, including know-how about contraception. Young people get more opportunities for sexual exploration, and sexual norms adapt to this situation.

The stress on the brides' industriousness, wealth, and chastity in collectivist societies is a consequence of the fact that marriage in such a society is a contract between families rather than between individuals. Industriousness, wealth, and chastity are the aspects that families can observe. In many collectivist societies, marriages are arranged by a broker, and the bride and groom may have little say in the choice of their partner; sometimes they are not even supposed to meet before the wedding day. This does not mean that such marriages are less happy. Research in India has shown more marital satisfaction in arranged marriages than in love marriages and more in Indian love marriages than in American marriages. While cultural individualism fosters the valuing of romantic love, certain aspects of individualism at the psychological level make developing intimacy problematic.[23] In a survey about the role of love in marriage, answered by female and male undergraduate students in eleven countries, one question ran: "If a man (woman) had all the other qualities you desired, would you marry this person if you were not in love with him (her)?" The answers varied with the degree of individualism in the eleven societies, from 4 percent "yes" and 86 percent "no" in the United States to 50 percent "yes" and 39 percent "no" in Pakistan.[24] In collectivist societies, considerations other than love weigh heavily in marriage.

Table 3.2 summarizes the key differences between collectivist and individualist societies described so far.

TABLE 3.2 Key Differences Between Collectivist and Individualist Societies: General Norm and Family

COLLECTIVIST	INDIVIDUALIST
People are born into extended families or other in-groups that continue protecting them in exchange for loyalty.	Everyone grows up to look after him- or herself and his or her immediate (nuclear) family only.
Children learn to think in terms of "we."	Children learn to think in terms of "I."
Harmony should always be maintained and direct confrontations avoided.	Speaking one's mind is a characteristic of an honest person.
Friendships are predetermined.	Friendships are voluntary and should be fostered.
Resources should be shared with relatives.	Individual ownership of resources, even for children.
High-context communication prevails.	Low-context communication prevails.
Trespassing leads to shame and loss of face for self and group.	Trespassing leads to guilt and loss of self-respect.
Brides should be young, industrious, and chaste; bridegrooms should be older.	Criteria for marriage partner are not predetermined.

Language, Personality, and Behavior in Individualist and Collectivist Cultures

A Japanese-Australian couple, Yoshi and Emiko Kashima, he a psychologist, she a linguist, studied the relationship between culture and language. Among other features of languages, they studied *pronoun drop*, the practice of omitting the first-person singular pronoun ("I") from a sentence (for example, "I love you" in Spanish: *te quiero* rather than *yo te quiero*). They included thirty-nine languages used in seventy-one different countries and looked for correlations with a number of other variables. The strongest correlation they found was with IDV.[25] Languages spoken in individualist cultures tend to require speakers to use the "I" pronoun when referring to themselves; languages spoken in collectivist cultures allow or prescribe dropping this pronoun. The English language, spoken in the most individualist countries in Table 3.1, is the only one we know of that writes "I" with a capital letter.

Languages change over time, but only slowly. The first-person singular pronoun was used in western European languages in medieval poetry. An Arab saying dating from the same period is "the satanic 'I' be damned!"[26] The link between culture scores and language features illustrates the very old roots of cultural differences.

The Chinese-American anthropologist Francis Hsu has argued that the Chinese language has no equivalent for *personality* in the Western sense. Personality in the West is a separate entity, distinct from society and culture—an attribute of the individual. The closest translation into Chinese is *ren*, but this includes not only the individual but also his or her intimate societal and cultural environment that makes his or her existence meaningful.[27]

The same point was made by two U.S. psychologists, Hazel Rose Markus and Shinobu Kitayama, the latter of Japanese descent. They argued that many Asian cultures have conceptions of individuality that insist on the fundamental relatedness of individuals to each other, while in America individuals seek to maintain their independence from others by focusing on the self and by discovering and expressing their unique inner attributes. The way people experience their self differs with the culture.[28] In our interpretation, individualist cultures encourage an independent self; collectivist cultures, an interdependent self.

U.S. psychologist Solomon E. Asch (1907–96) designed a rather nasty experiment to test to what extent U.S. individuals would stick to their own judgment against a majority. The subject believed he or she was a member of a group of people who had to judge which of two lines was longer. Unknown to the subject, all other group members were confederates of the experimenter and deliberately gave a false answer. In this situation, a sizable percentage of the subjects conformed to the group opinion against their own conviction. Since the 1950s this experiment has been replicated in a number of countries. The percentage of subjects conforming to the false judgment was negatively correlated with the countries' IDV score.[29]

Personality research is a core subject of psychology. There used to be a confusing variety of personality tests available, but since the 1990s a consensus has been building that there is a set of five dominant separate and useful dimensions of personality variation (the so-called Big Five):

O: Openness to experience versus rigidity

C: Conscientiousness versus undependability

E: Extraversion versus introversion

A: Agreeableness versus ill-temperedness

N: Neuroticism versus emotional stability

U.S. psychologists Paul T. Costa and Robert R. McCrae developed a self-scored personality test based on the Big Five, the Revised NEO Personality Inventory (NEO-PI-R). It has been translated from American English into a number of other languages. Mean scores on the five NEO-PI-R dimensions for comparative samples from thirty-three countries showed significant correlations with all four IBM culture dimensions. The highest correlation was between extraversion and IDV.[30] Extraversion (as opposed to introversion) combines the following set of self-scored personality facets that tend to go together: warmth, gregariousness, assertiveness, activity, excitement seeking, and positive emotions. What the correlations show is that on average, people in more individualist cultures rate themselves higher on these facets than people in more collectivist cultures. It may look surprising that people in cultures that encourage an independent self score themselves higher on gregariousness, but it is precisely when relationships between people are *not* prescribed by the culture that the conscious decision to get together becomes more important.

U.S. psychologist David Matsumoto analyzed a large number of studies of the recognition of emotions in facial expressions. Students classified the emotions from photos of faces into happiness, surprise, sadness, fear, disgust, and anger. For fifteen countries from the IBM set, percentages of observers correctly perceiving happiness were correlated positively with IDV, and those perceiving sadness negatively. Our interpretation is that individualist cultures encourage the showing of happiness but discourage the sharing of sadness; collectivist cultures do the opposite.[31] This is in line with the correlation between IDV and self-scored positive emotions as described in the previous paragraph.

U.S. professor Robert Levine asked his international students to collect data on the pace of life in their hometown. One measure collected was walking speed, defined as the stopwatch time it took seventy healthy adults (of both genders, fifty-fifty) to cover a distance of sixty feet in one of two uncrowded locations in each city, when walking alone on a clear summer day during main business hours. From thirty-one countries covered, twenty-three overlapped with the IBM set. Walking speed turned out to be strongly correlated with IDV. People in individualist cultures tended to walk faster.[32] We interpret this as a physical expression of their self-concept: people in more individualist cultures are more active in trying to get somewhere.

Powerful information about differences in behavior across countries can be obtained from consumer surveys. Dutch marketing professor and consultant Marieke de Mooij, comparing fifteen European countries, found many meaningful correlations between consumer behavior data and IDV.[33] Persons in high-IDV countries were more likely than those in low-IDV countries to live in detached houses and less likely to live in apartments or flats. They were more likely to have a private garden and to own a caravan (trailer, mobile home) for leisure. They more frequently had dogs as pets and especially cats, as measured by the household's consumption of pet food. (Cats are more individualistic animals than dogs!) They were more likely to possess home and life insurance. They more often engaged in do-it-yourself activities: painting walls and woodwork, wall papering, home carpentering, electric innovations and repairs, and plumbing. In all these cases, IDV explained the country differences better than national wealth. They all suggest a lifestyle in which the person tries to be self-supporting and not dependent on others.

In matters of information, persons in high-IDV countries read more books, and they were more likely to own a home computer and a telephone with voice mail. High-IDV country residents more often rated TV advertising useful for information about new products. They relied more on media and less on their social network.

There is no indication that individualist cultures are healthier or unhealthier than collectivist cultures, but the fact that people in high-IDV cultures are more focused on their self is visible in a greater concern for their own health than is found in low-IDV cultures. If we limit our analysis to the higher-income countries, where full medical provisions can be assumed to be available, people in countries with a more individualist culture spend a greater share of their private income on their health. Governments of the same countries also spend a greater share of public budgets on health care.[34]

Individualist and collectivist cultures deal differently with disability. A survey among Australian health-care workers showed different reactions to becoming disabled between the Anglo, Arabic-speaking, Chinese, German-speaking, Greek, and Italian immigrant communities. In the individualist communities (Anglo and German) the disabled tended to remain cheerful and optimistic, resent dependency and being helped, and plan for a future life as normal as possible. In the collectivist communities (Greek, Chinese, Arabic) there would be more expression of grief, shame, and pessimism; family members would be asked for advice and assistance, and they would make the main decisions about the disabled person's future. The Italians tended to be in the middle; northern Italy is more individualist, but a large share of Italian immigrants in Australia is from the collectivist South. Another study described the answers of the same panel of health-care workers about the way the different groups dealt with disabled children. Again in the individualist communities the dominant philosophy was to treat the disabled children as much as possible like other children, letting them participate in all activities where this was feasible. In the collectivist communities the disability would be seen as a shame on the family and a stigma on its members—especially if the child was a son—and the child would more often be kept out of sight.[35]

Table 3.3 summarizes the key differences between collectivist and individualist societies from this section.

Individualism and Collectivism at School

The relationship between the individual and the group that has been established in a child's consciousness during his or her early years in the family is further developed and reinforced at school. This is clearly visible in classroom behavior. In the context of development assistance, it often happens that teachers from a more individualist culture move to a more collectivist environment. A typical complaint from such teachers is that students do not speak up, not even when the teacher puts a question to the class. For the student who conceives of him- or herself as part of a group, it is illogical to speak up without being sanctioned by the group to do so. If the

TABLE 3.3 Key Differences Between Collectivist and Individualist Societies: Language, Personality, and Behavior

COLLECTIVIST	INDIVIDUALIST
Use of the word *I* is avoided.	Use of the word *I* is encouraged.
Interdependent self.	Independent self.
On personality tests, people score more introvert.	On personality tests, people score more extrovert.
Showing sadness is encouraged, and happiness discouraged.	Showing happiness is encouraged, and sadness discouraged.
Slower walking speed.	Faster walking speed.
Consumption patterns show dependence on others.	Consumption patterns show self-supporting lifestyles.
Social network is the primary source of information.	Media is the primary source of information.
A smaller share of both private and public income is spent on health care.	A larger share of both private and public income is spent on health care.
Disabled persons are a shame on the family and should be kept out of sight.	Disabled persons should participate as much as possible in normal day-to-day activities.

teacher wants students to speak up, the teacher should address a particular student personally.

Students in a collectivist culture will also hesitate to speak up in larger groups without a teacher present, especially if these are partly composed of relative strangers, or out-group members. This hesitation decreases in smaller groups. In a large, collectivist or culturally heterogeneous class, creating small subgroups is a way to increase student participation. For example, students can be asked to turn around in their seats and discuss a question for five minutes in groups of three or four. Each group is asked to appoint a spokesperson. In this way individual answers become group answers, and those who speak up do so in the name of their group. Often in subsequent exercises the students will spontaneously rotate the spokesperson role.

In the collectivist society in-group–out-group distinctions springing from the family sphere will continue at school, so that students from different ethnic or clan backgrounds often form subgroups in class. In an individualist society the assignment of joint tasks leads more easily to the formation of new groups than in a collectivist society. In the latter, students from the same ethnic or family background as the teacher or other school officials will expect preferential treatment on this basis. In an individualist society this would be considered nepotism and intensely immoral, but in a collectivist environment it is immoral *not* to treat one's in-group members better than others.

In the collectivist classroom the virtues of harmony and maintaining face reign supreme. Confrontations and conflicts should be avoided or at least formulated so as not to hurt anyone; students should not lose face if this can be avoided. Shaming (that is, invoking the group's honor) is an effective way of correcting offenders: they will be put in order by their in-group members. At all times, the teacher is dealing with the student as part of an in-group, never as an isolated individual.

In the individualist classroom, of course, students expect to be treated as individuals and impartially, regardless of their background. Group formation among students is much more ad hoc, according to the task or to particular friendships and skills. Confrontations and open discussion of conflicts are often considered salutary, and face-consciousness is weak or nonexistent.

The purpose of education is perceived differently between the individualist and the collectivist society. In the former it aims at preparing the individual for a place in a society of other individuals. This means learning to cope with new, unknown, unforeseen situations. There is a basically positive attitude toward what is new. The purpose of learning is less to know how to do as to know *how to learn*. The assumption is that learning in life never ends; even after school and university it will continue (for example, through post-academic courses). The individualist society in its schools tries to provide the competencies necessary for "modern man."

In the collectivist society there is a stress on adaptation to the skills and virtues necessary to be an acceptable group member. This leads to a premium on the products of tradition. Learning is more often seen as a one-time process, reserved for only the young, who have to learn *how to do* things in order to participate in society. It is an extended rite of passage.

The role of diplomas or certificates as a result of successful completion of a study is also different between the two poles of the individualism-collectivism dimension. In the individualist society the diploma improves the holder's economic worth but also his or her self-respect: it provides a sense of achievement. In the collectivist society a diploma is an honor to the holder (and his or her in-group) and entitles the holder to associate with members of higher-status groups—for example, to get a more attractive marriage partner. It is to a certain extent "a ticket to a ride." The social acceptance that comes with the diploma is more important than the individual self-respect that comes with mastering a subject, so that in collectivist societies the temptation is stronger to obtain diplomas in some irregular way, such as on the black market.

Individualism and Collectivism in the Workplace

Sons in collectivist societies are more likely than sons in individualist societies to follow in the occupation of their fathers.[36] We noticed that our operating as a father-and-son author team tends to be admired in collectivist cultures but is sometimes scorned in individualist ones. In more individualist societies, sons of fathers in manual occupations will more frequently move to nonmanual occupations, and vice versa. In more collectivist societies, occupational mobility is lower.

Employed persons in an individualist culture are expected to act according to their own interest, and work should be organized in such a way that this self-interest and the employer's interest coincide. Workers are supposed to act as "economic men," or as people with a combination of economic and psychological needs, but anyway as individuals with their own needs. In a collectivist culture an employer never hires just an individual, but rather a person who belongs to an in-group. The employee will act according to the interest of this in-group, which may not always coincide with his or her individual interest: self-effacement in the interest of the in-group belongs to the normal expectations in such a society. Often earnings have to be shared with relatives.

The hiring process in a collectivist society always takes the in-group into account. Usually preference is given to hiring relatives, first of all of the employer but also of other persons already employed by the company. Hiring persons from a family one already knows reduces risks. Also, relatives will be concerned about the reputation of the family and help to correct misbehavior of a family member. In the individualist society family relationships at work are often considered undesirable, as they may lead to nepotism and to a conflict of interest. Some companies have a rule that if one employee marries another, one of them has to leave.

The workplace itself in a collectivist society may become an in-group in the emotional sense of the word. In some countries this is more the case than in others, but the feeling that it should be this way is nearly always present. The relationship between employer and employee is seen in moral terms. It resembles a family relationship with mutual obligations of protection in exchange for loyalty. Poor performance of an employee in this relationship is no reason for dismissal: one does not dismiss one's child. Performance and skills, however, do determine what tasks one assigns to an employee. This pattern of relationships is best known from Japanese organizations. In Japan it applies in a strict sense only to the group of permanent employees that may be less than half the total workforce. Japan scores halfway on the IDV scale. In individualist societies the relationship between employer and employee is primarily conceived as a business transaction, a calculative relationship between buyers and sellers in a labor market. Poor performance on the part of the employee or a better pay offer from another employer are legitimate and socially accepted reasons for terminating a work relationship.

Christopher Earley, a management researcher from the United States, has illustrated the difference in work ethos between an individualist and a collectivist society very neatly with a laboratory experiment. In the experiment forty-eight management trainees from southern China and forty-eight matched management trainees from the United States were given an "in-basket task." The task consisted of forty separate items requiring between two and five minutes each, like writing memos, evaluating plans, and rating job candidates' application forms. Half the participants in either country were given a group goal of two hundred items to be completed in an hour by ten people; the other half were given each an individual goal of twenty items. Also, half the participants in either country, both from the group goal and from the individual goal subset, were asked to mark each item completed with their name, while the other half turned them in anonymously.

The Chinese collectivist participants performed best when operating with a group goal and anonymously. They performed worst when operating individually and with their name marked on the items produced. The American individualist participants performed best when operating individually and with their name marked but abysmally low when operating as a group and anonymously. All participants were also given a values test to determine their personal individualism or collectivism: a minority of the Chinese scored individualist, and these performed according to the U.S. pattern; a minority of the Americans scored collectivist, and these performed like the Chinese.[37]

In practice there is a wide range of types of employer-employee relationships *within* collectivist and individualist societies. There are employers in collectivist countries who do not respect the societal norm to treat their employees as in-group members, but then the employees in turn do not repay them in terms of loyalty. Labor unions in such cases may replace the work organization as an emotional in-group, and there can be violent union-management conflicts, as seen in parts of India. There are employers in individualist societies who have established a strong group cohesion with their employees, with the same protection-versus-loyalty balance that is the norm in the collectivist society. Organization cultures can to some extent deviate from majority norms and derive a competitive advantage from their originality. Chapter 8 will explore these issues in greater detail.

Management in an individualist society is management of individuals. Subordinates can usually be moved around individually; if incentives or bonuses are given, these should be linked to an individual's performance. Management in a collectivist society is management of groups. The extent to which people actually feel emotionally integrated into a work group may differ from one situation to another. Ethnic and other in-group differences within the work group play a role in the integration process, and managers within a collectivist culture will be extremely attentive to such factors. It often makes good sense to put persons from the same ethnic background into one crew, although individualistically programmed managers usually consider this dangerous and want to do the opposite. If the work group functions as an emotional in-group, incentives and bonuses should be given to the group, not to individuals.

Within countries with a dominant individualist middle-class culture, regional rural subcultures have sometimes retained strongly collectivist elements. The same applies to the migrant worker minorities that form majorities among the workforce in some industries in some individualist countries. In such cases a culture conflict is likely between managers and regional or minority workers. This conflict expresses itself, among other things, in the management's extreme hesitation to use group incentives in cases where these would suit the culture of the workforce.

Management techniques and training packages have almost exclusively been developed in individualist countries, and they are based on cultural assumptions that may not hold in collectivist cultures. A standard element in the training of first-line managers is how to conduct *appraisal interviews*, periodic discussions in which the subordinate's performance is reviewed. These can form part of Management by Objectives,[38] but even where MBO does not exist, conducting performance appraisals and the ability to communicate bad news are considered key skills for a successful manager. In a collectivist society discussing a person's performance openly with him or her is likely to clash head-on with the society's harmony norm and may be felt by the subordinate as an unacceptable loss of face. Such societies have more subtle, indirect ways of feedback—for example, by the withdrawal of a normal favor or verbally via an intermediary. We know of a case in which an older relative of the poorly performing employee, also in the service of the employer, played this intermediary role. He communicated the bad news to his nephew, avoiding the loss of face that a formal appraisal interview would have provoked.

For the same reason, training methods based on honest and direct sharing of feelings about other people, which have periodically been fashionable in the United States with labels like *sensitivity training, encounter groups*, or *transactional analysis*, are unfit for use in collectivist cultures.

The distinction between in-groups and out-groups that is so essential in the collectivist culture pattern has far-reaching consequences for business relationships, beyond those between employers and employees. It is the reason behind the cultural embarrassment of Mr. Johannesson and his Swedish superiors in Saudi Arabia, related at the beginning of this chapter. In individualist societies the norm is that one should treat everybody alike. In sociological jargon this is known as *universalism*. Preferential treatment of one customer over others is considered a bad business practice and unethical. In collectivist societies the reverse is true. As the distinction between "our group" and "other groups" is at the very root of people's consciousness, treating one's friends better than others is natural and ethical and is a sound business practice. Sociologists call this way of acting *particularism*.

A consequence of particularist thinking is that in a collectivist society a relationship of trust should be established with another person before any business can be done. Through this relationship the other is adopted into one's in-group and is from that moment onward entitled to preferential treatment. In Johannesson's case this process of adoption took two years. During this period the presence of the Swedish businessman as an intermediary was essential. After the adoption had taken place it became superfluous. The relationship, however, was with Johannesson personally and not with his company. To the collectivist mind only natural persons are worthy of trust, and via these persons their friends and colleagues, but not impersonal legal entities like a company. In summary, in the collectivist society *the personal relationship prevails over the task* and should be established first; whereas in the individualist society *the task is supposed to prevail over any personal relationships*. The naive Western businessman who tries to force quick business in a collectivist culture condemns himself to the role of out-group member and to negative discrimination.

Table 3.4 lists the key differences between collectivist and individualist societies related to school and the workplace.

Individualism, Collectivism, and the State

Alfred Kraemer, an American author in the field of intercultural communication, cited the following comment in a Russian literary journal by a poet, Vladimir Korotich, who had made a two-month lecturing tour of American universities:

> . . . *attempts to please an American audience are doomed in advance, because out of twenty listeners five may hold one point of view, seven another, and eight may have none at all.*[39]

What strikes the Western reader in this comment is not the described attitudes of American students but the fact that Korotich expected otherwise. He was obviously accustomed to audiences that held a common point of view, a characteristic of a collectivist culture. Table 3.1 shows Russia to score considerably more collectivist than Western countries.

Naive observers of the world political scene often see only the different political systems, but they are not aware of the different mind-sets of the populations that led to and maintain these different systems. If the commonly held value system is that collective interests should prevail over individual interests, this leads to a different kind of state than if the dominant feeling is that individual interests should prevail over collective ones.

TABLE 3.4 **Key Differences Between Collectivist and Individualist Societies: School and the Workplace**

COLLECTIVIST	INDIVIDUALIST
Students only speak up in class when sanctioned by the group.	Students are expected to individually speak up in class.
The purpose of education is learning how to do.	The purpose of education is learning how to learn.
Diplomas provide entry to higher-status groups.	Diplomas increase economic worth and/or self-respect.
Occupational mobility is lower.	Occupational mobility is higher.
Employees are members of in-groups who will pursue their in-group's interest.	Employees are "economic men" who will pursue the employer's interest if it coincides with their self-interest.
Hiring and promotion decisions take an employee's in-group into account.	Hiring and promotion decisions are supposed to be based on skills and rules only.
The employer-employee relationship is basically moral, like a family link.	The employer-employee relationship is a contract between parties on a labor market.
Management is management of groups.	Management is management of individuals.
Direct appraisal of subordinates spoils harmony.	Management training teaches the honest sharing of feelings.
In-group customers get better treatment (*particularism*).	Every customer should get the same treatment (*universalism*).
Relationship prevails over task.	Task prevails over relationship.

In American parlance the term *collectivist* is sometimes used to describe communist political systems. Countries in Table 3.1 that had or still have either communist or state capitalist governments are found on the medium to low IDV—that is, the collectivist side. The weaker the individualism in the citizens' mental software, the greater the likelihood of a dominating role of the state in the economic system.

Since the 1990s increasing individualism has been one of the forces leading to deregulation and reduction of public expenditures in Western countries. Even public monopolies like energy provision and public transport have sometimes been privatized at the expense of their performance and reliability, for ideological rather than for pragmatic reasons—which shows the power of cultural values.

The capitalist invention of the joint stock company—an enterprise owned by dispersed shareholders who can trade their shares at a stock exchange—was created in individualist Britain and for its functioning supposes an individualist mind-set among its actors.[40] In practice it is regularly threatened by particularist interests, and in a curious paradox, its supposedly free market needs strong regulation by government.

On the other hand, the economic life in collectivist societies, if not dominated by government, in any case is based on collective interests. Family enterprises abound; in the People's Republic of China, after the economic liberalization of the 1980s, villages, the army, and municipal police corps started their own enterprises.

Individualist countries tend to be wealthier and to have smaller power distances than collectivist ones. This is a statistical relationship that does not hold for all countries, but because of this relationship it is sometimes difficult to separate out the effects of wealth, individualism, and smaller power distance on government. For example, political scientists have developed an index of press freedom for a large number of countries. This index is significantly correlated with high IDV and low PDI, but most strongly with national wealth. Greater press freedom in wealthier countries is not only a matter of individualism and equality, but also of resources like more newspapers and TV channels and of interest groups having the means to disseminate their opinions.[41]

The right to privacy is a central theme in many individualist societies that does not find the same sympathy in collectivist societies, where it is seen as normal and right that one's in-group can at any time invade one's private life.

The difference between a universalist and a particularist treatment of customers, illustrated by the Johannesson case, applies to the functioning of the state as a whole. In the individualist society laws and rights are supposed to be the same for all members and applied indiscriminately to everybody (whether this standard is always met is another question). In the collectivist society laws and rights may differ from one category of people to another, if not in theory then in the way laws are administered, and this is not seen as wrong.

If differences in the political systems found in countries are rooted in their citizens' mental software, the possibility to influence these systems by propaganda, money, or arms from another country is limited. If the minds are not receptive for the message, propaganda and money are mostly spoiled. Even the most powerful foreign state cannot brainwash entire populations out of their deeply held values.

A main issue in international politics is national governments' respect for human rights. The Universal Declaration of Human Rights was adopted by the United Nations in 1948. Charles Humana, a former researcher for Amnesty International, calculated human rights ratings for a large number of countries on the basis of forty questions derived from UN criteria. Across fifty-two countries from the IBM set, Humana's human rights ratings correlated primarily with per capita GNP, which explained 50 percent of the differences; adding culture scores did not improve the explanation. The picture changed when we looked separately at the twenty-five wealthier countries: now the single explaining variable, accounting for 53 percent of the differences in human rights ratings, became IDV. For the remaining twenty-seven poorer countries, per capita GNP remained the single explaining variable, but it now accounted for only 14 percent of the differences.[42] Our conclusion from these relationships is that respect for human rights as formulated by the United Nations is a luxury that wealthy countries can afford more easily than poor ones; to what extent these wealthy countries do conform to UN criteria, however, depends on the degree of individualism in their culture. The Universal Declaration of Human Rights and other UN covenants were inspired by the values of the dominant powers at the time of their adoption, and these were individualistic.

Individualism, Collectivism, and Ideas

Individualist societies not only practice individualism but they also consider it superior to other forms of mental software. Most Americans feel that individualism is good and at the root of their country's greatness. On the other hand, the late chairman Mao Zedong of China identified individualism as evil. He found individualism and liberalism responsible for selfishness and aversion to discipline; they led people to placing personal interests above those of the group or simply to devoting too much attention to their own things. In Table 3.1 places with a predominantly Chinese population all score very low on IDV (Hong Kong 25, mainland China 20, Singapore 20, Taiwan 17).

In the European Values Survey, which preceded the World Values Survey, representative samples of the population in nine European countries in 1981 were asked to choose between the following statements:

> *A: I find that both freedom and equality are important. But if I were to make up my mind for one or the other, I would consider personal freedom more important, that is, everyone can live in freedom and develop without hindrance.*

> *B: Certainly both freedom and equality are important. But if I were to make up my mind for one of the two, I would consider equality more important, that is that nobody is underprivileged and that social class differences are not so strong.*[43]

This is, of course, an ideological choice. In most of the nine European countries, respondents on average preferred freedom over equality. The French sociologist Jean Stoetzel (1910–87), who published a brilliant analysis of the data, has computed a ratio for each country: preference for freedom divided by preference for equality. This ratio runs from about 1 in Spain (equal preference) to about 3 in Great Britain (freedom is three times as popular as equality). The values of the freedom/equality ratio for the nine countries were significantly correlated with IDV: the more individualist a country, the stronger its citizens' preference for freedom over equality.[44] Freedom is an individualist ideal, equality a collectivist ideal.

The choice between individualism and collectivism at the level of society has considerable implications for economic theories. Economics as a discipline was founded in Britain in the eighteenth century; among the founding fathers, Adam Smith (1723–90) stands out. Smith assumed that the pursuit of self-interest by individuals through an "invisible hand" would increase the wealth of nations. This is an individualist idea from a country that even today ranks high on individualism. Economics has remained an individualist science, and most of its leading contributors have come from strongly individualist nations, such as Britain and the United States. However, because of the individualist assumptions on which they are based, economic theories as developed in the West are unlikely to apply in societies in which group interests prevail. This has profound consequences on development assistance to poor countries and for economic globalization. There is a dire need for alternative economic theories that take into account the cultural differences on this dimension.

The degree of individualism or collectivism of a society affects the conceptions of human nature produced in that society. In the United States the ideas of Abraham Maslow (1908–70) about human motivation have been and are still quite influential, in particular for the training of management students and practitioners. Maslow's famous "hierarchy of human needs" states that human needs can be ordered in a hierarchy from lower to higher, as follows: physiological, safety and security, belongingness, esteem, and self-actualization.[45] In order for a higher need to appear, it is necessary that the lower needs have been satisfied up to a certain extent. A starving person, one whose physiological needs are not at all satisfied, will not be motivated by anything else than the quest for food, and so forth. The top of Maslow's hierarchy, often pictured as a pyramid, is taken by the motive of *self-actualization*: realizing to the fullest possible extent the creative potential present within the individual. This means doing one's own thing. It goes without saying that this can only be the supreme motivation in an individualist society. In a collectivist culture what will be actualized is the interest and honor of the in-group, which may very well ask for self-effacement from many of the in-group members. The interpreter for a group of young Americans visiting China in the late 1970s found the idea of "doing your own thing" untranslatable into Chinese. Harmony and consensus are more attractive ultimate goals for such societies than individual self-actualization.

Since *Culture's Consequences* first appeared in 1980, the individualism-collectivism dimension has gained great popularity among psychologists, especially those from the economically emerging Asian nations. The dimension implies that traditional psychology is as little a universal science as traditional economics: it is a product of Western thinking, caught in individualist assumptions. When these are replaced by more collectivist assumptions, another psychology emerges that differs in important respects. For example, individualist psychology is obviously universalist, opposing the "ego" to any "other." In collectivist psychology the ego is inseparable from its social context. People in collectivist societies make particularist distinctions: the in-group, which includes the ego, is opposed to all out-groups. This means that the results of psychological experiments in a collectivist society depend on whether participants belong to the same in-group or not.

Table 3.5 is a continuation of Tables 3.2, 3.3, and 3.4: it summarizes the key differences between collectivist and individualist societies from the last two sections.

TABLE 3.5 Key Differences Between Collectivist and Individualist Societies: The State and Ideas

COLLECTIVIST	INDIVIDUALIST
Opinions are predetermined by group membership.	Everyone is expected to have a private opinion.
Collective interests prevail over individual interests.	Individual interests prevail over collective interests.
The state holds a dominant role in the economic system.	The role of the state in the economic system is restrained.
Per capita GNP tends to be lower.	Per capita GNP tends to be higher.
Companies are owned by families or collectives.	Joint stock companies are owned by individual investors.
Private life is invaded by group(s).	Everyone has a right to privacy.
Laws and rights differ by group.	Laws and rights are supposed to be the same for all.
Lower human rights rating.	Higher human rights rating.
Ideologies of equality prevail over ideologies of individual freedom.	Ideologies of individual freedom prevail over ideologies of equality.
Imported economic theories are unable to deal with collective and particularist interests.	Native economic theories are based on pursuit of individual self-interests.
Harmony and consensus in society are ultimate goals.	Self-actualization by every individual is an ultimate goal.
Patriotism is the ideal.	Autonomy is the ideal.
Outcome of psychological experiments depends on in-group–out-group distinction.	Outcome of psychological experiments depends on ego-other distinction.

Origins of Individualism-Collectivism Differences

The origins of differences on the individualism-collectivism dimension, just like those on power distance, are a matter of conjecture. Yet statistical relationships with geographic, economic, and historic variables can support the guesswork.

As described in Chapter 1, it is a common assumption among archaeologists that the development of human societies started with groups of hunter-gatherer nomads, that subsequently people settled down into a sedentary existence as farmers, and that farming communities grew into larger settlements that became towns, cities, and finally modern megalopolises. Cultural anthropologists have compared present-day hunter-gatherer tribes, agricultural societies, and urbanized societies. They have found that from the most primitive to the most modern society, family complexity first increased and then decreased again. Hunter-gatherers tend to live in nuclear families or small bands. Sedentary agricultural societies mostly show complex extended families or village community in-groups. When farmers migrate to cities, the sizes of extended families become reduced and the typical urban family is again nuclear. In most countries today one finds only agricultural and urban subcultures. For these two types, modernization corresponds to individualization.

Information about one hunter-gatherer society comes from an Australian researcher, Ray Simonsen, who administered the VSM94 (the 1994 improved version of the IBM questionnaire) to Aboriginal entrepreneurs in Darwin, Northern Territory, and to a comparable group of white Australians. Aboriginal society is still largely based on hunting and gathering. While unlike the white Australians, the Aborigines scored high on power distance, low on masculinity, and high on uncertainty avoidance, on individualism they scored as high as their white compatriots.[46]

In Table 3.1 we find societies with a large traditional rural sector mostly at the collectivist side, and modern industrial societies at the individualist side. There are some exceptions, especially in East Asia, where Japan, South Korea, Taiwan, Hong Kong, and Singapore have retained considerable collectivism in spite of industrialization.

As in the case of PDI in Chapter 2, we used the statistical tool of stepwise multiple regression to determine what quantitative information about our countries best explained the differences in IDV scores. We found that a country's IDV score can be fairly accurately predicted from:

1. The country's wealth (richer countries are associated with higher IDV)
2. The country's geographic latitude (countries closer to the equator are associated with lower IDV)

Wealth (per capita GNP at the time of the IBM surveys) explained no less than 71 percent of the differences in IDV scores for the original fifty IBM countries. This is amazing, if we realize that the two measures come from entirely different sources and that both are rather imprecise—subject to measurement error.

A correlation does not show which of two related phenomena is cause and which is effect, or whether both could be caused by a third factor not shown in the graph. If individualism were the cause of wealth, one should find that IDV scores relate not only to national wealth per se but also to ensuing *economic growth*. The latter is measured by the World Bank as the average annual percentage increase in per capita GNP during a twenty-five-year period. If individualism leads to wealth, IDV should be positively correlated with economic growth in the period following the collection of the IDV data. However, the relationship between IDV scores (collected around 1970) and subsequent economic growth was, if anything, negative: the more individualist countries showed *less*, not more, economic growth than the less individualist ones.

We can draw the same conclusion by looking at the correlations of 1970 IDV with country wealth in later years. Wealth data from 1970 explained 71 percent of IDV differences, wealth in 1980 explained 62 percent, in 1990, 55 percent, and in 2000, 52 percent.[47] If causality went from IDV to subsequent GNP, the correlation should have become stronger over time.

The reverse causality, national wealth causing individualism, is more plausible. The IBM data bank allowed measuring shifts in individualism during the four-year period from 1968 to 1972. Out of twenty countries that had been surveyed in both years, nineteen had become richer, and all of these had shifted toward greater individualism. The only country in the set that had become poorer, Pakistan, shifted slightly toward the collectivist side.

Figure 3.2 plots IDV against GNP per capita for the year 2000. There is still a notable overall relationship, but the graph also shows which countries are wealthier and poorer than their IDV score would predict: for

FIGURE 3.2 GNP Per Capita in 2000 Versus Individualism

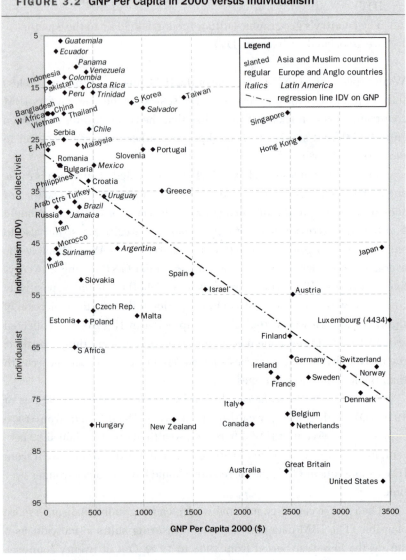

example, Singapore and Japan are wealthier, India and New Zealand are poorer.

When a country's wealth increases, its citizens get access to resources that allow them to "do their own thing." The storyteller in the village market is replaced by TV sets, first one per village, but soon more. In wealthy Western family homes, every family member may have his or her own TV set. The caravan through the desert is replaced by a number of buses, and these by a larger number of motor cars, until each adult family member drives a different car. The village hut in which the entire family lives and sleeps together is replaced by a house with a number of private rooms. Collective life is replaced by individual life. However, the negative relationship between individualism and economic growth for the very wealthy countries suggests that this development leads to its own undoing. Where wealth has progressed to a level at which most citizens can afford to do their own thing, this leads to friction losses, and the national economy grows less than in countries where people are still accustomed to doing at least a number of things together (for example, Japan). Reasons for the fast economic growth of East Asian countries will be further discussed in Chapter 6.

Besides national wealth the only other measure statistically related to IDV was geographic latitude: the distance from the equator of a country's capital city. It explained another 7 percent of the IDV differences. In Chapter 2 latitude was the *first* predictor of power distance scores. As we argued there, in countries with moderate and cold climates, people's survival depends more on their ability to fend for themselves. This favors educating children toward independence from more powerful others (lower PDI). It also seems to favor a degree of individualism.

The size of the population of a country, which contributed significantly to predicting power distance, did not relate to collectivism. The *growth* of the population (average percent per year over a ten-year period) did relate to collectivism, but its first correlation was with country wealth—in poor countries families tend to have more children. There are a number of reasons for this, most prominent being the poor education of women and the expectation that children will support their parents in old age. Children in larger families obviously are more likely to acquire collectivist rather than individualist values.

Historical factors, apart from economic ones, can also account for part of the country differences on this dimension, although not as clearly as in the case of the influence of the Roman Empire on power distance. The influence of the teachings of Confucius in the East Asian countries to which part of Chapter 6 will be devoted supports the maintenance of a collectivist value system. On the other hand, in parts of western Europe, in particular in England, Scotland, and the Netherlands, individualist values could be recognized centuries ago, when the average citizen in these countries was still quite poor and the economies were overwhelmingly rural. The migrants from Europe who populated North America, Australia, and New Zealand were by definition sufficiently individualist to leave their old environment, and they went to countries where, in the frontier spirit, every person had to fend for him- or herself.

The Future of Individualism and Collectivism

The deep roots of national cultures make it likely that individualism-collectivism differences, like power distance differences, will survive for a long time into the future. Yet if there is to be any convergence among national cultures it should be on this dimension. The strong relationship between national wealth and individualism is undeniable, with the arrow of causality directed, as shown earlier, from wealth to individualism. Countries having achieved fast economic development have experienced a shift toward individualism. Japan is an example: the Japanese press regularly publishes stories of breaches of traditional family solidarity. Care for the aged in the past was considered a task for the Japanese family, but provisions by the state have become necessary for cases where the family stops fulfilling its traditional duties.

Nevertheless, even at a level of per capita income equal to or larger than Western countries, Japanese society has conserved distinctive collectivist elements in its family, school, and work spheres. Between Western countries like Britain, Sweden, and Germany, in spite of a noticeable convergence toward individualism under the influence of common economic development, relationships between the individual and the group continue to differ. The cultures shift, but they shift together, so that their relative positions remain intact, and there is no reason why differences between them should disappear.

As far as the poor countries of the world are concerned, they cannot be expected to become more individualist as long as they remain poor. As previously mentioned, from 1968 to 1972 the only IBM country that had become poorer, Pakistan, had also become more collectivist. And if differences in wealth between rich and poor countries continue to increase (as in many instances they do), gaps on the individualism-collectivism dimension can only increase further.

Differences in values associated with the individualism-collectivism dimension will continue to exist and to play a big role in international affairs. Individualism versus collectivism as a dimension of national cultures is responsible for many misunderstandings in intercultural encounters. In Chapter 9 it will be shown that many problems of such encounters can be explained from differences on this dimension.

He, She, and (S)he

As a young Dutch engineer, Geert once applied for a junior management job with an American engineering company that had recently
settled in Flanders, the Dutch-speaking part of Belgium. He felt well
qualified: with a degree from the senior technical university of the country, good grades, a record of active participation in student associations,
and three years of experience as an engineer with a well-known
(although somewhat sleepy) Dutch company. He had written a short letter indicating his interest and providing some vital personal data. He
was invited to appear in person, and after a long train ride he sat facing
the American plant manager. Geert behaved politely and modestly, as he
knew an applicant should, and waited for the other man to ask the usual
questions that would enable him to find out how qualified Geert was. To
his surprise, the plant manager asked very few of the things that Geert
thought should be discussed. Instead, he wanted to know some highly

detailed facts about Geert's experience in tool design, using English words Geert did not know, and the relevance of which escaped him. Those were the things he could learn within a week once he worked there. After half an hour of painful misunderstandings, the interviewer said, "Sorry—we need a first-class man." And Geert was out in the street.

Assertiveness Versus Modesty

Years later Geert was the interviewer and he saw both Dutch and American applicants. Then he understood what had gone wrong in that earlier case. American applicants, to Dutch eyes, oversell themselves. Their curricula vitae are worded in superlatives, mentioning every degree, grade, award, and membership to demonstrate their outstanding qualities. During the interview they try to behave assertively, promising things they are very unlikely to realize—like learning the local language in a few months.

Dutch applicants, in American eyes, undersell themselves. They write modest and usually short CVs, counting on the interviewer to find out by asking how good they really are. They expect an interest in their social and extracurricular activities during their studies. They are careful not to be seen as braggarts and not to make promises they are not absolutely sure they can fulfill.

American interviewers know how to interpret American CVs and interviews, and they tend to discount the information provided. Dutch interviewers, accustomed to Dutch applicants, tend to upgrade the information. The scenario for cross-cultural misunderstanding is quite clear. To an uninitiated American interviewer, an uninitiated Dutch applicant comes across as a sucker. To an uninitiated Dutch interviewer, an uninitiated American applicant comes across as a braggart.

Dutch and American societies are reasonably similar on the dimensions of power distance and individualism described in the preceding two chapters, but they differ considerably on a third dimension, which opposes, among other things, the desirability of assertive behavior against the desirability of modest behavior. We will label it *masculinity versus femininity*.

Genders and Gender Roles

All human societies consist of men and women, usually in approximately equal numbers. They are biologically distinct, and their respective roles in biological procreation are absolute. Other physical differences between women and men, not directly related to the bearing and begetting of children, are not absolute but statistical. Men are *on average* taller and stronger, but many women are taller and stronger than quite a few men. Women have *on average* greater finger dexterity and, for example, faster metabolism, which makes them recover faster from fatigue, but some men excel in these respects.

The absolute and statistical biological differences between men and women are the same the world over, but their social roles in society are only partly determined by the biological constraints. Every society recognizes many behaviors, not immediately related to procreation, as more suitable to females or more suitable to males, but which behaviors belong to either gender differs from one society to another. Anthropologists having studied nonliterate, relatively isolated societies stress the wide variety of social sex roles that seem to be possible.[1] For the biological distinction this chapter will use the terms *male* and *female*; for the social, culturally determined roles *masculine* and *feminine*. The latter terms are *relative*, not absolute: a man can behave in a "feminine" way and a woman in a "masculine" way; this only means they deviate from certain conventions in their society.

Which behaviors are considered feminine or masculine differs not only among traditional but also among modern societies. This is most evident in the distribution of men and women over certain professions. Women dominate as doctors in Russia, as dentists in Belgium, and as shopkeepers in parts of West Africa. Men dominate as typists in Pakistan and form a sizable share of nurses in the Netherlands. Female managers are virtually nonexistent in Japan but frequent in the Philippines and Thailand.

In spite of the variety found, there is a common trend among most societies, both traditional and modern, as to the distribution of social sex roles. From now on this chapter will use the more politically correct term *gender roles*. Men are supposed to be more concerned with achievements outside the home—hunting and fighting in traditional societies, the same but translated into economic terms in modern societies. Men, in short, are supposed to be assertive, competitive, and tough. Women are supposed to be more concerned with taking care of the home, of the children, and of people in general—to take the tender roles. It is not difficult to see how this role pattern is likely to have developed: women first bore the children and then usually breast-fed them, so at least during this period they had to stay close to the children. Men were freer to move around, to the extent that they were not needed to protect women and children against attacks by other men and by animals.

Male achievement reinforces masculine assertiveness and competition; female care reinforces feminine nurturance and a concern for relationships and for the living environment.[2] Men, taller and stronger and freer to get out, tend to dominate in social life outside the home; inside the home a variety of role distributions between the genders is possible. The role pattern demonstrated by the father and mother (and possibly other family members) has a profound impact on the mental software of the small child, who is programmed with it for life. Therefore it is not surprising that one of the dimensions of national value systems is related to gender role models offered by parents.

The gender role socialization that started in the family continues in peer groups and in schools. A society's gender role pattern is daily reflected in its media: TV programs, motion pictures and children's books, newspapers, and women's journals. Gender role–confirming behavior is a criterion for mental health.[3] Gender roles are part and parcel of every society.

Masculinity-Femininity as a Dimension of Societal Culture

Chapter 3 referred to a set of fourteen work goals in the IBM questionnaire: "Try to think of those factors which would be important to you in an ideal job; disregard the extent to which they are contained in your present job." The analysis of the answers to the fourteen work goal items produced two underlying dimensions. One was *individualism versus collectivism*: the importance of personal time, freedom, and challenge stood for individualism, while the importance of training, physical conditions, and use of skills stood for collectivism.

The second dimension came to be labeled *masculinity versus femininity*. It was associated most strongly with the importance attached to the following work goal items:

For the masculine pole
1. **Earnings:** have an opportunity for high earnings.
2. **Recognition:** get the recognition you deserve when you do a good job.

3. **Advancement:** have an opportunity for advancement to higher-level jobs.
4. **Challenge:** have challenging work to do—work from which you can get a personal sense of accomplishment.

For the opposite, feminine, pole

5. **Manager:** have a good working relationship with your direct superior.
6. **Cooperation:** work with people who cooperate well with one another.
7. **Living area:** live in an area desirable to you and your family.
8. **Employment security:** have the security that you will be able to work for your company as long as you want to.

Note that the work goal *challenge* was also associated with the individualism dimension (Chapter 3). The other seven goals are only associated with masculinity or femininity.

The decisive reason for labeling the second work goals dimension *masculinity versus femininity* is that *this dimension is the only one on which the men and the women among the IBM employees scored consistently differently* (except, as will be shown, in countries at the extreme feminine pole). Neither power distance nor individualism nor uncertainty avoidance showed a systematic difference in answers between men and women. Only the present dimension produced such a gender difference, with men attaching greater importance to, in particular, the work goals 1 and 3 and women to 5 and 6. The importance of earnings and advancement corresponds to the masculine, assertive and competitive social role. The importance of relations with the manager and with the colleagues corresponds to the caring and social-environment-oriented feminine role.

Like in the case of the individualism versus collectivism dimension, the eight items from the IBM questionnaire do not cover all there is to the distinction between a masculine and a feminine culture in society. They just are the aspects of this dimension that were represented by questions in the IBM research. Again the correlations of the IBM country scores with non-IBM data about other characteristics of societies allow getting a full grasp of what the dimension encompasses.

The differences in mental programming between societies related to this new dimension are social, but even more emotional. Social roles can be imposed by external factors, but what people feel while playing them comes from the inside. This leads us to the following definition:

A society is called masculine *when emotional gender roles are clearly distinct: men are supposed to be assertive, tough, and focused on material success, whereas women are supposed to be more modest, tender, and concerned with the quality of life.*

A society is called feminine *when emotional gender roles overlap: both men and women are supposed to be modest, tender, and concerned with the quality of life.*

For the countries in the IBM database, masculinity index (MAS) values were calculated in a way similar to individualism index values (Chapter 3). MAS was based on the country's *factor score* in a *factor analysis* of the fourteen work goals. Scores were put into a range from about 0 for the most feminine to about 100 for the most masculine country through multiplying the factor scores by 20 and adding 50. For follow-up studies, an approximation formula was used in which MAS was directly computed from the mean scores of four work goals.

Country MAS scores can be read from Table 4.1. Like the scores for power distance and individualism, the masculinity scores represent *relative*, not absolute, positions of countries. Unlike individualism, masculinity is unrelated to a country's degree of economic development: we find rich and poor masculine and rich and poor feminine countries.

TABLE 4.1 Masculinity Index (MAS) Values for 74 Countries and Regions

COUNTRY/REGION	SCORE	RANK	COUNTRY/REGION	SCORE	RANK
Slovakia	110	1	Italy	70	7
Japan	95	2	Mexico	69	8
Hungary	88	3	Ireland	68	9–10
Austria	79	4	Jamaica	68	9–10
Venezuela	73	5	China	66	11–13
Switzerland German	72	6	Germany	66	11–13

continued

COUNTRY/REGION	SCORE	RANK	COUNTRY/REGION	SCORE	RANK
Great Britain	66	11–13	Taiwan	45	43–45
Colombia	64	14–16	Turkey	45	43–45
Philippines	64	14–16	Panama	44	46
Poland	64	14–16	Belgium Flemish	43	47–50
South Africa[1]	63	17–18	France	43	47–50
Ecuador	63	17–18	Iran	43	47–50
United States	62	19	Serbia	43	47–50
Australia	61	20	Peru	42	51–53
Belgium Walloon	60	21	Romania	42	51–53
New Zealand	58	22–24	Spain	42	51–53
Switzerland French	58	22–24	East Africa	41	54
Trinidad	58	22–24	Bulgaria	40	55–58
Czech Republic	57	25–27	Croatia	40	55–58
Greece	57	25–27	Salvador	40	55–58
Hong Kong	57	25–27	Vietnam	40	55–58
Argentina	56	28–29	Korea (South)	39	59
India	56	28–29	Uruguay	38	60
Bangladesh	55	30	Guatemala	37	61–62
Arab countries	53	31–32	Suriname	37	61–62
Morocco	53	31–32	Russia	36	63
Canada total	52	33	Thailand	34	64
Luxembourg	50	34–36	Portugal	31	65
Malaysia	50	34–36	Estonia	30	66
Pakistan	50	34–36	Chile	28	67
Brazil	49	37	Finland	26	68
Singapore	48	38	Costa Rica	21	69
Israel	47	39–40	Slovenia	19	70
Malta	47	39–40	Denmark	16	71
Indonesia	46	41–42	Netherlands	14	72
West Africa	46	41–42	Norway	8	73
Canada Quebec	45	43–45	Sweden	5	74

Scores for countries or regions in **bold type** were calculated from the IBM database. Scores for other countries or regions were based on replications or estimates.

1 The data were from whites only.

The most feminine-scoring countries (ranks 74 through 71) were Sweden, Norway, the Netherlands, and Denmark; Finland came close with a rank of 68. The lower third of Table 4.1 further contains some Latin countries: Costa Rica, Chile, Portugal, Guatemala, Uruguay, Salvador, Spain, Peru, and France; and some eastern European countries: Slovenia, Estonia, Russia, Croatia, Bulgaria, Romania, and Serbia. From Asia it contains Thailand, South Korea, Vietnam, and Iran. Other feminine-scoring cultures were the former Dutch colony of Suriname in South America, Flemish (Dutch-speaking Belgians), and countries from the East African region.

The top third of Table 4.1 includes all Anglo countries: Ireland, Jamaica, Great Britain, South Africa, the United States, Australia, New Zealand, and Trinidad. Also from Europe are Slovakia (with a rank of 1), Hungary, Austria, German-speaking Switzerland, Italy, Germany, Poland, and the French-speaking Belgians and Swiss. In Asia are Japan (rank 2), China, and the Philippines. From Latin America are the larger countries around the Caribbean—Venezuela, Mexico, and Colombia—and Ecuador.

The United States scored 62 on MAS (rank 19) and the Netherlands 14 (rank 72), so these two countries figuring in the story at the beginning of this chapter were markedly far apart.

Masculinity and Femininity in Other Cross-National Studies

Masculinity-femininity has been the most controversial of the five dimensions of national cultures. This is a matter not only of labeling (users are free to adapt the labels to their taste) but also of recognizing that national cultures do differ dramatically on the value issues related to this dimension. At the same time, ever since Geert's first publication on the subject in the 1970s, the number and scope of validations of the dimension has continued to grow.[*]

One reason the masculinity-femininity dimension is not recognized is that it is entirely unrelated to national wealth. For the other three IBM dimensions, wealthy countries are more often found on one of the poles (small power distance, individualist, and somewhat weaker uncertainty avoidance), and poor countries on the other. The association with wealth serves as an implicit justification that one pole must be better than the other. But for masculinity-femininity this does not work. There are just as many poor as wealthy masculine, or feminine, countries. So wealth is no clue to base one's values on, and this unsettles people. In several research projects, the influence of MAS became evident only after the influence of wealth had been controlled for.

From the six major replications of the IBM surveys presented in Table 1.1, five found a dimension similar to masculinity-femininity. The sixth, Shane's study among employees of six international companies (but not IBM), excluded the questions related to MAS because they were considered politically incorrect. What is not asked cannot be found. In Søndergaard's review of nineteen smaller replications, mentioned in Chapter 1, fourteen confirmed the MAS differences. This in itself is a statistically significant result.[5]

Schwartz's value study among elementary school teachers produced a country-level *mastery* dimension that correlated significantly with MAS.[6] Mastery combines the values ambitious, capable, choosing own goals, daring, independent, and successful, all on the positive pole. These values clearly confirm a masculine ethos.[7]

Masculinity Versus Individualism

In the literature the distinction between country-level masculinity and femininity is easily confused with the distinction between individualism and collectivism. Authors from the United States tend to classify feminine goals as collectivist; but a student from Korea in her master's thesis classified masculine goals as collectivist.

In reality the individualism-collectivism and masculinity-femininity dimensions are independent, as is evident in Figure 4.1, in which the two dimensions are crossed. All combinations occur with about equal frequency. The difference between them is that individualism-collectivism is about "I" versus "we," independence from versus dependence on in-groups. Masculinity-femininity is about a stress on ego versus a stress on relationship with others, regardless of group ties. Relationships in collectivist cultures are basically predetermined by group ties: "groupiness" is collectivist, not feminine. The biblical story of the Good Samaritan who helps a Jew in need—someone from another ethnic group—is an illustration of feminine and not of collectivist values.

Inglehart's analysis of the World Values Survey found a key dimension, well-being versus survival, that was associated with the combination of high IDV and low MAS.[8] This means that the highest stress on well-being

FIGURE 4.1   Masculinity Versus Individualism

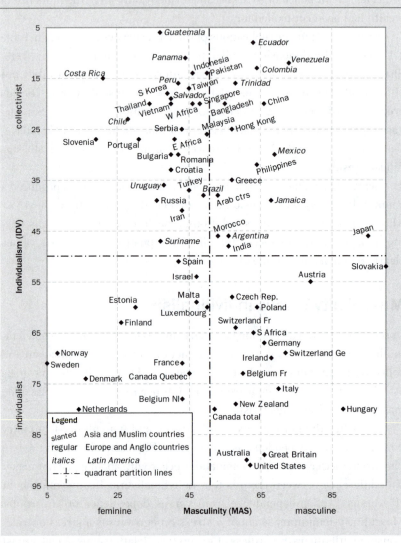

occurred in individualist, feminine societies (like Denmark), while the highest stress on survival was found in collectivist, masculine societies (like Mexico). In these societies there is a stress on group ego, also shown in a strong concern for group success and an identification with competitive sports.

Are Masculinity and Femininity One or Two Dimensions?

As in the case of individualism and collectivism, the objection is sometimes made that masculinity and femininity should be seen as two separate dimensions. Again the answer to this question is that it depends on our level of analysis. It depends on whether we try to compare the cultures of entire societies (which is what this book is about) or to compare individuals within societies. An individual can be both masculine and feminine at the same time,[9] but a country culture is either predominantly one or predominantly the other. We found that if in a country more people held masculine values, fewer people held feminine values.

Country Masculinity Scores by Gender and Gender Scores by Age

Country MAS scores were also computed separately for men and women.[10] Figure 4.2 shows in simplified form the relationship between masculinity by gender and masculinity by country and reveals that from the most feminine (tender) to the most masculine (tough) countries, both the values of men and of women became tougher but the country difference was larger for men than for women. In the most feminine countries, Sweden and Norway, there was no difference between the scores of men and women, and both expressed equally tender, nurturing values. In the most masculine countries in the IBM database, Japan and Austria, the men scored very tough and the women fairly tough, but the gender gap was largest. From the most feminine to the most masculine country, the range of MAS scores for men was about 50 percent wider than the range for women. Women's values differ less among countries than men's values do, and a country's femininity is more clearly reflected in the values of its men than in those of its women. Women across countries can be expected to agree more easily on issues in which ego values are at stake. A U.S. bestseller (by John Gray) was called *Men Are from Mars, Women Are from Venus*, but in feminine cultures both sexes are from Venus.[11]

Richard Lynn from Northern Ireland collected data about attitudes to competitiveness and money from male and female university students in forty-two countries. Overall, men scored higher than women on competi-

FIGURE 4.2 Country Masculinity Scores by Gender

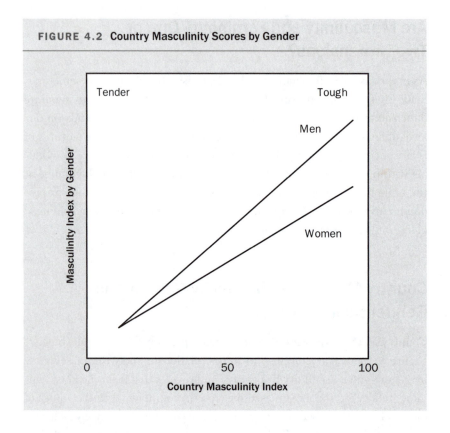

tiveness. In a reanalysis, Evert van de Vliert from the Netherlands showed that the ratio between men's and women's scores was significantly correlated with MAS. It was lowest in Norway, where the women rated their competitiveness higher than the men, and highest in Germany.[12]

Figure 4.3 shows schematically the age effects on masculinity values.[13] When people grow older they tend to become more social and less ego oriented (lower MAS). At the same time, the gap between women's and men's MAS values becomes smaller, and around age fifty it has closed completely. This is the age at which a woman's role as a potential child-bearer has ended; there is no more biological reason for her values to differ from a man's.

This development fits the observation that young men and women foster more technical interests (which could be considered masculine), and older men and women more social interests. In terms of values (but not necessarily in terms of energy and vitality), older persons are more suitable as people managers and younger persons as technical managers.

FIGURE 4.3   MAS Scores by Gender and Age

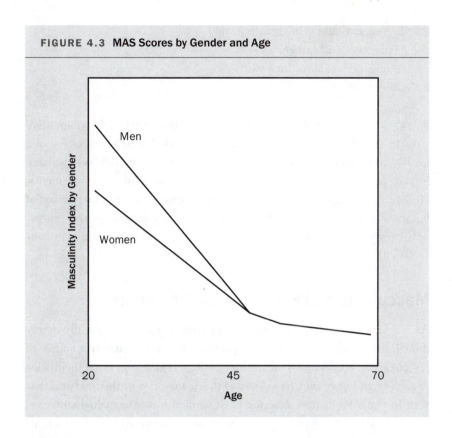

Masculinity and Femininity According to Occupation

In the IBM research, occupations could (on the basis of the values of those who exercised them) be ordered along a tough-tender dimension. It did make sense to call some occupations more masculine and others more feminine. Not surprisingly the masculine occupations were mostly filled by men, and the feminine occupations mostly by women. The differences in values, however, were not caused by the gender of the occupants. Men in feminine occupations held more feminine values than women in masculine occupations.

The ordering of occupations in IBM from most masculine to most feminine was as follows:

1. Sales representatives
2. Engineers and scientists

3. Technicians and skilled craftspeople
4. Managers of all categories
5. Semiskilled and unskilled workers
6. Office workers

Sales representatives were paid on commission, in a strongly competitive climate. Scientists, engineers, technicians, and skilled workers focused mostly on technical performance. Managers dealt with both technical *and* human problems, in roles with both assertive *and* nurturing elements. Unskilled and semiskilled workers had no strong achievements to boast of but usually worked in cooperative teams. Office workers also were less oriented toward achievements and were oriented more toward human contacts with insiders and outsiders.

Masculinity and Femininity in the Family

As only a small part of gender role differentiation is biologically determined, the stability of gender role patterns is almost entirely a matter of socialization. *Socialization* means that both girls and boys learn their place in society, and once they have learned it, the majority of them want it that way. In male-dominated societies, most women want the male dominance.

The family is the place where most people received their first socialization. The family contains two unequal but complementary role pairs: parent-child and husband-wife. The effects of different degrees of inequality in the parent-child relationship were related to the dimension of power distance in Chapter 2. The prevailing role distribution between husband and wife is reflected in a society's position on the masculinity-femininity scale.

Figure 4.4 crosses PDI against MAS. In the right half of the diagram (where PDI values are high), inequality between parents and children is a societal norm. Children are supposed to be controlled by obedience. In the left half, children are controlled by the examples set by parents. In the lower half of the diagram (where MAS scores are high), inequality between fathers' and mothers' roles (father tough, mother less tough) is a societal norm. Men are supposed to deal with facts, women with feelings. In the upper half, both men and women are allowed to deal with the facts and with the soft things in life.

Thus the lower right-hand quadrant (unequal and tough) stands for a norm of a dominant, tough father and a submissive mother who, although

FIGURE 4.4 Power Distance Versus Masculinity

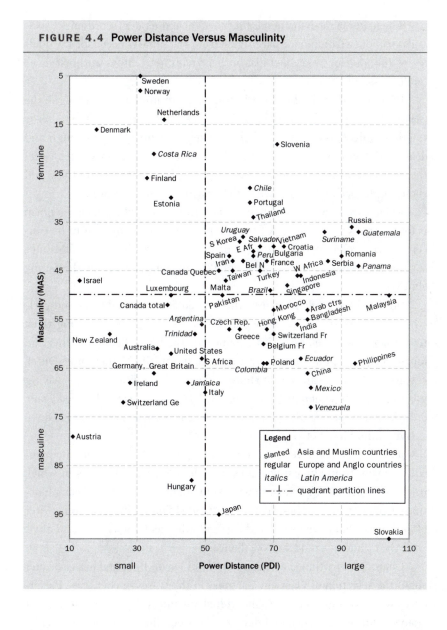

also fairly tough, is at the same time the refuge for consolation and tender feelings. This quadrant includes some of the Latin American countries, those where men are supposed to be macho. The complement of *machismo* for men is, for women, *marianismo* (being like the Virgin Mary) or *hembrismo* (from *hembra*, a female animal): a combination of near-saintliness, submissiveness, and sexual frigidity.[14]

The upper right-hand quadrant (unequal and tender) represents a societal norm of two dominant parents, sharing the same concern for the quality of life and for relationships, both providing at times authority *and* tenderness.

In the countries in the lower left-hand quadrant (equal and tough), the norm is for nondominant parents to set an example in which the father is tough and deals with facts and the mother is somewhat less tough and deals with feelings. The resulting role modeled is that boys should assert themselves and girls should please and be pleased. Boys don't cry and should fight back when attacked; girls may cry and don't fight.

Finally, in the upper left-hand quadrant (equal and tender), the norm is for mothers and fathers not to dominate and for them both to be concerned with relationships, with the quality of life, with facts *and* feelings, setting an example of a relative equality of gender roles in the family context.

Studies of schoolchildren in the United States asked boys and girls why they chose the games they played. Boys chose games allowing them to compete and excel; girls chose games for the fun of being together and for not being left out. Repeating these studies in the Netherlands, Dutch researcher Jacques van Rossum found no significant differences in playing goals between boys and girls; thinking he had made an error, he tried again, but with the same negative result. Child socialization in the feminine Dutch culture differs less between the sexes.[15]

The family context in Figure 4.4 depends also on individualism-collectivism. Individualist societies include one-parent families in which role models are incomplete or in which outsiders perform the missing functions. Collectivist societies maintain extended family links, and the center of authority could very well be the grandfather as long as he is still alive, with the father as a model of obedience.

Chapter 3 mentioned a massive study of David Buss and his associates about the selection of marriage partners in thirty-seven countries. Preferences were strongly related to individualism and collectivism, but further analysis showed that certain differences between the preferences for brides and for grooms were related to MAS. Masculine cultures tended to show a double moral standard in which the chastity and the industriousness of the partner were only considered important by the men. In feminine cultures, they were seen as equally important or unimportant by women and men alike.[16]

In 1993 a Japanese market research agency, Wacoal, asked young working women in eight Asian capital cities for their preferred characteristics of husbands and of steady boyfriends. In the masculine cultures husbands should be healthy, wealthy, and understanding, while boyfriends should have personality, affection, intelligence, and a sense of humor. In the more feminine cultures there was hardly any difference between the preferred characteristics of husbands and of boyfriends. If we see the boyfriend as the symbol of love and the husband as the symbol of family life, this means that in the masculine countries love and family life were more often seen as separate, whereas in the feminine countries they were expected to coincide. In the feminine countries the husband was the boyfriend. A unique aspect of this analysis was that the comparison with the IBM data was made exclusively across Asian countries, showing that the masculinity-femininity dimension could also be validated without including European countries.[17]

U.S. anthropologist Margaret Mead once observed that in the United States boys become less attractive sex partners by career failure, girls by career success.[18] In Japan a woman's marriage chances diminish if she has a career of her own.

Table 4.2 summarizes the key issues described so far on which masculine and feminine societies tend to differ.

Masculinity and Femininity in Gender Roles and Sex

The Wacoal survey also asked young working women in eight Asian cities whether they thought certain characteristics applied to men, to women, or to both. Answers differed between masculine and feminine countries. In the more masculine countries, sense of responsibility, decisiveness, liveliness, and ambitiousness were considered characteristics for men only, while caring and gentleness were seen as for women only. In the more feminine cultures, all these terms were considered as applying to both genders.[19]

Whereas gender roles *in the family* strongly affect the values about appropriate behavior for boys and for girls, they do not have immediate implications for the distribution of gender roles *in the wider society*. As argued earlier in this chapter, men, being on average taller and stronger and free to get out, have traditionally dominated in social life outside the home in virtually all societies. Only exceptional and usually upper-class

TABLE 4.2 Key Differences Between Feminine and Masculine Societies: General Norm and Family

FEMININE	MASCULINE
Relationships and quality of life are important.	Challenge, earnings, recognition, and advancement are important.
Both men and women should be modest.	Men should be assertive, ambitious, and tough.
Both men and women can be tender and focus on relationships.	Women are supposed to be tender and take care of relationships.
In the family both fathers and mothers deal with facts and feelings.	In the family fathers deal with facts and mothers with feelings.
Both boys and girls are allowed to cry, but neither should fight.	Girls cry, boys don't; boys should fight back, girls shouldn't fight at all.
Boys and girls play for the same reasons.	Boys play to compete, girls to be together.
Bridegrooms and brides are held to the same standards.	Brides need to be chaste and industrious, grooms don't.
Husbands should be like boyfriends.	Husbands should be healthy, wealthy, and understanding, and boyfriends should be fun.

women had the means to delegate their child-rearing activities to others and to step into a public role. If women entered dominant positions in society at all, this was mostly after the age of forty-five, when their mother status changed into grandmother status. Unmarried women were, and still are, rare in traditional societies and often discriminated against.

The much greater liberty of choice among social roles that women in modern industrialized societies enjoy, beyond those of wife, mother, and housekeeper, is a recent phenomenon. Its impact on the distribution of gender roles *outside* the home is not yet fully felt. Therefore a country's position on the masculinity-femininity scale need not be closely related to women's activities outside the family sphere. Economic possibilities and necessities play a bigger role in this respect than values.

A masculine gender role model is pictured in the following description of a popular U.S. motion picture:

> *Lucas, a 14-year-old boy, is unlike other kids. He's slight, inquisitive, and something of a loner, more interested in science and symphonies than in football and parties. But when he meets Maggie, a lovely 16-year-old girl who has just moved to town, things change. They become friends—but for Lucas it is more than friendship.*
>
> *During the summer they seem to have the same idea: football players and cheerleaders are superficial; but when school begins, Maggie shows an increasing interest in this side of school life, leaving Lucas out in the cold. He watches from the sidelines as Maggie becomes a cheerleader and starts dating Cappie Roew, the captain of the football team.*
>
> *Suddenly, Lucas wants to "belong," and in his attempt to win back Maggie, risks life and limb in the game of football. . . .*[20]

Mainstream movies are modern myths—they create hero models according to the dominant culture of the society in which they are made. Both Lucas and Maggie in this movie go through a *rite de passage* toward their rightful roles in a society where men fight while playing football and girls stand adoringly and adorably by the sidelines as cheerleaders.

Femininity should not be confused with feminism. *Feminism* is an ideology that wants to change the role of women in society. The masculinity-femininity dimension is relevant to this ideology because across countries we find a more masculine and a more feminine form of feminism. The masculine form claims that women should have the same possibilities as men have. In terms of Figure 4.2, it wants to move the female line up toward the male line; this could also be achieved by moving the entire society toward the right. The feminine form wants to change society, men included. Not only women's liberation, but men's lib as well. In Figure 4.2 this could be achieved by moving the male line downward toward the female line or by moving the entire society toward the left.

Obviously a country's position on the masculinity-femininity scale also affects its norms about sexual behavior.[21] Feelings about sex and ways in which sex is practiced and experienced are culturally influenced. Although individuals and groups within countries differ, too, women and men are affected by the written and unwritten norms of their country's culture.

The basic difference in sexual norms between masculine and feminine cultures follows the pattern of Figure 4.2. Masculine countries tend to maintain different standards for men and for women: men are the subjects, women the objects. In the section on family, we already found this double moral standard in masculine cultures with regard to the chastity of brides: women should be chaste, men need not. It can also be noticed in norms about nudity in photos and movies: the taboo on showing naked men is much stronger than on showing naked women. Feminine cultures tend to maintain a single standard—equally strict or equally loose—for both sexes, and there is no immediate link felt between nudity and sexuality.

Sex is more of a taboo subject in masculine than in feminine cultures. This is evident in information campaigns for the prevention of AIDS, which in feminine countries tend to be straightforward, whereas in masculine countries they are restricted by what can be said and what cannot. Paradoxically, the taboo also makes the subject more attractive, and there is more implicit erotic symbolism in TV programs and advertising in masculine than in feminine countries.

Double standards encourage an emphasis on sexual performance: "scoring" for men, and a feeling of being exploited for women. In single-standard feminine countries, the focus for both is primarily on the relationship between two persons.

In the 1980s Geert was involved in a large survey study on organizational cultures in Denmark and the Netherlands.[22] The questionnaire contained, among other items, a list of possible reasons for dismissal. In a feedback session in Denmark, Geert asked respondents why nobody in their company had considered "a married man having sexual relationships with a subordinate" as a valid reason for the man's dismissal. A woman stood up and said, "Either she likes it, and then there is no problem. Or she doesn't like it, and then she will tell him to go to hell." There are two assumptions in this answer: (most) Danish subordinates will not hesitate to speak up to their boss (small power distance), and (most) Danish bosses will "go to hell" if told so (femininity).

In a study of "sexual harassment" in four countries in the 1990s, Brazilian students of both sexes differed from their colleagues in Australia, the United States, and Germany. They saw sexual harassment less as an abuse of power, less as related to gender discrimination, and more as a relatively harmless pastime.[23] Brazil in the IBM research scored lower on MAS than the three other countries (49 versus 61, 62, and 66, respectively).

Attitudes toward homosexuality are also affected by the degree of masculinity in the culture. In a comparison between Australia, Finland, Ire-

land, and Sweden, it was found that young homosexuals had more problems accepting their sexual orientation in Ireland and Australia, less in
Finland, and least in Sweden. This is the order of the countries on MAS.
Homosexuality tends to be felt as a threat to masculine norms and rejected
in masculine cultures; this is accompanied by an overestimation of its frequency. In feminine cultures homosexuality is more often considered a fact
of life.[24]

Culture is heavy with values, and values imply judgment. The issues
in this section are strongly value-laden. They are about moral and immoral,
decent and indecent behavior. The comparisons offered should remind us
that morality is in the eye of the beholder, not in the act itself. There is no
one best way, neither in social nor in sexual relationships; any solution can
be the best according to the norms that come with it.

Table 4.3 follows on Table 4.2 and summarizes the key issues from
this section on which masculine and feminine societies were shown to differ.

Masculinity and Femininity in Education

A Dutch management consultant taught part of a course for Indonesian
middle managers from a public organization located all over the archipelago. In the discussion following one of his presentations, a Javanese par-
ticipant came up with a very lucid comment, and the teacher praised him
openly. The Javanese responded, "You embarrass me. Among us, parents
never praise their children to their face."[25]

This anecdote illustrates two things. First, it demonstrates how
strong, at least in Indonesia, is the transfer of behavior models from the
family to the school situation, the teacher being identified with the father.
Second, it expresses the virtue of modesty in the Javanese culture to an
extent that even surprised the Dutchman. Indonesia is a multiethnic country, one for which national culture scores may be misleading. Indonesians
agree that especially on the tough-tender dimension, ethnic groups within
the country vary considerably, with the Javanese taking an extreme position toward the tender side. The Dutch consultant said that even some of
the other Indonesians were surprised by the Javanese's feelings. A Batak
from the island of Sumatra said that he now understood why his Javanese
boss never praised him when he himself felt that praise should have been
due. In feminine cultures teachers will rather praise weaker students, to
encourage them, than openly praise good students. Awards for excel-

TABLE 4.3 **Key Differences Between Feminine and Masculine Societies: Gender and Sex**

FEMININE	MASCULINE
Being responsible, decisive, ambitious, caring, and gentle is for women and men alike.	Being responsible, decisive, and ambitious is for men; being caring and gentle is for women.
Girls don't cheer for boys.	Women's ambition is channeled toward men's success.
Women's liberation means that men and women take equal shares both at home and at work.	Women's liberation means that women are admitted to positions so far occupied by men.
Single standard: both sexes are subjects.	Double standards: men are subjects, women objects.
Same norm for showing male or female nudity.	Stronger taboo on showing male than female nudity.
Explicit discussion of sex, less implicit symbolism.	Taboo on explicit discussion of sex but implicit erotic symbolism.
Sex is a way for two persons to relate.	Performance for a man can be exploitation for a woman.
Sexual harassment is a minor issue.	Sexual harassment is a big issue.
Homosexuality is considered a fact of life.	Homosexuality is considered a threat to society.

lence—whether for students or for teachers—are not popular; in fact, *excellence* is a masculine term.[26]

For some years Geert taught U.S. students in a semester-long program of European studies at a Dutch university. He gave the assignment to some of the Americans to interview Dutch students about their goals in life. The Americans were struck by the fact that the Dutch seemed much less concerned with grades than they expected. Passing was considered enough; excelling was not an openly pronounced goal. Gert Jan's experiences with students from all over the world are similar. Students from masculine countries may ask to take an exam over again after passing with a mediocre grade—Dutch students never do so. Such experiences in teaching at home and abroad and discussions with teachers from different countries have led us to conclude that in the more feminine cultures the *average* student is considered the norm, while in more masculine countries the *best* students are the norm. Parents in these countries expect their children to try to match the best. The "best boy in class" in the Netherlands is a somewhat ridiculous figure.[27]

This difference is noticeable in classroom behavior. In masculine cultures students try to make themselves visible in class and compete openly with each other (unless collectivist norms put a limit to this; see Chapter 3).

In feminine countries assertive behavior and attempts at excelling are easily ridiculed. Excellence is not something one flaunts; it easily leads to jealousy. Gert Jan remembers being told by a classmate when he was fourteen: "We know you are smart—but you don't have to show it all the time."

In the feminine Scandinavian countries people call this the Law of Jante (*Janteloven*). The Law of Jante, a nickname chosen for a small Danish town, was codified in the 1930s by the Danish-born Norwegian author Aksel Sandemose, and in an English translation it runs as follows:

> *You should not believe that*
> *you are anything*
> *you are just as much as us*
> *you are wiser than us*
> *you are better than us*
> *you know more than we do*
> *you are more than we are*
> *or that you are good at anything*
> *You should not laugh at us*
>
> *You should not think*
> *that anybody likes you*
> *or that you can teach us anything.*[28]

Failing in school is a disaster in a masculine culture. In strongly masculine countries like Japan and Germany, the newspapers report each year about students who killed themselves after failing an examination. In a 1973 insider story, a Harvard Business School graduate reported four suicides—one teacher and three students—during his time at this elite American institution.[29] Failure in school in a feminine culture is a relatively minor incident. When young people in these cultures take their lives, it tends to be for reasons unrelated to performance.

Competitive sports play an important role in the curriculum in countries such as Britain and the United States. To a prominent U.S. sports coach is attributed the dictum "Winning isn't the most important thing— it's the only thing,"[30] which doesn't encourage friendly encounters in sports. In most other European countries sports are extracurricular and not a part of the school's main activities.

In an imaginative research project, ten- to fifteen-year-old children from five countries were shown a picture of one person sitting on the ground, with another standing over him saying, "Go ahead and fight back if you can!" They were asked to choose one of eight answers from a card. Aggressive answers were "You've hit me. Now I'm going to teach you a lesson," "I'll tell the teacher," "We are not friends anymore," and "You'll get caught by the police!" Appeasing answers were "We don't have to fight. Let's talk it over," "Let's not fight. Let's be friends," "I'm sorry. I was wrong," and "What if somebody gets hurt by fighting?"[31] An aggressive answer was chosen by 38 percent of the children in Japan, 26 percent in Britain, 22 percent in Korea, 18 percent in France, and 17 percent in Thailand. This almost exactly followed the countries' MAS scores.[32] It clearly shows the different socializing of children with regard to aggression. Another study, this time among university students in six countries, contained the question whether children in their country were allowed to express aggression. The percentages of "yes" answers varied from 61 in the United States to 5 in Thailand and again correlated significantly with MAS.[33]

The IBM research found Thailand to be the most feminine Asian country. A book about Thai culture by a British-Thai couple reads, "The Thai learns how to *avoid* aggression rather than how to *defend* himself against it. If children fight, even in defense, they are usually punished. The only way to stay out of trouble is to flee the scene."[34]

After the story at the beginning of this chapter about Geert's job interview, we wrote that U.S. applicants tend to oversell and Dutch applicants to undersell themselves. There is confirming evidence for this from two studies in a school or learning context.

In the first study some eight hundred U.S. and eight hundred Dutch youngsters, aged eleven to eighteen, completed questionnaires about their personal competencies and problems. The Americans reported many more problems *and* competencies than the Dutch. Some items on which Americans scored higher were "argues a lot," "can do things better than most kids," "stores up unneeded things," and "acts without thinking." The only item on which the Dutch scored higher was "takes life easy." Reports by parents and teachers showed no difference in problem behavior with these children, but U.S. parents rated their children's competencies higher than Dutch parents did.[35] Young people in U.S. society have been socialized to boost their ego: they take both their problems and their competencies seriously.[36] Young people in the Netherlands are socialized rather to efface their ego. An earlier comparison between the United States and (masculine) Germany had not found such differences.

The second study compared levels of literacy across seven countries. In 1994 representative samples of between two thousand and more than four thousand younger and older adults (age sixteen to sixty-five) all took the same tests to measure their literacy for three skills: reading, writing, and using numbers. From those with the best results (literacy levels 4 and 5 out of 5), 79 percent of the Americans rated their own skills "excellent," but only 31 percent of the Dutch did so[37]—this in spite of the fact that the tests had shown both groups to be equally good.

Criteria for evaluating both teachers and students differ between masculine and feminine cultures. On the masculine side teachers' brilliance and academic reputation and students' academic performance are the dominant factors. On the feminine side teachers' friendliness and social skills and students' social adaptation play a bigger role.

Interviews with teachers suggest that in masculine countries job choices by students are strongly guided by perceived career opportunities, while in feminine countries students' intrinsic interest in the subject plays a bigger role.

In feminine countries men and women more often follow the same academic curricula, at least if the country is wealthy. In poor countries boys almost always get priority in educational opportunities.[38]

Different job choices by women and men can be partly explained by differences in perceptual abilities. Psychologists studying human perception distinguish between *field-independent* and *field-dependent* persons.[39] Field-independent persons are able to judge whether a line, projected on a wall, is horizontal even if it is put within a frame that is slanted or if they themselves sit on a chair that is slanted. Field-dependent persons are influenced by the position of the frame and the chair. Field-independent persons rely on internal frames of reference; field-dependent persons take their clues from the environment. Therefore field-independent people tend to have better analytical skills, and field-dependent people better social and linguistic skills. Men are more often field-independent, women field-dependent. Masculine cultures tend to score more field-independent, feminine cultures more field-dependent,[40] and there is less difference in perceptual abilities between the genders in feminine than in masculine countries.

Segregation in job choice also determines who become teachers: women or men. In masculine societies women mainly teach younger children and men teach at universities. In feminine societies roles are more mixed and men also teach younger children. So on average, children in masculine societies are exposed longer to female teachers. This looks like a paradox, but the female teachers' status is often low so that they will be antiheroines rather than models for behavior.

Masculinity and Femininity in Shopping

Dutch marketing expert Marieke de Mooij studied consumer behavior data across sixteen affluent European countries.[41] She found several significant differences related to the masculinity-femininity dimension. One was the division of buying roles between the genders. In feminine culture countries a larger share of the family's food shopping is done by the husband. Other differences relate to the family car. In buying a new car, the husband in a feminine country will involve his partner. In a masculine country this tends to be the man's sovereign decision, in which the car's engine power plays an important role. In feminine cultures car owners often don't even know their car's engine power. The car has often been described as a sex symbol; to many it is certainly a status symbol. Masculine cultures have relatively more two-car families than feminine cultures; in the latter, husband and wife more often share one car.

Status purchases in general are more frequent in masculine cultures. People in masculine cultures buy more expensive watches and more real jewelry. They more often consider foreign goods as more attractive than local products. They more often fly business class on pleasure trips.

Feminine cultures spend more on products for the home. More people in these cultures take their "home" (their caravan or trailer) with them on vacation. They spend more on do-it-yourself carpentry, on making their own dresses, and, for smokers, on rolling their own cigarettes. Coffee is a symbol of togetherness; people in feminine cultures own more electric coffeemakers, guaranteeing that coffee in the home is always ready.

People in feminine cultures buy more fiction books, and people in masculine cultures more nonfiction. U.S. author Deborah Tannen has pointed to differences between male and female discourse: more "report talk" (transferring information) for men, more "rapport talk" (using the conversation to exchange feelings and establish a relationship) for women.[42] De Mooij's data show that at the culture level, too, masculine readers are more concerned with data and facts; readers from feminine cultures are more interested in the story behind the facts.

Table 4.4 is a continuation of Tables 4.2 and 4.3, summarizing the key issues from the past two sections.

Masculinity and Femininity in the Workplace

The Dutch manufacturing plant of a major U.S. corporation had lost three Dutch general managers in a period of ten years. To the divisional vice president in the United States, all these men had come across as "softies." They hesitated to implement unpopular measures with their personnel, claiming the resistance of their works council—a body elected by the employees and required by Dutch law that the vice president did not like anyway. After the third general manager had left, the vice president stepped in personally and nominated the plant controller as his successor, ignoring strong warnings by the human resources manager. To the vice president this controller was the only "real man" in the plant management team. He had always supported the need for drastic action, disregarding its popularity or unpopularity. In his reports he had indicated the weak spots. He should be able to maintain the prerogatives of management, without being sidetracked by this works council nonsense.

The new plant general manager proved the greatest disaster ever. Within six months he was on sick leave and the organization was in a state of chaos. Nobody in the plant was surprised. They had known the controller as a congenial but weak personality, who had compensated for his insecurity by using powerful language toward the American bosses. The assertiveness that impressed the American vice president was recognized within the Dutch environment as bragging. As a general manager he received no cooperation from anyone, tried to do everything himself, and suffered a nervous breakdown in the shortest possible time. Thus the plant

TABLE 4.4 Key Differences Between Feminine and Masculine Societies: Education and Consumer Behavior

FEMININE	MASCULINE
Average student is the norm; praise for weak students.	Best student is the norm; praise for excellent students.
Jealousy of those who try to excel.	Competition in class; trying to excel.
Failing in school is a minor incident.	Failing in school is a disaster.
Competitive sports are extracurricular.	Competitive sports are part of the curriculum.
Children are socialized to be nonaggressive.	Aggression by children is accepted.
Students underrate their own performance: ego-effacement.	Students overrate their own performance: ego-boosting.
Friendliness in teachers is appreciated.	Brilliance in teachers is admired.
Job choice is based on intrinsic interest.	Job choice is based on career opportunities.
Men and women partly study the same subjects.	Men and women study different subjects.
Women and men teach young children.	Women teach young children.
Women and men shop for food and cars.	Women shop for food, men for cars.
Couples share one car.	Couples need two cars.
More products for the home are sold.	More status products are sold.
More fiction is read (rapport talk).	More nonfiction is read (report talk).

lost both a good controller and another general manager. Both the plant and the controller were victims of a culturally induced error of judgment.

Historically, management is an Anglo-Saxon concept, developed in masculine British and American cultures. The English—and international—word *management* comes from the Latin *manus*, or "hand"; modern Italian *maneggiare* means "handling." But in French the Latin root is used in two derivations: *manège* (place where horses are drilled) and *ménage* (household); the former is the masculine side of management, the latter the feminine side. Classic American studies of leadership distinguished two dimensions: initiating structure versus consideration, or concern for work versus concern for people.[43] Both are equally necessary for the success of an enterprise, but the optimal balance between the two differs for masculine and feminine cultures.

A Dutchman who had worked with a prestigious consulting firm in the United States for several years joined the top management team of a manufacturing company in the Netherlands. After a few months he commented on the different function of meetings in his present job compared to his previous one. In the Dutch situation meetings were places where problems were discussed and common solutions were sought; they served for making consensus decisions.[44] In the U.S. situation as he had known it meetings were opportunities for participants to assert themselves, to show how good they were. Decisions were made by individuals elsewhere.

The masculinity-femininity dimension affects ways of handling industrial conflicts. In the United States as well as in other masculine cultures (such as Britain and Ireland) there is a feeling that conflicts should be resolved by a good fight: "let the best man win." The industrial relations scene in these countries is marked by such fights. If possible management tries to avoid having to deal with labor unions at all, and labor union behavior justifies their aversion.[45]

In feminine cultures like the Netherlands, Sweden, and Denmark, there is a preference for resolving conflicts by compromise and negotiation. In France, which scored moderately feminine in the IBM studies, there is occasionally a lot of verbal insult, both between employers and labor and between bosses and subordinates, but behind this seeming conflict there is a typically French "sense of moderation," which enables parties to continue working together while agreeing to disagree.[46]

Organizations in masculine societies stress results and try to reward it on the basis of equity—that is, to everyone according to performance. Organizations in feminine societies are more likely to reward people on the basis of equality (as opposed to equity)—that is, to everyone according to need.

The idea that small is beautiful is a feminine value. The IBM survey as well as public opinion survey data from six European countries showed that a preference for working in larger organizations was strongly correlated with MAS.[47]

The place work is supposed to take in a person's life differs between masculine and feminine cultures. Charles F. Kettering, a successful early twentieth-century U.S. inventor and businessman, is reputed to have said:

> *I often tell my people that I don't want any fellow who has a job working for me; what I want is a fellow whom a job has. I want the job to get the fellow and not the fellow to get the job. And I want that job to get hold of this young man so hard that no matter where he is the job has got him for keeps. I want that job to have him in its clutches when he goes to bed at night, and in the morning I want that same job to be sitting on the foot of his bed telling him it's time to get up and go to work. And when a job gets a fellow that way, he's sure to amount to something.[48]*

Kettering refers to a "young man" and not to a "young woman"—his is a masculine ideal. It would certainly not be popular in more feminine cultures; there such a young man would be considered a workaholic. In a masculine society the ethos tends more toward "live in order to work," whereas in a feminine society the work ethos would rather be "work in order to live."

A public opinion survey in the European Union in 1977 contained the question "If the economic situation were to improve so that the standard of living could be raised, which of the following two measures would you consider to be better: Increasing the salaries (for the same number of hours worked) or reducing the number of hours worked (for the same salary)?" Preferences varied from 62 percent in favor of salary in Ireland to 64 percent in favor of fewer hours worked in the Netherlands. The differences (percent preferring salary minus percent preferring fewer hours) were significantly correlated with MAS more than with national wealth. Although respondents in the poorer countries stressed the need for increasing salaries more, values (MAS) played a stronger role.[49]

Boys in a masculine society are socialized toward assertiveness, ambition, and competition. When they grow up they are expected to aspire to career advancement. Girls in a masculine society are polarized between those who want a career and the majority who don't. The family within a feminine society socializes children toward modesty and solidarity, and in these societies both men and women may or may not be ambitious and may or may not want a career.

The feminine side of management opens possibilities in any culture for women managers, who may be better able to combine manège and ménage than men. U.S. researcher Anne Statham interviewed matched groups of U.S. female and male managers and their secretaries, and she concluded that the women predominantly saw job and people orientation as interdependent, while to the men they were each other's opposites.[50]

Worldwide there is no relationship between the masculinity or femininity of a society's culture and the distribution of employment over men and women. An immediate relationship between a country's position on this dimension and the roles of men and women exists only within the home. Outside the home men have historically dominated, and only in the wealthier countries—and this only recently in history—have women in any numbers been sufficiently freed from other constraints to be able to enter the worlds of work and politics as men's equals. Lower-class women have entered work organizations before but only in low-status, low-paid jobs—not out of a need for self-fulfillment but out of a need for material survival of the family. Statistics therefore show no relationship between a country's share of women working outside the home per se and its degree of femininity. Wealthier feminine countries do have more working women in higher-level technical and professional jobs.[51]

Many jobs in business demand few skills and cause a qualitative underemployment of people. A need for "humanization of work" has been felt in industrialized masculine as well as feminine countries, but what is considered a humanized job depends on one's model of what it means to be human. In masculine cultures a humanized job should give more opportunities for recognition, advancement, and challenge. This is the principle of job enrichment as once defended, among others, by U.S. psychologist Frederick Herzberg.[52] An example is making workers on simple production tasks also responsible for the setting up and preventive maintenance of their machines, tasks that had previously been reserved for more highly trained specialists. Job enrichment represents a "masculinization" of unskilled and semiskilled work that, as shown earlier in this chapter, has a relatively "feminine" occupation culture.

In feminine cultures a humanized job should give more opportunities for mutual help and social contacts. Classic experiments were conducted in the 1970s by the Swedish car and truck manufacturers Saab and Volvo with assembly by autonomous work groups. These represent a reinforcement of the social side of the job: its "femininization." In 1974 six Detroit automobile workers, four men and two women, were invited to work for three weeks in a group assembly system in the Saab-Scania plant in Södertälje, Sweden. The experiment was covered by a U.S. journalist who reported on the Americans' impressions. All four men and one of the women said they continued to prefer the U.S. work system. "Lynette Stewart chose Detroit. In the Cadillac plant where she works, she is on her own and can make her own challenge, while at Saab-Scania she has to consider people in front and behind her."[53] Of course, this was precisely what made the group assembly system attractive to the Swedes.

Based on their cultural characteristics, masculine and feminine countries excel in different types of industries. Industrially developed masculine cultures have a competitive advantage in manufacturing, especially in large volume: doing things efficiently, well, and fast. They are good at the production of big and heavy equipment and in bulk chemistry. Feminine cultures have a relative advantage in service industries like consulting and transport, in manufacturing according to customer specification, and in handling live matter like in high-yield agriculture and biochemistry. There is an international division of labor in which countries are relatively more successful in activities that fit their population's cultural preferences than in activities that go against these. Japan is a world leader in high-quality consumer electronics; Denmark and the Netherlands excel in services, in agricultural exports, and in biochemical products like enzymes and penicillin.

Table 4.5 is a continuation of Tables 4.2, 4.3, and 4.4, summarizing the key issues from the past section on which masculine and feminine societies differ.

Masculinity, Femininity, and the State

National value patterns are present not only in the minds of ordinary citizens but, of course, also in those of political leaders, who, too, grew up as children of their society. As a matter of fact, people are usually elected or co-opted to political leadership *because* they are supposed to stand for certain values dear to citizens.

Politicians translate values dominant in countries into political priorities. The latter are most clearly visible in the composition of national gov-

TABLE 4.5 Key Differences Between Feminine and Masculine Societies: The Workplace

FEMININE	MASCULINE
Management as ménage: intuition and consensus.	Management as manège: decisive and aggressive.
Resolution of conflicts by compromise and negotiation.	Resolution of conflicts by letting the strongest win.
Rewards are based on equality.	Rewards are based on equity.
Preference for smaller organizations.	Preference for larger organizations.
People work in order to live.	People live in order to work.
More leisure time is preferred over more money.	More money is preferred over more leisure time.
Careers are optional for both genders.	Careers are compulsory for men, optional for women.
There is a higher share of working women in professional jobs.	There is a lower share of working women in professional jobs.
Humanization of work by contact and cooperation.	Humanization of work by job content enrichment.
Competitive agriculture and service industries.	Competitive manufacturing and bulk chemistry.

ernment budgets. The masculinity-femininity dimension affects priorities in the following areas:

- Solidarity with the weak versus reward for the strong
- Aid to poor countries versus investing in armaments
- Protection of the environment versus economic growth

Masculine culture countries strive for a performance society, feminine countries for a welfare society. They get what they pay for: in 1994–95 across ten developed industrial countries for which data were available, the share of the population living in poverty varied from 4.3 percent in feminine Norway to 17.6 percent in masculine Australia.[54] Across sixteen developed countries the share of the population earning less than half the median income varied from 5.1 percent in Finland to 16.9 percent in the United States. The share of functional illiterates (people who completed school but in actual fact cannot read or write) across thirteen developed countries varied from 7.5 percent in Sweden to 22.6 percent in Ireland. In all three cases the percentages were strongly correlated with MAS.[55]

In criticisms by politicians and journalists from masculine countries like the United States and Great Britain versus feminine countries like Sweden and the Netherlands, and vice versa, strong and quite different value positions appear. There is a common belief in, for example, the United States that economic problems in Sweden and the Netherlands are because of high taxes, while there is a belief in feminine European countries that economic problems in the United States are because of too much tax relief for the rich. Tax systems, however, do not just happen—they are created by politicians as a consequence of preexisting value judgments. Most Swedes feel that society should provide a minimum quality of life for everyone. It is normal that the financial means to that end are collected from those in society who have them. Even conservative politicians in northwestern Europe do not basically disagree with this view, only with the extent to which it can be realized.

The northwestern European welfare state is not a recent invention. The French philosopher Denis Diderot, who visited the Netherlands in 1773–74, described both the high taxes and the absence of poverty as a consequence of welfare payments, good medical care for all, and high standards of public education: "The poor in hospitals are well cared for: They are each put in a separate bed."[56]

The performance versus welfare antithesis is reflected in views about the causes of poverty. In 1990 a survey in the European Union countries included the following question: "Why, in your opinion, are there people who live in need? Here are four opinions, which is the closest to yours? (1) Because they have been unlucky; (2) Because of laziness and lack of will-power; (3) Because there is much injustice in our society; (4) It is an inevitable part of modern progress." Across the then twelve European Union member states, the percentages attributing poverty to having been unlucky varied from 14 percent in Germany to 33 percent in the Netherlands; they were significantly negatively correlated with MAS.[57] The percentages attributing poverty to laziness varied from 10 percent in the

Netherlands to 25 percent in Greece and Luxembourg; these were positively correlated with MAS. In masculine countries more people believe that the fate of the poor is their own fault, that if they would work harder they would not be poor, and that the rich certainly should not pay to support them.

Attitudes toward the poor are replicated in attitudes toward lawbreakers. A public opinion poll in nine European countries in 1981 asked to what extent a number of debatable acts were justifiable: joyriding, using soft drugs, accepting bribes, prostitution, divorce, and suicide. The answers were summarized in an index of permissiveness, which across countries was strongly correlated with femininity. Mother is less strict than father.[58]

The masculinity-femininity dimension is also related to opinions about the right way of handling immigrants. In general two opposing views are found. One defends *assimilation* (immigrants should give up their old culture), the other *integration* (immigrants should only adapt those aspects of their culture and religion that conflict with their new country's laws). In a public opinion survey in fourteen European Union countries in 1997, the public preference for integration over assimilation was strongly negatively correlated with MAS; there was a weaker additional correlation with GNP per capita.[59] Respondents in more masculine and poorer countries required assimilation; those in feminine and wealthier countries favored integration.

In wealthy countries the value choice between reward for the strong and solidarity with the weak is also reflected in the share of the national budget spent on development assistance to poor countries. In Figure 4.1, which plots MAS against IDV, the upper half of the diagram contains the collectivist (that is, mostly the poor) countries, and the lower half the individualist (that is, the rich) countries. Since the late 1950s development assistance money has flown from the rich to the poor countries—that is, from bottom to top in the diagram. However, the percentage of their gross national product that governments of rich countries have allocated to helping the poor ones has varied widely. In 2000 the United States spent 0.10 percent of its GNP and Italy 0.13 percent, while the Netherlands spent 0.84 percent and Denmark 1.06 percent.[60] The proportions spent are unrelated to the wealth of the donor countries and also unrelated to their former colonial ties or present trade flows. The only explanation of a high aid quote is a feminine national value system. The correlation between a donor country's MAS score and its aid spending in percent of GNP is strongly negative (high MAS, low aid).[61]

The journal *Foreign Policy* has computed, for twenty-one rich countries, a Commitment to Development Index (CDI) by not only measuring aid money flows but also positive and negative impacts of other policies: trade flows, migration, investment, peacekeeping, and environmental policies. Again the CDI was only significantly (negatively) correlated with MAS. The correlation was weaker than for money flows, as policies on behalf of welfare in the home country sometimes conflict with policies on help abroad.[62]

Countries that spend little money on helping the poor in the world probably spend more on armaments. Reliable data on defense spending are difficult to come by, however, as both the suppliers and the purchasers of arms have a vested interest in secrecy. The only conclusion we could draw from the available figures was that among donor countries, the less wealthy spent a greater share of their budgets on arms than the wealthier ones.[63]

Masculine countries tend to (try to) resolve international conflicts by fighting; feminine countries by compromise and negotiation (as in the case of work organizations). A striking example is the difference between the handling of the Åland crisis and of the Falkland crisis.

The Åland islands are a small archipelago halfway between Sweden and Finland; as part of Finland they belonged to the tsarist Russian Empire. When Finland declared itself independent from Russia in 1917, the thirty thousand inhabitants of the islands in majority wanted to join Sweden, which had ruled them before 1809. The Finns then arrested the leaders of the pro-Swedish movement. After emotional negotiations in which the newly created League of Nations participated, all parties in 1921 agreed to a solution in which the islands remained Finnish but with a large amount of regional autonomy.

The Falkland Islands are also a small archipelago disputed by two nations: Great Britain, which has occupied the islands since 1833, and nearby Argentina, which has claimed rights on them since 1767 and tried to get the United Nations to support its claim. The Falklands are about eight times as large as the Ålands but with less than one-fifteenth of the Ålands' population: about 1,800 poor sheep farmers. The Argentinean military occupied the Falkland Islands in April 1982, whereupon the British sent an expeditionary force that chased the occupants, at the cost of (officially) 725 Argentinean and 225 British lives and enormous financial expense. The economy of the islands, dependent on trade relations with Argentina, was severely jeopardized.

What explains the difference in approach and in results between these two remarkably similar international disputes? Finland and Sweden are both feminine cultures; Argentina and Great Britain are both masculine. The masculine symbolism in the Falkland crisis was evident in the language used on either side. Unfortunately the sacrifices resolved very little. The Falklands remain a disputed territory needing constant British subsidies and military presence; the Ålands have become a prosperous part of Finland, attracting many Swedish tourists.

In 1972 an international team of scientists nicknamed the Club of Rome published a report titled *Limits to Growth*, which was the first public recognition that continued economic growth and conservation of our living environment are fundamentally conflicting objectives. This report has been attacked on details, and for a time the issues it raised seemed less urgent. Its basic thesis, however, has never been refuted, and at least in our view it is irrefutable. Nothing can grow forever, and ignoring this basic fact is the greatest weakness of present-day economics. Governments have to make painful choices, and apart from local geographic and ecological constraints, these choices will be made according to the values dominant in a country. Governments in masculine cultures are more likely to give priority to growth and sacrifice the living environment for this purpose. Governments in feminine cultures are more likely to reverse priorities.[64] As environmental problems cross borders and oceans, international diplomacy is needed for solutions. A worldwide approach was laid down in the Kyoto Protocol, the result of a United Nations convention in 1997. After his election in 2001, U.S. President George W. Bush showed his masculine priorities by withdrawing from it.

The 1990–93 World Values Survey asked representative samples of the populations to place their political views on a scale from "left" to "right." Voters from masculine countries placed themselves mostly in the center; voters from feminine countries slightly more to the left. Few people placed themselves on the right.[65]

Masculinity or femininity in democratic politics is not only a matter of policy priorities; it is also reflected in the informal rules of the political game. In masculine cultures like Britain, Germany, and the United States, the style of political discourse is strongly adversarial. This is not a recent phenomenon. In 1876 the Dutch language newspaper *De Standaard* reported that "the American political parties eschewed no means to sling mud at their adversaries, in a way which foreigners find disgusting."[66] This statement is still valid today. In feminine cultures like the Nordic countries and the Netherlands, governments are nearly always coalitions between different parties that treat each other relatively gently.

In democratic countries with a more feminine culture, more women are elected to political office and occupy government posts, but large power distance and strong uncertainty avoidance (see Chapter 5) restrain this effect. In 2002 among twenty-two established parliamentary democracies, percentages of women in parliament were below 20 in Britain, France, Greece, Ireland, Israel, Italy, Japan, Portugal, and the United States and greater than 30 in Denmark, Finland, Germany, the Netherlands, New Zealand, Norway, and Sweden. Female ministers in 2000 were fewer than 20 percent in Australia, Belgium, Greece, Ireland, Israel, Italy, Japan, Portugal, and Spain and more than 40 percent in Denmark, Finland, New Zealand, Norway, and Sweden.[67] It is easier for women to advance in politics than in work organizations. The election process reacts faster to changes in society than co-optation processes in business. Capable women in business organizations still have to wait for aged gentlemen to retire or die.

Masculinity, Femininity, and Religion

The issues related to the masculinity-femininity dimension are central to any religion. Masculine cultures worship a tough God or gods who justify tough behavior toward fellow humans; feminine cultures worship a tender God or gods who demand caring behavior toward fellow humans.

Christianity has always maintained a struggle between tough, masculine and tender, feminine elements. In the Christian Bible as a whole, the Old Testament reflects tougher values (an eye for an eye, a tooth for a tooth), and the New Testament more tender values (turn the other cheek). God in the Old Testament is majestic. Jesus in the New Testament helps the weak and suffers himself. Catholicism has produced some very masculine, tough currents (Templars, Jesuits) but also some feminine, tender ones (Franciscans); outside Catholicism we find other groups with strongly masculine values (like the Mormons) and groups with very feminine values (like the Quakers and the Salvation Army). On average, however, countries with a Catholic tradition tend to maintain more masculine values and those with Protestant traditions more feminine values.[68]

Outside the Christian world there are also tough and tender religions. Buddhism in masculine Japan is very different from Buddhism in feminine Thailand. Some young men in Japan follow Zen Buddhist training aimed at self-development by meditation under a tough master. In the 1970s more than half of all young men in Thailand spent some time as a Buddhist monk, serving and begging.[69] In Islam Sunni is a more masculine version of the faith than Shia, which stresses the importance of suffering. In the IBM studies Iran, which is predominantly Shiite, scored more feminine than the predominantly Sunnite Arab-speaking countries.

In the 1990s Dutch sociologist Johan Verweij devoted his Ph.D. research to explaining differences in secularization (loss of religion) in Western Christianity. From the 1990–93 World Values Survey, he obtained data for various aspects of religiosity across sixteen Christian countries.[70] Existing theories sought the reason for secularization in the modernization of society, but these theories did not account for the situation in the United States, a modern country relatively untouched by secularization. To Verweij's surprise he found that the best available predictor of a country's degree of secularization was the degree of femininity of its culture, this in spite of the fact that women tend to be more religious than men. In masculine Christian countries people rated their religiosity higher and attached more importance in their lives to God, Christian rites, orthodoxy, and Christian world views. Countries with feminine values had secularized faster than those with masculine ones; this applied across the board, including the United States.

The Christian Gospel offers a choice of values for different positions on the masculinity-femininity scale. The New Testament carefully balances the importance of the relationships with God and with one's fellow humans. In one story Jesus is approached by a Pharisee, who asked, "What is the greatest command in the Law?"

Jesus replied, "You must love the Lord your God with your whole heart, with your whole soul, and with your whole mind. This is the greatest and chief command. There is a second like it: you must love your neighbor as yourself. The whole Law and the prophets hang upon these two commands."[71]

The comparison between Christian religiosity in more masculine and more feminine countries implies that the balance between these two commands is difficult to find. There are cultural necessities that lead Christians in some countries to stress the first, and Christians in other countries to stress the second.

One could argue that it is obvious that among Christian countries the tough, masculine societies endorse more strongly the importance of God—and other values derived from it. The Christian God is the Father: He is masculine. The importance of God as rated by the respondents to the European Values Survey and the masculinity index from the IBM studies were both correlated with the claimed observance of the Ten Commandments, but most strongly with the purely religious commandments (no other God, not abusing God's name, and honoring the Sabbath). Masculinity was less correlated with the claimed observance of the sexual commandments (no adultery, do not desire thy neighbor's wife) and least with the claimed observance of the moral commandments (honoring parents, no killing, no stealing, no false witnesses, do not desire thy neighbor's belongings). What was predominantly stressed in masculine cultures was the emotional and symbolic meaning of God's name.[72] The name of God the Father appeals strongly to the population of a masculine society—including the women who were socialized to inequality of gender values. In a feminine society the stress is more on the importance of relationships with fellow humans than with God.

Secularization in feminine countries does not imply a loss of civil morality. A comparison of 1981–82 with 1990 European/World Values Survey data for Ireland, the Netherlands, and Switzerland found no evidence for a relationship between the two.[73] Simplistic recipes that immoral behavior should be countered by a return to religion are thus proven false. On the contrary, it turns out that femininity, which as we saw correlates with secularization, relates positively to civil morality. In 1996 the results were published of an experiment by *Reader's Digest* magazine. Some two hundred wallets, each containing about $50 worth of cash, plus family snapshots and contact numbers of the putative owners, were "accidentally" dropped in public places in big and small cities in the United States and in fourteen European countries. From ten wallets dropped, all ten were returned in Oslo, Norway, and Odense, Denmark, but only two in Lausanne, Switzerland (one of them found by an Albanian!), Ravenna, Italy, and Weimar, Germany. The number returned was significantly correlated with the countries' femininity, with an additional influence of low power distance.[74]

A similar result was produced by another experiment, this one carried out by international students of U.S. psychology professor Robert Levine. These students in their twenty-three home cities "accidentally" dropped a pen in full view of a solitary pedestrian walking in the opposite direction. The score was the percentage of times the pedestrian warned the experimenter or picked up the pen and brought it to her or him. Percentages of helping pedestrians in twenty-three countries were significantly correlated with the countries' femininity score.[75]

All religions specify different religious roles for men and for women. In Christianity many Protestant churches now practice equality between men and women in their leadership and clergy, while the Roman Catholic Church strongly maintains the male prerogative to the priesthood. At the same time, in all Christian churches women are more religious than men. According to British author Tony Walter, "God is apparently not an equal opportunity employer: He has a bias to the women."[76] The European Values Survey showed that this applied in particular for women without paid jobs. Where the role of the woman changed from a housekeeper to a wage earner, her attitude to religion moved closer to the attitude of men.[77]

It should be no surprise that the same dimension, masculinity versus femininity, relates to both sexual and religious behavior. Religion is a way for humankind to influence the supernatural—to provide certainties beyond the unpredictable risks of human existence. Birth, marital fertility, and death figure foremost among these unpredictables. All religions accentuate and celebrate the events of procreation: births, weddings, and deaths. Fertility rites are known from virtually all human civilizations since prehistory; they survive to the present day, such as in wedding ceremonies and in sanctuaries devoted to prayers for pregnancy. In Judaism and most of Islam, circumcision of the male organ is a condition for being admitted to the religious community. In Hinduism the architecture of temples models the *lingam* and *yoni* (phallus and vulva). Chinese philosophy and religious practices give strong importance to the complementarity of *yang* and *yin*, the male and female elements.

Most or all religions contain do's and don'ts about love and sex. Human sexuality has the two facets of procreation and recreation, of reproduction and pleasure. Different religions, and currents within religions, have taken different positions toward the pleasure side of sex; the general trend is for religions in masculine cultures to stress procreation and for those in more feminine cultures to also value pleasure. Masculine Roman Catholicism has rejected sex for pleasure, institutionalizing celibacy for priests, the cult of the Virgin Mary, and marriage as a sacrament with the purpose of procreation and prohibiting divorce, contraception, and abortion. When they split from Rome, less masculine Protestant Christian churches did away with celibacy, did not consider marriage a sacrament, and accepted divorce. Orthodox Islam accepts sexual pleasure for men but considers sexual pleasure in women a danger. Currents in Hinduism have taken a positive attitude toward sexual pleasure, as manifested by the *Kamasutra* love guide and the erotic temples of Khajuraho and Konarak in

India. In feminine Buddhist Thailand the profession of prostitute carries less of a stigma than in the West. In feminine Sweden female prostitution is forbidden, but the visitor, not the woman, is punished.

In the domain of scientific theories about sex, it is remarkable that the work of Sigmund Freud (1856–1939) originated in Austria, a country with one of the highest MAS scores (79) in the IBM list. Freud, the founder of psychoanalysis, argues for the fundamental importance of sexuality in the development of the human personality; he attributed many psychopathological problems to the repression of sexuality. Freud attributed *penis envy* (jealousy about not having one) to all women. We wonder whether an author from a less masculine society would have imagined this. Every author or scientist is a child of his or her society; Freud's work comes directly out of the masculine Austrian context in which he was raised.

Table 4.6 complements Tables 4.2, 4.3, 4.4, and 4.5 by summarizing the key differences between feminine and masculine societies from the last two sections.

Origins of Masculinity-Femininity Differences

In human thinking the issue of equality or inequality between the sexes is as old as religion, ethics, and philosophy themselves. Genesis, the first book of the Judeo-Christian Old Testament (which was codified in the fifth century B.C.), contains two conflicting versions of the creation of the sexes. The first, Genesis 1:27–28, states:

> *So God created man in his own image, in the image of God created he him; male and female created he them. And God blessed them, and God said to them, Be fruitful, and multiply, and replenish the earth, and subdue it.*

This text suggests equal partnership between the sexes. The second version, Genesis 2:8ff. (which Old Testament experts suppose to have been derived from a different source document), contains the story of the garden in Eden, in which God first put "the man" alone. Then, in Genesis 2:18, it states:

> *And the Lord God said, It is not good that the man should be alone: I will make him a help meet for him.*[78]

TABLE 4.6 **Key Differences Between Feminine and Masculine Societies: The State and Religion**

FEMININE	MASCULINE
Welfare society ideal; help for the needy.	Performance society ideal; support for the strong.
Permissive society.	Corrective society.
Immigrants should integrate.	Immigrants should assimilate.
Government aid for poor countries.	Poor countries should help themselves.
The environment should be preserved: small is beautiful.	The economy should continue growing: big is beautiful.
International conflicts should be resolved by negotiation and compromise.	International conflicts should be resolved by a show of strength or by fighting.
More voters place themselves left of center.	More voters place themselves in the political center.
Politics are based on coalitions, polite political manners.	Political game adversarial, with frequent mudslinging.
Many women are in elected political positions.	Few women are in elected political positions.
Tender religions.	Tough religions.
In Christianity, more secularization; stress on loving one's neighbor.	In Christianity, less secularization; stress on believing in God.
Dominant religions stress complementarity of the sexes.	Dominant religions stress the male prerogative.
Religions are positive or neutral about sexual pleasure.	Religions approve sex for procreation rather than recreation.

Then follows the story of woman made from Adam's rib. This text gives clear priority to the male partner and defines the woman as "a help meet" (that is, appropriate) for him; it justifies a society in which there is male dominance.

In ancient Greece, Plato (in the fourth century B.C.) describes the sexes as equal in principle and (apart from their role in procreation) only statistically different. In *The Republic* he offers a design for an ideal state governed by an elite composed of men as well as women. Of course, in actual fact the Greek state was male dominated. So was the Roman state; but at least one Roman writer, C. Musonius Rufus (in the first century A.D.), defended the equality of the sexes and in particular the study of philosophy by women and men alike.

The German sociologist Norbert Elias argued that the balance of power between the genders varies with the development of a society. During the Roman Republic and early Empire (400 B.C. to A.D. 100), the influence and rights of patrician women improved gradually along with the development of the city-state into a world empire and of the senatorial class from peasant warriors into aristocrats. With the disintegration of the Roman Empire in the third century A.D., the status of women deteriorated. In an earlier book Elias described how around the eleventh century A.D. in Europe, and particularly in France, the gradual reestablishment of an orderly society and reduction of fighting gave the noble women a social and civilizing role. In the history of European civilization, the French nobility and court have been major models, being followed at a distance by other countries and classes. The present differences on the masculinity-femininity dimension between France, Spain, and Portugal on one side and Britain, Germany, and Italy on the other can be interpreted as different outcomes of this process.

Anthropologist Margaret Mead found in New Guinea very different gender role distributions among adjacent tribal groups. She showed that history and tradition allow the survival of considerable variety in gender roles. We did not find strong correlations with outside factors, which could explain why some countries have dominant masculine and others dominant feminine cultures. Feminine cultures are somewhat more likely in colder climates, suggesting that in this case an equal partnership between men and women improves chances of survival and population growth.

The concentration of feminine cultures in northwestern Europe (Denmark, Finland, Netherlands, Norway, Sweden) points to common historical factors. The elites in these countries consisted to a large extent of traders and seafarers. In trading and sailing, maintaining good interpersonal relationships and caring for the ships and the merchandise are essential virtues. The Viking period in the Scandinavian countries (A.D 800–

1000) also meant that the women had to manage the villages while the men were away on their long trips; but Vikings did not settle in the Netherlands for any length of time. The Hanseatic League (A.D. 1200–1500) covered all northwestern European countries, including the free cities of Hamburg, Bremen, and Lübeck in northern Germany and the Baltic states. The Hansa was a free association of trading towns in which women played an important role:

> *Although the wife did not share her husband's legal status, they usually formed a business team. Even in merchant circles, the family was the smallest functional cell of society, where the women and the children had a role to play. This meant that women had a certain degree of emancipation, and their independence and business skills increased. Indeed, some women managed to win the "battle for the trousers" even while their husbands were still alive.*[79]

Erasmus of Rotterdam in his *Colloquia* of 1524 compared the service in French and German inns—both of which he knew from experience. He referred to the charm of French innkeepers' wives and daughters, the quality of the food, and French *savoir vivre*. He opposed this to German strictness, inflexibility, and lack of manners. He actually used the word *masculine* to distinguish the German style from the French. At the same time, he recognized that the Germans maintained greater equality among customers.[80]

Comparing Britain and the Netherlands, the English statesman Sir Francis Walsingham wrote (in a political pamphlet in 1585) that England and the Low Countries "have been by common language resembled and termed as man and wife." Half a century later some Englishmen connected Dutch commercial success with the fact that they "generally breed their youth *of both sexes* more in the study of Geometry and Numbers than the English do." And elsewhere it was remarked that Dutch merchants *and their wives* were more conversant in trade than the English.[81] Although women in seventeenth-century Netherlands were excluded from public office, "within these limits they managed to assert themselves, both individually and collectively, in public life." And in paintings from this period, "fathers are occasionally shown participating in the work of caring for small children." Also, "Military glory . . . was liable to be regarded with more circumspection than enthusiasm in the Netherlands. . . . Even though professional soldiers . . . played a crucial role in the defense of the [Dutch]

Republic in the 17th century, they went conspicuously without honor in the patriotic culture of the time."[82] Military heroes belong to the history of masculine countries like Britain and the United States.

Symbolic personalities representing Western countries in the nineteenth and twentieth centuries were remarkably gendered according to their cultures' masculinity or femininity: John Bull for Britain and Uncle Sam for the United States but Marianne[83] for France and the Dutch maiden (called *Frau Antje* in Germany) for the Netherlands.

Latin American countries varied considerably on the masculinity-femininity scale. Small Central American countries, Peru, and Chile scored feminine; Mexico, Venezuela, Colombia, and Ecuador strongly masculine. One speculative explanation is that these differences reflect the inheritance of the different Indian civilizations dominant prior to the Spanish conquest. Most of Mexico inherited the tough Aztec culture, but the southern Mexican peninsula of Yucatan and the adjacent Central American republics the less militant Maya culture. Peru and northern Chile inherited the Inca culture, resembling the Maya.

All these historical examples show that differences between countries on the masculinity-femininity dimension were noticed and described centuries ago: the way in which a country deals with gender roles is deeply rooted.

The Future of Differences in Masculinity and Femininity

An extremely interesting relationship existed between MAS, wealth, and population growth. MAS and the number of children per family (leading to population growth) were negatively related for the wealthier countries but positively for the poorer countries. In other words, feminine cultures meant smaller families in poor countries and larger families in wealthy countries.[84] In these cultures women had a say in the number of children they bore: they adapted the family size to the available resources. In masculine cultures male choice prevailed in matters of family size and led to (too) large families in poor countries and to small families in wealthy countries. U.S. anthropologist Daniel Levinson, reviewing anthropological studies of traditional cultures, concluded that population increases in societies where females are subservient to males.[85] Family-planning programs stumble over the attitudes of men. UNICEF (United Nations Children's Fund) staff have calculated that if in all countries women could choose their family size, they would have an average of 1.41 fewer children, which amounts to 1.3 billion fewer people in the world in thirty-five years' time.[86] This relationship means that in the poor part of the world masculine cultures grow faster, and in the wealthy part feminine cultures grow faster.

For matched samples of the populations of ten wealthy European countries, we analyzed data from the European and World Values Surveys from around 1980, 1990, and 2000 about the public opinion and the changes in it, about "qualities children can be encouraged to learn at home." MAS scores in 2000 were positively correlated with children having to learn religious faith and negatively with children having to learn tolerance and respect. From 1980 via 1990 to 2000 the importance of learning religion had decreased, and the importance of learning tolerance and respect had increased. This confirms for these wealthy countries an overall reduction in masculinity.[87]

The shift toward more feminine values in wealthier countries can also be related to aging of the population. Figure 4.3 showed that masculinity scores decreased with age. The demographic development in the wealthy part of the world is toward lower birthrates, resulting in fewer young people.[88] An aging population will cause a shift toward more feminine values. When birthrates fall, this also implies that more women will be both available for and needed in the workforce (as there will be fewer young men). Again these influences predict for the wealthy countries a shift toward femininity.

Technology imposes changes on the work people do. In the wealthier countries the information revolution is moving on, eliminating old jobs and creating new ones. Jobs that can be structured will more and more be automated. What remains are activities that by their very nature cannot be automated. These are in the first place the jobs that deal with the setting of human and social goals, with defining the purpose of life for individuals and societies. These include all political and organizational top leadership functions. In the second place they are the creative jobs, those concerned with inventing new things and subjecting them to criteria of usefulness, beauty, and ethics. A third and sizable category of jobs that cannot be automated are those that deal with the unforeseeable: safety, security, defense, maintenance. Finally, there is a large category of jobs whose essence is human contact: supervision, entertainment, keeping people company, listening to them, helping them materially and spiritually, motivating them to learn. In these jobs computers can be introduced as resources, but they can never take over the job itself. For all these nonautomatable jobs, feminine values are as necessary in performing them as masculine ones, regardless of whether the job incumbents themselves are women or men. For the last category, in which human contact is the core of the task, feminine values are even superior. Tasks related with achievement can more easily be automated than nurturing tasks. In balance, technological developments are also likely to support a shift from masculine to feminine values in industrial societies.

For the poorer part of the world, as long as a country remains poor, it is unlikely to shift toward more feminine values. Masculinity-femininity differences play a role in what is becoming a dramatic problem for mainly Asian countries, the prevention or suppression of female births. Asia around 2000 counted some 100 million fewer females than would have been the result of normal birthrates. The reason is the desire of parents to have sons rather than daughters, the availability of ultrasound scanning of the sex of a fetus followed by selective abortion, and the old practice of killing baby girls. The female/male ratio in the population is higher in feminine cultures like Thailand and Indonesia than in masculine cultures like India and China. A surplus of men over women may further increase the masculinity of the societies in question.

Conservation of the global environment demands a worldwide nurturing mentality. The vicious circle from poverty to masculinity and back is bad for global survival. This is another good reason to strive for a fair distribution of resources throughout the world's population.

What Is Different Is Dangerous

In the 1960s Arndt Sorge did his military service in the West German army. Near his hometown, where he spent his free weekends, there were barracks of the British "Army on the Rhine." Sorge was keen on watching British motion pictures with the original sound track, which were shown in the British barracks, and he walked up to the sentry to ask whether he, as a German soldier, could attend. The sentry referred him to the sergeant of the guard, who called the second in command on the telephone and then tore a page out of a notebook, on which he wrote, "Mr Arndt Sorge has permission to attend film shows," and signed it, adding that permission was granted by the second in command.

Sorge used his privilege not only on that occasion but several other times, and the notebook page (in conjunction with his German army identity card) always opened the gate for him. After he was demobilized Sorge asked the British sentry whether he, now as a civilian, could continue to attend. The sentry looked at the notebook page, said, "This is for you personally," and let him in.

Arndt Sorge became an organization sociologist, and he remembers this experience as an example of how differently the British seemed to handle such an unplanned request from what he was accustomed to in the German army. The Germans would have taken more time and would have needed the permission of more authorities; they would have asked more information about the applicant and issued a more formal document. Finally, the document would have been issued to him as a member of the armed forces, and there would have been no question of his using it after his demobilization.[1]

The Avoidance of Uncertainty

Germany and Britain have a lot in common. Both are western European countries, both speak a Germanic language, their populations are of roughly equal size, and the British royal family is of German descent. Yet it does not take a very experienced traveler to notice the considerable cultural differences between the two countries.

Peter Lawrence is a British sociologist who wrote about Germany:

What strikes a foreigner traveling in Germany is the importance attached to the idea of punctuality, whether or not the standard is realized. Punctuality, not the weather, is the standard topic of conversation for strangers in railway compartments. Long distance trains in Germany have a pamphlet laid out in each compartment called a Zugbegleiter *(literally, "train accompanier") which lists all the stops with arrival and departure times and all the possible connections* en route. *It is almost a national sport in Germany, as a train pulls into a station, for hands to reach out for the Zugbegleiter* so that the train's progress may be checked against the digital watch. When trains are late and it happens, the loudspeaker announcements relay this fact in a tone which falls between the stoic and the tragic. The worst category of lateness which figures in these announcements is* unbestimmte Verspätung *(indeterminable lateness: we don't know how late it is going to be!) and this is pronounced as a funeral oration.[2]*

Sorge's surprise at the easygoing approach of the British sentry and Lawrence's at the punctual German travelers suggest that the two countries differ in their tolerance of the ambiguous and the unpredictable. In the IBM research Britain and Germany score exactly alike on the two dimensions of power distance (both 35) and masculinity (both 66). On individualism the British score considerably higher (89 versus 67). The largest difference between the two countries, however, is on a fourth dimension, labeled *uncertainty avoidance.*

The term *uncertainty avoidance* has been borrowed from American organization sociology, in particular from the work of James G. March.[3] March and his colleagues recognized it in American organizations. Ways of handling uncertainty, however, are part and parcel of any human institution in any country. All human beings have to face the fact that we do not know what will happen tomorrow: the future is uncertain, but we have to live with it anyway.

Extreme ambiguity creates intolerable anxiety. Every human society has developed ways to alleviate this anxiety. These ways belong to the domains of technology, law, and religion. Technology, from the most primitive to the most advanced, helps to avoid uncertainties caused by nature. Laws and rules try to prevent uncertainties in the behavior of other people. Religion is a way of relating to the transcendental forces that are assumed to control man's personal future. Religion helps to accept the uncertainties one cannot defend oneself against, and some religions offer the ultimate certainty of a life after death or of victory over one's opponents.

Anthropologists studying traditional societies have spent a good deal of their attention on technology, law, and religion. They have illustrated the enormous variety of ways in which human societies deal with uncertainty. Modern societies do not differ essentially from traditional ones in this respect. In spite of the availability of the same information virtually anywhere around the globe, technologies, laws, and religions continue to vary. Moreover, there are no signs of spontaneous convergence.

The essence of uncertainty is that it is a subjective experience, a feeling. A lion tamer may feel reasonably comfortable when surrounded by his animals, a situation that would make most of us almost die from fear. You may feel reasonably comfortable when driving on a crowded freeway at fifty-five miles per hour or more, a situation statistically probably about equally risky as the lion tamer's.

Feelings of uncertainty not only are just personal but may also be partly shared with other members of one's society. Like the values discussed in the past three chapters, feelings of uncertainty are acquired and learned. Those feelings and the ways of coping with them belong to the cultural heritage of societies. They are transferred and reinforced through basic institutions like the family, the school, and the state. The collectively held values of the members of a particular society reflect them. Their roots are nonrational. They lead to collective patterns of behavior in one society that may seem aberrant and incomprehensible to members of other societies.

Measuring the (In)tolerance of Ambiguity in Society: The Uncertainty Avoidance Index

After power distance, individualism-collectivism, and masculinity-femininity comes uncertainty avoidance (from strong to weak), the fourth dimension found in the IBM research project. Each country and region in this project could be assigned an uncertainty avoidance index (UAI) score.

Differences between countries on uncertainty avoidance were originally discovered as a by-product of power distance. It all started with a question about job stress. This question runs "How often do you feel nervous or tense at work?" with answers ranging from (1) I always feel this way to (5) I never feel this way. Geert had been struck by the regularity of answer patterns on this question from country to country. For example, British employees always scored less nervous than German employees, be they managers, engineers, secretaries, or unskilled factory workers. Across all countries in the IBM database, however, differences in stress were unrelated to power distance.

Close scrutiny of all questions producing stable country differences revealed that the country mean scores on the following three items were strongly correlated:

1. Job stress, as just described (mean score on a 1 to 5 scale).
2. Agreement with the statement "Company rules should not be broken—even when the employee thinks it is in the company's best interest" (mean score on a 1 to 5 scale). This item was labeled *rule orientation*.
3. The percentage of employees expressing their intent to stay with the company for a long-term career. The question was "How long do you think you will continue working for IBM?" and the answers ran (1) Two years at the most; (2) From two to five years; (3) More than

five years (but I probably will leave before I retire); and (4) Until I retire. The percentage in a country answering 3 or 4 was correlated with the mean answers on items 1 and 2.

At first the combination of these three items did not make sense. Why should someone who feels under stress also want rules to be respected and his or her career to be long-term? But this is a false interpretation. The data do not suggest that "someone" shares these three attitudes. When we looked at the answers of individual "someones," the answers to the three questions were not correlated. It was the *differences in mean answers by country* for the three questions that were correlated. So if in a country more people felt under stress at work, in that same country more people wanted rules to be respected and more people wanted to have a long-term career. But the individuals who held each of these feelings did not need to be the same persons.

The culture of a country—or other category of people—is not a combination of properties of the "average citizen" nor a "modal personality." It is, among other things, a set of likely reactions of citizens with a common mental programming. One person may react in one way (such as feeling more nervous), and another in another way (such as wanting rules to be respected). Such reactions need not be found within the same *individuals*, but only statistically more often in the same *society*.

The interpretation of the association between questions 1 through 3 *at the society level* does make sense. We assume that all three are expressions of the level of anxiety that exists in a particular society in the face of an uncertain future. This level of anxiety forms part and parcel of the shared mental programming of people in that society, in the family, at school, and in adult life. Because of this anxiety level, a relatively larger share of individuals will feel nervous or tense at work (question 1). The idea of breaking a company rule—for whatever good reason—is rejected by more people (question 2), because it introduces ambiguity: what if everybody would just start doing as they pleased? Finally, changing employers is less popular in such a country (question 3), for it means venturing into the unknown.

Uncertainty avoidance can therefore be defined as *the extent to which the members of a culture feel threatened by ambiguous or unknown situations*. This feeling is, among other things, expressed through nervous stress and in a need for predictability: a need for written and unwritten rules.

The UAI values for seventy-four countries and regions are listed in Table 5.1. In a way similar to the computation of the power distance index (Chapter 2), the index value for each country was computed from the mean scores of questions 1 and 2 and the percentage score for question 3. The formula used is based on simple mathematics: adding or subtracting the three scores after multiplying each by a fixed number, and finally adding another fixed number. The formula was developed such that (1) each of the three questions would contribute equally to the final index and (2) index values would range from around 0 for the country with the weakest uncertainty avoidance to around 100 for the strongest. The latter objective was not completely attained, because after the formula had been developed, some more countries were added that produced scores greater than 100.

TABLE 5.1 Uncertainty Avoidance Index (UAI) Values for 74 Countries and Regions

COUNTRY/REGION	SCORE	RANK	COUNTRY/REGION	SCORE	RANK
Greece	112	1	Chile	86	17–22
Portugal	104	2	Costa Rica	86	17–22
Guatemala	101	3	France	86	17–22
Uruguay	100	4	Panama	86	17–22
Belgium Flemish	97	5	Spain	86	17–22
Malta	96	6	Bulgaria	85	23–25
Russia	95	7	Korea (South)	85	23–25
Salvador	94	8	Turkey	85	23–25
Belgium Walloon	93	9–10	Hungary	82	26–27
Poland	93	9–10	Mexico	82	26–27
Japan	92	11–13	Israel	81	28
Serbia	92	11–13	Colombia	80	29–30
Suriname	92	11–13	Croatia	80	29–30
Romania	90	14	Brazil	76	31–32
Slovenia	88	15	Venezuela	76	31–32
Peru	87	16	Italy	75	33
Argentina	86	17–22	Czech Republic	74	34

continued

COUNTRY/REGION	SCORE	RANK	COUNTRY/REGION	SCORE	RANK
Austria	70	35–38	**Australia**	51	55–56
Luxembourg	70	35–38	Slovakia	51	55–56
Pakistan	70	35–38	Norway	50	57
Switzerland French	70	35–38	**New Zealand**	49	58–59
Taiwan	69	39	South Africa[1]	49	58–59
Arab countries	68	40–41	**Canada total**	48	60–61
Morocco	68	40–41	Indonesia	48	60–61
Ecuador	67	42	**United States**	46	62
Germany	65	43	**Philippines**	44	63
Thailand	64	44	**India**	40	64
Bangladesh	60	45–47	Malaysia	36	65
Canada Quebec	60	45–47	**Great Britain**	35	66–67
Estonia	60	45–47	**Ireland**	35	66–67
Finland	59	48–49	China	30	68–69
Iran	59	48–49	Vietnam	30	68–69
Switzerland German	56	50	**Hong Kong**	29	70–71
Trinidad	55	51	**Sweden**	29	70–71
West Africa	54	52	**Denmark**	23	72
Netherlands	53	53	Jamaica	13	73
East Africa	52	54	**Singapore**	8	74

Scores for countries or regions in **bold type** were calculated from the IBM database. Scores for other countries or regions were based on replications or estimates.

1 The data were from whites only.

Table 5.1 shows a new grouping of countries, unlike the ones found for any of the previous three dimensions. High scores occur for Latin American, Latin European, and Mediterranean countries (from 112 for Greece to 67 for Ecuador). Also high are the scores of Japan and South Korea (92 and 85). Medium high are the scores of the German-speaking countries Austria, Germany, and Switzerland (70, 65, and 56). Medium to low are the scores of all Asian countries other than Japan and Korea (from 69 for Taiwan to 8 for Singapore), for the African countries, and for the Anglo and

Nordic countries plus the Netherlands (from 59 for Finland to 23 for Denmark). As already noted, Germany scored 65 (rank 43), and Great Britain scored 35 (rank 66–67). This confirms a culture gap between these otherwise similar countries with regard to the avoidance of uncertainty, as illustrated in the story with which this chapter opened.

Uncertainty Avoidance and Anxiety

Anxiety is a term taken from psychology and psychiatry that expresses a diffuse "state of being uneasy or worried about what may happen."[4] It should not be confused with *fear*, which has an object. We are afraid of something, but anxiety has no object. The idea that levels of anxiety may differ between countries goes back to the French sociologist Émile Durkheim (1858–1917), who as early as 1897 published a study on the phenomenon of suicide. This showed that suicide rates in different countries and regions were surprisingly stable from year to year. He used this stability as proof that a highly individual act like taking one's life could nevertheless be influenced by social forces that differed between countries and remained largely the same over time.

High suicide rates are one, but only one, possible outcome of anxiety in a society. In the 1970s the results were published of a large study of anxiety-related phenomena in eighteen developed countries by the Irish psychologist Richard Lynn. Lynn used data from official health and related statistics and showed that a number of indicators were correlated across countries: the suicide death rate, alcoholism (measured by the death rate resulting from liver cirrhosis), the accident death rate, and the rate of prisoners per ten thousand population. These together formed a factor that he labeled *anxiety* or *neuroticism*. Some other indicators were negatively related with the anxiety factor: the consumption of caffeine (in coffee and tea), the average daily intake of calories of food, the death rate resulting from coronary heart disease, and the occurrence of chronic psychosis (measured through the number of patients per one thousand population). Lynn calculated scores for the strength of the anxiety factor of each of his eighteen countries, based on data from 1960. He found Austria, Japan, and France to score highest, and New Zealand, Great Britain, and the Republic of Ireland lowest. There is a strong correlation between Lynn's country anxiety scores and the UAI scores found in the IBM studies and listed in Table

5.1.[5] Because the two studies use completely different sources of data, the agreement between their results is supportive of the solidity of their conclusions: anxiety levels differ from one country to another. Some cultures are more anxious than others.

Anxious cultures tend to be expressive cultures. They are the places where people talk with their hands, where it is socially acceptable to raise one's voice, to show one's emotions, to pound the table. Japan may seem to be an exception in this respect; like other Asians, the Japanese generally behave unemotionally in Western eyes. In Japan, however, and to some extent also in Korea and Taiwan, there is the outlet of getting drunk among colleagues after working hours. During these parties men release their pent-up aggression, even toward superiors; but the next day business continues as usual. Such drinking bouts represent one of the major institutionalized places and times for anxiety release.

In weak uncertainty avoidance countries, anxiety levels are relatively low. According to Lynn's study, more people in these countries die from coronary heart disease. This can be explained by the lower expressiveness of these cultures. Aggression and emotions are not supposed to be shown: people who behave emotionally or noisily are socially disapproved of. This means that stress cannot be released in activity; it has to be internalized. If this happens again and again, it may cause cardiovascular damage.

Lynn explains the larger number of chronic psychosis patients in low-anxiety countries from a lack of mental stimuli in such societies, a certain gloom or dullness. Coffee and tea are stimulating drugs, and these societies show a high consumption of such caffeine carriers. Alcohol has the opposite effect; that is, it releases stress. Weak uncertainty avoidance societies tend to have low average alcohol consumption figures as manifested by their low frequency of liver sclerosis deaths. Many people in the Scandinavian countries show a particular pattern of periodic excessive drinking—in which case, the alcohol does act as a stimulus, but for a short period only—followed by longer periods of abstention; the *average* alcohol consumption in the Scandinavian countries is low compared to the rest of Europe.

A comparison across thirty-three countries of UAI with national norms for the Big Five personality test showed that in more uncertainty avoiding cultures, respondents scored themselves higher on neuroticism and lower on agreeableness. Neuroticism scores increased further if the culture was also masculine.[6] Neuroticism (the opposite of emotional stability) combines the following set of self-scored personality facets: anxiety, angry hostility, depression, self-consciousness, impulsiveness, and vulnerability. Agreeableness, on which more uncertainty-avoiding cultures score lower, combines trust, straightforwardness, altruism, compliance, modesty, and tender-mindedness.

These correlations explain why people from strong uncertainty avoidance cultures may come across as busy, fidgety, emotional, aggressive, suspicious and why people from weak uncertainty avoidance countries may give the impression of being dull, quiet, easygoing, indolent, controlled, lazy. These impressions are in the eye of the beholder: they show the difference with the level of emotionality in the observer's own culture.

Uncertainty Avoidance Is Not the Same as Risk Avoidance

Uncertainty avoidance should not be confused with risk avoidance. Uncertainty is to risk as anxiety is to fear. Fear and risk are both focused on something specific: an object in the case of fear, an event in the case of risk. Risk is often expressed as a percentage of probability that a particular event may happen. Anxiety and uncertainty are both diffuse feelings. Anxiety, it was argued earlier, has no object. Uncertainty has no probability attached to it. It is a situation in which anything can happen and we have no idea what. As soon as uncertainty is expressed as risk, it ceases to be a source of anxiety. It may become a source of fear, but it may also be accepted as routine, such as the risks of driving a car or practicing a sport.

Rather than leading to reducing risk, uncertainty avoidance leads to a reduction of *ambiguity*. Uncertainty avoiding cultures shun ambiguous situations. People in such cultures look for a structure in their organizations, institutions, and relationships that makes events clearly interpretable and predictable. Paradoxically, they are often prepared to engage in risky behavior in order to reduce ambiguities, like starting a fight with a potential opponent rather than sitting back and waiting.

The analysis of the IBM data shows a correlation between the strength of uncertainty avoidance in a (developed) country and the maximum speeds allowed in freeway traffic in that country. The relationship is positive: stronger uncertainty avoidance means faster driving. Faster driving, other things being equal, means more fatal accidents, thus more risk. However, this is a *familiar* risk, which uncertainty avoiding cultures do not mind running. Their emotionality provides them with a sense of stress, of urgency, which in turn leads to wanting to drive faster. The higher speed limits in stronger uncertainty avoidance countries show, in fact, a priority of saving time over saving lives.

In countries with weaker uncertainty avoidance, there is less of a prevailing sense of urgency, and therefore more public acceptance of a lower speed limit. Not only familiar but also unfamiliar risks are accepted, such as those involved in a change of jobs or in engaging in activities for which there are no rules.

Uncertainty Avoidance According to Occupation, Gender, and Age

It is easy to imagine more and less uncertainty avoiding occupations (such as bank clerk versus journalist). Nevertheless, the analysis of the IBM data across the thirty-eight available occupations did not permit the use of the UAI for characterizing occupations. The reason is that the three questions used to compute the index for countries (stress, rule orientation, and intent to stay) had different meanings for different occupations, so that across occupations, the three were not correlated. If anybody wants to measure the amount of uncertainty avoidance in occupations, she or he will have to use other questions.

The same holds for gender differences. Women and men *in the same countries and occupations* showed exactly the same stress levels and rule orientation. Only their intent to stay differed (men on average wanting to stay longer), but this does not express their greater avoidance of uncertainty: it just shows that the IBM population contained a percentage of younger women who planned to stop working for some time when they had small children.

The only aspect of the IBM population other than nationality that did show a close relationship with the uncertainty avoidance index was average age. In countries where IBM employees were older, we found higher stress, more rule orientation, and a stronger intent to stay. There is a circular logic in the relationship between UAI and age: in countries with stronger uncertainty avoidance, people not only intended to but did change employers less frequently. Therefore IBM employees in these countries on average had been with the company longer and were older.[7]

Uncertainty Avoidance in the Family

An American couple spent two weeks in a small Italian town babysitting their grandchildren, whose American parents, temporarily located in Italy, were away on a trip. The children loved to play in the public piazza, amidst lots of Italian children with their mothers or nannies. The American children were allowed to run around; they would fall down but get up again, and the grandparents felt there was little real danger. The Italians, however, reacted quite differently. They would not for a moment lose their children from sight, and when a child fell down, an adult would immediately pick it up, brush it off, and console it.[8]

Among the first things a child learns are the distinctions between clean and dirty and between safe and dangerous. What is considered clean and safe, or dirty and dangerous, varies widely from one society to the next, and even among families within a society. What a child has to learn is to classify clean things from dirty things and safe things from dangerous things. In strongly uncertainty avoiding cultures, classifications with regard to what is dirty and dangerous are tight and absolute. The Italian mothers and nannies (UAI 75) saw dirt and danger in the piazza, where the American grandparents (UAI 46) saw none.

British American anthropologist Mary Douglas has argued that dirt—that which pollutes—is a relative concept, depending entirely on cultural interpretation. Dirt is basically matter out of place. Dangerous and polluting are things that do not fit our usual frameworks of thinking, our normal classifications.[9]

Dirt and danger are not limited to matter. Feelings of dirt and danger can also be held about people. Racism is bred in families. Children learn that persons from a particular category are dirty and dangerous. They learn to avoid children from other social, ethnic, religious, or political out-groups as playmates.

Ideas, too, can be considered dirty and dangerous. Children in their families learn that some ideas are good and others taboo. In some cultures the distinction between good and evil ideas is sharp. There is a concern about Truth with a capital *T*. Ideas that differ from this Truth are dangerous and polluting. Little room is left for doubt or relativism.

The stronger systems of rules and norms in strongly uncertainty avoiding societies make children more often feel guilty and sinful. In fact, the education process in high-UAI societies develops in its children stronger *superegos* (the concept was developed by Sigmund Freud in high-UAI Austria). Children in these societies are more likely to learn that the world is a hostile place and are more likely to be protected from experiencing unknown situations.

Weak uncertainty avoidance cultures also have their classifications of dirt and danger, but these are less precise and more likely to give the benefit of the doubt to unknown situations, people, and ideas. In these societies rules are more flexible, superegos weaker, the world is pictured as basically benevolent, and experiencing novel situations is encouraged.

The tighter system of rules and norms for children in stronger uncertainty avoiding cultures is also reflected in their language. Data about the structure of languages presented by Kashima and Kashima, whose work we already met in Chapter 3, show that languages in uncertainty avoiding cultures more often have different modes of address for different persons, like *tu* and *vous* in French. Children learning such languages face more choices according to tight cultural rules. Languages in lower-UAI cultures tend to have fewer such rules.[10]

The strong uncertainty avoidance sentiment can be summarized by the credo of xenophobia: "What is different is dangerous." The weak uncertainty avoidance sentiment, on the contrary, is: "What is different is curious."

Family life in high-UAI societies is inherently more stressful than if UAI is low. Feelings are more intense, and both parents and children express their positive as well as their negative sentiments more emotionally. Data from the World Values Survey showed that in balance, satisfaction with home life was negatively correlated with UAI, at least in the more affluent countries. When poorer countries were included, satisfaction with home life related more to individualism and femininity.[11]

In Chapter 4 we described the complex relationship between masculinity, family size, and wealth. Worldwide there was and still is a strong correlation of fertility with national poverty. Poor feminine countries, however, tended to have lower fertility than poor masculine countries, and the reverse was true for wealthy countries. This relationship was based on fertility and wealth data measured at the time of the IBM surveys, 1960–70. In the next thirty-five years, birthrates nearly all over the world dropped. In the wealthy countries they even sank below the level necessary for a stable population without immigration (2.1 children per family). Our analysis for twenty-one affluent Western countries shows that in the 1970s national levels of fertility were only correlated (negatively) with wealth: wealthier countries had smaller families. In 1995–2000 fertility levels were primarily correlated, also negatively, with UAI. Uncertainty avoiding affluent societies had smaller families than uncertainty accepting societies. The lower satisfaction with home life also meant wanting fewer children.[12]

Table 5.2 summarizes the key differences between weak and strong uncertainty avoidance societies described so far. Obviously the descriptions refer to the extreme poles of the dimension, and most countries are really somewhere in between, with considerable variation *within* each country.

TABLE 5.2   Key Differences Between Weak and Strong Uncertainty Avoidance Societies: General Norm and Family

WEAK UNCERTAINTY AVOIDANCE	STRONG UNCERTAINTY AVOIDANCE
Uncertainty is a normal feature of life, and each day is accepted as it comes.	The uncertainty inherent in life is a continuous threat that must be fought.
Low stress and low anxiety.	High stress and high anxiety.
Aggression and emotions should not be shown.	Aggression and emotions may at proper times and places be ventilated.
In personality tests, higher scores on agreeableness.	In personality tests, higher scores on neuroticism.
Comfortable in ambiguous situations and with unfamiliar risks.	Acceptance of familiar risks; fear of ambiguous situations and of unfamiliar risks.
Lenient rules for children on what is dirty and taboo.	Firm rules for children on what is dirty and taboo.
Weak superegos developed.	Strong superegos developed.
Similar modes of address for different others.	Different modes of address for different others.
What is different is curious.	What is different is dangerous.
Family life is relaxed.	Family life is stressful.
In affluent Western countries, more children.	In affluent Western countries, fewer children.

Uncertainty Avoidance, Happiness, and Health

The 1990 World Values Survey included a question about happiness in life. Happiness was negatively correlated with UAI, both for the wealthier countries and for all countries together.[13] Higher UAI goes together with less subjective well-being. Dutch sociologist Ruut Veenhoven compiled data about happiness in nations for a period of more than fifty years. For all countries together and for the period before 1990, happiness was primarily correlated with wealth (richer countries were happier). For the affluent countries and for all countries since 1990, the first correlation of happiness was with UAI.[14]

Veenhoven included a measure for the distribution (dispersion) of happiness scores within each country. These dispersion scores were positively correlated with UAI.[15] Very happy people could be found in both high- and low-UAI countries, but very unhappy people existed especially in high-UAI countries.

An ingenious indirect measurement of happiness was supplied by Peter Smith's comparison of national levels of acquiescence in large international surveys, as described in Chapter 3. *Acquiescence* is the tendency to give positive answers to any question, regardless of its content. For questions dealing with values, this tendency was correlated with collectivism and large power distance. For questions dealing with descriptions of the actual situation, the tendency to give positive answers all across was correlated with weak uncertainty avoidance. In high-UAI countries people showed a negative tendency in describing their work and life situation.[16]

In 1979 a study of human values was conducted among a broad sample of the population in thirteen countries around the world. People in high-UAI countries as compared to those in low-UAI countries described themselves more often as living sincerely and seriously, as living independently, and as being concerned about peace in the world. They more often worried about money and about their health.[17]

The World Values Survey also included a question about health. Satisfaction with health was again negatively correlated with UAI, both for the wealthier countries and for all countries together.[18] People in lower-UAI countries felt healthier, although medical data showed no evidence of objective health differences. One is as healthy as one feels.

Health-care practices vary considerably between countries, as any traveler who has consulted a doctor abroad can testify. Theories and practices of medicine are tightly interwoven with cultural traditions, in which uncertainty avoidance plays an important role. Lynn Payer, a medical journalist, described her personal experiences as a patient in Britain, France, Germany, and the United States. One of her examples is that low blood pressure was seen as a reason for living longer (and maybe getting a lower life insurance premium) in Britain and the United States, but it was treated as a disorder in (higher-UAI) Germany, where several drugs are on the market to cure it.[19] It is said that when in France a village is slowly depopulating, the local pharmacy survives longer than the local pub. This is certainly not the case in (lower-UAI) Ireland.

A country's uncertainty avoidance norm is also reflected in the way health-care resources are spent. For thirty-six countries in the IBM studies, the *Human Development Report 1999*, issued by the United Nations Development Programme, lists the number of doctors and the number of nurses per 100,000 inhabitants. Dividing the number of nurses by the number of doctors provides an index of nurses per doctor that is independent of the absolute size of the health budget (that is, of the country's wealth). There is a significant negative correlation between nurses per doctor and UAI, meaning that uncertainty avoiding countries tend to spend more money on doctors, uncertainty accepting countries on nurses. In high-UAI cultures more tasks are performed by the doctor himself, who is seen as the indispensable expert.[20]

Uncertainty Avoidance at School

The International Teachers Program (ITP) around 1980 was a summer refresher course for teachers in management subjects. In a class of fifty there might be twenty or more different nationalities. Such a class offered excellent opportunities to watch the different learning habits of the students (who were teachers themselves at other times) and the different expectations they had of the behavior of those who taught them.

One dilemma Geert experienced when teaching in the ITP was choosing the proper amount of structure to be put into the various activities. Most Germans, for example, favored structured learning situations with precise objectives, detailed assignments, and strict timetables. They liked situations in which there was one correct answer that they could find. They expected to be rewarded for accuracy. These preferences are typical for stronger uncertainty avoidance countries. Most British participants, on the other hand, despised too much structure. They liked open-ended learning situations with vague objectives, broad assignments, and no timetables at all. The suggestion that there could be only one correct answer was taboo with them. They expected to be rewarded for originality. Their reactions are typical for countries with weak uncertainty avoidance.

Students from strong uncertainty avoidance countries expect their teachers to be the experts who have all the answers. Teachers who use cryptic academic language are respected; some of the great gurus from these countries write such difficult prose that one needs commentaries by more ordinary creatures explaining what the guru really meant. "German students are brought up in the belief that anything which is easy enough for them to understand is dubious and probably unscientific."[21] French academic books not infrequently contain phrases of half a page long.[22] Students in these countries will not, as a rule, confess to intellectual disagreement with their teachers. A Ph.D. candidate who finds him- or herself in conflict with a thesis adviser on an important issue has the choice of changing his or her mind or finding another adviser. Intellectual disagreement in academic matters is felt as personal disloyalty.

Students from weak uncertainty avoidance countries accept a teacher who says, "I don't know." Their respect goes to teachers who use plain language and to books that explain difficult issues in ordinary terms. Intellectual disagreement in academic matters in these cultures can be seen as a stimulating exercise, and we know of thesis advisers whose evaluation of a Ph.D. candidate is positively related to the candidate's amount of well-argued disagreement with the professor's position.

In similar situations students in low-UAI countries were more likely to attribute their achievements to their own ability, students in high-UAI countries to circumstances or luck. In two different studies, each covering students from five countries, the relative tendency to attribute achievement to ability was significantly negatively correlated with UAI.[23]

The examples used so far stem from university and postacademic teaching and learning situations, but the behavior and expectations of both students and teachers in these examples were clearly developed during earlier school experiences. One more difference related to uncertainty avoidance that operates specifically at the elementary and secondary school level is the expected role of parents versus teachers. In cultures with strong uncertainty avoidance, parents are sometimes brought in by teachers as an audience, but they are rarely consulted. Parents are laypersons and teachers are experts who know. In countries with weak uncertainty avoidance, teachers often try to get parents involved in their children's learning process: they actively seek parents' ideas.

Uncertainty Avoidance in Shopping

The previous chapter already referred to the studies of Dutch marketing expert Marieke de Mooij. She found many significant links between the IBM indices and consumer behavior differences among sixteen affluent European countries.[24] Next to masculinity-femininity, uncertainty avoidance played an important role.

In shopping for food and beverages, higher UAI stands for valuing purity and basic products. Uncertainty avoiding cultures used mineral water rather than tap water, even where the tap water was of good quality. They ate more fresh fruits and used more pure sugar. Uncertainty accepting cultures valued convenience rather than purity: they consumed more ready-made products, such as ice cream, frozen foods, confectionery, savory snacks, and cereals.

Uncertainty avoiding cultures believed more in cleanliness: they used more textile-washing powders. On the other hand, uncertainty accepting cultures valued looks more than cleanliness: they used more beauty products, such as cosmetics, lipstick, body lotions, deodorants, hair conditioner, facial moisturizing cream, face cleaner, and mascara.

People in uncertainty avoiding cultures bought new cars rather than used ones. People in uncertainty accepting cultures would more often do jobs in the home themselves—for example, painting and wallpapering. In high-UAI countries people preferred playing it safe and leaving such jobs to experts.

Customers in uncertainty avoiding cultures tend to be hesitant toward new products and information. They were slower in introducing electronic communication tools (e-mail, Internet), even if eventually they may use them as much as people in uncertainty accepting cultures. The latter also read more books and newspapers.

Advertising campaigns, in print and on TV, for uncertainty avoiding cultures frequently feature experts, such as doctors in white coats, who recommend the product. Ads in uncertainty accepting cultures more frequently use humor.

In financial matters people from high-UAI countries take fewer risks: they tend to invest less in stocks and more in precious metals and gems.

They are also slower in paying their bills, which may be a problem in trade with uncertainty accepting countries.[25]

Table 5.3 continues the summary of key differences between weak and strong uncertainty avoidance societies started in Table 5.2. Again the descriptions refer to extremes, and most countries are really somewhere in between, with considerable variation *within* each country.

TABLE 5.3 Key Differences Between Weak and Strong Uncertainty Avoidance Societies: Health, Education, and Shopping

WEAK UNCERTAINTY AVOIDANCE	STRONG UNCERTAINTY AVOIDANCE
People feel happier.	People feel less happy.
People have fewer worries about health and money.	People have more worries about health and money.
People have more heart attacks.	People have fewer heart attacks.
There are many nurses but few doctors.	There are many doctors but few nurses.
Students are comfortable with open-ended learning situations and concerned with good discussions.	Students are comfortable in structured learning situations and concerned with the right answers.
Teachers may say, "I don't know."	Teachers are supposed to have all the answers.
Results are attributed to a person's own ability.	Results are attributed to circumstances or luck.
Teachers involve parents.	Teachers inform parents.
In shopping the search is for convenience.	In shopping the search is for purity and cleanliness.
Used cars, do-it-yourself home repairs.	New cars, home repairs by experts.
There is fast acceptance of new products and technologies, like e-mail and the Internet.	There is a hesitance toward new products and technologies.
More books and newspapers.	Fewer books and newspapers.
Risky investments.	Conservative investments.
Appeal of humor in advertising.	Appeal of expertise in advertising.

Uncertainty Avoidance in the Workplace

One of the components of the UAI was the percentage of IBM employees expressing their intent to stay with the company for a long-term career. This was not only an IBM phenomenon; in higher-UAI countries, other factors being equal, more employees and managers look for long-term employment.

Laws, rules, and regulations were mentioned in the beginning of this chapter as ways in which a society tries to prevent uncertainties in the behavior of people. Uncertainty avoiding societies have more formal laws and informal rules controlling the rights and duties of employers and employees. They also have more internal regulations controlling the work process, although in this case the power distance level plays a role, too. Where power distances are large, the exercise of discretionary power by superiors replaces to some extent the need for internal rules.

The need for rules in a society with a strong uncertainty avoidance culture is emotional. People—employers and employees but also civil servants and members of governments—have been programmed since their early childhood to feel comfortable in structured environments. Matters that can be structured should not be left to chance.

The emotional need for laws and rules in a strong uncertainty avoidance society can lead to rules or rule-oriented behaviors that are purely ritual, inconsistent, or even dysfunctional. Critics from countries with weaker uncertainty avoidance do not realize that ineffective rules can also satisfy people's emotional need for formal structure. What happens in reality is less important. Philippe d'Iribarne, in his comparative study of a French, a U.S., and a Dutch manufacturing plant, remarked that some procedures in the French plant were formally followed but only after having been divested of any practical meaning. He compared this to what has been written about the French ancien régime (the eighteenth-century, pre-Napoleon monarchy): "une règle rigide, une pratique molle" ("a strict rule, but a lenient practice").[26]

Countries with weak uncertainty avoidance can show the opposite, an emotional horror of formal rules. People think that rules should only be established in case of absolute necessity, such as to determine whether traffic should keep left or right. They believe that many problems can be solved without formal rules. Germans, coming from a fairly uncertainty avoiding culture, are impressed by the public discipline shown by the British in forming neat queues for bus stops and in shops. There is no law in Britain governing queuing behavior; it is based on a public habit continuously reinforced by social control. The paradox is that although rules in countries with weak uncertainty avoidance are less sacred, they are often better followed.

British queuing behavior is facilitated by the unemotional and patient nature of most British subjects. As argued earlier in this chapter, weak uncertainty avoidance also stands for low anxiety. At the workplace the anxiety component of uncertainty avoidance leads to noticeable differences between strong and weak uncertainty avoidance societies. In strong uncertainty avoidance societies, people like to work hard or at least to be always busy. Life is hurried, and time is money. In weak uncertainty avoidance societies, people are able to work hard if there is a need for it, but they are not driven by an inner urge toward constant activity. They like to relax. Time is a framework to orient oneself in, but not something one is constantly watching.

In the 1970s, during courses at INSEAD business school in Fontainebleau, France, Professor André Laurent surveyed managers from ten industrialized countries about their beliefs regarding organization. Items for which the country mean scores correlated with UAI were:

- Most organizations would be better off if conflict could be eliminated forever.
- It is important for a manager to have at hand precise answers to most of the questions that his subordinates may raise about their work.
- If you want a competent person to do a job properly, it is often best to provide him with very precise instructions on how to do it.
- When the respective roles of the members of a department become complex, detailed job descriptions are a useful way of clarifying.
- An organizational structure in which certain subordinates have two direct bosses should be avoided at all costs.[27]

All of these items show a dislike of ambiguity and a need for precision and formalization in organizations in high-UAI countries. In low-UAI countries ambiguity and chaos are sometimes praised as conditions for creativity.

Uncertainty avoiding cultures also have a strong belief in expertise on the work floor; their organizations count more specialists. Uncertainty accepting cultures have an equally strong belief in common sense and in generalists; a well-known example is the British tradition of considering studying classic literature at a good university a valid entry ticket for a business management career.

A study of top management control in British, French, and German companies by Jacques Horovitz from France concluded that in Britain top managers occupied themselves more with strategic problems and less with daily operations; in France and Germany the reverse was the case.[28] In the IBM studies France and Germany scored considerably higher on UAI than Britain (86 and 65, respectively, versus 35). Strategic problems, being by definition unstructured, demand a greater tolerance for ambiguity than do operational problems. During the period in which Horovitz did his study, the French and German economies did better than the British, so weak uncertainty avoidance leading to more strategic planning does not necessarily increase business effectiveness. Strategic planning is rather a matter of faith. The economic success of companies and countries depends on many more factors.

U.S. researcher Scott Shane found that across thirty-three countries the number of new trademarks granted to nationals was negatively correlated with UAI. He concluded that uncertainty avoiding cultures were slower in innovating.[29] Shane and his colleagues also surveyed employees of four multinational companies in thirty countries about their role in innovation processes. In stronger uncertainty avoidance countries, employees felt more often constrained by existing rules and regulations.[30]

A different story, however, is told by d'Iribarne. In the early 1990s two European car manufacturers, Renault of France and Volvo of Sweden, created a joint venture. In the IBM studies France scored high on UAI, Sweden quite low. A mixed team of engineers and technicians from both nations worked on the design of a new model. After a few years the venture was dissolved. French and Swedish social scientists interviewed the actors to find out what went wrong and possibly learn from the experience. D'Iribarne described what they found:

In the joint team, the French rather than the Swedes produced the more innovative designs. French team members did not hesitate to try out new ideas and to defend these aggressively. The Swedes, on the other hand, were constantly seeking consensus. The need for consensus limited what ideas they could present, even what ideas they could conceive of. To the Swedes the expression of ideas was subject to the need for agreement between people; to the French, it was only subject to the search for technical truth. The French were primarily concerned with the quality of decisions; the Swedes with the legitimacy of the decision process. In the negotiations within the team, the French usually won. They had the support of their superiors who were involved all along, while the Swedish superiors had delegated the responsibility to the team members and were nowhere to be seen. The danger of this asymmetric structure was discovered too late. A mutual distrust had developed at top management level that led to the termination of the venture.[31]

This case suggests that stronger uncertainty avoidance does not necessarily constrain creativity, nor does weaker uncertainty avoidance guarantee its free flow. Comparing the conclusions by Shane and by d'Iribarne, we are also warned that the results of social research are not independent of the nationality of the researcher.

The IBM surveys had already found that people in high-UAI countries preferred larger over smaller companies to work for. In the organizational literature, large companies are often supposed to be less innovative than small ones, unless they reward *intrapreneurs* who dare to break rules. This term is a pun on the word *entrepreneurs,* the independent self-starters who, according to the Austrian American economist Joseph Schumpeter (1883–1950), are the main source of innovation in a society. Schumpeter's ideas played a role in a research project in which Geert (together with a number of Dutch colleagues) took part. The project looked for economic and cultural factors affecting levels of self-employment in twenty-one industrialized countries. Comparing self-employment levels to the countries' UAI scores produced a surprise. While one would expect that in strong uncertainty avoidance cultures fewer people would risk self-employment, the opposite turned out to be the case: self-employment rates were consistently *positively* correlated with UAI. A further search revealed that, in particular, one aspect associated with strong uncertainty avoidance accounted for the correlation: low subjective well-being (happiness) in a society. Self-employment was therefore more often chosen in countries where people were dissatisfied with their lives, not in countries with a higher tolerance for the unknown.[32]

If Schumpeter was right that entrepreneurs innovate more than nonentrepreneurs, we thus found a reason for expecting more, not less, innovation in high-UAI countries. Innovation, however, has more than one face. It may be true that weak uncertainty avoidance cultures are better at basic innovations, but they seem to be at a disadvantage in developing these into new products or services. Implementation of new processes demands a considerable sense of detail and punctuality. The latter are more likely to be found in strong uncertainty avoidance countries. Britain has produced more Nobel Prize winners than Japan, but Japan has put more new products on the world market. There is a strong case here for synergy between innovating and implementing cultures—the first supplying ideas, the second developing them.

Uncertainty Avoidance, Masculinity, and Motivation

The motivation of employees is a classic concern of management and probably even more of management trainers and of the authors of management books. Differences in uncertainty avoidance imply differences in motivation patterns, but the picture becomes clearer when we simultaneously consider the masculinity-femininity dimension described in Chapter 4. Figure 5.1 therefore presents a two-dimensional plot of country scores on uncertainty avoidance (vertically) and masculinity (horizontally).

The usefulness of combining UAI and MAS for studying motivation patterns was suggested by a comparison of the IBM survey results with the work of Harvard University psychologist David McClelland, who in 1961 issued a now-classic book, *The Achieving Society*. In this book he attempted to trace different dominant motivation patterns in different countries. He distinguished three types of motives: achievement, affiliation (associating with other people), and power. The strength of each motive for each country was measured through a content analysis of the stories appearing in children's readers. McClelland argued that the stories read by second- to fourth-grade schoolchildren, their first readings, are to modern nations what folktales are to traditional societies. Folktales have been widely used by field anthropologists to infer motives of nonliterate peoples; McClelland wanted to do the same for modern nations.

McClelland's research team analyzed children's stories from a large number of countries dating from 1925 and from 1950. For each country and either period, twenty-one stories were studied. Each story and each country was scored on need for achievement, need for affiliation, and need for power. McClelland's own hypothesis was that the need for achievement in children's stories would predict a country's rate of economic develop-

FIGURE 5.1 Masculinity Versus Uncertainty Avoidance

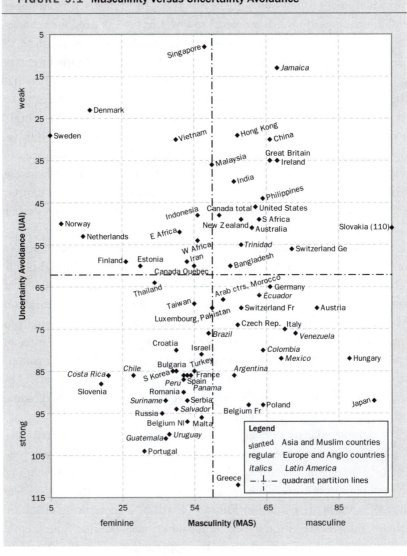

ment at the time when these children grew up. On this account later events did not prove him right. A comparison of McClelland's country scores with the IBM dimension scores, however, revealed that the need for achievement as measured from 1925 children's books (the more traditional ones) was strongly correlated with *weak* uncertainty avoidance and even more strongly with the combination of weak uncertainty avoidance and strong masculinity.[33]

This means that McClelland's 1925 ranking of countries on their need for achievement follows a diagonal line through Figure 5.1, from upper right (strong need for achievement) to lower left (weak need for achievement). Low UAI means willingness to run unfamiliar risks, and high MAS the importance of having visible results. Both are components of entrepreneurial activity in the American tradition. It should be no surprise that the United States and the other Anglo countries in Figure 5.1 are to be found in the upper right-hand quadrant, where UAI is low, MAS is high, and need for achievement is strong. In choosing the achievement motive, the American McClelland has promoted a typical Anglo value complex to a *universal* recipe for economic success. A Frenchman, Swede, or Japanese would have been unlikely to conceive of a worldwide achievement motive. Even the word *achievement* is difficult to translate in most languages other than English.[34]

Leaving McClelland's work aside, the combination of cultural uncertainty avoidance and masculinity-femininity in Figure 5.1 highlights different motivation patterns for different clusters of countries. A point of departure is the "hierarchy of human needs" formulated by Abraham Maslow and referred to in Chapter 3. Maslow has ordered needs from lower to higher: physiological, safety and security, belongingness, esteem, and self-actualization. Chapter 3 took issue with the individualistic assumptions in putting *self*-actualization on top. In view of the cultural variety in the world with regard to uncertainty avoidance and masculinity, some other provisos should also be made.

Safety or security is likely to prevail over other needs where uncertainty avoidance is strong. Belongingness (human relationships) will prevail over esteem in a feminine culture, but esteem prevails over belonging in a masculine culture. Thus the supreme motivators—other things like type of work being equal—in Figure 5.1 will be achievement (of self or group) and esteem in the upper right-hand corner (United States, etc.); achievement and belongingness in the upper left-hand corner (Sweden, etc.); security and esteem in the lower right-hand corner (Japan, Germany, etc.); security and belongingness in the lower left-hand corner (Spain, etc.).

In this classification Maslow's five categories have been maintained, but they have been reshuffled according to a country's prevailing culture pattern. An additional question is whether other needs should be added, which were missing in Maslow's model because they were not recognized in his mid-twentieth-century U.S. middle-class cultural environment. Candidate needs identified in the previous chapters could be respect, harmony, face, and duty.

Table 5.4 summarizes the key differences between weak and strong uncertainty avoidance societies related to work, organization, and motivation. Again most real situations will be somewhere in between.

TABLE 5.4 Key Differences Between Weak and Strong Uncertainty Avoidance Societies: The Workplace, Organization, and Motivation

WEAK UNCERTAINTY AVOIDANCE	STRONG UNCERTAINTY AVOIDANCE
More changes of employer, shorter service.	Fewer changes of employer, longer service.
There should be no more rules than strictly necessary.	There is an emotional need for rules, even if these will not work.
Hard-working only when needed.	There is an emotional need to be busy and an inner urge to work hard.
Time is a framework for orientation.	Time is money.
There is tolerance for ambiguity and chaos.	There is a need for precision and formalization.
Belief in generalists and common sense.	Belief in experts and technical solutions.
Top managers are concerned with strategy.	Top managers are concerned with daily operations.
More new trademarks.	Fewer new trademarks.
Focus on decision process.	Focus on decision content.
Intrapreneurs are relatively free from rules.	Intrapreneurs are constrained by existing rules.
There are fewer self-employed people.	There are more self-employed people.
Better at invention, worse at implementation.	Worse at invention, better at implementation.
Motivation by achievement and esteem or belonging.	Motivation by security and esteem or belonging.

Uncertainty Avoidance, the Citizen, and the State

In countries with strong uncertainty avoidance, there tend to be more and more precise laws than in those with weak uncertainty avoidance. Germany, for example, has laws for the event that all other laws might become unenforceable (*Notstandsgesetze*), while Britain does not even have a written constitution. Labor-management relations in Germany have been codified in detail, while attempts to pass an Industrial Relations Act in Britain have never succeeded.

In countries with weak uncertainty avoidance, a feeling prevails that if laws do not work, they should be withdrawn or changed. In countries with strong uncertainty avoidance, laws can fulfill a need for security even if they are not followed—very similar to religious commandments.

Establishing laws is one thing; applying them is another. Legal experts from the World Bank, in cooperation with law firms in more than one hundred countries, have collected information on the practical duration in each country of two relatively simple civil procedures: collecting a bounced check (one refused by the bank) and evicting a tenant for nonpayment of rent. The figures varied between forty days and three years, and across sixty-seven countries for which culture indices were available, the duration of either procedure was highly significantly correlated with UAI and not with any of the other indices or with national wealth.[35] More uncertainty avoiding cultures are well provided with laws, but for the citizen to make them work in these two simple cases takes more time—possibly so much that citizens may not even try.

The effect of uncertainty avoidance on a society's legislation depends also on its degree of individualism or collectivism. In Figure 5.2 these two dimensions have been plotted against each other. Whereas in strongly uncertainty avoiding, individualist countries, rules will tend to be explicit and written into laws (low-context communication; see Chapter 3), in strongly uncertainty avoiding, collectivist countries, rules are often implicit and rooted in tradition (high-context communication). The latter is clearly the case in Japan, and it represents a bone of contention in the negotiations between Western countries and Japan about the opening of the Japanese markets for Western products. The Japanese rightly argue that there are no formal rules preventing the foreign products to be brought in, but the Western would-be importers run up against the many implicit rules of the Japanese distribution system, which they do not understand.

FIGURE 5.2   Uncertainty Avoidance Versus Individualism

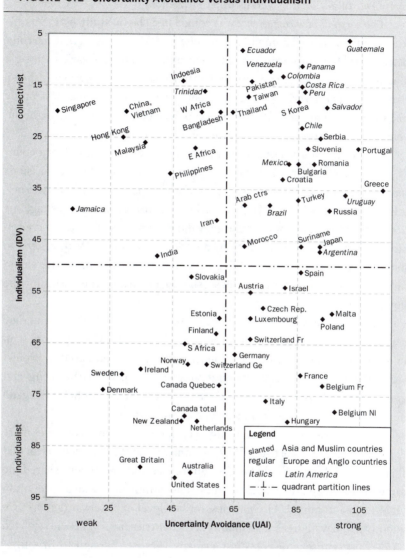

The implications of uncertainty avoidance for the relationship between authorities and citizens differ from those of power distance, as described in Chapter 2. In high-PDI countries authorities have more unchecked power, status, and material rewards than in low-PDI countries. In high-UAI countries authorities are supposed to have more expertise than in low-UAI countries. The inequality in this latter case is not in the *power* but in the *competence* of authorities versus other citizens.

The term *citizen competence* was coined in a classic study by U.S. political scientists Gabriel Almond and Sidney Verba: they found that the competence attributed to ordinary citizens versus authorities varied strongly among five countries in their research.[36] In *Culture's Consequences* it is shown that Almond and Verba's citizen competence measure correlates strongly negatively with uncertainty avoidance: perceived competence is higher in countries that scored lower on uncertainty avoidance.

In another study, citizens from strong uncertainty avoidance countries were less optimistic about their possibilities to influence decisions made by authorities than were citizens of weak uncertainty avoidance societies. Few citizens in high-UAI countries were prepared to protest against decisions by the authorities, and if they did their means of protest were relatively conventional, like petitions and demonstrations. With regard to more extreme protest actions like boycotts and sit-ins, most citizens in high-UAI countries thought these should be firmly repressed by the government.

Citizens from weak uncertainty avoidance countries believed that they could participate in political decisions at the lowest, local level. More than in strong uncertainty avoidance countries, they were prepared to protest against government decisions, and they sympathized with strong and unconventional protest actions if the milder actions did not help. They did not think the government should repress such protests.[37]

Not only were citizens in strong uncertainty avoidance countries more dependent on the expertise of the government, but they seemed to feel that this was how things should be. The authorities and the citizens shared the same norms about their mutual roles. The authorities tended to think in legal terms: in high-UAI countries, higher-level civil servants more frequently had law degrees than in low-UAI countries (a 1977 article reported 65 percent with law degrees in Germany versus 3 percent in Britain).[38] Civil servants in high-UAI countries tended to have negative feelings about politicians and the political process; in low-UAI countries their feelings were more positive.

Citizens of strong uncertainty avoidance countries were less interested in politics and less inclined to trust their country's politicians and civil servants. While we observed that these countries tend to have more laws and bylaws, this did not imply a greater trust in the legal system.[39] Citizens of weak uncertainty avoidance countries participated more often in voluntary associations and activities for the benefit of their society.

An American family living in a suburb of Brussels, Belgium, worried about the increasing noise level caused by a nearby airport. They went around with a petition to the authorities to demand measures for noise reduction. Only the foreign families in the neighborhood were prepared to sign. The Belgians (from a high-UAI culture) either denied the problem ("What noise?") or declined to sign, claiming the authorities would pay no attention anyway.[40]

Chapter 4 described the "dropped pen" experiment by U.S. psychology professor Robert Levine and his international students. This was part of a project on helping behavior across cultures. The same project included an experiment on "helping a blind person across the street." Students assumed the role of a blind person at a busy pedestrian traffic light. "Helping" meant that within sixty seconds after the light went green, someone informed the "blind person" that it was green or helped him or her across. Percentages of helping pedestrians in twenty-three countries were significantly positively correlated with the countries' UAI score. In more uncertainty avoiding cultures, members of the public could not stand by and see a blind person wait while the light was green.[41] In this case uncertainty avoidance had a *positive* effect on citizens taking responsibility—but the other party was not their government.

In higher-UAI countries in Europe, citizens are obliged to carry identity cards in order to be able to legitimate themselves whenever requested to do so by an authority figure. In the weak uncertainty avoidance countries, no such obligation exists, and the burden of proof of identifying the citizen is on the authorities. The identity card obligation splits fourteen countries of western Europe almost exactly according to UAI.[42]

In high-UAI countries there is more conservatism, even within parties that call themselves progressive, and a stronger need for law and order. The public in low-UAI countries tends to be more liberally minded. In these countries a positive attitude toward young people prevails, whereas in high-UAI countries youngsters are more often considered as suspect.[43] High-UAI countries are more likely to harbor extremist minorities within their political landscape than low-UAI countries, and they are also more likely to ban political groups whose ideas are considered dangerous.

Banned groups may continue an underground existence or even resort to terrorism. These countries have more native terrorists.

Table 5.5 summarizes key differences between weak and strong uncertainty avoidance societies related to politics and the state.

TABLE 5.5 Key Differences Between Weak and Strong Uncertainty Avoidance Societies: The Citizen and the State

WEAK UNCERTAINTY AVOIDANCE	STRONG UNCERTAINTY AVOIDANCE
Few and general laws or unwritten rules.	Many and precise laws or unwritten rules.
If laws cannot be respected, they should be changed.	Laws are necessary, even if they cannot be respected.
Fast result in case of appeal to justice.	Slow result in case of appeal to justice.
Citizens competent toward authorities.	Citizens incompetent toward authorities.
Citizen protest is acceptable.	Citizen protest should be repressed.
Civil servants do not have law degrees.	Civil servants have law degrees.
Civil servants positive toward political process.	Civil servants negative toward political process.
Citizens are interested in politics.	Citizens are not interested in politics.
Citizens trust politicians, civil servants, and the legal system.	Citizens are negative toward politicians, civil servants, and the legal system.
There is high participation in voluntary associations and movements.	There is low participation in voluntary associations and movements.
The burden of proof of identifying a citizen is on the authorities.	Citizens should be able to identify themselves at all times.
Liberalism.	Conservatism, law and order.
Positive attitudes toward young people.	Negative attitudes toward young people.
Tolerance, even of extreme ideas.	Extremism and repression of extremism.

Uncertainty Avoidance, Xenophobia, and Nationalism

In 1983 a sixteen-year-old high school student from Rotterdam, whom we will call Anneke, participated in a youth exchange program between the Netherlands and Austria. She stayed with the family of a high school teacher in a middle-sized Austrian town. There were Dr. Riedl, his wife, their daughter Hilde (of Anneke's age), and two younger boys.

Anneke went to school with Hilde. Her German improved quickly. On Sundays she went to Mass with the Riedls, who were pious Roman Catholics. Anneke was a Protestant, but she did not mind; she liked the experience and the singing. She had brought her violin, and after school she played pieces for violin and piano with Hilde.

One day when Anneke had been with the Riedls for about two months, the dinner conversation somehow turned to the subject of Jewish people. The Riedls seemed to be tremendously prejudiced on the subject. Anneke became upset. She asked Mrs. Riedl whether she knew any Jewish people. "Of course not!" was the answer.

Anneke felt the blood go to her face. "Well, you know one now," she said. "I am Jewish. At least, my mother is from a Jewish family, and according to Jewish tradition anybody born from a Jewish mother is also Jewish."

The dinner ended in silence. The next morning Dr. Riedl took Anneke aside and told her that she could no longer eat with the Riedls. They would serve her separately. Nor could she go to church with them. They should have been told that she was a Jew. Anneke returned to the Netherlands a few days later.[44]

Among European Union members, Austria and other central European countries in the IBM studies and their replications scored relatively high on uncertainty avoidance. In this part of Europe, ethnic prejudice, including anti-Semitism, has been rampant for centuries. Until the 1930s there was a large Jewish community in Vienna. Many of the leading Austrian scholars were Jewish, among them Sigmund Freud. In 1936 Nazi Germany invaded Austria. Large numbers of Jewish Austrians fled, many to the United States. Those who did not flee perished in the Nazi Holocaust. Since 1945 there have been few Jews in Austria.[45] Our true story shows that prejudice can survive, perhaps even thrive unchecked, long after its object has disappeared.

The Riedl parents in our story were programmed with the feeling that what is different is dangerous, and they transferred this feeling to their children. We don't know how the Riedl children experienced the incident or whether they became as prejudiced as their parents. Feelings of danger may be directed toward minorities (or even minorities from the past), toward immigrants and refugees, and toward citizens of other countries. Data from the European Commission report *Racism and Xenophobia in Europe* (1997) showed that the opinion that immigrants should be sent back was strongly correlated with uncertainty avoidance. In IBM it had already been found that foreign managers were less well accepted in high-UAI countries.[46]

Feelings toward other nations vary not only with uncertainty avoidance but also with masculinity. The combination was illustrated in Figure 5.1. The Axis powers from World War II (Germany, Italy, and Japan) were all located in the lower right-hand quadrant: strong uncertainty avoidance plus masculinity. Under the conditions prior to the war, ethnocentric, xeno-phobic, and aggressive tendencies could get the upper hand in these countries more easily than in countries with different culture patterns. Fascism and racism find their most fertile ground in cultures with strong uncertainty avoidance plus pronouncedly masculine values. The paradox is that these same values in the postwar period contributed to these countries' fast economic recovery. A culture's weaknesses may in different circumstances become its strengths.

In weak uncertainty avoidance countries, aggressive nationalism has little appeal. The 1990–93 World Values Survey, however, showed that the public in weak uncertainty avoidance countries declared themselves more proud of their nationality and more willing to fight for their country than in strong uncertainty avoidance countries. The generally positive attitude in low-UAI countries toward authorities and politics extends to a positive attitude toward their country as a whole.

The combination of uncertainty avoidance and individualism, illustrated in Figure 5.2, clarifies the different ways in which societies deal with intergroup conflict. The presence within the borders of a country of different ethnic, linguistic, or religious groups is a historical fact; some countries are more homogeneous than others. How a population and a government deal with such conflict, however, is a cultural phenomenon. In countries in the upper right-hand corner, strong uncertainty avoidance ("what is different is dangerous") is combined with collectivist particularism (strong identification with in-groups). Such countries often attempt to eliminate intergroup conflict by denying it and trying either to assimilate or to repress minorities. The chances of violent intergroup strife within these countries are considerable, as the minorities often hold the same strong uncertainty avoiding, collectivist values. Countries with severe intergroup conflicts within the upper right-hand quadrant of Figure 5.2 are Serbia, Arab countries, and Turkey. Indonesia and African countries are close to this quadrant.

Countries in the upper left-hand corner of Figure 5.2, like Malaysia, may contain different groups with strong group identities but are more likely to find a modus vivendi in which groups tolerate and complement each other. Countries in the lower right-hand corner often harbor considerable antagonism against minorities and ethnic, religious, or linguistic opponent groups (Belgium!), but the universalism of the individualist state tries to guarantee that everybody's rights are respected; extremism versus others is restricted to the political margin. Finally, in countries in the lower left-hand corner, like the United States, a majority will at least in theory support integration of minorities and equal rights for all. An event like the terrorist attack on September 11, 2001, puts this tolerance to a rough test, as Arab and Arab-looking Americans have experienced.

Strong uncertainty avoidance leading to intolerance of deviants and minorities has at times been costly to countries. The expulsion of the Jews from Spain and Portugal by the Catholic kings after the Reconquista of the Iberian Peninsula from the Moors (1492) has deprived these countries of some of their most enterprising citizens and is supposed to have contributed to the decadence of the empire in the following centuries. One group of Iberian Jews settled in the Netherlands and played an important role in the seventeenth-century Dutch colonial expansion. Others went to Costa Rica, which even today is a favorable exception to Latin American *personalismo* and stagnation (see Chapter 3). In recent history the exodus of top scientists, many of them Jewish, from Hitler's Germany enabled the Americans to develop the atomic bomb.

Uncertainty Avoidance, Religion, and Ideas

Earlier in this chapter religion was mentioned as one of the ways in which humankind avoids anxiety. Religious beliefs and rituals help us to accept the uncertainties we cannot defend ourselves against. Some religions offer the ultimate certainty of a life after death.

The grouping of countries according to UAI score in Table 5.1 is somewhat associated with their dominant religion. Most Orthodox and Roman Catholic Christian countries score high; exceptions are the Philippines and Ireland. Muslim countries tend to score in the middle, Protestant Christian countries below average, and Buddhist and Hindu countries medium to very low, with Japan as an exception.

A problem in classifying countries by religion is that the great religions of the world are all internally heterogeneous. Polish, Peruvian, Italian, and Dutch Roman Catholicism are very different. Indonesian, Iranian, Saudi, and Balkan Islam mean quite different things to their believers and to their countries. Thai, Singaporean, and Japanese Buddhism have quite dissimilar affective and practical consequences.

It is evident, as was already suggested in Chapter 1, that religious conversion does not cause a total change in cultural values. The value complexes described by the dimensions of power distance, individualism or collectivism, masculinity or femininity, and uncertainty avoidance seem to have survived religious conversions. These value complexes may even have influenced to what extent a population has been receptive to certain religions and how the accepted religion has evolved in that country. Indonesian (Javanese) mysticism has survived Hindu, Buddhist, Muslim, and Christian conversions. In the Christian countries the Reformation has separated almost exactly those European countries once under the Roman Empire from the rest. All former Roman countries (the ones now speaking Romance languages) refuted the Reformation and remained Roman Catholic; most others became Protestant or mixed. Poland and Ireland were never part of the Roman Empire, but in their case, Roman Catholicism provided them with an identity against non-Catholic oppressors.

In establishing a relationship between uncertainty avoidance and religious belief, it makes sense to distinguish between Western and Eastern religions. This distinction will be taken up again in Chapter 6. The Western religions (Judaism, Christianity, and Islam) are based on divine revelation, and all three originated from what is now called the Middle East. What distinguishes the Western from the Eastern religions is their concern with Truth with a capital T. The Western revelation religions share the assumption that there is an absolute Truth that excludes all other truths and which man can possess. The difference between strong and weak uncertainty avoidance societies adhering to these religions lies in the amount of certainty one needs about having this Truth. In strong uncertainty avoidance cultures, the belief is more frequent that "There is only one Truth and we have it. All others are wrong." Possessing this Truth is the only road to salvation and the main purpose in a person's life. The consequence of the others being wrong may be trying to convert them, avoiding them, or killing them.

Weak uncertainty avoidance cultures from the West still believe in Truth, but they have less of a need to believe that they alone possess it. "There is only one Truth and we are looking for it. Others are looking for it as well, and we accept as a fact of life that they look in different directions." One certainty of these cultures is that God wants nobody to be persecuted for their beliefs.

For centuries the Roman Catholic Church maintained an Inquisition, which sent many people with deviant ideas to their deaths and banned or burned books; some books are banned by the Roman Catholic Church even today. In Iran, Ayatollah Ruhollah Khomeini, shortly before his death in 1989, banned the book *The Satanic Verses* by Salman Rushdie and invited all believers to kill the author and his publishers. It is somewhat amazing that many people in Christian countries were so shocked by this in view of their own countries' histories of religious intolerance. With some exceptions, and Khomeini's action is one of them, Islam in history has been more tolerant of other religions than has Roman Catholic Christianity. The medieval Crusades, which cost hundreds of thousands of lives, were a product of Christian, not of Muslim, intolerance. In the Muslim Turkish Empire, People of the Book (that is, Jews and Christians) were tolerated and could exercise their religions, as long as they paid a special tax. On the other hand, even Protestant Christians, generally considered as more broad-minded, have made victims of religious intolerance, such as Michael Servetus, who was burned to death by John Calvin's followers in Geneva in 1553. Protestant nations have also in past centuries burned supposed witches. In the early twenty-first century, fundamentalist Christian preachers denounced J. K. Rowling's Harry Potter series as a work of the devil.

Confession of sins is a practice that fits the strong uncertainty avoidance culture pattern. If a rule cannot be kept, confession is a way to preserve the rule and put the blame on the individual. The Roman Catholic practice of confession is relatively mild and discreet; militant communism in the Soviet Union in the days of Stalin made it a public show. In weak uncertainty avoidance cultures, there will be more of a tendency to change a rule if it is evident that it cannot be respected.

Eastern religions are less concerned about Truth. The assumption that there is one Truth that man can possess is absent in their thinking. Buddhism instead stresses the acquisition of insight by meditation. Thus in the East, people will easily absorb elements of different religions. Most Japanese perform both Buddhist and Shinto rituals, although by standards of Western logic the two religious traditions are mutually exclusive.

Across all countries with a Christian majority there is a strong correlation between the percentage of Catholics in the population (as opposed to Protestants) and the country's UAI. A second correlation is with masculinity, implying that where Catholicism prevails, masculine values tend to prevail as well—for instance, in refusing to admit women to leadership positions (see Chapter 4).[47] The correlation with uncertainty avoidance is easy to interpret as the Catholic Church supplies its believers with a certainty that most Protestant groups (apart from some of the smaller sects) lack. The Catholic Church appeals to cultures with a need for such certainty. Within the Protestant nations the dominant cultures have equipped people with a lesser need for certainty. Those who do need it find a spiritual home in sects and fundamentalist groups.

Both within Islam and within Judaism there is also a clearly visible conflict between more and less uncertainty avoiding factions, the first dogmatic, intolerant, fanatical, and fundamentalist ("There is only one Truth and we have it"), the second pragmatic, tolerant, liberal, and open to the modern world. In recent years the fanatic wings in all three revelation religions have been quite active and vocal. In history fanaticism has always led to its own undoing, so there is some hope that the excesses will not last.

What holds for religions applies also to political ideologies that can become secular neoreligions. Marxism in many places has been an example. When East Germany was still solidly communist, the facade of the University of Leipzig was decorated with an enormous banner reading "*Der Marxismus ist allmächtig, weil er wahr ist!*" ("Marxism is all-powerful, because it is True!")[48] In strong uncertainty avoidance cultures we find intolerant political ideologies, in weak uncertainty avoidance cultures tolerant ones. The respect of what are commonly called human rights assumes a tolerance for people with different political ideas. Violation of human rights in some countries is rooted in the strong uncertainty avoidance that is part and parcel of their culture. In other countries it is rather an outcome of a power struggle (and related to power distance) or of collectivist intergroup strife.

In the area of philosophy and science,[49] grand theories are more likely to be conceived within strong uncertainty avoidance cultures than in weak uncertainty avoidance ones. The quest for Truth is an essential motivator for a philosopher. In Europe, Germany and France have produced more great philosophers than Britain and Sweden (for example, Descartes, Hegel, Kant, Marx, Nietzsche, and Sartre). Weak uncertainty avoidance cultures have produced great empiricists, people developing conclusions from observation and experiments rather than from pure reflection (like Newton, Linnaeus, and Darwin).

In serving as peer reviewers of manuscripts submitted to scientific journals, we notice that papers written by Germans and French often present broad conclusions unsupported by data. Manuscripts written by British and Americans present extensive data analysis but shy away from bold conclusions. Germans and French tend to reason by deduction, British and Americans by induction.[50]

Scientific disputes sometimes hide cultural assumptions. A famous example is the discussion between the German physicist Albert Einstein (1879–1955) and his Danish colleague Niels Bohr (1885–1962) on whether certain processes inside the atom are governed by laws or random. "I cannot imagine God playing dice," Einstein is supposed to have said. Bohr could; recent research has proven him right, not Einstein. Denmark scores very low on uncertainty avoidance (rank 72, score 23).

A practical consequence of a society's level of uncertainty avoidance is whether people who hold different convictions can be personal friends. Stories of scientists who severed their links of friendship after a scientific disagreement tend to come from high-UAI countries. The conflict between psychiatrists Sigmund Freud (Austria) and Carl Gustav Jung (Switzerland) is one example. In weak uncertainty avoidance countries, different scientific opinions do not necessarily bar friendships.

Before and during World War II many German and Austrian scientists of Jewish descent or who were otherwise anti-Nazi fled their countries, mostly to Britain and the United States. Examples are Albert Einstein, Sigmund Freud, Karl Popper, Kurt Lewin, and Theodor Adorno. This "brain injection" has been highly beneficial to the host countries. The younger among the refugees made substantial contributions to their scientific field in the new country. They brought synergy between the Middle European taste for theory (rooted in strong uncertainty avoidance) and the Anglo-American sense for empiricism fostered by weak uncertainty avoidance.

Some of the refugees experienced scientific culture shock. Former Frankfurt sociologist Herbert Marcuse, when preaching his critique of modern society in California, met with what he labeled *repressive tolerance*. This is a nonsensical term because repression and tolerance are mutually exclusive. The term, however, reflects Marcuse's embarrassment at trying to provoke and expecting heated debate in the German style, but instead meeting with intellectual tolerance American style.

Marieke de Mooij has pointed out that cultural values can be recognized in both the subjects and the style of literary fiction produced in a country. As examples of world literature from high-UAI countries, she mentions Franz Kafka's *The Castle* from Czechia and Goethe's *Faust* from Germany. In the former the main character is haunted by impersonal rules; in the latter the hero sells his soul for knowledge of Truth. Low-UAI Britain has produced literature in which the most unreal things happen: Lewis Carroll's *Alice in Wonderland*, J. R. R. Tolkien's *Lord of the Rings*, and J. K. Rowling's Harry Potter series.[51]

Table 5.6 completes the summary of key differences between weak and strong uncertainty avoidance societies started in Table 5.2, adding issues covered in the past two sections.

Origins of Uncertainty Avoidance Differences

Possible origins of power distance differences were explored in Chapter 2. The grouping of countries suggested that the roots of the differences go back as far as the Roman Empire, two thousand years ago. In East Asia it assumed roots in the even older Chinese Empire. Both empires left a legacy of large power distances.

On uncertainty avoidance we again find the countries with a Romance language together. These heirs of the Roman Empire all scored on the strong uncertainty avoidance side. The Chinese-speaking countries Taiwan, Hong Kong, and Singapore scored lower on uncertainty avoidance, as did countries with important minorities of Chinese origin: Thailand, Indonesia, Philippines, and Malaysia.

The Roman and Chinese Empires were both powerful centralized states, supporting a culture pattern in their populations prepared to take orders from the center. The two empires differed, however, in an important respect. The Roman Empire had developed a unique system of codified laws that in principle applied to all people with citizen status regardless of origin. The Chinese Empire never knew this concept of law. The main continuous principle of Chinese administration has been described as "government of man" in contrast to the Roman idea of "government by law."

TABLE 5.6 Key Differences Between Weak and Strong Uncertainty Avoidance Societies: Tolerance, Religion, and Ideas

WEAK UNCERTAINTY AVOIDANCE	STRONG UNCERTAINTY AVOIDANCE
More ethnic tolerance.	More ethnic prejudice.
Positive or neutral toward foreigners.	Xenophobia.
Refugees should be admitted.	Immigrants should be sent back.
Defensive nationalism.	Aggressive nationalism.
Lower risk of violent intergroup conflict.	High risk of violent intergroup conflict.
One religion's truth should not be imposed on others.	In religion, there is only one Truth and we have it.
If commandments cannot be respected, they should be changed.	If commandments cannot be respected, we are sinners and should repent.
Human rights: nobody should be persecuted for their beliefs.	More religious, political, and ideological intolerance and fundamentalisms.
In philosophy and science, there is a tendency toward relativism and impericism.	In philosophy and science, there is a tendency toward grand theories.
Scientific opponents can be personal friends.	Scientific opponents cannot be personal friends.
Literature dealing with fantasy worlds.	Literature dealing with rules and Truth.

Chinese judges were supposed to be guided by broad general principles, like those attributed to Confucius (see Chapter 6).

The contrast between the two intellectual traditions explains the fact that IBM employees from countries with a Roman inheritance scored higher on uncertainty avoidance than their colleagues from countries with a Chinese inheritance. It is another powerful illustration of the deep historical roots of national culture differences. Their long history should make us modest about expectations of fundamental changes in these value differences within our lifetime.

Power distance differences in Chapter 2 were found to be statistically related to geographic latitude, population size, and national wealth. For uncertainty avoidance no such broad relationships could be found, except a weak negative correlation of national wealth with UAI, meaning that on average, weak UAI countries were slightly wealthier than those with strong UAI.

For the wealthy countries only, a strong correlation was found between UAI and economic growth after 1960. This relationship is particular to this period. Nobel Prize laureate Simon Kuznets has calculated economic growth rates for countries since 1865.[52] Until 1925 no systematic relationship between the UAI scores from the IBM study and Kuznets's figures for economic growth can be found. For the period 1925–50 the correlation is *negative*, meaning that the weak uncertainty avoidance countries grew faster. This is because the strong uncertainty avoidance countries were more actively belligerent in World War II, and their economy suffered badly. Only after 1950 does the relationship reverse. Part of this may be a catching-up operation. All in all, the statistical analysis does not allow us to identify any general sources of weak or strong uncertainty avoidance, other than history.

The Future of Uncertainty Avoidance Differences

The IBM studies allow a comparison of scores collected around 1968 with those collected around 1972. During this relatively short period, scores on the question about job stress had increased in all countries but mostly in those that were already highly stressed in 1968, indicating divergence, not convergence, among countries. Rule orientation and intent to stay, the other two questions composing the UAI index, had not changed systematically.

Earlier in this chapter the correlation was described between IBM uncertainty avoidance scores and the country anxiety factor scores for 1960 developed by Richard Lynn. In a later publication Lynn calculated anxiety scores for different years: 1935, 1950, 1955, 1960, 1965, and 1970. For 1940 and 1945 no data were available because of World War II.[53]

Lynn's anxiety scores for eighteen countries show an overall high for 1950, shortly after the war, and an overall low for 1965. The five countries with the highest anxiety scores in 1935 were Austria, Finland, Germany, Italy, and Japan (the World War II Axis powers and two countries that got involved in the war on their side). From 1935 to 1950 all countries defeated or occupied during World War II (1939–45) increased in anxiety level, while six out of the nine countries not defeated or occupied decreased. After the overall low of 1965, the anxiety scores for fourteen out of the eighteen countries increased sharply. The only countries where the scores decreased from 1965 to 1970 were Finland, France, Japan, and Norway. The 1965–70 period overlaps partly with the 1968–72 period, for which the IBM data also show an overall increase in stress (and the IBM stress scores were strongly correlated with Lynn's anxiety scores).

Lynn's data from 1935 to 1970 suggest that national anxiety levels fluctuate and that high anxiety levels are associated with wars. It seems a reasonable assumption that a similar wave of anxiety earlier accompanied World War I and the various wars before it. The process could be as follows: when anxiety levels in a country increase, uncertainty avoidance increases. This is noticeable in intolerance, xenophobia, religious and political fanaticism, and all the other manifestations of uncertainty avoidance described in this chapter. Leadership passes in the hands of fanatics, and these may drive the country toward war. War, of course, pulls in other countries that did not show the same fanaticism but that will develop increasing anxiety because of the war threat.

In countries experiencing war on their territory, anxiety mounts further. After the war the stress is released, first for the countries not directly touched and some years later for the others, which start reconstructing. Anxiety decreases and tolerance increases, but after a number of years the trend is reversed and a new wave of anxiety sets in that could be the prelude to a new conflict. Economic processes play a role: prosperity breeds tolerance, and poverty breeds anxiety.

Breaking this vicious spiral demands international concerted action. The European Union among partners that less than a half century before were deadly enemies is an example. The ultimate recourse is the United Nations, and it has no substitute in terms of legitimizing actions on behalf of world peace.

Yesterday, Now, or Later?

The *Dream of the Red Chamber* is a famous Chinese novel that was published around 1760. In it the author, Cao Xueqin, describes the rise and fall of two branches of an aristocratic family who live in adjacent plots in Beijing. In between their properties they have laid out a magnificent common garden with several pavilions for the young, mostly female, members of both families. The maintenance of such a big garden poses many problems, until one of the young women, Tan Chun, is put in charge. She announces a new business plan:

> *I think we ought to pick out a few experienced trustworthy old women from among the ones who work in the Garden—women who know something about gardening already—and put the upkeep of the Garden into their hands. We needn't ask them to pay us rent; all we need ask them for is an annual share of the produce. There would be four advantages in this arrangement. In the first place, if we have people whose sole occupation is to look after trees and flowers and so on, the condition of the Garden will*

improve gradually year after year and there will be no more of those long periods of neglect followed by bursts of feverish activity when things have been allowed to get out of hand. Secondly there won't be the spoiling and wastage we get at present. Thirdly the women themselves will gain a little extra to add to their incomes, which will compensate them for the hard work they put in throughout the year. And fourthly, there's no reason why we shouldn't use the money we should otherwise have spent on nurserymen, rockery specialists, horticultural cleaners, and so on for other purposes.[1]

As the story goes on, Tan Chun's privatization is successfully carried through. Cao has described a society in which entrepreneurial spirit could be taken for granted, among old women as much as among others. It was in the software of their minds.

National Values and the Teachings of Confucius

In Chapter 1 we described why and how Michael Bond developed the Chinese Value Survey (CVS). In the analysis of country data obtained with the CVS, three dimensions were significantly correlated with dimensions from the IBM surveys. The fourth CVS dimension was not correlated with the fourth IBM dimension: uncertainty avoidance had no equivalent in the CVS. Instead, the fourth CVS dimension grouped values based on the teachings of Confucius.

Confucius (or Kong Ze, as he is called in Chinese) was an intellectual of humble origins in China around 500 B.C. He sought, rather unsuccessfully, to serve various local rulers in the divided China of his day. He did, however, gain a reputation for wit and wisdom and in his later life was surrounded by a host of disciples who recorded his ideas. Confucius thus held a position rather similar to Socrates in ancient Greece, who was his virtual contemporary (Confucius was born about eighty years before Socrates).

Confucius's teachings are lessons in practical ethics without a religious content. Confucianism is not a religion but a set of pragmatic rules for daily life derived from Chinese history. The following are the key principles of Confucian teaching:

1. *The stability of society is based on unequal relationships between people.* This part of Confucius's teaching was already described in Chapter 2. He distinguished five basic relationships (the *wu lun*): ruler-subject, father-son, older brother–younger brother, husband-wife, and senior

friend–junior friend. These relationships are based on mutual and complementary obligations: for example, the junior partner owes the senior respect and obedience, and the senior owes the junior partner protection and consideration.

2. *The family is the prototype of all social organizations.* A person is not primarily an individual; rather, he or she is a member of a family. Children should learn to restrain themselves, to overcome their individuality so as to maintain the harmony in the family (if only on the surface; one's thoughts remain free). Harmony is found when everybody maintains face in the sense of dignity, self-respect, and prestige. The importance of face in the collectivist family and society has been described in Chapter 3. Losing one's dignity in the Chinese tradition is equivalent to losing one's eyes, nose, and mouth. Social relations should be conducted in such a way that everybody's face is maintained. Paying respect to someone is called *giving face.*

3. *Virtuous behavior toward others consists of not treating others as one would not like to be treated oneself.* In Western philosophy this is known as the Golden Rule, but without the double *not.* Confucius prescribes a basic human benevolence toward others, but it does not go as far as the Christian injunction to love one's enemies. Geert heard the Confucian comment that if one should love one's enemies, what would remain for one's friends?

4. *Virtue with regard to one's tasks in life consists of trying to acquire skills and education, working hard, not spending more than necessary, being patient, and persevering.* Conspicuous consumption is taboo, as is losing one's temper. Everything should be done with moderation, a rule that was also formulated by Socrates.

The fourth CVS dimension combined on the one side these values:

- Persistence (perseverance)
- Thrift
- Ordering relationships by status[2]
- Having a sense of shame

And on the opposite side:

- Reciprocation of greetings, favors, and gifts
- Respect for tradition

- Protecting one's "face"
- Personal steadiness and stability

Geert embraced this dimension as an essential addition to his earlier four, a fifth general dimension labeled *long-term versus short-term orientation.*

Michael Bond had earlier described the positive pole as "Confucian work dynamism." The values on *both* poles are Confucian, but the positive pole expresses a dynamic orientation toward the future (especially perseverance and thrift); the negative pole stands for a static orientation toward the past and the present. As country scores on the dimension were collected from all continents, mostly from respondents who never heard of Confucius, Geert chose a label referring to the nature of the values involved, rather than to their origin.

Long- and Short-Term-Oriented National Cultures

A definition of the fifth dimension is as follows: *long-term orientation* (LTO) stands for *the fostering of virtues oriented toward future rewards—in particular, perseverance and thrift.* Its opposite pole, *short-term orientation,* stands for *the fostering of virtues related to the past and present—in particular, respect for tradition, preservation of "face," and fulfilling social obligations.*

Table 6.1 lists the scores for thirty-eight countries and one region (Quebec, French-speaking Canada) on the long- versus short-term orientation dimension. From these, twenty-three (in bold type) were based on the student samples in the CVS study. These scores were converted to a scale between 0 and 100 in the same way as the scores for the IBM survey results in Chapters 2 through 5. (The score for China, which exceeds 100, was added after the scale had been fixed.) The remaining scores are based on replications.[3] As was the case for the other dimensions, figures represent *relative* positions of countries, not absolutes.

The top six positions in Table 6.1 are occupied by East Asian countries: China, Hong Kong, Taiwan, Japan, Vietnam, and South Korea; Singapore comes in the eleventh position. Japan, Hong Kong, Taiwan, South Korea, and Singapore were known in the last decades of the twentieth century as the "Five Dragons" because of their remarkable economic dash. The highest scoring non-Asian country is Brazil (which has a sizable Japanese minority). All other Asian countries except the Philippines and Pakistan

TABLE 6.1 Long-Term Orientation Index (LTO) Values for 39 Countries and Regions

COUNTRY/REGION	SCORE	RANK	COUNTRY/REGION	SCORE	RANK
China	118	1	Slovakia	38	20–21
Hong Kong	96	2	Italy	34	22
Taiwan	87	3	Sweden	33	23
Japan	80	4–5	Poland	32	24
Vietnam	80	4–5	Austria	31	25–27
Korea (South)	75	6	Australia	31	25–27
Brazil	65	7	Germany	31	25–27
India	61	8	Canada Quebec	30	28–30
Thailand	56	9	New Zealand	30	28–30
Hungary	50	10	Portugal	30	28–30
Singapore	48	11	United States	29	31
Denmark	46	12	Great Britain	25	32–33
Netherlands	44	13–14	Zimbabwe	25	32–33
Norway	44	13–14	Canada	23	34
Ireland	43	15	Philippines	19	35–36
Finland	41	16	Spain	19	35–36
Bangladesh	40	17–18	Nigeria	16	37
Switzerland	40	17–18	Czech Republic	13	38
France	39	19	Pakistan	0	39
Belgium total	38	20–21			

Scores for countries or regions in **bold type** were calculated from the original Chinese Value Survey database. Scores for other countries or regions were based on replications.

are in the higher LTO range (the left column of numbers in the table). European countries occupy a middle range. Great Britain and its Anglo partners Australia, New Zealand, the United States, and Canada score on the short-term side. The African countries Zimbabwe and Nigeria scored very short-term, as did the Philippines and Pakistan.

The short-term orientation in the United States is illustrated by the fact that the values thrift and persistence were missing in the Rokeach

Value Survey, which is supposed to have been based on a complete inventory of American values around 1970. Spending, not thrift, seems to have been a U.S. value in the second part of the twentieth century, both at the individual and at the government level.[4] When asked why Americans did not save more, Herbert Stein, former chairman of the Council of Economic Advisers of two Republican U.S. presidents, said:

> *Economists have been unable to answer this question. Our savings quote . . . has always been lower than elsewhere. . . . It is most likely a reflection of the American lifestyle, although this is no explanation.*[5]

The LTO dimension is definitely not Confucianism. As we saw, *both* opposing poles of the dimension contain Confucian values. Confucianism during the first half of the twentieth century was blamed as the reason for the "backwardness" of East Asia, and this can be understood when we realize that the term stands for a very mixed bag of values.[6] Moreover, some non-Confucian countries like Brazil and India also scored quite high on LTO. A number of very Confucian values were *not* related to the dimension—for example, filial piety, which in the CVS was associated with collectivism.

Table 6.2 summarizes the key aspects of the long- versus short-term orientation norm as it differs between countries.

TABLE 6.2 Key Differences Between Short- and Long-Term Orientation Societies: General Norm

SHORT-TERM ORIENTATION	LONG-TERM ORIENTATION
Efforts should produce quick results.	Perseverance, sustained efforts toward slow results.
Social pressure toward spending.	Thrift, being sparing with resources.
Respect for traditions.	Respect for circumstances.
Concern with personal stability.	Concern with personal adaptiveness.
Concern with social and status obligations.	Willingness to subordinate oneself for a purpose.
Concern with "face."	Having a sense of shame.

Long- and Short-Term Orientation and the Family

In all human societies, children have to learn an amount of self-restraint and deferment of gratification in order to be accepted as civilized persons. The German sociologist Norbert Elias (1897–1990) described self-control and developing a longer-term view on life as essential steps in the civilization process.[7] Within societies, deferment of gratification increases with social class: children of lower classes seek more immediate reward in spending their time and their money than middle-class children.[8] Between societies, deferment of gratification varies with LTO.

Marriage in high-LTO countries is a pragmatic, goal-oriented arrangement. Questions in the 1990–93 World Values Survey about "things that make a marriage successful" showed that in families of high-LTO countries, living with in-laws was considered normal and differences in tastes and interests between spouses did not matter. In another study students in high-LTO countries agreed most with the statement "If love has completely disappeared from a marriage, it is best for the couple to make a clean break and start new lives." At the same time, actual divorce rates in these high-LTO countries were lower.[9]

Chapter 4 cited a survey by the Japanese market research company Wacoal, asking young working women in eight Asian cities about traits preferred in husbands versus steady boyfriends. The trait that differentiated most between high- and low-LTO countries was affection. In high-LTO cultures affection was associated with the husband, in low-LTO countries with the boyfriend. In the section of the Wacoal study dealing with gender stereotypes, the trait that differentiated most between high- and low-LTO countries was humility. In the high-LTO cultures humility was considered a general human virtue; in low-LTO countries humility was seen as feminine. As a Chinese student in one of Geert's classes wrote: "Without a sense of humility we become worse than an animal." He saw humility is the consequence of "having a sense of shame."[10]

Another study in nineteen countries surveyed students' views about aging. The age at which a person was described as "old" (an overall mean of sixty for men and sixty-two for women) correlated positively with national wealth and (across ten overlapping countries) negatively with LTO. In poorer countries, but also in high-LTO cultures, old age was seen as starting earlier. But the same survey showed that the high-LTO countries' students expected to be more satisfied with their life when they were old.[11]

In the 1990–93 World Values Survey section about "things that make a marriage successful," mentioned earlier, another question correlated with LTO was whether children of preschool age suffer when their mother does not stay at home. Respondents in high-LTO countries thought the children would suffer.

A study in Australia asked mothers from two ethnic categories what was on their mind when choosing presents for their children. White Australian mothers mentioned making the children feel good and gaining their love. First-generation Chinese Vietnamese immigrant mothers mentioned contributing to their children's education and financial situation; these mothers did not mention any benefits to themselves. The first group went for short-term, the second for long-term benefits.[12]

Data from another section in the 1990–93 World Values Survey showed that among eleven qualities that children can be encouraged to learn at home, thrift had the highest priority in the high-LTO countries. On the other hand, tolerance and respect for other people scored higher in the low-LTO countries. The high-LTO family tends to keep themselves to themselves.

In high-LTO country families elder brothers and sisters hold authority over younger ones, illustrating the Confucian rule of ordering relationships by status and observing this order. In low-LTO country families this is not necessarily so.[13]

In summary, family life in the high-LTO culture is a pragmatic arrangement but is supposed to be based on real affection and with attention paid to small children. The children learn thrift, not to expect immediate gratification of their desires, tenacity in the pursuit of their goals, and humility. Chinese parents don't tolerate self-assertion.[14]

These are Confucian values, and they are transferred by practicing, not by preaching. As an overseas Chinese entrepreneur told Professor Gordon Redding of Hong Kong University: "I have a feeling that if I have to tell my son about all the virtues and so on it becomes hypocritical. So a lot of these are implied, and a matter of leading by example."[15]

While the norm in high-LTO countries is an industrious and satisfying family, reality may fall short of this ideal. In 1922 Chinese philosopher Liang Shu-Ming published the book *Eastern and Western Cultures*, a patriotic argument for the superiority of the former. A Chinese reviewer of the book, Yen Chi-Cheng, wrote the following in a review: "Do not tell me that

Mr. Liang has not heard of those many kinds of hostility and enmity, such as brothers fighting over property inheritance or friends breaking up because of calculating self-interest. Do not tell me that Mr. Liang does not know about the jealousy, the secret plots, and the many kinds of misery almost universally present in [Chinese] family life."[16]

Children growing up in a *low*-LTO culture experience two sets of norms. One is toward respecting "musts": traditions, face saving, being seen as a stable individual, respecting the social codes of marriage even if love has gone, tolerance and respect for others as a matter of principle, and reciprocation of greetings, favors, and gifts as a social ritual. The other is toward immediate need gratification, spending, and sensitivity to social trends in consumption ("keeping up with the Joneses"). There is a potential tension between these two sets of norms that leads to a great variety of individual behaviors.

Long- and Short-Term Orientation and School

Several studies have shown that Asian more than Western students tend to attribute success to effort and failure to lack of it, so they are likely to put in more effort.[17] Yet there is more to the performance of Asian students in school than hard work.

In 1997 the Organisation for Economic Co-operation and Development sponsored an international comparative test of mathematics and science performance. Participants were fourth-grade students (age about ten) in twenty-six countries and eighth-grade students (age about fourteen) in forty-one countries. For the older students, Singapore obtained the highest scores in both subjects, and South Africa the lowest. U.S. students scored twenty-eighth on math and seventeenth on science.[18] Across eleven overlapping countries for the younger students and thirteen for the older ones, math scores correlated significantly with LTO. Science scores were not correlated with LTO at all, although science and math scores were strongly correlated among each other. Wealthier countries did slightly better than poorer countries, but the math performance was more correlated with LTO than with national wealth.[19]

So the argument that Asian students simply work harder is insufficient, because then they should show an equally good performance in science as in math, which was not the case. The correlations between math performance and LTO suggest that there is something common in the mental programming dominant in the high-LTO cultures and in the mental requirement for performing well in basic mathematics.

A traditional assumption has been that Asian students focus on rote learning instead of comprehension, but the superior performance of high-LTO culture students in basic mathematics refutes this. That which Western minds interpret as rote learning may in fact be a way toward understanding. Teaching and learning are culturally conditioned, and apparently similar behaviors may have different deep meanings.[20]

Basic mathematics poses well-defined problems in which goals are explicitly stated—that is, "formal" rather than "open" problems.[21] Students from high-LTO cultures prove to be well equipped for solving such problems. Professor Redding, who spent many years at Hong Kong University, wrote:

> The Chinese student, if he has been initially educated in his own culture, and in his own language, will have begun to use a set of cognitive processes which give him a "fix" on the world of a very distinctive kind. . . . It is possible to see some rationale for the noticeable tendency of Chinese to excel in certain subjects, particularly the applied sciences, where "the individual and the concrete" is paramount, and for their tendency not to move naturally into the abstract realms of philosophy and sociology.
>
> It is a common question why an active tradition of scientific investigation failed to develop in China in the way it did in the West. The most appealing explanations for it center upon differences in cognitive structures of a fundamental kind.[22]

The "hard work" argument may apply in the case of the Singapore eighth graders who were at the top in both math and science. "Singapore Chinese children are taught that industriousness is good and play is bad."[23] In the eyes of other East Asians, Singaporeans have a rather immodest and pushy image. Singapore's LTO score in Table 6.1 is lower than those for the other "Dragon" countries (Taiwan, South Korea, Hong Kong, and Japan).

Table 6.3 summarizes key issues associated with the long- versus short-term orientation dimension from the past two sections.

TABLE 6.3 Key Differences Between Short- and Long-Term Orientation Societies: Family and School

SHORT-TERM ORIENTATION	LONG-TERM ORIENTATION
Marriage is a moral arrangement.	Marriage is a pragmatic arrangement.
Living with in-laws is a source of trouble.	Living with in-laws is normal.
Young women associate affection with a boyfriend.	Young women associate affection with a husband.
Humility is for women only.	Humility is for both men and women.
Old age is an unhappy period but it starts late.	Old age is a happy period and it starts early.
Preschool children can be cared for by others.	Mothers should have time for their preschool children.
Children get gifts for fun and love.	Children get gifts for education and development.
Children should learn tolerance and respect for others.	Children should learn how to be thrifty.
Birth order is not a matter of status.	Older children in the family have authority over younger children.
Students attribute success and failure to luck.	Students attribute success to effort and failure to lack of it.
Talent for thoretical, abstract sciences.	Talent for applied, concrete sciences.
Less good at mathematics and at solving formal problems.	Good at mathematics and at solving formal problems.

Long- and Short-Term Orientation, Work, and Business

U. T. Qing went to Singapore in 1921 when he was twenty and started peddling embroidered textiles, mainly to expatriate clients. In 1932 he opened his own shop. After World War II a son and a nephew joined him in the business, which kept expanding and grew into a major upscale department store.

In her Ph.D. dissertation about the culture of the Qing store, Chew-Lim Fee Yee wrote:

> *The structure at the store was familial and the culture, simple. The founder was autocratic and respected by his obedient and docile followers. The Qings led in decision-making and supervision while workers complemented with their obedience, and harmony prevailed. All shared values of thrift, a habitual respect for hierarchy, perseverance, and focused on one objective of profit maximization. The old-timers said they "didn't think very much" which meant that their thoughts were not distracted by ambitions. They merely did their jobs to the utmost of their ability in the hope that their performance was accepted.*[24]

In the long-term–oriented environment, family and work are not separated. Family enterprises are normal. The values at the LTO pole support entrepreneurial activity. *Persistence* (perseverance), or tenacity in the pursuit of whatever goals, is an essential asset for a beginning entrepreneur. *Ordering relationships by status and observing this order* reflects the Confucian stress on unequal relationship pairs. A sense of a harmonious and stable hierarchy and complementarity of roles makes the entrepreneurial role easier to play. *Thrift* leads to savings and the availability of capital for reinvestment by oneself or one's relatives. The value of *having a sense of shame* supports interrelatedness through sensitivity to social contacts and a stress on keeping one's commitments.

At the short-term orientation pole, *personal steadiness and stability*, if overstressed, discourage the initiative, risk seeking, and changeability required of entrepreneurs in quickly changing markets. *Protecting one's face* if exaggerated would detract from getting on with the business at hand. Even if there is in fact a lot of face saving going on in East Asia, the scores show that at the conscious level, the student respondents wanted to de-emphasize it. Too much *respect for tradition* impedes innovation. Part of the secret of the Dragons' economic success is the ease with which they have accepted Western technological innovations. In this respect they have been less traditional than many Western countries, and this confirms the Dragons' relatively low scores on respect for tradition. Finally, *reciprocation of greetings, favors, and gifts* is a social ritual more concerned with good manners than with performance. Again, although definitely still very present in the East Asian countries, in the CVS study it was consciously de-emphasized. In Western countries the equivalent of face, tradition, and reciprocation is a sensitivity to social trends in consumption, to "keeping up with the Joneses," which is at odds with thrift and persistence.

Adaptiveness was described by one of Confucius's disciples as follows:

> *The superior man goes through his life without any one preconceived action or any taboo. He merely decides for the moment what is the right thing to do.*[25]

Sixty senior business leaders from the five Dragons plus Thailand and an equivalent group in the United States were asked to rank seventeen possible work values. The top seven values selected by the Asians were hard work, respect for learning, honesty, openness to new ideas, accountability, self-discipline, and self-reliance. The Americans selected freedom of expression, personal freedom, self-reliance, individual rights, hard work, personal achievement, and thinking for oneself.[26] This confirms both the LTO differences (hard work, learning, openness, accountability, self-discipline) and the IDV differences (freedoms, rights, thinking for self) between East Asia and the United States. In the 1990–93 World Values Survey, the relative importance in one's life of leisure time compared with family, work, friends, religion, and politics was negatively correlated with LTO.[27]

Investing in building up strong market positions, at the expense of immediate results, is supposed to be a characteristic of Asian, high-LTO companies.[28] Managers (often family members) are allowed time and resources to make their own contribution. In short-term-oriented cultures the bottom line (the results of the past month, quarter, or year) is a major concern; control systems are focusing on it and managers are constantly judged by it. This state of affairs is supported by arguments assumed to be rational, but this rationality rests on cultural—that is, pre-rational—choices. The cost of short-term decisions in terms of "pecuniary considerations, myopic decisions, work process control, hasty adoption and quick abandonment of novel ideas"[29] is evident; managers are rewarded or victimized by today's bottom line even where that is clearly the outcome of decisions made by their predecessors or pre-predecessors years ago, yet the force of a cultural belief system perpetuates the system.

Supported by a network of associates, Geert studied the goals that part-time MBA students in fifteen countries ascribed to their country's business leaders. The combination of the importance of "profits 10 years from now" and the *un*importance of "this year's profits" was significantly correlated with LTO.[30]

East Asian entrepreneurship is not only based on the values of the entrepreneurs. The story at the beginning of this section, and the way the CVS scores were found (by surveying student samples), suggests that the decisive values are held broadly within entire societies, among entrepreneurs and future entrepreneurs, among their employees and their families, and among other members of the society.

Gordon Redding, in a book based on interviews with overseas Chinese businessmen, divided the reasons for their efficiency *and* failure into four parts: vertical cooperation, horizontal cooperation, control, and adaptiveness. About *vertical cooperation* he wrote:

> *[The] atmosphere is not . . . one in which workers and owner/managers naturally divide into two camps psychologically. They tend to be similar socially, in terms of their values, their behavior, their needs, and their aspirations. . . . One of the outcomes of this vertical cooperativeness is willing compliance. This tendency is also reinforced by early conditioning of people during childhood and education, and the respect for authority figures, deeply ingrained in the Confucian tradition, tends to be maintained throughout life. . . . An extension of this willingness to comply is willingness to engage diligently in routine and possibly dull tasks, something one might term perseverance. This nebulous but nonetheless important component of Overseas Chinese work behavior, a kind of micro form of the work ethic, pervades their factories and offices. . . . [T]he huge diligence required to master the Chinese language has played a part here, as has also the strict order of a Confucian household.[31]*

We recognize the LTO components of ordering relationships by status and maintaining this order and perseverance; the latter functions not only in the sustained efforts of the entrepreneur in building a business but also in those of his or her workers in carrying out their daily tasks.

An international public opinion survey of human values and satisfactions asked respondents to choose between two opinions:

1. There is too much emphasis upon the principle of equality. People should be given the opportunity to choose their own economic and social life according to their individual abilities.
2. Too much liberalism has been producing increasingly wide differences in people's economic and social life. People should live more equally.

The percentages of respondents choosing opinion 2 varied from 30 in France to 71 in Japan and were correlated significantly with LTO.[32] *Long-term orientation* stands for a society in which wide differences in economic and social conditions are considered undesirable. *Short-term orientation* stands for meritocracy, differentiation according to abilities.

Horizontal cooperation refers to networks. The key concept of *guanxi* in Asian business is by now known worldwide. It refers to personal connections; it links the family sphere to the business sphere. In high-LTO societies, having one's personal network of acquaintances is essential for success. This is an evident consequence of collectivism (relationships before task), but it also demands a long-term orientation. One's capital of *guanxi* lasts a lifetime, and one would not want to damage it for short-term, bottom-line reasons.[33]

One consequence of adaptiveness in business *plus* the importance of networks is that high-LTO exporting countries on average score higher on the Bribe Payers Index (BPI) than do low-LTO countries (see the section on corruption in Chapter 2). High-LTO country companies will more easily use side payments and services to their customers and prospects abroad, which Transparency International considers to be bribing.[34]

Long- and Short-Term Orientation and Economic Growth

After World War II (1939–45) the victorious powers claimed a new world order (with universal human rights) led by the United Nations. The first issue on the world's agenda in the 1950s and '60s was political independence. The colonial era ended and many former colonies of rich countries became new states. Around 1970 priorities shifted to economic development. Three international organizations already founded in 1944—the World Bank, the International Monetary Fund (IMF), and the World Trade Organization—made a commitment to end poverty.

Poverty, however, did not disappear. From 1970 to 2000 some countries were extremely successful in moving from "rags to riches." The absolute winners were the five Dragons: Taiwan, South Korea, Singapore, Hong Kong, and Japan—this in spite of a serious economic crisis in their region in the 1990s. In U.S. dollars of the year, Taiwan's 2000 GNP per capita was thirty-six times as high as its 1970 GNP per capita. Japan's nominal GNP per capita increased by a factor of eighteen. On the other hand, the GNPs per capita of the countries of sub-Saharan Africa and the countries of the former Soviet bloc did not even increase enough to compensate for inflation—they became poorer in this same period.

The economic success of the Dragons had not been predicted by economists. Even after it happened, some failed for a time to recognize it. A forecast for the region by prominent World Bank economists in the *American Economic Review* in 1966[35] did not even include Hong Kong and Singapore, because they were considered insignificant; it underrated the performances of Taiwan and South Korea and overrated those of India and Sri Lanka. Fifteen years later Singapore with a population of 2.5 million exported more than India with 700 million.

After the Dragons' economic miracle had become undeniable, economics had no explanation for it. By economic criteria, Colombia, for example, should have outperformed South Korea, while the reverse was true.[36] The American futurologist Herman Kahn (1922–83)[37] formulated a neo-Confucian hypothesis. He suggested that the economic success of the countries of East Asia could be attributed to Confucian values, common cultural roots going back far into history.

Kahn's hypothesis remained unproven until the Chinese Value Survey appeared. Economic growth in the last three decades of the twentieth century is significantly correlated with LTO, an index related to Confucian values.[38] This is visible from Figure 6.1, in which the available LTO scores (for thirty-eight countries) are plotted against the ratio between 2000 and 1970 GNP per capita. As far as we know, LTO is the first external variable found that relates to economic growth. None of the four IBM dimensions correlated with growth in the years after the surveys, neither for all countries, nor for the poor ones, nor for wealthy ones.

The correlation between economic growth and LTO not only confirms Herman Kahn's neo-Confucian hypothesis, but it also indicates *which* of the various Confucian values were associated with economic growth: thrift and persistence. It is remarkable that it took an East Asian instrument—

FIGURE 6.1 Long-Term Orientation Versus GNP Per Capita Growth Rate 1970–2000

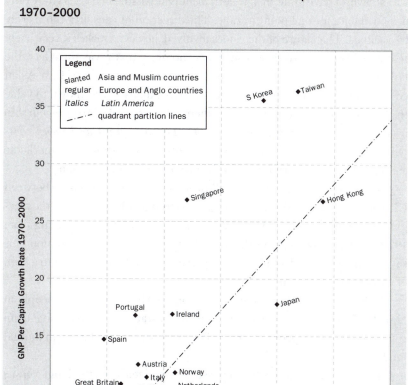

the CVS—to prove the role of culture in the development of East Asia and to provide an explanation of the economic success of the Dragons.

A correlation does not prove a causal link. Causality could have gone either way, or there could have been a third factor acting as a common cause. Chapter 3 showed that national wealth was associated with individualism index scores, and, based on data from two points in time, causality was shown to have gone *from* wealth *to* individualism. The CVS study only provided data for one point in time. The direction of causality can merely be assumed. The nature of the values involved, however, makes it very likely that these values were the cause and economic growth was the effect, the link between the two being formed by the unique success of East Asian entrepreneurship. The Japanese and overseas Chinese were known to value thrift and perseverance long before their boom started. Entrepreneurship was already evident in the quote from *The Dream of the Red Chamber*, written about 250 years ago. East Asian countries have shown a remarkable ability to break with traditions in the interest of modernization.

A U.S. political scientist, Russell Read, proved the relationship between LTO and various measures of saving. The strongest link was with the marginal propensity to save (MPS), the change in real per capita saving from 1970 to 1990, in percents of the total changes in private consumption plus saving. MPS ranged from a low of 3 percent in the United States to a high of 64 percent in Singapore.[39]

In her analysis of consumer behavior, de Mooij found that people in high-LTO countries invested more in real estate, which is a long-term commitment, while people in low-LTO countries invested more in mutual funds.[40]

Table 6.4 summarizes the key issues associated with the long- versus short-term orientation dimension from the past two sections.

Economic Growth and Politics

Culture in the form of certain dominant values is a necessary but not a sufficient condition for economic growth. Two other conditions are the existence of a market and a political context that allows development. The need for a market explains why the growth of the Dragons started only after 1955, when for the first time in history a truly global market started to develop. The need for a supportive political context was met in all five Dragon countries, but in very different ways, with the role of government varying from active support to laissez-faire. Labor unions were weak and company oriented in all five countries, and a relatively egalitarian income distribution meant that support for revolutionary social changes was weak. The Confucian sense of moderation affected political life as well, in spite of occasional outbreaks of unrest and violence.

TABLE 6.4 Key Differences Between Short- and Long-Term Orientation Societies: Business and Economics

SHORT-TERM ORIENTATION	LONG-TERM ORIENTATION
Main work values include freedom, rights, achievement, and thinking for oneself.	Main work values include learning, honesty, adaptiveness, accountability, and self-discipline.
Leisure time is important.	Leisure time is not important.
Focus is on bottom line.	Focus is on market position.
Importance of this year's profits.	Importance of profits 10 years from now.
Managers and workers are psychologically in two camps.	Owner-managers and workers share the same aspirations.
Meritocracy, reward by abilities.	Wide social and economic differences are undesirable.
Personal loyalties vary with business needs.	Investment in lifelong personal networks, *guanxi*.
There was slow or no economic growth between 1970 and 2000.	There was fast economic growth between 1970 and 2000.
Small savings quote, little money for investment.	Large savings quote, funds available for investment.
Investment in mutual funds.	Investment in real estate.

The influence of the political context was evident in the country that was the cradle of Confucianism, mainland China, suitably the top scorer on LTO. Overseas Chinese were at the core of the economic miracles in Hong Kong, Singapore, and Taiwan and contributed to the emerging economies of Indonesia, Malaysia, Thailand, and the Philippines. They seem to have been able to use their entrepreneurial skills better than their relatives who stayed in the mother country.

In 1970 the Chinese currency was not convertible, which led to an overestimate of 1970 GNP per capita and an underestimated 2000/1970 ratio. But China's economic growth also suffered from political events: the disasters of the Great Leap Forward (1958–59) and the Great Proletarian

Cultural Revolution (1966–76) and the backlash after the dramatic suppression of student demonstrations at the Square of the Gate of Heavenly Peace (Tiananmen Square) in Beijing in 1989. On the other hand, tight political control, by enforcing a one-child family policy, prevented a population explosion that would have diluted per capita growth. From 1975 to 2000 the Chinese population grew by 37 percent, from 0.93 to 1.28 billion, an average of 1.3 percent a year. The forecast for the period until 2015 is 0.7 percent a year. With less effective population control, the population of India in the same period grew by 62 percent, from 0.62 to 1.01 billion, an average of 1.9 percent a year. Without any planned population control at all, the population of Nigeria grew by 107 percent, from 55 to 114 million, an average of 2.9 percent a year.[41]

The challenge for China's rulers is to cope with the domestic political consequences of the country's economic opening toward the rest of the world. Turning around a nation of 1.3 billion people without falling into despotism, anarchy, or fatal destruction of the environment is immensely more difficult than modernizing an island with 4 million inhabitants (like Singapore). If a solution to these dilemmas is found, the mainland Chinese seem to have the mental software to make their country into a sixth and giant Dragon.

The same holds true for Vietnam, a country devastated by its 1964–73 war with the United States. Here, too, the political leadership has been torn between permitting the economic freedom needed for further development and maintaining tight political control. In the early 1990s Vietnam showed fast economic progress, but afterward the politicians reinstated controls and the economy fell back. Vietnamese immigrants in other countries are remarkably successful as entrepreneurs. Culturally, Vietnam should to be able to produce a new economic miracle.

In Figure 6.1, after the five Dragons, three European countries appear as fast growers: Ireland, Portugal, and Spain. These countries benefited greatly from joining the European Union. In fact, fourteen out of the fifteen countries that were EU members in 2003 (all except Sweden) grew faster than the United States. The EU is a good example of how peaceful politics paved the way for economic progress.

Slow growers (or shrinkers) in Figure 6.1 are eastern European countries once under communist rule: Poland, Hungary, the Czech Republic, and Slovakia. In the former Soviet bloc, currencies in 1970 were not convertible, which, like in China, led to an overestimate of 1970 GNP per capita and an underestimated 2000/1970 ratio. After the downfall of communism these countries were exposed to an economic shock treatment by the IMF that was hardly successful; the country that best resisted IMF pressures, Poland, suffered least.[42] These countries entered the European Union in May 2004, and this may offer new chances for economic progress.

Among the shrinkers in Figure 6.1 are also the two African countries, Nigeria and Zimbabwe. We will come back to the African situation later in this chapter.

Long- and Short-Term Orientation and Rates of Imprisonment

One striking difference among modern nations is their rate of imprisonment: the share of the population that is locked up in a penitentiary institution. This share is particularly large in the United States: in 2002 almost 2 million people (equivalent to the population of a country like Slovenia or of a city like Paris or Houston) were imprisoned, a rate of 690 per 100,000 inhabitants. The only country coming near that was Russia, with 625; after that the next was Romania, with 230. Among thirty-one nations the lowest was Japan, with an imprisonment rate of 48 per 100,000 inhabitants.[43]

An analysis of factors explaining these huge differences pointed to the role of short- versus long-term orientation. The picture was as follows: country ranks on the rate of imprisonment list were strongly negatively influenced by two factors operating independently of each other, national wealth and LTO. Across twenty-four countries for which both imprisonment rate and LTO were available, poverty alone explained 42 percent of the differences in rank on the imprisonment scale and short-term orientation alone explained 38 percent; the two together explained 58 percent. Adding a third variable, individualism, increased the percentage to 67.[44]

Our interpretation of this pattern of relationships is that poverty leads to crime; poorer countries on average have more punished criminals. This, of course, does not at all account for the position of the United States. Another factor influencing the imprisonment rate is the purpose of punishment. The short-term solution, practiced in the United States and to a lesser extent in Britain, is to protect society by locking criminals away. This leads to long prison sentences. The long-term solution is to reform criminals and recycle them into productive citizens, leading to shorter sentences and lower rates of imprisonment. Strongly individualist societies are more likely to see the criminal as the problem and punish him or her; less individualist societies are more likely to see the crime as the problem and focus on correcting its causes.

Long- and Short-Term Orientation, Religion, and Ways of Thinking

Dr. Rajendra Pradhan was a Nepalese anthropologist who in 1987–88 did a ten-month field research project in the Dutch village of Schoonrewoerd. He thus reversed the familiar pattern of Western anthropologists doing field research in Eastern villages. Schoonrewoerd was a typical Dutch village in the rural heart of the province of South Holland, with 1,500 inhabitants and two churches from different Calvinist Protestant denominations. Dr. Pradhan became a regular churchgoer in both, and he established his contacts with the local population predominantly through the congregations. He was often invited to people's homes for coffee after church, and the topic, usually, was religion. He used to explain that his parents respected Hindu rituals but that he stopped doing this, because it would take him too much time. His Dutch hosts always wanted to know what he *believed*—an exotic question to which he did not have a direct answer. "Everybody over here talks about believing, believing, believing," he remarked, bewildered. "Where I come from, what counts is the ritual, in which only the priest and the head of the family participate. The others watch and make their offerings. Over here so much is *mandatory*. Hindus will never ask 'Do you believe in God?' Of course one should believe, but the important thing is what one *does*."[45]

The Chinese Value Survey research revealed an important difference between Eastern and Western thinking. The CVS questionnaire, designed by Eastern minds, did not detect the uncertainty avoidance dimension. The IBM and RVS questionnaires, both designed by Western minds, did not detect long- versus short-term orientation.

The other three dimensions emerged in all three studies. We called them power distance, individualism-collectivism, and masculinity-femininity. They deal with basic human relationships that were recognized by the questionnaire designers both in the East and in the West.

Uncertainty avoidance was described in Chapter 5. It deals ultimately with a society's search for Truth. Uncertainty avoiding cultures foster a belief in an absolute Truth, and uncertainty accepting cultures take a more relativistic stance. In Western thinking this is an important choice, reflected in key values. In Eastern thinking the question of Truth is less relevant.

Long- versus short-term orientation can be interpreted as dealing with a society's search for Virtue. It is no accident that this dimension relates to the teachings of Confucius. As mentioned earlier in this chapter, Confucius was a teacher of practical ethics without a religious content. He dealt with Virtue but he left open the question of Truth. In Eastern thinking the search for Virtue is key. In Western thinking Virtue is secondary to Truth.

The 1990–93 World Values Survey asked respondents to choose between two statements:

1. There are absolutely clear guidelines about what is good and evil. These always apply to everyone, whatever the circumstances.
2. There can never be absolutely clear guidelines about what is good and evil. What is good and evil depends entirely upon the circumstances at the time.

The agreement with statement 1 varied from 60 percent in Nigeria and 50 percent in the United States to 19 percent in Sweden and 15 percent in Japan. On average, poorer countries believed more in absolute guidelines. When the influence of wealth was eliminated, answers were correlated with LTO.[46] Respondents in high-LTO countries believed less in universal guidelines about what is good and evil and more in considering the circumstances. This enlightens the differences in imprisonment described in the previous section: if good and evil are clearly separated, evil people should be locked away. If good and evil reside within every person, those who committed evil should learn to be good.

Eastern religions (Hinduism, Buddhism, Shintoism, and Taoism) are separated from Western religions (Judaism, Christianity, and Islam) by a deep philosophical dividing line. The three Western religions belong to the same thought family; historically, they grew from the same roots. As argued in Chapter 5, all three are based on the existence of a Truth that humans can possess. All three have a Book. In the East neither Confucianism, which is a nonreligious ethic, nor any major religion is based on the assumption that there is a Truth that a human community can embrace. They offer various ways in which a person can improve him- or herself; however, these do not consist in believing, but in ritual, meditation, or ways of living. Some of these may lead to a higher spiritual state, eventually to unification with God or gods. This explains why Dr. Pradhan was so puzzled by the question about what he believed—it is an irrelevant question in the East. What one *does* is important. U.S. mythologist Joseph Campbell, in his comparison of Western and Eastern religious myths, concluded that Judaism, Christianity, and Islam separate matter and spirit, while Eastern religions and philosophers have kept them integrated.[47] This difference in thinking explains why a questionnaire invented by Western minds produced a fourth dimension dealing with Truth; a questionnaire invented by Eastern minds found a fourth dimension dealing with Virtue.

Data from the public opinion survey of human values and satisfactions mentioned earlier showed that people in high-LTO countries were more satisfied than people in low-LTO countries with their personal contribution to "Being attentive to daily human relations, deepening human bonds in family, neighborhood and friends or acquaintances" and with "Making efforts to correct social inequality and injustice, bringing about fair and equal life for everybody."[48] Respondents in short-term-oriented cultures felt less satisfied with their contribution to these good causes. In a culture that believes in absolute criteria for good and evil, it is difficult to be satisfied with one's own efforts at doing good. In long-term-oriented cultures a strong concern for Virtue allows a pragmatic integration of morals and practice. Virtue is not based on absolute standards for good and evil; what is virtuous depends on the circumstances, and when behaving virtuously one doesn't feel a strong need to do more for correcting social injustice.

The Western concern with Truth is supported by an axiom in Western logic that a statement excludes its opposite: if A is true, B (which is the opposite of A) must be false. Eastern logic does not have such an axiom. If A is true, its opposite B may also be true, and together they produce a wisdom superior to either A or B. Human truth in this philosophical approach is always partial. People in East and Southeast Asian countries see no problem in adopting elements from different religions or adhering to more than one religion at the same time. In countries with such a philosophical background, a practical nonreligious ethical system like Confucianism can become a cornerstone of society. In the West ethical rules tend to be derived from religion: Virtue from Truth.

According to Danish Sinologist Verner Worm, the Chinese give priority to common sense over rationality. Rationality is abstract, analytical, and idealistic with a tendency to logical extremes, whereas the spirit of common sense is more human and in closer contact with reality.[49]

Western psychology assumes people seek cognitive consistency, meaning that they avoid mutually conflicting bits of information. This seems to be less the case in East and Southeast Asian countries.[50] In comparison with North Americans, Chinese viewed disagreement as less harmful to personal relationships than injury or disappointment. A different opinion did not hurt their egos.[51]

Korean psychologist Uichol Kim believes the Western way of practicing psychology does not fit in East Asia:

> *[P]sychology . . . is deeply enmeshed with Euro-American cultural values that champion rational, liberal, and individualistic ideals. . . . This belief affects how conferences are organized, research collaborations are developed, research is funded, and publications are accepted. In East Asia, human relationships that can be characterized as being "virtue-based" rather than "rights-based" occupy the center stage. Individuals are considered to be linked in a web of inter-relatedness and ideas are exchanged through established social networks.*[52]

In science and technology, Western Truth stimulated analytical thinking, and Eastern Virtue, synthetic thinking. A Chinese student told Geert:

> *The biggest difference between the Chinese and the Western society is that the Western society worships the hero and the Chinese worship the saint. If one is good in doing one thing, one can be a hero. To be a saint, you have to be good in everything.*

During the Industrial Revolution in the West, the search for Truth led to the discovery of laws of nature that could then be exploited for the sake of human progress. Chinese scholars, despite their high level of civilization, never discovered Newton's laws. They were simply not looking for laws. The Chinese script exemplifies this lack of interest in generalizing. It needs three thousand or more different characters, one for each syllable, while by splitting the syllables into separate letters Western languages need only about thirty signs. Western analytical thinking focused on elements, while Eastern synthetic thinking focused on wholes. A Japanese Nobel Prize winner in physics is quoted as having said that "the Japanese mentality is unfit for abstract thinking."[53]

By the middle of the twentieth century, the Western concern for Truth gradually ceased to be an asset and turned instead into a liability. Science may benefit from analytical thinking, but management and government are based on the art of synthesis. With the results of Western, analytically derived technologies freely available, Eastern cultures could start putting these technologies into practice using their own superior synthetic abilities. What is true or who is right is less important than what works and how the efforts of individuals with different thinking patterns can be coordinated toward a common goal. Japanese management, especially with Japanese employees, is famous for this pragmatic synthesis. It is a misconception to think that it can be exported to parts of the world where different ways of thinking prevail.

Table 6.5 summarizes the key aspects of the long- versus short-term orientation dimension from this section. Together with Tables 6.2, 6.3, and 6.4, it presents an overview of what research about the connotations of the dimension has so far produced.

TABLE 6.5 Key Differences Between Short- and Long-Term Orientation Societies: Religion and Ways of Thinking

SHORT-TERM ORIENTATION	LONG-TERM ORIENTATION
Concern with possessing the Truth.	Concern with respecting the demands of Virtue.
There are universal guidelines about what is good and evil.	What is good and evil depends upon the circumstances.
Higher rates of imprisonment.	Lower rates of imprisonment.
Dissatisfaction with own contributions to daily human relations and to correcting injustice.	Satisfaction with own contributions to daily human relations and to correcting injustice.
Matter and spirit are separated.	Matter and spirit are integrated.
If A is true, its opposite B must be false.	If A is true, its opposite B can also be true.
Priority given to abstract rationality.	Priority given to common sense.
There is a need for cognitive consistency.	Disagreement does not hurt.
Analytical thinking.	Synthetic thinking.

Fundamentalisms as Short-Term Orientation

As argued earlier, Judaism, Christianity, and Islam are three Western religions, belonging to the same thought family and having historically grown from the same roots. All three derive Virtue from Truth. All three have modern wings, focusing on the present, and fundamentalist wings, focusing on wisdom from the past. Religious fundamentalisms represent the extreme short-term pole of the long-term versus short-term dimension. Decisions are not based on what works today but on an interpretation of what has been written in the old holy books. Fundamentalisms are unable to cope with the problems of the modern world. British philosopher Bertrand Russell (1872–1970) wrote:

> *[A]ll fanatical creeds do harm. This is obvious when they have to compete with other fanaticisms, since in that case they promote hatred and strife. But it is true even when only one fanatical creed is in the field. It cannot allow free inquiry, since this might shake its hold. It must oppose intellectual progress. If, as is usually the case, it involves a priesthood, it gives great power to a caste professionally devoted to maintenance of the intellectual status quo, and to a pretence of certainty where in fact there is no certainty.*[54]

Politically influential fundamentalisms that represent a threat to world peace and prosperity exist within all three Western religions. The opposing modern wings are weakest in Islam. There has been a period in history, from about the ninth to the fourteenth century A.D., when the Muslim world was not only militarily but also scientifically advanced while Christian Europe was backward. With the Renaissance and the Reformation, Christian countries entered the road to modernization, while the world of Islam withdrew into traditionalism.

U.S. Islamologist Bernard Lewis has described the attitude of Muslim scholars after the fourteenth century as a "feeling of timelessness, that nothing really changes" and a lack of interest in what happened in the rest of the world. Knowledge was seen as a "corpus of eternal verities which could be acquired, accumulated, transmitted, interpreted, and applied but not modified or transformed." Innovation was bad and similar to heresy. While in Europe printing had been invented around 1450, the first printing press in Turkey was installed in 1729 and was closed down again in 1742 by conservative Muslims. Lewis writes:

> *The contrast has sometimes been drawn between the very different responses of the Islamic world and of Japan to the challenge of the West. Their situations were very different. Muslim perceptions of Europe were influenced, indeed dominated, by an element which had little or no effect on the Japanese—namely religion. Like the rest of the world, Europe was perceived by Muslims first and foremost in religious terms, i.e., not as Western or European or white but as Christian—and in the Middle East, unlike the Far East, Christianity was familiar and discounted. What lesson of value could be learned from the followers of a flawed and superseded religion?*[55]

Today modern technology has penetrated into the Muslim world. There are traditional and modern forms of Islam, but the former are still strong and aggressive. Confronted with backwardness and poverty, some groups react by calling for reinstating the *sharia*, the laws from the Prophet Muhammad's days. Muslim countries that temporarily collected enormous riches from their oil resources have hardly adapted better to the modern world than those that remained poor. The oil benefits seem to have been a liability rather than an asset. None of the five Dragons had any natural resources worth mentioning besides the mental software of their populations.

Table 6.1 contains data from only two entirely Muslim countries, Bangladesh scoring medium (40) and Pakistan extremely short (0). Islam by itself does not stand for a short-term orientation, but the strength of its fundamentalisms does.

In the second half of the twentieth century, many Muslims migrated to Western countries. In Europe this has created a European Islamic community with, as of 2000, some ten million believers. Many of these have moved into the working and middle classes and have become Islamic Westerners; some have failed to integrate, remained underclass, and retreated into ghettos. The modern Euro-Muslims can play an important role in paving Islam's roadway into prosperity.

Short-Term Orientation in Africa

Africa, and particularly sub-Saharan Africa, is a development economist's headache. In the 2003 World Development Report, eleven out of the twelve poorest countries are African.[56] African countries are plagued by a population explosion, with growth rates of 3 percent annually, leading to an anticipated doubling of the population within twenty-five years. They are also plagued by AIDS and other epidemics, by extremely bloody wars and massacres, and by ineffective governments perceived as corrupt and as enemies by their own people. In many of the fifty African states, with a few favorable exceptions, basic governmental tasks such as health care have deteriorated or disappeared.

The extreme case is Somalia, where Siad Barre, president since 1969, fled in 1991, leaving the country in chaos in the hands of competing warlords. The next year President George H. W. Bush, with the UN's blessing, sent U.S. troops to Somalia in Operation Restore Hope. Against everybody's expectations after the successful first Gulf War in Kuwait in 1991, the Somalia intervention became a disaster. The most powerful warlord, Aideed, could not be apprehended; the population remained hostile, and the Americans discovered that they were seen as oppressors, not as liberators. When TV pictures appeared of cheering Somalis dragging a dead U.S. soldier through the streets of Mogadishu, U.S. public opinion reversed. In 1994 the Americans left Somalia, and in 1995 the UN ended its activities in the country. Somalia was left to its own anarchy; its seat in the United Nations remained unoccupied.[57]

It was evident that Western logic often did not apply in Africa. The example of Bond's Chinese Value Survey led Geert to suggest a similar exercise for Africa: asking Africans to develop a values questionnaire, administer this in both African and non-African countries, and see whether any new dimension emerged that explained why Western recipes for development don't seem to work in Africa.

The project was undertaken at Geert's former institute, the Institute for Research on Intercultural Cooperation,[58] by his successor, Niels Noorderhaven, with Bassirou Tidjani from Senegal. African scientists in Africa and African students abroad were asked to suggest value survey items. Through a "Delphi" approach the first results were anonymously fed back to the contributors, and their comments were incorporated. More than one hundred draft items were collected and then reduced to eighty-two by the elimination of overlaps. The questionnaire, in an English or a French version, was then administered to samples of male and female students in the African countries of Cameroon, Ghana, Senegal, South Africa, Tanzania, and Zimbabwe and outside Africa in Belgium, Germany, Great

Britain, Guyana, Hong Kong, Malaysia, the Netherlands, and the United States. There was a total of 1,100 respondents in fourteen countries.[59]

Unlike the Chinese Value Survey, the African Value Survey did not reveal a new, African-inspired value dimension. It produced six factors. Four of these were significantly correlated each with one of the IBM dimensions. One was trivial, caused by differences between the two language versions.[60] The remaining factor (the second strongest in Noorderhaven and Tidjani's analysis), traditional wisdom, was significantly correlated with LTO and opposed the African (and some of the European) to the Asian countries in the study.[61] Distinctive items on the short-term pole of this dimension were "Wisdom is more important than knowledge" and "Wisdom comes from experience and time, not from education." These statements fiercely oppose Confucian values.

This result of the African Value Survey as well as the low LTO scores for Zimbabwe and Nigeria based on the CVS suggest that short-term thinking prevails in these African countries. Expecting wisdom without knowledge and education does not encourage studying today for reaping benefits tomorrow.

Africans often do not attribute effects to causes obvious to outsiders. An example was the initial refusal of President Thabo Mbeki of South Africa to recognize the link between HIV contagion and AIDS (he changed his mind in 2000). A widespread belief in witchcraft supports blaming others and occult forces for evils that, according to outsiders, Africans have brought over themselves.

The value scores do not imply that all Africans are short-term thinkers, nor that all East Asians are long-term thinkers. They do mean that these ways of thinking are sufficiently general to affect common behavior patterns and the structure and functioning or malfunctioning of national institutions. Through these, thinking affects economic development.

Since 1980 Africa has more and more become the world's poorhouse, a terrible irony considering the abundant natural resources present on the continent. Nearly all African countries became dependent on foreign aid and loans from the IMF. According to Joseph Stiglitz, former chief economist of the World Bank and 2001 Nobel Prize winner in economics, Africa's economic problems have been compounded by the conditions for loans dictated by the IMF. Even more than the World Bank, the IMF has been dominated by short-term-oriented market fundamentalism. This has led to a stress on budget discipline at the expense of education, health, and infrastructure and to forced liberalization of imports while keeping Western markets closed for African exports, ruining fledgling local enterprises.[62] In fact, the IMF advisers were as much caught in a short-term-oriented mind-set as their African clients.

Very short-term values (LTO of − 10) were also found in a study of Australian Aborigines, already mentioned in Chapter 3. This, too, is a group whose economic development is problematic.[63] Also in their case, conditions created by short-term-oriented white policies often compound their problem.

The Future of Long- and Short-Term Orientation

The second time Duke Ching called Confucius to an audience, he again asked him, "What is the secret of good government?" Confucius replied, "Good government consists in being sparing with resources."[64]

The future is by definition a long-term problem. Our grandchildren and their grandchildren will have to live with the long-term consequences of our present actions.

The question Duke Ching put before Confucius some 2,500 years ago is still as topical as ever: What is good government? In 1999–2000 social scientists from East Asia (China, Japan, and South Korea) and from Nordic Europe (Denmark, Finland, and Sweden) in a joint project surveyed representative samples of the populations of their countries about the same issue. The survey showed differences in opinions about how the relationship between rulers and citizens should be, reflecting the countries' different positions on the power distance and uncertainty avoidance dimensions. On the role of government the survey showed remarkable consensus. A majority in all six countries supported "a strong government to handle today's complex economic problems" and did not believe that "the free market can handle these problems without governmental involvement." Next to its role in the economy, the government tasks about which there was the strongest consensus were fighting environmental pollution and maintaining harmonious social relations.[65]

The report on the Asian-Nordic study takes issue with the ongoing process of *globalization*, perceived by the Asians as "Westernization" and by the Nordic Europeans as "Americanization." It signals a values discrepancy between all six countries and what the authors see as the values behind this kind of globalization.[66]

In our interpretation the main value-based objections of these Asians and northern Europeans were directed against the short-term focus of this kind of globalization. In Table 6.1 the countries participating in this research project all scored more long-term than the United States. Their respondents saw good government as future directed, while the ongoing U.S.- and IMF-led globalization stressed quick fixes. In fact, according to economist Joseph Stiglitz, it was based on a market fundamentalism that as much as other fundamentalisms was based on maintaining or returning to past positions rather than guided by a view of a common future for humankind as a whole.

Responsible thinking about the long term cannot be separated from the conclusion that in a finite world, any growth has its limits. The human population cannot continue growing forever, nor can the economy of a state, unless its growth comes at the expense of other states. Few politicians have been prepared to face this reality. The most evident area where this applies is the environment. Climate changes through global warming, water shortage, and radioactive waste deposits are examples of environmental costs of unbridled growth, with which good government should take issue.

Religious, political, and economic fundamentalisms are aggressive enemies of long-term thinking. They are based on the past and tend to escape their share of responsibility for the future, putting it in the hands of God or the market. For example, in many parts of the world an immediate threat for peace, health, and justice is human overpopulation. Adequate methods of family planning exist, but religious and economic fundamentalists in a remarkable consensus try to resist making it widely accessible.

The economic importance of East Asia in this twenty-first century is likely to increase. One precious gift the wise men and women from the East can bring the others would be a shift toward global long-term thinking.

CULTURES IN ORGANIZATIONS

Pyramids, Machines, Markets, and Families: Organizing Across Nations

Somewhere in western Europe a middle-sized textile printing company struggled for survival. Cloth, usually imported from Asian countries, was printed in multicolored patterns according to the desires of customers, firms producing fashion clothing for the local market. The company was run by a general manager to whom three functional managers reported: one for design and sales, one for manufacturing, and one for finance and personnel. The total work force numbered about 250.

The working climate in the firm was often disturbed by conflicts between the sales and manufacturing managers. The manufacturing manager had an interest, as manufacturing managers have the world over, in producing smoothly and in minimizing product changes. He preferred grouping customer orders into large batches. Changing colors and/or designs implied cleaning the machines, which cut into productive time and also wasted costly dyestuffs. The worst was changing from a dark color set into a light one, because every bit of dark-colored dye left would show on the cloth and spoil the product quality. Therefore the manufacturing planners tried to start on a clean machine with the lightest shades and gradually move toward darker ones, postponing the need for an overall cleaning round as long as possible.

The design and sales manager tried to satisfy his customers in a highly competitive market. These customers, fashion clothing firms, were notorious for short-term planning changes. As their supplier, the printing company often got requests for rush orders. Even when these orders were small and unlikely to be profitable, the sales manager hated to say no. The customer might go to a competitor, and then the printing firm would miss that big order the sales manager was sure would come afterward. The rush orders, however, usually upset the manufacturing manager's schedules and forced him to print short runs of dark color sets on a beautifully clean machine, thus forcing the production operators to start cleaning all over again.

There were frequent hassles between the two managers over whether a certain rush order should or should not be taken into production. The conflict was not limited to the department heads: production personnel publicly expressed doubts about the competence of the salespeople, and vice versa. In the cafeteria production and salespeople would not sit together, although they had known each other for years.

Implicit Models of Organizations

This story describes a quite banal problem of a kind that occurs regularly in all kinds of organizations. Like most organization problems, it has both structural and human aspects. The people involved react according to their mental software. Part of this mental software consists of people's ideas about what an organization should be like.

From the four dimensions of national culture described in Chapters 2 through 5, power distance and uncertainty avoidance in particular affect our thinking about organizations. Organizing always requires answering two questions: (1) who has the power to decide what? and (2) what rules or procedures will be followed to attain the desired ends? The answer to the first question is influenced by cultural norms of power distance; the answer to the second question, by cultural norms about uncertainty avoidance. The remaining two dimensions, individualism and masculinity, affect our thinking about people in organizations, rather than about organizations themselves.

Power distance and uncertainty avoidance have been plotted against each other in Figure 7.1, and if the preceding analysis is correct, the posi-

FIGURE 7.1 Power Distance Versus Uncertainty Avoidance

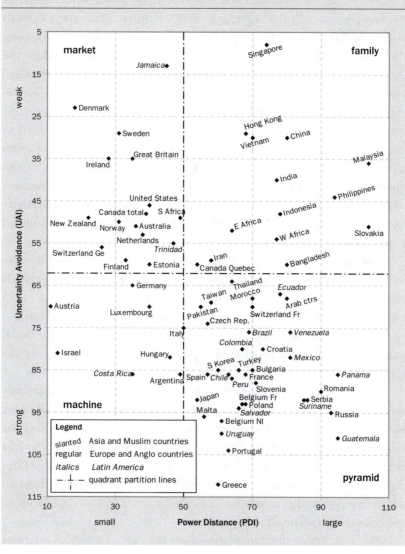

tion of a country in this diagram should tell us something about a country's way of solving organizational problems.

There is empirical evidence for the relationship between a country's position within the PDI-UAI matrix and models of organizations implicit in the minds of people from that country that affect the way problems are tackled. In the 1970s Owen James Stevens, an American professor at

INSEAD business school in Fontainebleau, France, used as an examination assignment for his organizational behavior course a case study similar to the one presented in the beginning of this chapter. This case, too, dealt with a conflict between two department heads within a company. Among the INSEAD MBA (master of business administration) students taking the exam, the three largest national contingents were the French, the Germans, and the British. In Figure 7.1 we find their countries in the lower-right, lower-left, and upper-left quadrants, respectively.

Stevens had noticed earlier that the students' nationality seemed to affect their way of handling this case. He had kept a file of the examination work of about two hundred students, in which, with regard to the case in question, the students had written down, individually, (1) their diagnosis of the problem and (2) their suggested solution. Stevens had sorted these exams by the nationality of the author, and he went separately through all French, all German, and all British answers.

The results were striking. The French in majority diagnosed the case as negligence by the general manager to whom the two department heads reported. The solution preferred by the French was for the opponents to take the conflict to their common boss, who would issue orders for settling such dilemmas in the future. Stevens interpreted the implicit organization model of the French as a "pyramid of people": the general manager at the top of the pyramid and each successive level at its proper place below.

The majority of the Germans diagnosed the case as a lack of structure. The competence of the two conflicting department heads had never been clearly laid down. The solution preferred by the Germans was the establishment of procedures. Ways to develop these could be calling in a consultant, nominating a task force, or asking the common boss. The Germans, Stevens felt, saw an organization ideally as a "well-oiled machine" in which management intervention is limited to exceptional cases because the rules should settle all daily problems.

The majority of the British diagnosed the case as a human relations problem. The two department heads were poor negotiators, and their skills in this respect should be developed by sending them to a management course, preferably together. The implicit model of an organization in the minds of the British, Stevens thought, was a "village market" in which neither hierarchy nor rules but rather the demands of the situation determine what will happen.

Stevens's experience happened to coincide with the discovery, in the context of the IBM research project, of power distance and uncertainty avoidance as dimensions of country cultures. These two dimensions resembled those found a few years earlier through a piece of academic research commonly known as the Aston Studies. From 1961 through 1973 Aston University in Birmingham, England, hosted an Industrial Administration Research Unit. Among the researchers involved were Derek Pugh, David Hickson, and John Child.[1] The Aston Studies represented a large-scale attempt to assess quantitatively—that is, to measure—key aspects of the structure of different organizations. At first the research was limited to the United Kingdom, but later on it was replicated in a number of other countries. The principal conclusion from the Aston Studies was that the two major dimensions along which structures of organizations differ are concentration of authority and structuring of activities. It did not take much imagination to associate the first with power distance and the second with uncertainty avoidance.

The Aston researchers had tried to measure the "hard" aspects of organization structure: *objectively* assessable characteristics. Power distance and uncertainty avoidance indices measure "soft" (*subjective*) characteristics of the people within a country. A link between the two would mean that organizations are structured in order to meet the subjective cultural needs of their members. Stevens's implicit models of organization in fact provided the proof. French INSEAD MBA students with their "pyramid of people" model, coming from a country with large power distance *and* strong uncertainty avoidance, advocated measures to concentrate the authority *and* structure the activities. Germans with their "well-oiled machine" model, coming from a country with strong uncertainty avoidance but small power distance, wanted to structure the activities *without* concentrating the authority. British INSEAD MBA students with a "village market" model and a national culture characterized by small power distance and weak uncertainty avoidance, advocated neither concentrating authority nor structuring activities. And all of them were dealing with the same case study. People with international business experience have confirmed many times over that, other things being equal, French organizations *do* concentrate authority more, German ones do need more structure, and people in British ones *do* believe more in resolving problems ad hoc.

Stevens's three implicit models leave one quadrant in Figure 7.1 unexplained. The upper right-hand corner contains no European countries, only Asian and African ones (except for, marginally, Quebec). People from these countries were rare at INSEAD, so there were insufficient data from this group. A discussion of Stevens's models with Indian and Indonesian col-

leagues led to the suggestion that the equivalent implicit model of an organization in these countries is the (extended) "family," in which the owner-
manager is the almighty (grand)father. It corresponds to large power
distance but weak uncertainty avoidance, a situation in which people would
resolve the conflict we pictured by permanent referral to the boss: concentration of authority without structuring of activities. Anant Negandhi and
S. Benjamin Prasad, two Americans originally from India, quoted a senior
Indian executive with a Ph.D. from a prestigious American university:

> *What is most important for me and my department is not what I do or
> achieve for the company, but whether the Master's favor is bestowed on me.
> . . . This I have achieved by saying "yes" to everything the Master says or
> does. . . . To contradict him is to look for another job. . . . I left my freedom
> of thought in Boston.*[2]

More recently, psychologist Jan Pieter van Oudenhoven of the Netherlands collected spontaneous descriptions of local organizations from
more than seven hundred business administration students in ten different
countries.[3] They were asked to describe a company they knew well in a
number of freely chosen adjectives. The seven hundred stories were content analyzed, and the adjectives used were combined into opposing pairs.
One pair was bureaucratic versus nonbureaucratic. The frequency of
"bureaucratic" correlated with the country's power distance and uncertainty avoidance. Another pair was teamwork versus individual work, and
the frequency of "individual work" correlated with individualism. A third
was friendly versus hostile work ambiance, and the frequency of "hostile
work ambiance" correlated with masculinity.[4] So the way these students
described organizations in their country reflected aspects of their national
culture.

A network of political scientists coordinated by Poul Erik Mouritzen
of Denmark and James Svara of the United States studied local government administration in more than four thousand municipalities from fourteen Western democracies. Among other things, they collected scores on
national cultures, through survey answers by the top civil servant in each
municipal administration. Their study is one of the larger replications of
the IBM survey (see Table 1.1). They distinguished four ways in which

local government was organized, dividing roles between elected political leaders and appointed civil servants:

1. The *strong-mayor form*, in which an elected mayor controls the majority of the city council and is in charge of all executive functions. The top civil servant serves at the mayor's will. This form was found in France, Italy, Portugal, and Spain, as well as in major cities in the United States.

2. The *council-manager form*, in which all executive functions are in the hand of the top civil servant, who is appointed by an elected council that has responsibility for setting policies but not for their execution. This form was found in Australia, Finland, Ireland, and Norway and in the smaller municipalities in the United States.

3. The *committee-leader form*, in which the executive functions are shared between the political leader (with or without the title of mayor), standing committees composed of elected politicians, and the top civil servant. This form was found in Denmark, Sweden, and the United Kingdom.

4. The *collective form*, in which all executive functions are in the hands of an executive committee of elected politicians presided by an appointed mayor to whom the top civil servant reports. This form was found in Belgium and the Netherlands. As of 2004 the Dutch government announced plans for a system change replacing the appointed mayor by an elected mayor, which should move the country into category 3. In Belgium, too, plans exist to switch to an elected mayor.

The researchers relate these forms to the national cultural dimensions of power distance and uncertainty avoidance, as measured by the top civil servant's answers on the culture survey. These measures were significantly correlated with, but not identical with, those found in the IBM studies. On this basis and within this group of fourteen countries, the strong-mayor form was found where uncertainty avoidance was relatively strong. The council-manager form was found where uncertainty avoidance was relatively weak and power distance medium. The committee-leader form was found where uncertainty avoidance was relatively weak and power distance small.[5]

Management Professors Are Human

Not only organizations are culture bound; theories about organizations are equally culture bound. The professors who wrote the theories are children of a culture; they grew up in families, went to schools, worked for employers. Their experiences represent the material on which their thinking and writing have been based. Scholars are as human and as culturally biased as other mortals.

For each of the four corners of Figure 7.1 we selected a classical author who described organizations in terms of the model belonging to his corner of the diagram: the pyramid, the machine, the market, or the family. The four authors are approximate contemporaries; all were born in the mid-nineteenth century.

Henri Fayol (1841–1925) was a French engineer whose management career culminated in the position of *président-directeur-général* of a mining company. After his retirement he formulated his experiences in a groundbreaking text on organization: *Administration industrielle et générale* (1916). On the issue of the exercise of authority, Fayol wrote:

> *We distinguish in a manager his* statutory *authority which is in the office, and his* personal *authority which consists of his intelligence, his knowledge, his experience, his moral value, his leadership, his service record, etc. For a good manager, personal authority is the indispensable complement to statutory authority.*[6]

In Fayol's conception the authority is both in the person *and* in the rules (the statute). We recognize the model of the organization as a pyramid of people with both personal power *and* formal rules as principles of coordination.

Max Weber (1864–1920) was a German academic with university training in law and some years of experience as a civil servant. He became a professor of economics and a founder of German sociology. Weber quotes a seventeenth-century Puritan Protestant Christian textbook about "the sinfulness of the belief in authority, which is only permissible in the form of an impersonal authority."[7] In his own design for an organization, Weber describes the bureaucracy. The word was originally a joke, a classic Greek ending grafted on a modern French stem. Nowadays it has a distinctly negative connotation, but to Weber it represented the ideal type for any large organization. About the authority in a bureaucracy, Weber wrote:

> *The authority to give the commands required for the discharge of (the assigned) duties should be exercised in a stable way. It is strictly delimited by rules concerning the coercive means . . . which may be placed at the disposal of officials.*[8]

In Weber's conception the real authority is in the rules. The power of the "officials" is strictly delimited by these rules. We recognize the model of the organization as a well-oiled machine that runs according to the rules.

Frederick Winslow Taylor (1856–1915) was an American engineer who, contrary to Fayol, had started his career in industry as a worker. He attained his academic qualifications through evening studies. From chief engineer in a steel company, he became one of the first management consultants. Taylor was not really concerned with the issue of authority at all; his focus was on efficiency. He proposed to split the task of the first-line boss into eight specialisms, each exercised by a different person. Thus each worker would have eight bosses, each with a different competence. This part of Taylor's ideas was never completely implemented, although we find elements of it in the modern *matrix organization* in which an employee has two (or even three) bosses, usually one concerned with productivity and one with technical expertise.

Taylor's book *Shop Management* (1903) appeared in a French translation in 1913, and Fayol read it and devoted six full pages from his own 1916 book to Taylor's ideas. Fayol shows himself generally impressed but shocked by Taylor's "denial of the principle of the Unity of Command" in the case of the eight-boss system. "For my part," Fayol writes, "I do not believe that a department could operate in flagrant violation of the Unity of Command principle. Still, Taylor has been a successful manager of large organizations. How can we explain this contradiction?"[9] Fayol's rhetorical question had been answered by his compatriot Blaise Pascal (1623–62) about two and a half centuries before: there are truths in one country that are falsehoods in another.

In a 1981 article André Laurent, another of Fayol's compatriots, demonstrated that French managers in a survey reacted strongly against a suggestion that one employee could report to two different bosses, while, for example, Swedish and U.S. managers in the same survey showed fewer misgivings in this respect.[10] Matrix organization has never become as popular in France as it has in the United States. It is amusing to read Laurent's suggestion that in order to make matrix organizations acceptable in France they should be translated into hierarchical terms—that is, one real boss plus one or more staff experts. Exactly the same solution was put forward by Fayol in his 1916 discussion of the Taylor system; in fact, Fayol writes that he supposes this is how the Taylor system really worked in Taylor's companies.

Whereas Taylor dealt only implicitly with the exercise of authority in organizations, another American pioneer of organization theory, Mary Parker Follett (1868–1933), did address the issue squarely. She wrote:

> *How can we avoid the two extremes: too great bossism in giving orders, and practically no orders given? . . . My solution is to depersonalize the giving of orders, to unite all concerned in a study of the situation, to discover the law of the situation and to obey that. . . . One* person *should not give orders to another* person, *but both should agree to take their orders from the situation.*[11]

In the conception of Taylor and Follett, the authority is neither in the person nor in the rules but rather, as Follett puts it, in the situation. We recognize the model of the organization as a market, in which market conditions dictate what will happen.

Sun Yat-sen (1866–1925), from China, was a scholar from the fourth corner of the power distance–uncertainty avoidance diagram. He received a Western education in Hawaii and Hong Kong and became a political revolutionary. As China started industrialization much later than the West, there is no indigenous theorist of industrial organization contemporary with Fayol, Weber, and Taylor. However, Sun was concerned with organization, albeit political. He wanted to replace the ailing government of the Manchu emperors by a modern Chinese state. He eventually became for a short period nominally the first president of the Chinese Republic. Sun's design for a Chinese form of government represents an integration of Western and traditional Chinese elements. From the West, he introduced the *trias politica*: the executive, legislative, and judicial branches. Unlike in the West, however, all three are placed under the authority of the president. Two more branches are added, both derived from Chinese tradition—the examination branch (determining access to the civil service) and the control branch, supposed to audit the government—bringing the total up to five.[12]

This remarkable mix of two systems is formally the basis of the present government structure of Taiwan, which has inherited Sun's ideas through the Kuomintang party. It stresses the authority of the president (large power distance): the legislative and judicial powers, which in the West are meant to guarantee government by law, are made dependent on the ruler and paralleled by the examination and control powers that are based on government of man (weak uncertainty avoidance). It is the family model with the ruler as the country's father and whatever structure there is, based on personal relationships.

Paradoxically, in the other China (which expelled the Kuomintang), the People's Republic, the 1966–76 Cultural Revolution experiment can also be interpreted as an attempt to maintain the authority of the ruler (in this case Chairman Mao Zedong [1893–1976]) while rejecting the authority of the rules, which were felt to suffocate the modernization of the minds. The Cultural Revolution is now publicly recognized as a disaster. What passed for modernization may in fact have been a revival of centuries-old unconscious fears.

In the previous paragraphs the models of organization in different cultures have been related to the theories of the founding fathers (including one founding mother) of organization theory. The different models can also be recognized in more recent theories.

In the United States in the 1970s and '80s, it became fashionable to look at organizations from a point of view of transaction costs. Economist Oliver Williamson opposed hierarchies to markets.[13] The reasoning is that human social life consists of economic transactions between individuals. These individuals will form hierarchical organizations when the cost of the economic transactions (such as getting information, finding out whom to trust, etc.) is lower in a hierarchy than if all transactions took place on a free market. What is interesting about this theory from a cultural point of view is that *the "market" is the point of departure or base model*, and the organization is explained from market failure. A culture that produces such a theory is likely to prefer organizations that internally resemble markets to organizations that internally resemble more structured models, like pyramids. The ideal principle of control in organizations in the "market" philosophy is *competition* between individuals.

Williamson's colleague William Ouchi, an American of Japanese descent, has suggested two alternatives to markets: "bureaucracies" and "clans"; they come close to what earlier in this chapter we called the "machine" and the "family" model, respectively.[14] If we take Williamson's and Ouchi's ideas together, we find all four organizational models described. The market, however, takes a special position as the theory's starting point, and this can be explained by the nationality of the authors.

In the work of both German and French organization theorists, markets play a modest role. German books tend to focus on formal systems— on the running of the machine.[15] The ideal principle of control in organizations is a system of *formal rules* on which everybody can rely. French books usually stress the exercise of power and sometimes the defenses of the individual against being crushed by the pyramid.[16] The principle of control is *hierarchical authority*; there is a system of rules, but contrary to the German case, the personal authority of the superiors prevails over the rules.

In China, in the days of Mao and the Cultural Revolution, it was neither markets nor rules nor hierarchy but *indoctrination* that was the attempted principle of control in organizations, in line with a national tradition that for centuries used comparative examinations as a test of adequate indoctrination.

Models of organizations in people's minds vary also *within* countries. In any given country, banks will function more like pyramids, post offices like machines, advertising agencies like markets, and orchestras like (autocratically led) families. We expect such differences, but when we cross national borders we run into differences in organizational models that were not expected. More about this will follow in Chapter 9.

Culture and Organizational Structure: Elaborating on Mintzberg

Henry Mintzberg from Canada is one of today's leading authorities on organizational structure, at least in the English-speaking world. His merit has been to summarize the academic state of the art into a small number of concepts, highly practical and easy to understand.

To Mintzberg, all good things in organizations come in fives.[17] Organizations in general contain up to five distinct parts:

1. The operating core (the people who do the work)
2. The strategic apex (the top management)

3. The middle line (the hierarchy in between)
4. The technostructure (people in staff roles supplying ideas)
5. The support staff (people in staff roles supplying services)

Organizations in general use one or more of five mechanisms for coordinating activities:

1. Mutual adjustment (of people through informal communication)
2. Direct supervision (by a hierarchical superior)
3. Standardization of work processes (specifying the contents of work)
4. Standardization of outputs (specifying the desired results)
5. Standardization of skills (specifying the training required to perform the work)

Most organizations show one of five typical configurations:

1. **The simple structure.** Key part: the strategic apex. Coordinating mechanism: direct supervision.
2. **The machine bureaucracy.** Key part: the technostructure. Coordinating mechanism: standardization of work processes.
3. **The professional bureaucracy.** Key part: the operating core. Coordinating mechanism: standardization of skills.
4. **The divisionalized form.** Key part: the middle line. Coordinating mechanism: standardization of outputs.
5. **The adhocracy.** Key part: the support staff (sometimes with the operating core). Coordinating mechanism: mutual adjustment.

Mintzberg recognized the role of values in the choice of coordinating mechanisms. For example, about formalization of behavior within organizations (a part of the standardization of work processes) he wrote:

> *Organizations formalize behavior to reduce its variability, ultimately to predict and control it . . . to coordinate activities . . . to ensure the machine-like consistency that leads to efficient production . . . to ensure fairness to clients . . . Organizations formalize behavior for other reasons as well, of more questionable validity. Formalization may, for example, reflect an arbitrary desire for order. . . . The highly formalized structure is above all the neat one; it warms the heart of people who like to see things orderly.*[18]

Mintzberg's reference to "questionable validity" obviously represents his own values choice. He did not go as far as recognizing the link between values and nationality. The IBM research has demonstrated to what extent values about the desirability of centralization (reflected in power distance) and formalization (reflected in uncertainty avoidance) affect the implicit models of organizations in people's minds and to what extent these models differ from one country to another. This suggests that it should be possible to link Mintzberg's typology of organizational configurations to national culture profiles based on the IBM data. The link means that, other factors being equal, people from a particular national background will prefer a particular configuration because it fits their implicit model and that otherwise similar organizations in different countries will resemble different Mintzberg configuration types because of different cultural preferences.

The link between Mintzberg's five configurations and the quadrants of the power distance–uncertainty avoidance diagram is easy to make; it is presented in Figure 7.2.

Mintzberg uses the term *machine* in a different sense than Stevens and we do: in his machine bureaucracy Mintzberg stresses the role of the technostructure (that is, the higher educated specialists) but not the role of the highly trained workers, who belong to his operating core. Therefore Mintzberg's machine bureaucracy does not correspond with Stevens's machine but with his pyramid. In order to avoid confusion, we have in Figure 7.2 renamed it "full bureaucracy." This is the term used for a very similar configuration in the Aston Studies (referenced earlier in this chapter).

The adhocracy corresponds with the "village market" implicit organization model, the professional bureaucracy with the "well-oiled machine" model, the full (machine) bureaucracy with the "pyramid" model, and the simple structure with the "family" model, while the divisionalized form takes a middle position on both culture dimensions, containing elements of all four models. A typical country near the center of the diagram of Figure 7.2 is the United States, where the divisionalized form has been developed and enjoys great popularity.

Figure 7.2 explains a number of national characteristics known from the professional and anecdotal literature about organizations; these are especially clear in the preferred coordination mechanisms. *Mutual adjustment* fits the market model of organizations and the stress on ad hoc negotiation in the Anglo countries. *Standardization of skills* explains the traditional emphasis in countries like Germany and Switzerland on the professional qualification of workers and the high status in these countries of appren-

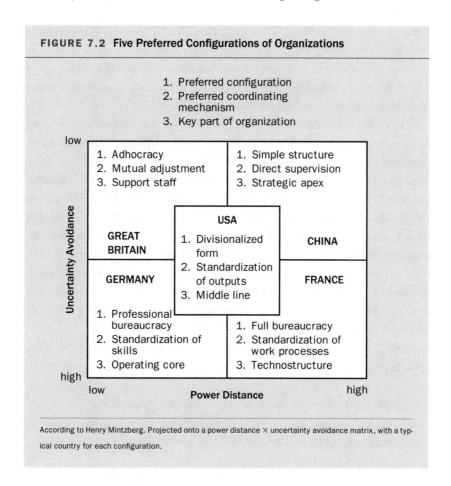

FIGURE 7.2 Five Preferred Configurations of Organizations

According to Henry Mintzberg. Projected onto a power distance × uncertainty avoidance matrix, with a typical country for each configuration.

tice systems. *Standardization of work processes* fits the French concept of bureaucracy.[19] *Direct supervision* corresponds to what we know about Chinese organizations, also outside mainland China, which emphasize coordination through personal intervention of the owner and his relatives. *Standardization of outputs* is very much the preferred philosophy in the United States, even in cases where outputs are difficult to assess.

Planning, Control, and Accounting

Planning and control processes in organizations are strongly influenced by culture. Planning and control go together: planning tries to reduce uncertainty, and control is a form of power. So planning and control processes in a country are likely to vary according to the prevailing uncertainty avoidance and power distance norms. Planning and control systems are often considered rational tools, but in fact they are partly ritualistic. It is extremely difficult to know how effective planning and control really are. The ritual elements make an objective evaluation impossible—there will always be believers and nonbelievers.

Therefore it is difficult to identify effective and ineffective planning and control systems in other cultures. Let us take the case of strategic planning and control by top management. In Chapter 5 we referred to a study (published in 1980 by the Frenchman Jacques Horovitz) of top management in France, Germany, and Great Britain. According to the criteria set by the U.S. designers of planning and control systems, British managers did a better job of strategic planning than their German and French counterparts; the latter two focused on details and short-term feedback. Yet the national economies of France and Germany at that time did at least as well as those of the United Kingdom and the United States. Mintzberg, himself a North American, has expressed strong skepticism about the effects of strategic planning.[20] Rituals are effective for those who believe in them.

Some of the ways in which national power distance and uncertainty avoidance affect planning and control processes in organizations are:[21]

- Higher PDI supports political rather than strategic thinking.
- Higher PDI supports personal planning and control rather than impersonal systems. The higher in the hierarchy, the less formal is the planning and control.
- Lower PDI control systems place more trust in subordinates; in higher-PDI cultures such trust is lacking.
- Higher UAI makes it less likely that strategic planning activities are practiced because these may call into question the certainties of today.
- Higher UAI supports a need for more detail in planning and more short-term feedback.
- Higher UAI implies leaving planning to specialists.
- Higher UAI implies a more limited view of what information is relevant.

When companies go international, their planning and control systems continue to be strongly influenced by their national culture. Dutch researchers Anne-Wil Harzing and Arndt Sorge collected information on how multinationals controlled their subsidiaries' performance. The decisive influence was the *home country* of the multinational, not the subsidiary. It explained the variations in the use of both impersonal control by systems and personal control by expatriates.[22]

National cultures are also reflected in the role of accountants in organizations. Not only managers and management professors but even accountants are human; moreover, they play a particular role in the culture of a society.[23]

In Chapter 1 culture was shown to be manifested in the form of symbols, heroes, rituals, and values. Accounting is said to be the language of business: this means that accounting is the handling of *symbols* that have meaning only to those initiated in business. At the level of symbols one also finds money. Money has no intrinsic value, nor an intrinsic meaning, other than that which is attributed to it by convention. It also means different things to different people. For example, it means something else in the culture of accountants than in the culture of bankers. There is a national component to the meaning of money: in Chapter 4 the importance of money was associated with masculinity. In more masculine societies, such as the United States and Germany, accounting systems stress the achievement of purely financial targets more than in more feminine societies, like Sweden and the Netherlands. In shorter-term-oriented societies, such as the United States, the systems' stress is obviously more on short-term results than in longer-term-oriented societies.

Accountants themselves are unlikely to ever become *heroes* in organizations, but they have an important role in identifying and anointing heroes elsewhere in the organization, because they determine who are the good or the bad guys. Their major device for this purpose is *accountability*: holding someone personally responsible for results. As measurable results are more important in masculine societies than in feminine ones, the former's accounting systems are more likely to present results in such a way that a responsible manager is pictured as a hero or as a villain.

From a cultural point of view, accounting systems in organizations are best understood as uncertainty-reducing *rituals*, fulfilling a cultural need for certainty, simplicity, and truth in a confusing world, regardless of whether this truth has any objective base. Trevor Gambling, a professor and former accountant from the United Kingdom, has written that much of accounting information is after-the-fact justification of decisions that were taken for nonlogical reasons in the first place. The main function of accounting information, according to Gambling, is maintaining morale in the face of uncertainty. The accountant "enables a distinctly demoralized modern industrial society to live with itself, by reassuring that its models and data can pass for truth."[24]

This explains the lack of consensus across different countries on what represents proper accounting methods. For the United States these are collected in the accountant's holy book of generally accepted accounting principles, the *GAAP Guide*. Being "generally accepted" within a certain population is precisely what makes a ritual a ritual. It does not need any other justification. Once you have agreed on the ritual, a lot of problems become technical again, such as how to perform the ritual most effectively. To a naive observer, accounting practice has a lot in common with religious practice (which also serves to avoid uncertainty). British journalist Graham Cleverley called accountants the "priests" of business.[25] Sometimes we find explicit links between religious and accounting rules, such as in Islam in the Koranic ban on calculating interest.

Geert's doctoral research in the 1960s dealt with the behavioral consequences of budgeting, and it unwittingly supported the ritual nature of budget accounting. This is remarkable, because the budget process is probably one of the most action-oriented parts of the accounting system. In those days Geert worked as a production manager in a Dutch textile mill, and he had been struck by a number of behavioral paradoxes when a budget system was introduced: observable behavior that was the opposite of what the system intended.

The main conclusion of the research was captured in the title of the dissertation: *The Game of Budget Control.*[26] It was based on a field study in five Dutch business companies. It did not refer to rituals or culture, but it found that for budget control to have a positive impact on results, it should be played as a game. Games in all human societies are a very specific form of ritual: they are activities carried out for their own sake. Basically the research showed that the proper ritual use of the system was a prime condition for its impact on results. The technical aspects of the system used— the things the professional literature worried and still worries most about—did not affect the results very much. The way the game was played gave the system its meaning in the minds of the actors, and this determined the impact. This was a cultural interpretation *avant la lettre*.

If accounting systems are uncertainty avoiding rituals, one can expect that a society's score on uncertainty avoidance will strongly affect its accounting practices: more strongly uncertainty avoiding societies will have more precise rules on how to handle different cases; in less strongly uncertainty avoiding societies more will be left to the discretion of the organization or even of the accountant.

Behind the symbols, heroes, and rituals in accounting there are *values*. The less an activity is determined by technical necessity, the more it is ruled by values and thus influenced by cultural differences. Accounting is a field in which the technical imperatives are weak: historically based conventions are more important to it than laws of nature. So it is logical for accounting systems and the ways they are used to vary along national cultural lines.

In large-power-distance countries, accounting systems will be frequently used to justify the decisions of the top power holder(s): they are seen as the power holder's tool to present the desired image, and figures will be twisted to this end. The accounting scandals in the United States in 2002 (of which the Enron Corporation case is the most infamous example) fit the picture of a shift in U.S. society to larger power distances, signaled at the end of Chapter 2.

Power distance also affects the degree to which people at lower levels in organizations will be asked to participate in setting accounting standards. When three large state enterprises in Thailand tried to introduce a participative costing system designed in the United States, this met with strong resistance, because redistribution of power went against Thai values.[27]

In stronger uncertainty avoidance countries like Germany and France, accounting systems will be not only more detailed, as argued previously, but they will also to a larger extent be theoretically based—pretending to derive from consistent general economic principles. In weak uncertainty avoidance countries, systems will be more pragmatic, ad hoc, and folkloristic. An example mentioned above are the Generally Accepted Accounting Principles in the United States. In Germany and Japan, annual reports to shareholders are supposed to use the same valuation of the company's assets as is used for fiscal purposes; in the Dutch, British, and U.S. systems, reports to the fiscal authorities are a completely different thing from reports to shareholders.

In individualist cultures the information in the accounting system will be taken more seriously and considered more indispensable than in collectivist ones. The latter—being "high-context," according to Edward Hall—possess many other and more subtle clues to find out about the well-being of organizations and the performance of people, so they rely less on the explicit information produced by the accountants. The accounting profession in such societies is therefore likely to carry lower status; the work of accountants is a ritual without practical impact on decisions.

Multinationals, when going abroad, have to impose universal accounting rules for consolidation purposes. If, as the research in IBM showed, even in this tightly coordinated corporation employees in different countries hold quite different personal values, it is likely that interpretations of accounting rules in the subsidiaries of multinationals will often deviate from what headquarters expect.

Differences among occupational value systems play a role in the communication between accountants and other organization members. U.S. students majoring in accounting were found to attribute higher value to being clean and responsible and lower value to being imaginative than other students, which suggests a self-selection on uncertainty avoiding values.[28] In a Dutch and an international sample, Geert found that accountants stress the *form* of information, where people in operating roles will stress its *content*.[29]

Accountants are also the people who determine the value of the organization's assets. Ways of valuing assets reflect underlying nonrational value systems, such as the fact that machines are considered assets while people are not. Hardware is less uncertain than software.

Corporate Governance and Business Goals

Traditionally, patterns of *corporate governance*, the ownership and control of corporations, differ vastly between countries. A study across twelve European countries, published in 1997,[30] showed that while in Britain 61 of the hundred largest companies had dispersed shareholders (no single owner holding more than 20 percent), in Austria and Italy no large companies at all had this ownership type. The percentages of dispersed ownership were significantly correlated with IDV.[31]

Capitalism is historically linked to individualism. The United Kingdom inherited the ideas of the Scot Adam Smith about the market as an invisible hand. In the individualist value pattern, the relationship between the individual and the organization is *calculative* both for the owners and for the employees; it is based on enlightened self-interest. In more collectivist societies, the link between individuals and their organizations is *moral* by tradition (Chapter 3). A hire-and-fire but also a buy-and-sell approach is considered immoral or indecent. Sometimes firing employees is even prohibited by law. If it is not, selling companies and firing redundant employees still carry a high cost in terms of loss of public image and of goodwill with authorities.

Differences in power distance also affect corporate governance. Across the same twelve European countries, dominant ownership of the one hundred largest companies (one person, family, or company owning between 20 and 50 percent) was positively correlated with power distance.[32] In high-PDI France banking, the development of large companies, and foreign trade were historically strongly directed and controlled by the state according to the principle of mercantilism; other fairly large companies continue to be family owned.

In the Nordic countries of Denmark, Finland, Norway, and Sweden, but also in Austria, ten or more of the one hundred largest corporations were owned by a cooperative; in Britain and Italy, virtually none. The share of cooperatively owned corporations was negatively correlated with masculinity.[33] Cooperatives appeal to the need for cooperation in a feminine society.

A Russian economist, Radislav Semenov, compared (in 2000) the systems of corporate governance in seventeen Western countries[34] and showed that culture scores explained their differences better than any of the economic variables suggested in the literature. By a combination of power distance, uncertainty avoidance, and masculinity, he was able to classify countries in terms of market, bank, or other control; concentration of ownership; mind-sets of politicians, directors, employees, and investors; formation and implementation of economic policy; and industrial relations. In a separate analysis he studied ownership of firms across forty-four countries worldwide and found a significant relationship with uncertainty avoidance only. His study shows the importance of cultural considerations when exporting one country's solutions to another, as was frequently tried in eastern Europe in the 1990s.

Corporate governance is also related to corporate financial goals. It is a naive assumption that such goals are culture free. In interviews by the Dutch researcher Jeroen Weimer with Dutch, German, and U.S. business executives, besides about making profits, the Dutch talked about assets, the Germans about independence from banks, and the Americans about shareholder value.[35] This reflects the institutional differences between the countries (the strong role of banks in Germany) but also the prevailing ideologies (the shareholder as a culture hero in the United States).

Personal goals of top business executives are not only financial; the challenge lies in how you find out what they really are. Asking the executives themselves will predictably produce mostly rehearsed responses and window dressing. Geert resolved this dilemma by asking junior managers and professionals attending evening MBA courses to rate the goals used by successful top managers in their country. Part-time MBA students who work in companies during the day are probably among the best-informed judges available. With the help of an international network of colleagues, Geert and three coauthors polled more than 1,800 part-time MBA students at twenty-one local universities in fifteen countries, using a list of fifteen potential goals.[36] Across the countries there was an overall order of goals in which growth, continuity, and profits were on top. After all, these were business companies. But relative to this overall list, the MBA students from different countries ascribed different priorities to their country's successful business leaders. The countries could be divided into seven clusters. The relative ordering of goals within these clusters is listed in Table 7.1. It suggests seven different "archetypal" business leader roles.

The U.S. archetype of the "executive" (on which there was virtual consensus among five different universities from all parts of the country) puts the strongest stress on growth, short-term profits, personal wealth and power, staying within the law (the United States is supposed to have the highest density of lawyers in the world), and respecting ethical norms (reflecting a concern with the choice between good and evil). All other countries deviate from this pattern in several respects. For example, "responsibility toward employees" appears in Germany and the Netherlands, as well as in Britain and New Zealand—countries in which organized labor has traditionally played a strong role in society. "Family interests" appears in clusters 2 and 3, mainly in Latin countries and India, where business is still often a family affair. The goal of "profits ten years from now" is most prominent in Hong Kong and among the Hawaiian Americans of Asian descent.

Some of the goals chosen were directly correlated with the countries' culture indices. Power distance was especially important: it related to the ascribed importance of "power," of "honor, face, reputation," and of "family interests" and the *un*importance of "staying within the law." Long-term orientation related to the ascribed importance of "profits ten years from now" against "this year's profits."

TABLE 7.1   Six *Relatively* Most Important Perceived Goals of Successful Business Leaders in Seven (Sub)Clusters of Countries

Cluster 1a (United States)
"The Executive"
Growth of the business
This year's profits
Personal wealth
Power
Staying within the law
Respecting ethical norms

Cluster 1b (Britain, New Zealand)
"The Manager"
This year's profits
Staying within the law
Responsibility toward employees
Continuity of the business
Patriotism, national pride
Respecting ethical norms

Cluster 2 (India, Jamaica, Bahamas)
"The Family Manager"
Continuity of the business
Family interests
Patriotism, national pride
Personal wealth
Profits ten years from now
This year's profits

Cluster 3 (Latin countries, Australia, Hungary)
"The Family Entrepreneur"
Family interests
Personal wealth
Power
This year's profits
Game and gambling spirit
Growth of the business

Cluster 4a (Hong Kong, Hawaii-Asian)
"The Entrepreneur"
Profits ten years from now
Creating something new
Game and gambling spirit
Growth of the business
Honor, face, reputation
Personal wealth

Cluster 4b (Germany, Netherlands)
"The Founder"
Responsibility toward employees
Responsibility toward society
Creating something new
Game and gambling spirit
Continuity of the business
Honor, face, reputation

Cluster 5 (China)
"The Mandarin"
Respecting ethical norms
Patriotism, national pride
Honor, face, reputation
Power
Responsibility toward society
Profits ten years from now

Some people assume that globalization and the acquisition of compa- nies across borders will wipe out the differences shown in Table 7.1 and that all business leaders will become like the American "executive" arche- type. The fact that these archetypes are the products of national cultures that have centuries-old roots makes that assumption unlikely. Conflicting goals between leaders from different countries, and between expatriate leaders and their local personnel, are predictable.

Different national business goals limit the exportability of "agency theory." *Agency* refers to the delegation of discretionary power by a prin- cipal to an agent, and since the 1980s the term has in particular been applied to the delegation by owners to managers. Agency theories are based on implicit assumptions about societal order, contractual relationships, and motivation. Such assumptions are bounded by national borders.

Motivation Theories and Practices

Motivation is an assumed force operating inside an individual, inducing him or her to choose one action over another. Culture as collective program- ming of the mind thus plays an obvious role in motivation. Culture influ- ences our behaviors but also the explanations we give for our behaviors. Thus an American may explain putting in extra effort for her job by the money received, a French person by her honor, a Chinese by mutual obli- gations, and a Dane by collegiality.

Different assumptions about motivation lead to different motivation theories. The founding father of motivation theory was the Austrian Sig- mund Freud, but ironically he is rarely quoted in relation to management.[37] The classic motivation theorists in a management context are Americans. We met Abraham Maslow's hierarchy of human needs in Chapters 3 and 5 and David McClelland's theory of the achievement motive in Chapter 5. A third popular theory about work motivation that reflects its U.S. origin is Frederick Herzberg's motivation versus hygiene.

Herzberg and two coworkers in 1959 published a now-classic study,[38] which argued that the work situation contains elements with a positive motivation potential (the real motivators) and elements with a negative potential (the hygiene factors). The motivators are the work itself, achieve- ment, recognition, responsibility, and advancement. These were labeled the *intrinsic* elements of the job. The hygiene factors, which have to be present in order to prevent lack of motivation but cannot motivate by themselves, are company policy and administration, supervision, salary, and working conditions: *extrinsic* elements of the job. Herzberg assumed this distinction to be a universal characteristic of human motivation. He proposed that it is the *job content*, not the job context, that makes people act.

Herzberg's conclusion resembles the quote from his compatriot Mary Parker Follett earlier in this chapter, where she defends that people should seek the law of the situation: "take their orders from the situation." Culturally both fit an environment in which power distances are small and uncertainty avoidance is weak: neither dependence on more powerful superiors nor a need for rules is supposed to be functional or necessary for making people act. The theory fits the cultures of the upper left-hand corner of Figure 7.1.

In countries of the lower left-hand corner of Figure 7.1, contrary to Herzberg's theory, rules as part of what Herzberg called "company policy and administration" should not only be seen as hygiene. Enforced by a superego (see Chapter 5; in ordinary language, by a sense of duty) they can be real motivators in these countries.

In a similar way within countries in the right-hand half of Figure 7.1, "supervision" should not be seen as a hygienic factor. When power distances are large, dependence on more powerful people is a basic need that can be a real motivator. In the lower right-hand corner, incorporating most Latin countries, the motivator could be labeled the *boss* in the sense of the formally appointed superior. At INSEAD business school in Fontainebleau (where Stevens did his analysis reported earlier in this chapter), leaderless discussion groups composed entirely of French participants were known to often lose their time in internal fights for leadership at the expense of productivity, unlike groups of German or British students and also unlike internationally mixed groups including French participants.

In the upper right-hand corner, where we find Asian and African countries, the motivator should rather be labeled the *master*. He differs from the boss in that his power is based on tradition and charisma more than on formal position.

In summary, Herzberg's theory, like the other U.S. theories of motivation considered in previous chapters, is only valid in the cultural environment in which it was conceived. It is culturally constrained and reflects the one section of the U.S. environment in which its author grew up and did his research.

Another classic U.S. motivation theory is Douglas McGregor's distinction between "Theory X" and "Theory Y." McGregor's work carries a strong humanistic missionary flavor characteristic of the 1950s, when his ideas were formulated. The main thrust of Theory X is that the average human being has an inherent dislike of work and will avoid it if he can; therefore people must be coerced, punished, and controlled to make them contribute to organizational objectives. The main thrust of Theory Y is that the expenditure of physical and mental effort in work is as natural as play or rest, and that under proper conditions, people will not only accept but even seek responsibility and exercise effort toward achieving organizational objectives. McGregor evidently defended Theory Y.

In the 1980s Geert was invited to speak at a seminar on human resource development in Jakarta, Indonesia. Someone suggested he should address the problem of how to train Indonesian managers to replace Theory X with Theory Y. This made him reflect on the basic, unspoken cultural assumptions present in *both* Theories X *and* Y. He arrived at the following list:

1. Work is good for people. It is God's will that people should work.
2. People's capacities should be maximally utilized. It is God's will that people should use their capacities to the fullest extent.
3. There are "organizational objectives" that exist apart from people.
4. People in organizations behave as unattached individuals.

These assumptions reflect the value positions of an individualist, masculine society, like the United States, in which McGregor grew up. None of them applies in Indonesia or other Southeast Asian cultures. Southeast Asian assumptions differ in their beliefs:

1. Work is a necessity, but not a goal in itself.
2. People should find their rightful place, in peace and harmony with their environment.
3. Absolute objectives exist only with God. In the world, persons in authority positions represent God, so their objectives should be followed.
4. People behave as members of a family and/or group. Those who do not are rejected by society.

Because of these different culturally determined assumptions, McGregor's Theory X–Theory Y distinction is irrelevant in Southeast Asia. A distinction more in line with Southeast Asian cultures would not oppose mutually exclusive alternatives that disrupt the norm of harmony. The ideal model would be one in which opposites complement each other and fit harmoniously together. Let us call them Theory T and Theory T+, in which *T* stands for "Tradition."

Theory T could be:

1. There is an order of inequality in this world in which everyone has his or her rightful place. High positions and low positions are protected by this order that is willed by God.
2. Children have to learn to fulfill their duties at the place where they belong by birth. They can improve their place by studying under a good teacher, working with a good patron, and/or marrying a good partner.
3. Tradition is a source of wisdom. Therefore the average human being has an inherent dislike of change and will rightly avoid it if he or she can.

Without contradicting Theory T, Theory T+ would affirm:

1. In spite of the wisdom in traditions, the experience of change in life is natural, as natural as work, play, or rest.
2. Commitment to change is a function of the quality of leaders who lead the change, the rewards associated with the change, and the negative consequences of not changing.
3. The capacity to lead people to a new situation is widely, not narrowly, distributed among leaders in the population.
4. The learning capacities of the average family are more than sufficient for modernization.

Thus a Southeast Asian equivalent of human resource development might be based on something like Theories T and T+ and not on an irrelevant import like the Theory X–Theory Y distinction.[39]

National differences in motivation patterns are reflected in different ways of compensation. Wages and other conditions are established by comparison with others in the same national labor market. A study across twenty-four countries found significant correlations between compensation practices and our culture indices, as follows:[40]

- Employers in small-power-distance countries more often gave workplace child care for managers and professional and technical staff and stock options for nonmanagers.
- Employers in individualist countries more often paid for individual performance and gave stock options to managers.
- Employers in masculine countries more often paid commission to nonmanagerial employees; in feminine countries they more often gave flexible benefits and workplace child care and maternity leave to clerical and manual workers.
- Employers in uncertainty avoiding countries more often related pay to seniority and skill and less often to performance.

Leadership, Decision Making, and Empowerment

One of the oldest theorists of leadership in the world literature is Niccolò Machiavelli (1469–1527).[41] He was a former statesman, and his book *The Ruler* described the most effective techniques for manipulation and remaining in power, including deceit, bribery, and murder, which has given him a bad reputation in the centuries afterward. In truth Machiavelli just described what he had observed—today he would be called a sociologist. Machiavelli wrote in and about the Italy of his day, and what he described was clearly a large-power-distance, masculine context. Power distances in Italy in the IBM studies were found to be medium large, and in the sixteenth century they were probably considerably larger. Italy in the IBM studies still scored highly masculine.

As we argued in Chapter 2, leadership and subordinateship in a country are inseparable. Vertical relations in organizations are based on the common values of superiors *and* subordinates. Beliefs about leadership reflect the dominant culture of a country. Asking people to describe the qualities of a good leader is a way of asking them to describe their culture. The leader is a culture hero, in the sense of acting as a model for behavior (refer back to Figure 1.2).

Authors from individualist countries tend to treat leadership as an independent characteristic that a person can acquire, without reference to its context. In the management literature from individualist, masculine cultures like Australia, Britain, and the United States, romanticized descriptions of masculine leaders are popular. They describe what the readers like to be and to believe. What really happens depends on leaders, on followers, and very much on the situation.

Feminine cultures believe in modest leaders. A prestigious U.S. consulting firm was once asked to analyze decision making in a leading Dutch corporation. The firm's report criticized the corporation's decision-making style for being, among other things, "intuitive" and "consensus-based."[42] The in-depth comparison of a U.S., a Dutch, and a French organization by d'Iribarne (see Chapter 2) showed that the consensus principle was precisely the essence of the success of the Dutch plant. The Dutch "polder" consensus model is supposed to have been a keystone of the country's economy. Imposing a foreign leadership model (believed to be universal) in such a situation is a destruction of cultural capital.

Danish researcher Jette Schramm-Nielsen interviewed Danish managers working in French manufacturing companies, as well as French managers working in Danish manufacturing companies, asking them to compare Danish and French ways of arriving at decisions. The statements mostly betray the large UAI gap between the two countries.

A Dane said:

> *The French tend to think that the Danes are not thorough enough, and the Danes think that the French are too complicated. At his desk, the Frenchman tends to keep on working on a case. He agrees neither with his surroundings nor with himself. This means that when he has analysed a case and has come to a conclusion, then he would like to go over it once more.*

One Frenchman said:

> *The French are rational, yes, but this statement has to be graded. They are rational in their reasoning, but much more subjective in their actions and their reactions.*

And another Frenchman said:

> *Danes are more pragmatic. . . . The rationality of the Danes tends to be modulated by their actions and their knowledge of the practical side of things.*[43]

Two U.S. researchers, Ellen Jackofsky and John Slocum, analyzed descriptions of chief executives in the management press in five countries. French CEOs were described as taking autocratic initiatives (high PDI); Germans as stressing the training and responsibilities of their managers and workers (low PDI, high UAI); Japanese as practicing patience and letting the organization run itself, aiming at long-term market share (high LTO); Swedes as taking entrepreneurial risks and at the same time caring for their people's quality of working life (low UAI, low MAS); and the one Taiwanese CEO in the sample stressed hard work and the family (high LTO, low IDV).[44]

Ingrid Tollgerdt-Andersson from Sweden compared more than 1,400 job advertisements for executives from eight European countries. She looked for whether the ads mentioned personal and social abilities, like the ability to cooperate. This was the case in 80 percent or more of the ads in Sweden, Denmark, and Norway but only in some 50 percent in Italy and Spain. Weak uncertainty avoidance explains most of the differences. Ability to cooperate is a soft criterion considered more valid in low-UAI countries. Femininity explains nearly all the remaining differences: cooperation is a more important value in feminine than in masculine cultures.[45]

Studies of the satisfaction and productivity of subordinates under different types of leaders show the influence of national cultures. French IBM technicians were most satisfied when they saw their boss as persuasive or paternalistic, unlike their British and German colleagues, who more often liked consultative and democratic bosses. Workers from Peru liked close supervision, unlike similar workers from the United States. Indian assistants showed the highest satisfaction and performance when working under foremen who behaved like elder brothers. What represents appropriate leadership in one setting does not have to be appropriate for a differently programmed group of subordinates.[46]

Leadership behaviors and leadership theories that do not take collective expectations of subordinates into account are basically dysfunctional. Harry Triandis described how the U.S. leadership style was dysfunctional in Greece and the Greek leadership style in the United States.[47] What usually happens when foreign theories are taught abroad is that they are preached but not practiced. Wise local managers silently adapt the foreign ideas to fit the values of their subordinates. A country in which this has happened a lot is Japan.[48] Not-so-wise managers may once try an unfitting approach, find out it does not work, and fall back into their old routine.

The existence and functioning of *grievance channels,* through which lower-level organization members can complain about those at the top, is obviously very much culturally influenced. Grievance channels in large-power-distance environments are difficult to establish. On the one hand, subordinates will fear retaliation (for good reason); on the other hand, there will be more unrealistic and exaggerated grievances, and the channels may be used for personal revenge against a superior who is not accessible otherwise. Uncertainty avoidance plays a role, too: allowing complaints means allowing the unpredictable.

The term *empowerment* became fashionable in the 1990s. It can refer to any kind of formal and informal means of sharing decision-making power and influence between leaders and subordinates. Earlier terms for such processes were *participative management, joint consultation, Mitbestimmung, industrial democracy, worker representation, worker self-management, shop floor consultation,* and *codetermination.* Their feasibility depends on the value systems of the organization members—of the subordinates at least as much as of the leaders. The first cultural dimension involved is again power distance. Distributing influence comes more naturally to low- than to high-PDI cultures.[49] Ideologies may go the other way around; in the IBM surveys the statement "Employees in industry should participate more in the decisions taken by management" was more strongly endorsed in high- than in low-PDI countries, showing how an ideology can compensate for reality.

Classic mid-twentieth-century U.S. leadership models like Douglas McGregor's Theory Y (discussed earlier), Rensis Likert's System 4, and Robert Blake and Jane Mouton's Managerial Grid[50] reflected small but not very small power distances (in the IBM studies the United States ranked moderately low on PDI). They all advocated participative management in the sense of participation by subordinates in the superior's decisions, *but at the initiative of the superior.* In countries with still lower PDI values—like Sweden, Norway, Germany, and Israel—models of management were developed assuming the initiatives to be taken by the subordinates. In the United States this tends to be seen as infringing upon management prerogatives, but in the lowest-PDI countries people do not think in these terms. A Scandinavian was cited as remarking to an American lecturer: "You are against participation for the very reason we are in favor of it— one doesn't know where it will stop. We think that is good."[51] On the other hand, U.S. theories of participative management are also unlikely to apply in countries much higher on the power distance scale. Harry Triandis reported the embarrassment of a Greek subordinate when his expatriate U.S. boss asked his opinion on how much time a job should take: "He is the boss. Why doesn't he tell me?"[52] One of the critical notes about the GLOBE Research Project about societal culture, organizational culture, and leadership (see Chapter 1) is that the questionnaires were designed on the basis of a U.S. concept of leadership.[53]

The choice of informal versus formal empowerment is affected by the country's level of uncertainty avoidance. Thus both PDI and UAI should be taken into account, and the four quadrants of Figure 7.1 represent four different forms of dividing power. In the upper left-hand corner (Anglo countries, Scandinavia, Netherlands: PDI and UAI both low), the stress is on informal and spontaneous forms of participation on the shop floor. In the lower left-hand corner (German-speaking countries: PDI low, UAI higher), the stress is on formal, legally determined systems (*Mitbestimmung*). On the right-hand side (high PDI), distributing power is basically a contradiction; it will meet with strong resistance from elites and sometimes even from underdogs or their representatives, such as labor unions. Where it is tried it has to be pushed by a powerful leader—by a father type such as an enlightened entrepreneur in the high-PDI, low-UAI countries (upper right-hand corner) or by political leadership using legislative tools in the high-PDI, high-UAI countries (lower right-hand corner). Both mean imposed participation, which, of course, is a paradox. One way of making it function is to limit participation to certain spheres of life and to maintain tight control in others; this is the Chinese solution, in which participative structures in work organizations can be combined with a strictly controlled hierarchy in ideological issues.[54] That this has a long history too is evident from the story with which Chapter 6 opened: eighteenth-century participative management in the *Dream of the Red Chamber* garden.

Performance Appraisal and Management by Objectives

Any organization in any culture depends on the performance of people. Monitoring the performance of subordinates is a theme in most management development programs right from the lowest management level upward. Often there is a formal performance appraisal program requiring periodic written and/or oral evaluations by the superior. Exporting such programs across national borders once more calls for adaptation. In collectivist countries social harmony is an important ingredient for organizational functioning, even more crucial than formal performance, and a program that harms the former eventually damages the latter.[55] Personal criticism may have to be given in an indirect way or through a trusted intermediary, like an older relative. Geert remembers a case in Pakistan in which the personnel department of a multinational company produced all the paperwork of an internationally prescribed appraisal system to the satisfaction of its international head office—but the local managers carefully avoided conducting the expected appraisal interviews.

In the United States, management guru Peter Drucker developed performance appraisal into *Management by Objectives.*[56] MBO was probably the most popular management technique of the twentieth century. It is based on a cybernetic control-by-feedback philosophy that is supposed to spread a results orientation throughout the organization. MBO has been considerably more successful where results are objectively measurable than where they are a matter of subjective interpretation. It reflects an American value position in that it presupposes each of the following:

- That the subordinate is sufficiently independent to have a meaningful dialogue with the boss (not too high PDI)
- That both superior and subordinate are prepared to accept some ambiguity (low UAI)
- That high performance is seen as an important goal by both (high MAS)

Let us now take the case of Germany. This is also a below-average PDI country, so the dialogue element in MBO should present no problem. Germany scored considerably higher on UAI, however; consequently the acceptance of ambiguity is weaker. MBO in Germany has been strongly formalized and converted into "Management by joint goal setting."[57]

In France MBO was first introduced in the early 1960s; it became extremely popular for a time after the student revolts that shook up the Western world in 1968. People expected that this new technique would lead to the long-overdue democratizing of organizations. DPO (*direction par objectifs*), the French name for MBO, became DPPO (*direction participative par objectifs*). After a few years, however, a French management author wrote, "I think that the career of DPPO is terminated, or rather that it has never started, and it won't ever start as long as we in France continue our tendency to confound ideology and reality." The journal editor added, "French blue- and white-collar workers, lower-level and higher-level managers, and *patrons* all belong to the same cultural system which maintains dependency relations from level to level. Only the deviants really dislike this system. The hierarchical structure protects against anxiety; DPO, however, generates anxiety."[58]

Management Training and Organization Development

It will be evident from all that has been written in this book and, in particular, in this chapter that there is no single formula for developing successful managers that can be used in all cultures. Not only is success defined differently in different cultures, but systems of education in schools and training on the job are also markedly different.

Developing managers across cultural barriers could thus be seen as an impossible task, but fortunately programs should not be judged exclusively on the basis of their subject matter. They have other important functions, too. They bring people from different cultures and subcultures together and by this fact broaden their outlook. In many organizations international management development programs have become *rites de passage*, which signal to the manager-participant as well as to his or her environment that from now on he or she belongs to the manager caste. They provide a socialization for the managerial subculture, either company-specific or in general. They also provide a break with the job routine that stimulates reflection and reorientation.

Management development packages have been developed in the United States since the middle of the twentieth century. Some approaches have used intensive discussion of interpersonal processes, such as sensitivity training and transactional analysis. Culturally these assumed low PDI, low UAI, medium to high IDV, and medium to low MAS; the latter made it somewhat countercultural in the United States.

In cases where such programs were used with international participants, dysfunctional behaviors occurred, which their trainers rarely understood. With Japanese, for example, the giving and receiving of personal feedback appeared virtually impossible and, when tried, resulted in ritualized behavior: the receiver of feedback felt that he must have insulted the sender in some way. Japanese participants in such programs concentrated on tasks rather than interpersonal process issues. Most Germans also did not appreciate talking about process issues, because this was seen as a wasteful deviation from the task.[59]

A parallel trend was *organization development*, in which managers and others tried to learn and resolve actual common problems at the same time. It sometimes also included intensive interpersonal process analysis.

In Latin countries, trainers—themselves Latin—gave a wide range of reasons all showing the organization development program's cultural incompatibility:

- We Latins (high PDI) lack the equality ethos needed for such programs.
- We Latins don't believe in self-development.
- We Latins tend to interpret interpersonal feedback competitively, unless it comes from a person seen as superior.
- The organization development process creates insecurity, which we Latins cannot tolerate.
- Our Latin languages and discussion styles are more suitable for abstract discussions than for actual problem solving.
- Our Latin organizations are not changed by development but by crisis and revolution.[60]

Conclusion: Nationality Defines Organizational Rationality

In 1980 Geert published an article in the U.S. journal *Organizational Dynamics* entitled "Motivation, Leadership, and Organization: Do American Theories Apply Abroad?" It had a stormy history; after the untimely demise of the editor who had invited and accepted it, the article was at first refused and then published hesitatingly by his successor. He asked a U.S. and an Australian colleague to write assuaging comments, which were published in a later volume, with Geert's reply.[61] The article caused an upheaval far beyond what Geert had expected. Many reprints were ordered, especially from Canada.

The idea that the validity of a theory is constrained by nationality was more obvious in Europe, with all its borders, than in a huge borderless country like the United States. In Europe the cultural relativity of the laws that govern human behavior had been recognized as early as the sixteenth century in the skepticism of Michel de Montaigne (1533–92). Pascal's quote referred to earlier in this chapter—"There are truths on this side of the Pyrénées which are falsehoods on the other" (the Pyrénées being the border mountains between France and Spain)—was in fact inspired by Montaigne.[62] Since Montaigne and Pascal, the link between nationality and ways of thinking has sometimes been recognized but more often forgotten.

The previous chapters have demonstrated five ways in which national cultures differ; all of these have implications for organization and management processes. Theories, models, and practices are basically culture-specific; they may apply across borders, but this should always be proven. The naive assumption that management ideas are universal is not only found in popular literature. In scholarly journals—even in those explicitly addressing an international readership—the silent assumption of universal validity of culturally restricted findings is common. Articles in such journals often do not even mention the country in which the data were collected (which usually is the United States, as can be concluded from the affiliations of the authors). As a matter of scientific etiquette we suggest that articles written for an international public should always mention the country or countries—and the time period—in which the data were collected.

Unawareness of national limits causes management and organization ideas and theories to be exported without regard for the values context in which they were developed. Fad-conscious publishers and gullible readers in those other countries encourage such exports. Unfortunately, to rephrase a famous dictum, there is nothing as impractical as a bad theory.[63]

The economic success of the United States in the decades before and after World War II has led some people in other parts of the world to believe that U.S. ideas about management must be superior and therefore should be copied. They forgot to ask about the kind of society in which these ideas were developed and applied—*if* they were really applied as the books and articles claimed. U.S. management researchers Mark Peterson and James Hunt wrote, "A question for many American normative theories is whether they even apply in the United States."[64] U.S. ethnopsychologist Edward Stewart wrote, "North American decision-makers do not observe rational decision making in their own work and lives, as a general rule, but they restructure past events according to a decision making model. . . . Thus, in the United States rational decision making is a myth."[65] U.S. business historian Robert Locke described how the successful industrialization of the United States took place in a very distinct historical context and owed much more to external circumstances than to the quality of the management principles used.[66]

The belief in the superiority of American theories is reinforced by the fact that most "international" management journals are published in the United States with U.S. editors, making it notoriously difficult for non-North American authors to get their papers accepted.[67] British professors David Hickson and Derek Pugh in their anthology *Great Writers on Organizations* included seventy-one names, of whom forty-eight were American, fifteen British, and two Canadian; only six were non-Anglo.[68]

U.S. business professor and consultant Michael Porter analyzed why some nations succeeded much better than others in the international competition of the latter part of the twentieth century. His "diamond" of the determinants of national advantage recognized four attributes: (1) factor conditions, by which he meant the availability of necessary production factors like skilled labor and infrastructure, (2) demand conditions, (3) related and supporting industries, and (4) firm strategy, structure, and rivalry. Porter stopped short of the question of *why* some countries get better diamonds than others. He still assumed universal applicability of the ethnocentric laws of competitive markets.[69]

Just as certain nations excel in certain sports, others are associated with specific disciplines. Psychology, including social psychology, is predominantly a U.S. discipline: individualist and mostly masculine. Sociology is predominantly European,[70] but even European sociologists rarely consider the influence of their nationality on their thinking. The great French sociologist Pierre Bourdieu fiercely rejected critiques explaining his ideas from his being French.[71] In our eyes, far from invalidating Bourdieu's theories, recognizing the fact of their French origin makes them more understandable to others—just as U.S. models become more useful if we realize their American origin.

In organization theories the nationality of the author reflects the implicit assumptions as to what organizations came from, are, and try to achieve. These national paradigms all begin "In the beginning was . . . " After God had created men, men made organizations—but what did they have in mind when making them? Here is Geert's list of the paradigms he observed: *In the beginning was . . .*

In the United States	the market
In France	power
In Germany	order
In Poland and Russia	efficiency
In the Netherlands	consensus
In Nordic countries	equality
In Britain	systems
In China	the family
In Japan	Japan

In Paris in 1994 U.S. economist Oliver Williamson engaged in a public discussion with two French social scientists, economist Olivier Favereau and sociologist Emmanuel Lazega. Williamson defended an "efficiency approach" for studying organizations, even for the phenomena of power and authority. "I submit that there is less to power than meets the eye," he said. Favereau and Lazega criticized Williamson's concept of "transaction cost" as being too thin a concept to be the basis of a general theory of organization; efficiency as being a weak incentive; and Williamson's conception of power as too limited. The discussion had been announced as dealing with a supposed *con*vergence between economics and sociology, but in fact it dealt with a *di*vergence of implicit national paradigms, opposing United States (market) to France (power). All the sources Williamson cited were American; all the sources Favereau and Lazega cited were French. But neither side seemed to be aware that the other spoke from a different context, not even that there was such a thing as a national context from which theories are written and criticized.[72]

The lack of universal solutions to management and organization problems does not mean that countries cannot learn from each other. On the contrary, looking across the border is one of the most effective ways of getting new ideas for management, organization, or politics. But their export calls for prudence and judgment. Nationality constrains rationality.

The Elephant and the Stork: Organizational Cultures

Heaven's Gate BV (HGBV) is a sixty-year-old production unit in the chemical industry of the Netherlands. Many of its employees are old-timers. Stories about the past abound. Workers tell about how heavy the jobs used to be, when loading and unloading was done by hand. They tell about heat and physical risk. HGBV used to be seen as a rich employer. For several decades the demand for its products exceeded the supply. Products were not sold but were distributed. Customers had to be nice and polite in order to be served. The money was made very easily.

HGBV's management style used to be paternalistic. The old general manager made his daily morning walk through the plant, shaking hands with everyone he met. This, people tell, is the root of a tradition that still exists and which they call the "HGBV-grip": when one arrives in the morning, one shakes hands with one's colleagues. This greeting ritual would be normal in France, but in the Netherlands it is unusual. Rich and paternalistic, HGBV has long been considered a benefactor, both to its employees in times of need and to the local community. Some of this has survived. Employees still feel HGBV to be a desirable employer, with good pay, benefits, and job security. A job with HGBV is still seen as a job for life. HGBV is a company one would like one's children to join. Outside, HGBV is a regular sponsor of local sports and humanitarian associations. "No appeal to HGBV has ever been made in vain."

The working atmosphere is good-natured, with a lot of freedom given to employees. The plant has been pictured as a club, a village, a family. Twenty-five-year and forty-year anniversaries are given lots of attention; the plant's Christmas parties are famous. These celebrations represent rituals with a long history, which people still value. In HGBV's culture—or, as people express it, "the HGBV way"—unwritten rules for social behavior are very important. One doesn't live in order to work; one works in order to live. What one does counts less than *how* one does it. One has to fit into the informal network, and this holds for all hierarchical levels. *Fitting* means avoiding conflicts and direct confrontations; covering other people's mistakes; loyalty, friendliness, modesty, good-natured cooperation. Nobody should be too conspicuous, either in a positive or in a negative sense.

HGBVers grumble, but never directly about other HGBVers. Also, grumbling is reserved for one's own circle: toward superiors or outsiders, one does not soil the nest. This concern for harmony and group solidarity fits well into the regional culture of the geographic area in which HGBV is located. Newcomers are quickly accepted, as long as they adapt. The quality of their work counts less than their social adaptation. Whoever disrupts the harmony is rejected, however good a worker she or he is. Disturbed relationships may take years to heal. "We prefer to let a work problem continue for another month, even if it costs a lot of money, above resolving it in an unfriendly manner." Company rules are never absolute. The most important rule, one interviewee said, is that rules are flexible. One may break a rule if one does it gently. It is not the rule breaker who is at risk, but rather the one who makes an issue of it.

Leadership in HGBV, in order to be effective, should be in harmony with the social behavior patterns. Managers should be accessible, fair, and good listeners. The present general manager is such a leader. He does not give himself airs. He has an easy contact with people of all levels and is felt by employees to be one of them. Careers in HGBV are made primarily on the basis of social skills. One should not behave too conspicuously; one need not be brilliant, but one does need good contacts; one should know one's way in the informal network, being invited rather than volunteering. One should belong to the tennis club. All in all, one should respect what someone called the strict rules for being a nice person.

This romantic picture, however, has recently been disturbed by outside influences. First, market conditions have changed, and HGBV finds itself in an unfamiliar competitive situation with other European suppliers. Costs had to be cut and manpower reduced. In the HGBV tradition this problem was resolved without collective layoffs, but instead through early retirement. Yet the old-timers who had to leave prematurely were shocked that the company did not need them anymore.

Second, and even more seriously, HGBV has been attacked by environmentalists because of the pollution it causes, a point of view that has received growing support in political circles. It is not impossible that the licenses necessary for HGBV's operation will one day be withdrawn. HGBV's management has tried to counter this problem with an active lobby with the authorities, with a press campaign, and through organizing public visits to the company, but their success is by no means certain. Inside HGBV this threat is belittled. People are unable to imagine that one day there may be no more HGBV. "Our management has always found a solution. There will be a solution now." In the meantime attempts are made to increase HGBV's competitiveness through quality improvement and product diversification. These also imply the introduction of new people from the outside. These new trends, however, clash head-on with HGBV's traditional culture.[1]

The Organizational Culture Craze

The short case study just presented is a description of an organization's culture. People working for Heaven's Gate BV have a specific way of acting and interacting that sets them apart from people working for other organizations, even within the same region. In the earlier chapters this book has mainly associated culture with nationality. English-language literature attributing cultures to organizations first appeared in the 1960s: *organizational culture* became a synonym for *organizational climate*. The equivalent *corporate culture*, coined in the 1970s, gained popularity after the book *Corporate Cultures*, by Terrence Deal and Allan Kennedy, appeared in the United States in 1982. It became common parlance through the success of a companion volume—like the former, from a McKinsey–Harvard Business School team: Thomas Peters and Robert Waterman's *In Search of Excellence*, which appeared in the same year.[2] After that, an extensive literature in different languages developed on the topic.

Peters and Waterman wrote:

> *Without exception, the dominance and coherence of culture proved to be an essential quality of the excellent companies. Moreover, the stronger the culture and the more it was directed toward the marketplace, the less need was there for policy manuals, organization charts, or detailed procedures and rules. In these companies, people way down the line know what they are supposed to do in most situations because the handful of guiding values is crystal clear.*[3]

Talking about the culture of a company or an organization became a fad, among managers, among consultants, and, with somewhat different concerns, among academics. Fads pass, and so did this one, but not without having left its traces. Organizational, or corporate, culture has become as fashionable a topic as organizational structure, strategy, and control. There is no standard definition of the concept, but most people who write about it would probably agree that organizational culture is:

- **Holistic:** referring to a whole that is more than the sum of its parts
- **Historically determined:** reflecting the history of the organization
- **Related to the things anthropologists study:** like rituals and symbols
- **Socially constructed:** created and preserved by the group of people who together form the organization
- **Soft:** although Peters and Waterman assured their readers that "soft is hard"
- **Difficult to change:** although authors disagree on *how* difficult

In Chapter 1 culture in general was defined as "the collective programming of the mind that distinguishes the members of one group or category of people from another." Consequently organizational culture can be defined as "the collective programming of the mind that distinguishes the members of one organization from another." An organization's culture, however, is maintained not only in the minds of its members but also in the minds of its other "stakeholders," everybody who interacts with the organization (such as customers, suppliers, labor organizations, neighbors, authorities, and the press).

Organizations with strong cultures, in the sense of the quote from Peters and Waterman, arouse positive feelings in some people, negative in others. The universal desirability of having a strong culture from an organizational point of view has frequently been questioned; it could be a source of fatal rigidity.[4] The attitude toward strong organizational cultures is partly affected by national culture elements. The culture of the IBM Corporation, one of Peters and Waterman's most excellent companies, was depicted with horror by Max Pagès, a leading French social psychologist, in a 1979 study of IBM France; he called it *"la nouvelle église"* ("the new church").[5] French society as compared to U.S. society is characterized by a greater dependence of the average citizen on hierarchy and on rules (see Chapters 2, 5, and 7). French academics are also children of their society and therefore more likely than American academics to stress intellectual rules—that is, rational elements in organizations. At the same time, French culture according to Chapter 3 is individualistic, so there is a need to defend the individual against the rational system.[6]

Dutch sociologist Joseph Soeters showed the similarity between the descriptions of Peters and Waterman's "excellent companies" and of social movements preaching civil rights, women's liberation, religious conversion, or withdrawal from civilization. In the United States itself cards were sold with the slogan "I'd rather be dead than excellent." In a more dispassionate way, Soeters's compatriot Cornelis Lammers showed that the "excellent companies" were simply the latest scion of an entire genealogy within organizational sociology of ideal types of "organic organizations" described already by the German sociologist Joseph Pieper in 1931, if not by others before, and reiterated in the sociological literature on both sides of the Atlantic.[7]

Another type of reaction was found in the Nordic countries Denmark, Sweden, and, to some extent, Norway and Finland. In their case society is *less* built on hierarchy and rules than in the United States. The idea of "organizational cultures" in these countries was greeted with approval because it tended to stress the irrational and the paradoxical. This did not at all prevent a basically positive attitude toward organizations.[8]

In a review of twenty years of organizational culture literature, Swedish sociologist Mats Alvesson distinguishes eight metaphors used by different authors:

1. Control mechanism for an informal contract
2. Compass, giving direction for priorities
3. Social glue for identification with the organization
4. Sacred cow to which people are committed
5. Affect regulator for emotions and their expression
6. Mixed bag of conflict, ambiguity, and fragmentation
7. Taken-for-granted ideas leading to blind spots
8. Closed system of ideas and meanings, preventing people to critically explore new possibilities[9]

Probably the most basic distinction among writers on organizational cultures exists between those who see culture as something an organization *has* and those who see it as something an organization *is*. The former leads to an analytic approach and a concern with change. It predominates among managers and management consultants. The latter supports a synthetic approach and a concern with understanding and is almost exclusively found among pure academics.[10]

Differences Between Organizational and National Cultures: The IRIC Project

Using the word *culture* for both nations and organizations suggests that the two kinds of culture are identical phenomena. This is incorrect: a nation is not an organization, and the two types of culture are of a different nature.

The difference between national and organizational cultures is based on their different mix of values and practices, as illustrated in Figure 8.1, which is based on Figure 1.3. *National cultures* are part of the mental software we acquired during the first ten years of our lives, in the family, in the living environment, and at school, and they contain most of our basic values. *Organizational (or corporate) cultures* are acquired when we enter a work organization as young or not-so-young adults, with our values firmly in place, and they consist mainly of the organization's practices[11]—they are more superficial.

In Figure 8.1 we also located several other levels of culture: a gender level, even more basic than nationality; a social class level, with some pos-

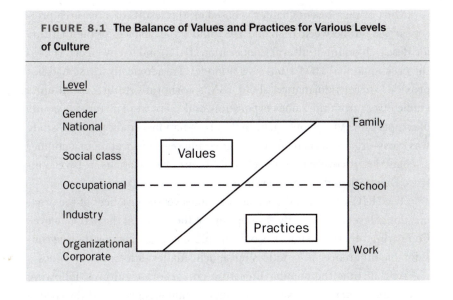

FIGURE 8.1   The Balance of Values and Practices for Various Levels of Culture

Level

Gender
National — Family

Social class — Values

Occupational — School

Industry

Organizational — Practices
Corporate — Work

sibilities of ascent or descent; an occupational level, linked to the kind of school education chosen; and an industry level between occupation and organization. An industry, or line of business, employs specific occupations *and* maintains specific organizational practices, for logical or traditional reasons.

Among national cultures—comparing otherwise similar people—the IBM studies found considerable differences in values, in the sense described in Chapter 1 of broad, nonspecific feelings of good and evil, and so on. This is notwithstanding similarities in practices among IBM employees in similar jobs but in different national subsidiaries.

When people write about national cultures in the modern world becoming more similar, the evidence cited is usually taken from the level of practices: people dress the same, buy the same products, and use the same fashionable words (symbols); they see the same television shows and movies (heroes); they perform the same sports and leisure activities (rituals). These relatively superficial manifestations of culture are sometimes mistaken for all there is; the deeper, underlying level of the values, which moreover determine the meaning for people of their practices, is overlooked. Studies at the values level continue to show impressive differences between nations; this is true for not only the IBM studies and their various replications (Table 1.1) but also the successive rounds of the World Values Survey based on representative samples of entire populations.[12]

Most of the present chapter is based on the results of a research project carried out between 1985 and 1987 under the auspices of the Institute
for Research on Intercultural Cooperation (IRIC) and led by Geert. It used
the cross-national IBM studies as a model. Paradoxically, these had not
provided direct information about IBM's corporate culture, as all units
studied were from the same corporation, and there were no outside points
of comparison. As a complement to the cross-national study, the IRIC study
was cross-organizational: instead of covering one corporation in a number
of countries, it covered a number of different organizations in two countries, Denmark and the Netherlands.

The IRIC study found the roles of values versus practices at the organizational level to be exactly the opposite of their roles at the national level.
Comparing otherwise similar people in different organizations showed considerable differences in practices but much smaller differences in values.

At that time the popular literature on corporate cultures, following
Peters and Waterman, insisted that shared values represented the core of
a corporate culture. The IRIC project showed that *shared perceptions of
daily practices* should be considered the core of an organization's culture.
Employees' values differed more according to their gender, age, and education (and, of course, their nationality) than according to their membership in the organization per se.

The difference between IRIC's findings and the statements by Peters
and Waterman and their followers can be explained by the fact that the
U.S. management literature tends to describe the values of corporate heroes
(founders and significant leaders), whereas IRIC asked the ordinary members of the organization who are supposed to carry the culture. IRIC
assessed to what extent leaders' messages had come across to members.
The values of founders and key leaders undoubtedly shape organizational
cultures, but the way these cultures affect ordinary members is through
shared practices. Founders' and leaders' values become members' practices.

Effective shared practices are the reason that multinational corporations can function at all. Employing personnel from a variety of nationalities, they cannot assume common values. They coordinate and control
their operations through worldwide practices inspired by their national
origin (be it U.S., Japanese, German, Dutch, etc.) but that can be learned
by employees from a variety of other national origins.[13]

If members' values depend primarily on criteria other than membership in the organization, the way these values enter the organization is

through the hiring process: a company hires people of a certain nationality, gender, age, or education. Their subsequent socialization in the organization is a matter of learning the practices: symbols, heroes, and rituals.

Two Dutch researchers, Joseph Soeters and Hein Schreuder, compared employees in Dutch and foreign accounting firms operating in the Netherlands. They found differences in values between the two groups, but they could prove that these were based on self-selection by the candidates, not on socialization to the firm's values after entering.[14] Human resources departments that preselect the people to be hired play an important role in maintaining an organization's values (for better or for worse), a role of which HR managers (and their colleagues) are not always conscious.

Qualitative and Quantitative Approaches in the IRIC Project

The original design of the IRIC project idea had been to compare only organizations within one country (the Netherlands). Finding a sufficient number of Dutch participants willing to grant access *and* share in the project's cost proved too difficult. Generous help by a Danish consultant resulted in adding a number of Danish units. The final project was carried out on twenty units from ten different organizations: five each in Denmark and the Netherlands. On the IBM national culture dimensions these two countries scored fairly similar: both belong to the same Nordic-Dutch cluster. Within these national contexts IRIC sought access to a wide range of different work organizations. By seeing how different organization cultures can be, one acquires a better insight into how different is different, and how similar is similar. Units of study were both entire organizations and parts of organizations, which their management assumed to be culturally reasonably homogeneous (the research outcome later allowed to test this assumption).

Table 8.1 lists the activities the twenty units were engaged in. Unit sizes varied from 60 to 2,500 persons. The number of units was small enough to allow studying each unit in depth, qualitatively, as a separate case study. At the same time, it was large enough to permit statistical analysis of comparative quantitative data across all cases.

The first, qualitative phase of the research consisted of in-depth person-to-person interviews of two to three hours in duration each with nine informants per unit (thus a total of 180 interviews). These interviews

TABLE 8.1 Organizations Participating in the IRIC Project

Private manufacturing companies (electronics, chemicals, consumer goods)	
Total divisions or production units	6
Head office or marketing units	3
Research and development units	2
Private service companies (banking, transport, trade): units	5
Public institutions (telecommunications, police): units	4
Total number of units studied	**20**

served both to get a qualitative feel for the whole (the gestalt) of the unit's culture and to collect issues to be included in the questionnaire for the ensuing survey. Informants were handpicked in a discussion with the person who served as the researchers' contact in the unit, on the basis that they would have something interesting and informative to tell about the culture. The group of informants included in all cases the unit's top manager and his (never her) secretary; additionally, it comprised a selection of people in different jobs from all levels, both old-timers and newcomers, women and men. Sometimes the gatekeeper or doorman was found to be an excellent informant; an employee representative (equivalent to a shop steward) was always included.

The interviewer team consisted of eighteen members (Danish or Dutch), most of them with a social science training, but deliberately naive about the type of activity going on in the unit studied. Each unit's interviews were divided between two interviewers, one woman and one man, as the gender of the interviewer might affect the observations obtained. All interviewers received the same project training beforehand, and all used the same broad checklist of open-ended questions.

The interview checklist contained questions like the following:

- **About organizational symbols:** What are special terms here that only insiders understand?
- **About organizational heroes:** What kind of people are most likely to advance quickly in their career here? Who do you consider as particularly meaningful persons for this organization?

- **About organizational rituals:** In what periodic meetings do you participate? How do people behave during these meetings? Which events are celebrated in this organization?
- **About organizational values:** What things do people very much like to see happening here? What is the biggest mistake one can make? What work problems can keep you awake at night?

Interviewers were free to probe for more and other information if they felt it was there. Interviews were taped, and the interviewers wrote a report for each interview using a prescribed sequence, quoting as much as possible the respondents' actual words.

The second, quantitative phase of the project consisted of a paper-and-pencil survey with precoded questions, administered contrary to the first phase to a strictly *random* sample from the unit. This sample was composed of about twenty-five managers (or as many as the unit contained, if fewer than twenty-five), twenty-five college-level nonmanagers ("professionals"), and twenty-five non-college-level nonmanagers. The questions in the survey included those used in the cross-national IBM study plus a number of later additions; most, however, were developed on the basis of the interviews of the first phase. Questions were formulated about all issues that the interviewers suspected to differ substantially between units. These included in particular many perceptions of daily practices, which had been missing in the cross-national studies.

The results of both the interviews and the surveys were discussed with the units' management and sometimes fed back to larger groups of employees if the management agreed with it.

Results of the In-Depth Interviews: The SAS Case

The twenty units studied produced as many case studies, insightful descriptions of each unit's culture composed by the interviewers after the interviews and with the survey results as a check on their interpretations. The case of Heaven's Gate BV at the beginning of this chapter was taken from the survey results. One more case will now be described: the Scandinavian Airlines System (SAS) Copenhagen passenger terminal.

SAS in the early 1980s went through a spectacular turnaround process. Under the leadership of a new president, Jan Carlzon, the company switched from a product-and-technology orientation to a market-and-service orientation. Before, planning and sales had been based on realizing a maximum number of flight hours with the most modern equipment available. Pilots, technicians, and disciplinarian managers were the company's heroes. Deteriorating results forced the reorganization.

Carlzon was convinced that in the highly competitive air transport market success depended on a superior way of catering to the needs of the present and potential customers. These needs should be best known by the employees with daily face-to-face customer contact. In the old situation these people had never been asked for their opinions: they were a disciplined set of uniformed soldiers, trained to follow the rules. Now they were considered "the firing line," and the organization was restructured to support them rather than order them around. Superiors were turned into advisers; the firing line received considerable discretion in dealing with customer problems on the spot. They only needed to report their decisions to superiors after the fact—which meant a built-in acceptance of employees' judgment with all risks involved.[15]

One of the units participating in the IRIC study was the SAS passenger terminal at Copenhagen airport. The interviews were conducted three years after the turnaround operation. The employees and managers were uniformed, disciplined, formal, and punctual. They seemed to be the kind of people who *like* to work in a disciplined structure. People worked shift hours with periods of tremendous work pressure alternating with periods of relative inactivity. They showed considerable acceptance of their new role. When talking about the company's history, they tended to start from the time of the turnaround; only some managers referred to the earlier years.

The interviewees were proud of the company: their identity seemed to a large extent derived from it. Social relationships outside the work situation were frequently with other SAS people. Carlzon was often mentioned as a company hero. In spite of their being disciplined, relationships between colleagues seemed to be good-natured, and there was a lot of mutual help. Colleagues who met with a crisis in their private lives were supported by others and by the company. Managers of various levels were visible and accessible, although clearly managers had more trouble accepting the new role than nonmanagers. New employees entered via a formal introduction and a training program with simulated encounters with problem clients. This served also as a screening device, showing whether the newcomer had the values and the skills necessary for this profession. Those who successfully completed the training felt quickly at home in the department.

Toward clients the employees demonstrated a problem-solving attitude: they showed considerable excitement about original ways in which to resolve customers' problems, ways in which some rules could be stretched in order to achieve the desired result. Promotion was from the ranks and was felt to go to the most competent and supportive colleagues.

It is not unlikely that this department benefited from a certain "Hawthorne effect"[16] because of the key role it had played in a successful turnaround. At the time of the interviews the euphoria of the successful turnaround was probably at its peak. Observers inside the company commented that people's values had not really changed but that the turnaround had transformed a discipline of obedience toward superiors into a discipline of service toward customers.

Results of the Survey: Six Dimensions of Organizational Cultures

The IBM studies had led to the identification of four dimensions of *national* cultures (power distance, individualism-collectivism, masculinity-femininity, and uncertainty avoidance). These were dimensions of *values*, because the national IBM subsidiaries primarily differed on the cultural values of their employees. The twenty units studied in the IRIC cross-organizational study, however, differed only slightly with respect to the cultural values of their members, but they varied considerably in their practices.

Most questions in the paper-and-pencil survey measured *people's perceptions of the practices in their work unit.* These were presented in a "Where I work . . ." format; for example:

Where I work:

Meeting times are kept very punctually	1	2	3	4	5	Meeting times are only kept approximately
Quantity prevails over quality	1	2	3	4	5	Quality prevails over quantity

Each item thus consisted of two opposite statements: which statement was put in the right column and which in the left was decided on a random basis, so that their position could not suggest their desirability.

All sixty-one "Where I work . . ." questions were designed on the basis of the information collected in the open interviews and were subjected to a statistical analysis quite similar to the one used in the IBM studies. They produced six entirely new dimensions: of practices, not of values. What was used was a factor analysis of a matrix of sixty-one questions by twenty units; for each unit a mean score was computed on each question across all respondents (who were one-third managers, one-third professionals, and one-third nonprofessionals). This analysis produced six clear factors reflecting dimensions of (perceived) practices distinguishing the twenty organizational units from each other. These six dimensions were mutually independent; that is, they occurred in all possible combinations.

Choosing labels for empirically found dimensions is a subjective process: it represents the step from data to theory. The labels chosen have been changed several times. Their present formulation was discussed at length with people in the units. As much as possible, the labels had to avoid suggesting a "good" and a "bad" pole for a dimension. Whether the score of a unit on a dimension should be interpreted as good or bad depends entirely on where those responsible for managing the unit wanted it to go. The terms finally arrived at are the following:

1. Process oriented versus results oriented
2. Employee oriented versus job oriented
3. Parochial versus professional
4. Open system versus closed system
5. Loose control versus tight control
6. Normative versus pragmatic

The order of the six cross-organizational dimensions (their number) reflects the order in which they appeared in the analysis, but it has no theoretical meaning; that is, number 1 is not more important than number 6. A lower number only shows that the questionnaire contained more questions dealing with dimension 1 than with dimension 2, and so on; but this can very well be seen as a reflection of the interests of the researchers who designed the questionnaire.

For each of the six dimensions three key "Where I work . . ." questions were chosen to calculate an index value of each unit on each dimension, very much the same way as index values in the IBM studies were computed for each country on each cross-national dimension. The unit scores of the three questions chosen were strongly correlated with each other.[17] Their content was such that together they would convey the essence of the dimension, as the researchers saw it, to the managers and the employees of the units in the feedback sessions.

Dimension 1 opposes a concern with means (*process oriented*) to a concern with goals (*results oriented*). The three key items show that in the process-oriented cultures, people perceived themselves as avoiding risks and spending only a limited effort in their jobs, while each day was pretty much the same. In the results-oriented cultures, people perceived themselves as comfortable in unfamiliar situations and as putting in a maximal effort, while each day was felt to bring new challenges. On a scale from 0 to 100, in which 0 represents the most process-oriented and 100 the most results-oriented unit among the twenty, HGBV, the chemical plant described earlier, scored 2 (very process oriented, little concern for results), while the SAS passenger terminal scored 100: it was the most results-oriented unit of all. For this dimension it is difficult not to attach a "good" label to the results-oriented pole and a "bad" label to the other side. Nevertheless, there are operations for which a single-minded focus on the process is essential. The most process-oriented unit (score 0) was a production unit in a pharmaceutical firm. Drug manufacturing is an example of a risk-avoiding, routine-based environment in which it is doubtful whether one would want its culture to be results oriented. Similar concerns exist in many other organizational units. So even a results orientation is not always "good" and its opposite not always "bad."

One of the main claims from Peters and Waterman's book *In Search of Excellence* was that "strong" cultures are more effective than "weak" ones. A problem in verifying this proposition was that in the corporate culture literature one would search in vain for a practical (operational) measure of culture strength. As the issue seemed important, the IRIC project developed a method for measuring the strength of a culture. A strong culture was interpreted as a homogeneous culture—that is, one in which all survey respondents gave about the same answers on the key questions, regardless of their content. A weak culture was a heterogeneous one: this occurred when answers among different people in the same unit varied widely. The survey data showed that across the twenty units studied, culture strength (homogeneity) was significantly correlated with results orientation.[18] To the extent that *results oriented* stands for *effective*, Peters and Waterman's proposition about the effectiveness of strong cultures was therefore confirmed.

Dimension 2 opposes a concern for people (*employee oriented*) to a concern for completing the job (*job oriented*). The key items selected show that in the employee-oriented cultures, people felt their personal problems were taken into account, that the organization took a responsibility for employee welfare, and that important decisions were made by groups or committees. In the job-oriented units, people experienced a strong pressure to complete the job; they perceived the organization as only interested in the work employees did, not in their personal and family welfare; and they reported that important decisions were made by individuals. On a scale from 0 to 100, HGBV scored 100 and the SAS passenger terminal 95—both of them extremely employee oriented. Scores on this dimension reflected the philosophy of the unit or company's founder(s), but also the possible scars left by past events: units that had recently been in economic trouble, especially if this had been accompanied by collective layoffs, tended to score job oriented, even if according to informants the past had been different. Opinions about the desirability of a strong employee orientation differed among the leaders of the units in the study. In the feedback discussions some top managers wanted their unit to become more employee oriented, but others desired a move in the opposite direction.

The employee-oriented versus job-oriented dimension corresponds to the two axes of a classic U.S. leadership model: Robert Blake and Jane Mouton's *Managerial Grid*.[19] Blake and Mouton developed an extensive system of leadership training on the basis of their model. In this training employee orientation and job orientation are treated as two independent dimensions: a person can be high on both, on one, or on neither. This seems to be at conflict with our placing the two orientations at opposite poles of a single dimension. Blake and Mouton's grid applies to individuals, however, while the IRIC study compared organizational units. What the IRIC study shows is that while individuals may well be both job *and* employee oriented at the same time, organizational cultures tend to favor one or the other.

Dimension 3 opposes units whose employees derive their identity largely from the organization (*parochial*) to units in which people identify with their type of job (*professional*). The key questions show that members of parochial cultures felt the organization's norms cover their behavior at home as well as on the job; they felt that in hiring employees, the company took their social and family background into account as much as their job competence; and they did not look far into the future (they probably assumed the organization would do this for them). On the other side, members of professional cultures considered their private lives their own business, they felt the organization hired on the basis of job competence only, and they did think far ahead. U.S. sociologist Robert Merton has called this distinction *local versus cosmopolitan*, the contrast between an internal and an external frame of reference.[20] The parochial type of culture is often associated with Japanese companies. Predictably in the IRIC survey, unit scores on this dimension were correlated with the unit members' level of education: parochial units tended to have employees with less formal education. SAS passenger terminal employees scored quite parochial (24); HGBV employees scored about halfway (48).

Dimension 4 opposes *open systems* to *closed systems*. The key items show that in the open system units, members considered both the organization and its people open to newcomers and outsiders, almost anyone would fit into the organization, and new employees needed only a few days to feel at home. In the closed system units, the organization and its people were felt to be closed and secretive, even among insiders; only very special people fitted into the organization; and new employees needed more than a year to feel at home (in the most closed unit, one member of the managing board confessed that he still felt like an outsider after twenty-two years). On this dimension HGBV again scored halfway (51) and SAS extremely open (9). What this dimension describes is the communication climate. It was the only one of the six "practices" dimensions associated with nationality: it seemed that an open organizational communication climate was a characteristic of Denmark more than of the Netherlands. One Danish organization, however, scored very closed.

Dimension 5 refers to the amount of internal structuring in the organization. According to the key questions, people in *loose control* units felt that no one thought of cost, meeting times were only kept approximately, and jokes about the company and the job were frequent. People in *tight control* units described their work environment as cost-conscious, meeting times were kept punctually, and jokes about the company and/or the job were rare. It appears from the data that a tight formal control system is associated, at least statistically, with strict unwritten codes in terms of dress and dignified behavior. On a scale where 0 equals loose and 100 equals tight, SAS with its uniformed personnel scored extremely tight (96), and HGBV scored once more halfway (52); but halfway was quite loose for a production unit, as comparison with other production units showed.

Dimension 6, finally, deals with the popular notion of customer orientation. *Pragmatic* units were market-driven; *normative* units perceived their task toward the outside world as the implementation of inviolable rules. The key items show that in the normative units, the major emphasis was on correctly following organizational procedures, which were more important than results; in matters of business ethics and honesty, the unit's standards were felt to be high. In the pragmatic units, there was a major emphasis on meeting the customer's needs, results were more important than correct procedures, and in matters of business ethics, a pragmatic rather than a dogmatic attitude prevailed. The SAS passenger terminal was the top scoring unit on the pragmatic side (100), which shows that Jan Carlzon's message had come across. HGBV scored 68, also on the pragmatic side. In the past as it was described in the HGBV case study, the company might have been more normative toward its customers, but it seemed to have adapted to its new competitive situation.

The Scope for Competitive Advantages in Cultural Matters

Inspection of the scoring profiles of the twenty units on the six dimensions shows that dimensions 1, 3, 5, and 6 (process versus results, parochial versus professional, loose versus tight, and normative versus pragmatic) relate to the type of work the organization does and to the type of market in which it operates. These four dimensions partly reflect the industry (or business) culture (see Figure 8.1). On dimension 1 most manufacturing and large office units scored process oriented; research-and-development and service units scored more results oriented. On dimension 3 units with a traditional technology scored parochial; high-tech units scored professional. On dimension 5 units delivering precision or risky products or services (such as pharmaceuticals or money transactions) scored tight; those with innovative or unpredictable activities scored loose. To the researchers' surprise the two city police corps studied scored on the loose side (16 and 41). The work of a police officer, however, is highly unpredictable, and police personnel have considerable discretion in the way they want to carry out their tasks. On dimension 6 service units and those operating in competitive markets scored pragmatic; units involved in the implementation of laws and those operating under a monopoly scored normative.

While the task and market environment thus affect the dimension scores, the IRIC study also has produced its share of surprises: production units with an unexpectedly strong results orientation even on the shop floor, or a unit like HGBV with a loose control system in relation to its task. These surprises represent the distinctive elements in a unit's culture (as compared to similar units) and the competitive advantages or disadvantages of a particular organizational culture.

The other two dimensions, 2 and 4 (employee versus job and open versus closed), seem to be less constrained by task and market but rather based on historical factors like the philosophy of the founder(s) and recent crises. In the case of dimension 4, open versus closed system, the national cultural environment was already shown to play a role as well.

Figure 8.1 indicates that although organizational cultures are *mainly* composed of practices, they do have a modest values component. The cross-organizational IRIC survey included the values questions from the cross-national IBM studies. The organizations differed somewhat on three clusters of values. The first resembled the cross-national dimension of uncertainty avoidance, although the differences showed up on other survey questions than those used for computing the country UAI scores. The cross-organizational uncertainty avoidance measure was correlated with dimension 4 (open versus closed), with weak uncertainty avoidance obviously on the side of an open communication climate. The relationship was reinforced by the fact that the Danish units, with one exception, scored more open than the Dutch ones. Denmark and the Netherlands, though similar on most national culture scores, differed most on their national uncertainty avoidance scores, with Denmark scoring much lower.

A second cluster of cross-organizational values bore some resemblance to power distance. It was correlated with dimension 1 (process oriented versus results oriented): larger power distances were associated with process orientation and smaller ones with results orientation.

Clusters of cross-organizational value differences associated with individualism and masculinity were not found in the IRIC study. It is possible that this was because the study was restricted to business organizations and public institutions. If, for example, health and welfare organizations had been included, the study might have shown a wider range of values with regard to helping other people, which would have produced a feminine-masculine dimension.

Questions that in the cross-national study composed the individualism and masculinity dimensions appeared in the cross-organizational study in a different configuration. It was labeled *work centrality* (strong or weak): the importance of work in one's total life pattern. It was correlated with dimension 3: parochial versus professional. Obviously work centrality is stronger in professional organization cultures. In parochial cultures people do not take their work problems home.

From the six organizational culture dimensions, numbers 1, 3, and 4 were thus to some extent associated with values. For the other three dimensions—2, 5, and 6—no link with values was found at all. These dimensions just described practices to which people had been socialized without their basic values being involved.

Organizational Culture and Other Organizational Characteristics

In the IBM studies, a national culture's antecedents and consequences were proven by correlating the country scores with all kinds of external data. These included such economic indicators as the country's per capita gross national product, political measures like an index of press freedom, and demographic data like the population growth rate. Comparisons were also made with the results of other surveys covering the same countries but using different questions and different respondents. The IRIC cross-organizational study included a similar "validation" of the dimensions against external data. This time, of course, the data used consisted of information about the organizational units obtained in other ways and from other sources.

Besides the interviews and the survey, the IRIC study included the collection of quantifiable data about the units as wholes. Examples of such information (labeled *structural data*) are total employee strength, budget composition, economic results, and the ages of key managers. All structural data were personally collected by Geert. Finding out what meaningful structural data *could* be obtained was a heuristic process that went along with the actual collection of the data. This process was too complicated to be shared across researchers. The informants for the structural data were the top manager, the chief personnel officer, and the chief budget officer. They were presented with written questionnaires, followed up by personal interviews.

Out of a large number of quantifiable characteristics tried, about forty provided usable data. For these forty characteristics, the scores for each of the twenty units were correlated with the unit scores on the six practices dimensions.[21] In the following paragraphs, for each of the six practice dimensions the most important relationships found are described.

There was a strong correlation between the scores on practice dimension 1, process versus results orientation, and the balance of labor versus material cost in the operating budget (the money necessary for daily functioning). An operation can be characterized as labor-intensive, material-intensive, or capital-intensive, depending on which of the three categories of cost takes the largest share of its operating budget. Labor-intensive units (holding number of employees constant) scored more results oriented, while material-intensive units (again holding number of employees constant) scored more process oriented. If an operation is labor-intensive, the effort of people by definition plays an important role in its results. This appears more likely to breed a results-oriented culture. The yield of material-intensive and capital-intensive units tends to depend on technical processes, which fact seems to stimulate a process-oriented culture. It is therefore not surprising that one finds research-and-development and service units on the results-oriented side; manufacturing and office units, subject to more automation, are more often found on the process-oriented side.

The second highest correlation of results orientation was with lower absenteeism. This is a nice validation of the fact that, as one of the key questions formulated it, "people put in a maximal effort." Next there were three significant correlations between results orientation and the structure of the organizations. Flatter organizations (larger span of control for the unit top manager) scored more results oriented. This confirms one of Peters and Waterman's maxims: "simple form, lean staff." Three simplified scales were used based on the Aston Studies of organizational structure, referred to in Chapter 7,[22] measuring centralization, specialization, and formalization. Both specialization and formalization were negatively correlated with results orientation: more specialized and more formalized units tend to be more process oriented. Centralization was not correlated with this dimension. Results orientation was also correlated with having

a top management team with a lower education level and promoted from
the ranks. Finally, in results-oriented units, union membership among
employees tended to be lower.

The strongest correlations with dimension 2 (employee versus job orientation) were with the way the unit was controlled by the organization to
which it belonged. Where the top manager of the unit stated that his superiors evaluated him on profits and other financial performance measures,
the members scored the unit culture as job oriented. Where the top manager of the unit felt his superiors evaluated him on performance versus a
budget, the opposite was the case: members scored the unit culture to be
employee oriented. It seems that operating against external standards
(profits in a market) breeds a less benevolent culture than operating against
internal standards (a budget). Where the top manager stated he allowed
controversial news to be published in the employee journal, members felt
the unit to be more employee oriented, which validated the top manager's
veracity.

The remaining correlations of employee orientation were with the
average seniority (years with the company) and age of employees (more
senior employees scored a more job-oriented culture), with the education
level of the top management team (less-educated teams correspond with a
more job-oriented culture), and with the total invested capital (surprisingly, not with the invested capital per employee). Large organizations with
heavy investment tended to be more employee than job oriented.

On dimension 3 (parochial versus professional), units with a traditional
technology tended to score parochial, and high-tech units professional. The
strongest correlations of this dimension were with various measures of size:
not surprisingly, the larger organizations fostered the more professional
cultures. Also not surprisingly, professional cultures had less labor union
membership. Their managers had a higher average education level and age.
Their organizational structures showed more specialization. An interesting
correlation was with the time budget of the unit top manager: the way the
unit top manager claimed to spend his time. In the units with a professional
culture, the top managers claimed to spend a relatively large share of their
time in meetings and person-to-person discussions. Finally, the privately
owned units tended to score more professional than the public ones.

Dimension 4 (open versus closed system) was responsible for the single
strongest correlation with external data—that is, between the percentage
of women among the employees and the openness of the communication

climate.[23] The percentage of women among *managers* and the presence of at least one woman in the top management team were also correlated with openness. This correlation, however, was affected by the binational composition of the research population. Among developed European countries, Denmark at the time of the research had one of the highest participation rates of women in the workforce, and the Netherlands one of the lowest. Also, as mentioned earlier, Danish units as a group (with one exception) scored more open than Dutch units. This does not necessarily exclude a causal relationship between the participation of women in the workforce and a more open communication climate: it could very well be the explanation *why* the Danish units were so much more open.

Also connected with the open versus closed dimension were associations of formalization with a more closed culture (a nice validation of both measures), of admitting controversial issues in the employee journal with an open culture (obviously), and of higher average seniority with a more open culture.

The strongest correlation of dimension 5 (loose versus tight control) was with an item in the self-reported time budget of the unit top manager: where the top manager claimed to spend a relative large part of his time reading and writing reports and memos from inside the organization, control was found to be tighter. This makes perfect sense. We also found that material-intensive units have more tightly controlled cultures. As the results of such units often depend on small margins of material yields, this makes sense, too.

Tight control was also correlated with the percentage of female managers and of female employees, in this order. This was most likely a consequence of the simple, repetitive, and clerical activities for which, in the organizations studied, the larger number of women tended to be hired. Tighter control was found in units with a lower education level among male and female employees and also among its top managers. This reminds us of the finding in Chapter 2 that employees in lower-educated occupations maintained larger power distances. In units in which the number of employees had recently increased, control was felt to be looser; where the number of employees had been reduced, control was perceived as tighter. Employee layoffs are obviously associated with budget squeezes. Finally, absenteeism among employees was lower where control was perceived to be less tight. Absenteeism is evidently one way of escape from the pressure of a tight control system.

For dimension 6 (normative versus pragmatic) only one meaningful correlation with external data was found. Privately owned units in the sample were more pragmatic, public units (such as the police corps) more normative.

Missing from the list of external data correlated with culture were measures of the organizations' performance. This does not mean that culture is not related to performance, only that the research did not find comparable yardsticks for the performance of so varied a set of organizational units.

The relationships described in this section show objective conditions of organizations that were associated with particular culture profiles. They point to the things one has to change in order to modify an organization's culture—for example, certain aspects of its structure or the priorities of the top manager. We will come back to this at the end of this chapter.

Organizational Subcultures

A follow-up study by IRIC investigated organizational subcultures.[24] In 1988 a Danish insurance company commissioned IRIC to study the cultures of all its departments, surveying its total population of 3,400 employees. The study used the same approach as the previous Danish-Dutch project: open-ended interviews leading to the composition of a survey questionnaire.

The total respondent population could be divided into 131 "organic" working groups. These were the smallest building blocks of the organization, whose members had regular face-to-face contact. Managers were not included in the groups they managed but were combined with colleagues at their level of the hierarchy.

On the basis of their survey answers, the 131 groups could be sorted into three clearly distinct subcultures: a *professional,* an *administrative,* and a *customer interface* subculture. The first included all managers and employees in tasks for which a higher education was normally required, the second included all the (mostly female) employees in clerical departments, and the third included two groups of employees dealing directly with customers: salespeople and claim handlers.

Using the six dimensions from the Danish-Dutch study, the researchers showed various culture gaps between the three subcultures. The professional groups were the most job oriented, professional, open, tightly controlled, and pragmatic; the administrative groups the most parochial and normative; the customer interface groups the most results and employee oriented, closed, and loosely controlled. The customer interface subculture represented a counterculture to the professional culture that included higher management.

Just before the survey was held, the company had gone through two cases of internal rebellion: from the salespeople and from the women. The sales rebellion had been a conflict about working conditions and compensation; a sales strike had only just barely been prevented. This problem can be understood from the wide gap between the professional and customer interface subcultures. This rift on the culture map of the company proved quite dangerous. The customer interface people generate the business—without them, an insurance company cannot survive. The managers and professionals who made the key decisions in this company belonged to a quite different subculture: a high-profile, glorified environment in which big money, business trends, and market power were daily concerns—far from the crowd who did the actual work and brought in the daily earnings.

The women's rebellion was about a lack of careers for women, and it happened when the share of female employees had passed the 50 percent mark. The rebellion can be understood by looking at the gap between the professional and the administrative subcultures. Management from their professional subculture saw women as belonging to the administrative subculture: employees in routine jobs, not upwardly mobile. But this image was no longer accurate, if it ever had been so. From the 1,700 women in the company, 700 had a higher education; many worked in professional roles, and even those in administrative roles were nearly as much interested in a career as their male colleagues. The interviews had revealed that managers believed most women to experience conflicts between their work and their private and family lives. The survey, however, showed that whereas 21 percent of the women employees claimed to suffer from such conflicts, 30 percent of the men did. The women's explanation of this result was that if a woman took a job, she had to have her family problems resolved, whereas many men never consciously resolved them.

For an understanding of the culture of this insurance company, the subculture split was essential. Unfortunately the management—caught in their professional culture—did not recognize the alarming aspects of the culture rifts. They took little action as a result of the survey. Soon afterward the company started losing money; a few years later it changed ownership and top management.

Individual Perceptions of Organizational Cultures: Flowers, Bouquets, and Gardens

Different individuals within the same organizational unit do not necessarily give identical answers to questions about how they see their organization's practices. The IRIC study did not look at differences between individuals: its concern was with differences between organizational cultures. Michael Bond at the Chinese University of Hong Kong, who was interested in individual differences, offered to re-analyze the IRIC database from this point of view. Chung Leung Luk, at that time Bond's assistant, performed the necessary computer work. His results show the structure in the variation of individual scores around the means of the organizational units: in what ways individuals' answers differed *after organization culture differences were eliminated.* This extension of the IRIC project has been described in a joint paper by Hofstede, Bond, and Luk.[25]

The individual perceptions study first analyzed the values questions and the practices questions separately. Not surprisingly, individuals within the same unit differed more in their values, which were private, than in their perceptions of the unit's practices, in which they shared. Yet it became clear that for individuals, values and perceptions of practices were related, so in the further analysis they could be combined. This combination produced six dimensions of individuals' answers:

1. Alienation, a state of mind in which all perceptions of practices were negative. Alienated respondents were misers: they scored the organization as less professional, felt management to be more distant, trusted colleagues less, saw the organization as less orderly, felt more hostile to it, and perceived less integration between the organization and its employees. Alienation was stronger among employees who were younger, less educated, and nonmanagerial.

2. A commitment to work, which the researchers labeled "workaholism" (for example, the job is more important than leisure time), as opposed to a need for a supportive organization (for example, wanting to work in a well-defined job situation). The commitment to work was stronger

among employees who were younger, more educated, male, and managerial.

3. A personal need for achievement (for example, wanting to contribute to the success of the organization and wanting opportunities for advancement).

4. Personal masculinity, "machismo" (for example, parents should stimulate children to be best in their class, and when a man's career demands it, the family should make sacrifices).

5. Orderliness; employees saw the organization as more orderly when they personally had more orderly minds.

6. Authoritarianism (for example, it is undesirable that management authority can be questioned). Authoritarianism was stronger for employees who were less educated and female.

Systematic individual differences in perceptions of organizational cultures are most likely based on personality. In fact, five of the dimensions listed above resemble the "Big Five" dimensions of personality already described in Chapter 3: Openness to experience, conscientiousness, extraversion, agreeableness, and neuroticism. The individual perceptions dimensions can be associated with Big Five dimensions as follows:[26]

1. Alienation with neuroticism
2. Workaholism with extraversion (which includes *active* and *energetic*)
3. Need for achievement with openness to experience
4. Machismo negatively with agreeableness
5. Orderliness with conscientiousness

No personality factor was available for an association with authoritarianism. This may be a candidate for extending the Big Five into a Big Six; it is somewhat surprising that a corresponding factor is not included in the Big Five.

The choice of a level of analysis has played an important role in the present chapter. When we compared the same kind of data across countries, across organizational units, and across individuals, we found three different sets of dimensions, belonging to three different social science disciplines: anthropology, sociology, and psychology.

The cross-national study of the IBM data took what were first supposed to be psychological data and aggregated them to the country level. At that level they melted into concepts describing societies, like collectivism versus individualism, which really belong to anthropology and/or to political science. The database of the IRIC organizational culture study, analyzed at the level of organizational units, produced basic distinctions from organizational sociology, like Merton's local versus cosmopolitan. The same database, analyzed at the level of individual differences from the organizational unit's mean, supported the results of personality research in individual psychology.

Societies, organizations, and individuals represent the gardens, bouquets, and flowers of social science. Our research has shown that the three are related and part of the same social reality. To understand our social environment, we cannot have ourselves fenced in into one level only: we should be prepared to count with all three.[27]

Occupational Cultures

In Figure 8.1 an occupational culture level was placed halfway between national and organizational, suggesting that entering an occupational field means the acquisition of both values and practices; the place of socialization is the school, apprenticeship, or university, and the time is between childhood and entering work.

We know of no broad cross-occupational study that allows identifying dimensions of occupational cultures. Neither the five national culture (values) dimensions nor the six organizational culture (practices) dimensions will automatically apply to the occupational level. From the five cross-national dimensions, only power distance and masculinity-femininity were applicable to occupational differences in IBM. Chapter 3 showed that IBM occupations could not be described in terms of "individualist" or "collectivist," but rather as "intrinsic" or "extrinsic" according to what motivated most of those exercising the occupation, the work itself or the conditions and the material rewards provided.

From a review of the literature[28] and some guesswork, we predict that in a systematic cross-occupational study the following dimensions of occupational cultures may well be found:

1. Handling people versus handling things (for example, nurse versus engineer)
2. Specialist versus generalist, or from a different perspective, professional versus amateur (for example, psychologist versus politician)

3. Disciplined versus independent (for example, police officer[29] versus shopkeeper)
4. Structured versus unstructured (for example, systems analyst versus fashion designer)
5. Theoretical versus practical (for example, professor versus sales manager)
6. Normative versus pragmatic (for example, judge versus advertising agent)

These dimensions will have stronger associations with practices than the national culture dimensions and stronger associations with values than the organizational culture dimensions. They may also be used for distinctions *within* professions; for example, medical specialists can be placed on the "handling people versus handling things" continuum, with pediatricians landing far on the "handling people" side (they often deal with not only the child but the family as well) and surgeons and pathologists, who focus on details of the body, far on the "handling things" side.

Conclusions from the IRIC Research Project: Dimensions Versus Gestalts

The IRIC research project produced a six-dimensional model of organizational cultures, defined as perceived common practices: symbols, heroes, and rituals. The research data came from twenty organizational units in two northwestern European countries, and one should therefore be careful not to claim that the same model applies to any organization anywhere. Certain important types of organizations, like those concerned with health and welfare, government, and the military, were not included.[30] We do not know what new practice dimensions may still be found in other countries. Nevertheless, we believe that the fact that organizational cultures can be meaningfully described by a number of practice dimensions is probably universally true. Also it is likely that such dimensions will generally resemble, and partly overlap with, the six described in this chapter.[31]

The geographic and industry limitations of the six-dimensional model imply that our questionnaire is not suitable for blanket replications. Interpreting the results is a matter of comparison. The formulas we used for computing the dimension scores were made for comparing an organization with the twenty units in the IRIC study, but they are meaningless in other environments and at other times. New studies should choose their own units to compare and develop their own standards for comparison. They should again start with interviews across the organizations to be included in order to get a feel for the organizations' gestalts and then compose their own questionnaire covering the crucial differences in the practices of these organizations.[32]

The dimensions found describe the culture of an organization, but they are not prescriptive: no position on one of the six dimensions is intrinsically good or bad. In Peters and Waterman's book *In Search of Excellence,* eight conditions for excellence were presented as norms. Their book suggested there is one best way toward excellence. The results of the IRIC study refute this. What is good or bad depends in each case on where one wants the organization to go, and a cultural feature that is an asset for one purpose is unavoidably a liability for another. Labeling positions on the dimension scales as more or less desirable is a matter of strategic choice, and this will vary from one organization to another. For example, a stress on customer orientation (becoming more pragmatic on dimension 6) is highly relevant for organizations engaged in services and the manufacturing of custom-made quality products but may be unnecessary or even harmful for, for example, the manufacturing of standard products in a competitive price market.

This chapter referred earlier to the controversy about whether an organization *is* or *has* a culture. On the basis of the IRIC research project, we propose that practices are features an organization *has.* Because of the important role of practices in organizational cultures, the latter can be considered somewhat manageable. We saw that changing collective values of adult people in an intended direction is extremely difficult, if not impossible. Collective practices, however, depend on organizational characteristics like structures and systems and can be influenced in more or less predictable ways by changing these organizational characteristics. Organizations are sometimes compared to animals; thus HGBV could be pictured as an elephant (slow, bulky, self-confident) and the SAS passenger terminal as a stork (reliable, caring, transporting). Nevertheless, as argued earlier, organizational cultures are also in a way integrated wholes or gestalts, and a gestalt can be considered something the organization *is.* The animal metaphor suggests limits to the changeability of the gestalt; one cannot train an elephant to become a racehorse, let alone to become a butterfly.

Changes in practices represent the margin of freedom in influencing these wholes, the kind of things the animals can learn without losing their essence. Because they are wholes, an integrating and inspiring type of leadership is needed to give these structural and systems changes a meaning for the people involved. The outcome should be a new and coherent cultural pattern, as was illustrated by the SAS case.

Managing (with) Organizational Culture

Back in the 1980s, when Geert tried to sell participation in the organizational culture research project to top managers of organizations, he claimed that "organizational culture represents the psychological assets of the organization that predict its material assets in five years' time." As we see it now, the crucial element is not the organizational culture itself, but what (top) management does with it. Four aspects have to be balanced (Figure 8.2).[33]

The performance of an organization should be measured against its objectives, and top management's role is to translate objectives into strategy—even if by default all that emerges is a laissez-faire strategy. *Strate-*

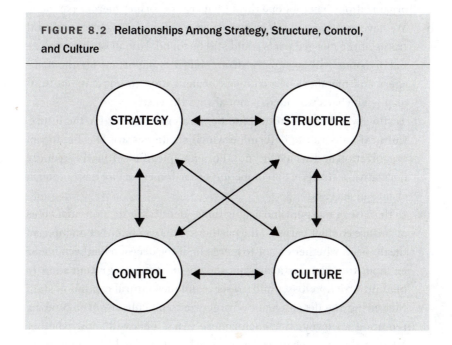

FIGURE 8.2 Relationships Among Strategy, Structure, Control, and Culture

gies are carried out via the existing *structure* and *control* system, and their outcome is modified by the organization's *culture*—and all four of these elements influence each other.

The IRIC study has shown that, as long as quantitative studies of organizational cultures are not used as isolated tricks but are integrated into a broader approach, they are both feasible and useful. In a world of hardware and bottom-line figures, the scores make organizational culture differences visible, and by becoming visible they move up on management's priority list.

Practical uses of such a study for managers and members of organizations, as well as for consultants, are:

1. Identifying the subcultures in one's own organization. The extension of the IRIC project to the insurance company demonstrated the importance of this. As Figure 8.3 illustrates, organizations may be culturally divided according to hierarchical levels: top management, middle- and lower-level managers, professional employees, and other employees (office or shop floor). Other potential sources of internal cultural divisions are functional area (such as sales versus production versus research), product/market division, country of operation, and, for organizations having gone through mergers, former merger partners. We have met cases in which twenty years after a merger the cultural traces of the merged parts could still be found. Not all of these potential divisions will be equally strong, but it is important for the managers and members of a complex organization to know its cultural map—which, as we found, is not always the case.

2. Testing whether the culture fits the strategies set out for the future. Cultural constraints determine which strategies are feasible for an organization and which are not. For example, if a culture is strongly normative, a strategy for competing on customer service has not much chance of success.

3. In the case of mergers and acquisitions, identifying the potential areas of culture conflict between the partners. This can be either an input to the decision whether or not to merge or, if the decision has been made, an input to a plan for managing the postmerger integration so as to minimize friction losses and preserve unique cultural capital.

4. Measuring the development of organizational cultures over time, by repeating a survey after one or more years. This will show whether attempted culture changes have, indeed, materialized, as well as what

FIGURE 8.3 Potential Subdivisions of an Organization's Culture

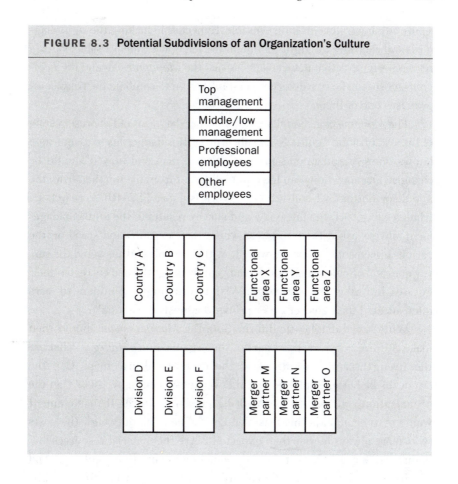

have been the cultural effects of external changes that occurred after the previous survey.

In practice, what can one do about one's organization's culture? First, this depends on one's position in, or with regard to, the organization. A classic study by Professor Eberhard Witte from Germany concluded that successful innovations in organizations required the joint action of two parties: a *Machtpromotor* and a *Fachpromotor* (a power holder and an expert, respectively).[34] Witte's model was developed on German data and may well be entirely valid only for countries like Germany with small power distance (accessibility of power holders) and fairly strong uncertainty avoidance (belief in experts). Nevertheless, in any national culture it makes sense to distinguish the two roles. Both are crucial for culture innovations. The support of a power holder—preferably a person with some charisma, not a pure administrator—is indispensable. Expertise in making the right diagnosis and choosing the right therapy, however, is also indispensable. Witte's research suggests that in Germany at least the *Machtpromotor* and the *Fachpromotor* should be two different persons; trying to combine the roles compromises one of them.

The *Fachpromotor* should provide a proper diagnosis of the present state of the organization's culture and subcultures. It is dangerous to assume one knows one's organization's present cultural map and how it should be changed. Organizations can look quite different from the top than from the middle or bottom, where the actual work is done. The IRIC researchers, when feeding back the interview and survey results to the units' management, always asked them to guess where their organization stood on the various dimensions, before showing how their people had answered the survey questions. Some managers were uncannily insightful and correct in their guesses, but others were way off. Wishful thinking and unfounded fears often affected their answers. So a proper diagnosis is essential.

With sound diagnostic information, the *Machtpromotor* should then make cultural considerations part of the organization's *strategy*. What are the strengths and weaknesses of the present cultural map? Can the strengths be better exploited and the weaknesses circumvented? Can the organization continue to live with its present culture? If management wants it to change, is this feasible? Do the benefits outweigh the costs (which are always higher than expected)? Are the material resources and human skills available that will be needed for changing the culture? And if it has been decided that the culture should change, what steps will be taken to implement the changes? Does the *Machtpromotor* realize his or her own crucial and lasting role in this process? Will he or she be given enough time by superiors, directors, or banks to take the process to its completion (and it always takes longer than one thinks)? Can a sufficient amount of support for the necessary changes be mobilized within the organization? Who will be the supporters? Who will be the resisters? Can the latter be circumvented or put in positions where they can do no harm?

Although culture is a "soft" characteristic, changing it calls for "hard" measures. *Structural changes* may mean closing departments, opening other departments, merging or splitting activities, or moving people and/or groups geographically. The general rule is that when people are moved as individuals, they will adapt to the culture of their new environment; when people are moved as groups, they will bring along their group culture. People in groups have developed, as part of their culture, ways of interacting that are quite stable and difficult to change. Changing them means that all interpersonal relationships have to be renegotiated. If new tasks or a new environment force such a renegotiation, however, there is a good chance that undesirable aspects of the old culture will be cleaned up.

Process changes mean implementing new procedures, eliminating controls or establishing new controls, implementing or discontinuing automation, and short-circuiting communications or introducing new communication links.

A bulk chemicals company wanted to move into the more profitable specialty chemicals market. They were successful only after they had renounced their usual detailed process figures and replaced them by checks on delivery time and on customer satisfaction.

Processes can be controlled on the basis of their outputs or through their inputs. The former, if possible, is more effective. Especially in the public sector, activities whose outputs can be clearly defined are often only controlled by their inputs, for traditional budget reasons.

Personnel changes mean new hiring and promoting policies. The gatekeeper role of the human resources department should be recognized. HR managers unconsciously maintain hero models for the organization that in a new culture may have to be revised. Could the hero be a heroine? Can a man with an earring be promoted? Training programs, often the first thing managers think of when wanting to change cultures, are only functional after the need for retraining has been established by structural, process, and personnel changes (as in the SAS case). Training programs without the support of hard changes usually remain at the level of lip service and are a waste of money. In general one should always be suspicious about suggestions to train *someone else*. Training is only effective if the trainee wants to be trained.

In attempted culture changes, new symbols often receive a lot of attention. They are easily visible: new name, logo, uniforms, slogans, and portraits on the wall—all that belongs to the fashionable area of *corporate identity*. But symbols are only the most superficial level of culture. New symbols without the support of more fundamental changes at the deeper levels of heroes, rituals, and the values of key leaders just mean a lot of hoopla, the effects of which wear out quickly.

Culture change in an organization asks for persistence, as well as sustained attention by the *Machtpromotor*. If the process started by a culture diagnosis, it is evidently useful to repeat this diagnosis after sufficient time has passed for the planned changes to become noticeable. In this way a process of monitoring is started, in which changes actually found are compared with intended changes and further corrections can be applied. If organizational culture is *somewhat* manageable, this is the way to go about it.

In Table 8.2 the main steps in managing (with) culture have been summarized as a practical checklist.

TABLE 8.2 Managing (with) Organizational Culture

- Is a task of top management that cannot be delegated
- Demands both power and expertise
- Should start with a cultural map of the organization
- Demands strategic choices
  - Is present culture matched with strategy?
  - If not, can strategy be adapted?
  - If not, what change of culture is needed?
  - Is this change feasible—do we have the people?
  - What will be the costs in management attention and money?
  - Do the expected benefits outweigh these costs?
  - What is a realistic time span for the changes?
  - If in doubt, better change strategy anyway.
  - Different subcultures may demand different approaches.
- Create a network of change agents in the organization
  - Some key people at all levels.
  - If key people start, others will follow.
  - Can resisters be circumvented?
- Design necessary structural changes
  - Opening or closing departments.
  - Merging or splitting departments or tasks.
  - Should groups or individuals be moved?
  - Are tasks matched with talents?

continued

- Design necessary process changes
  - Eliminating or establishing controls.
  - Automating or eliminating automation.
  - Establishing or cutting communication links.
  - Replace control of inputs by control of outputs?
- Revise personnel policies
  - Reconsider criteria for hiring.
  - Reconsider criteria for promotion.
  - Is human resource management up to its new task?
  - Design timely job rotation.
  - Be suspicious of plans to train others.
  - The need for training has to be felt by trainees themselves.
- Continue monitoring development of organizational culture
  - Persistence, sustained attention.
  - Periodically repeat culture diagnosis.

IMPLICATIONS

Intercultural Encounters

The English Elchi [ambassador] had reached Tehran a few days before we arrived there, and his reception was as brilliant as it was possible for a dog of an unbeliever to expect from our blessed Prophet's own lieutenant.... The princes and noblemen were enjoined to send the ambassador presents, and a general command issued that he and his suite were the Shah's guests, and that, on the pain of the royal anger, nothing but what was agreeable should be said to them.

All these attentions, one might suppose, would be more than sufficient to make infidels contented with their lot; but, on the contrary, when the subject of etiquette came to be discussed, interminable difficulties seemed to arise. The Elchi was the most intractable of mortals. First, on the subject of sitting. On the day of his audience of the Shah, he would not sit on the ground, but insisted upon having a chair; then the chair was to be placed so far, and no farther, from the throne. In the second place, of shoes, he insisted upon keeping on his shoes, and not walking barefooted upon the pavement; and he would not even put on our red cloth stockings. Thirdly, with respect to hats: he announced his intention of pulling his off to make his bow to the king, although we assured him that it was an act of great indecorum to uncover the head. And then, on the article of dress, a most violent dispute arose: at first, it was intimated that proper dresses should be sent to him and his suite, which would cover their persons (now too indecently exposed) so effectually that they might be fit to be seen by the king; but this proposal he rejected with derision. He said that he would appear before the Shah of Persia in the same dress he wore when before his own sovereign.

—JAMES MORIER, *The Adventures of Hajji Baba of Ispahan,* 1824, Chapter LXXVII

James J. Morier (1780–1849) was a European, and *The Adventures of Hajji Baba of Ispahan* is a work of fiction. Morier, however, knew what he wrote about. He was born and raised in Ottoman Turkey as a son of the British consul at Constantinople (now Istanbul). Later on he spent altogether seven years as a British diplomat in Persia (present-day Iran). When *Hajji Baba* had been translated into Persian, the readers refused to believe that it had been written by a foreigner. "Morier was by temperament an ideal traveler, reveling in the surprising interests of strange lands and peoples, and gifted with a humorous sympathy that enabled him to appreciate the motives actuating persons entirely dissimilar to himself," to quote the editor of the 1923 version of his book.[1] Morier obviously read and spoke Turkish and Persian. For all practical purposes he had become multicultural.

Intended Versus Unintended Intercultural Conflict

Human history is composed of wars between cultural groups. Joseph Campbell (1904–87), an American author on comparative mythology, finds the primitive myths of nonliterate peoples without exception affirming and glorifying war. In the Old Testament, a holy book of both Judaism and Christianity and a source document for the Muslim Koran, there are several quotes like the following:

But in the cities of these people that the Lord your God gives you for an inheritance, you shall save alive nothing that breathes, but you shall utterly destroy them, the Hittites and the Amorites, the Canaanites and the Perizzites, the Hivites and the Jebusites, as the Lord your God has commanded.

—*Deuteronomy 20:16–18*

This is a religiously sanctified call for genocide.[2] The fifth commandment, "Thou shalt not kill," from the same Old Testament obviously only applies to members of the in-group. Territorial expansion of one's own tribe by killing off others is not only permitted but supposed to be ordered by God. Not only in the land of the Old Testament but also in many other parts of the world, territorial conflicts involving the killing or expelling of other groups continue to this day. The Arabic name of the modern Palestinians who dispute with the Israelis the rights on the land of Israel is Philistines, the same name by which their ancestors are described in the Old Testament.

Territorial expansion is not the only *casus belli* ("reason for war"). Human groups have found many other excuses for collectively attacking others. An external enemy has always been one of the most effective ways to maintain internal cohesion. In Chapter 5 it was shown how a basic belief in many cultures is "what is different is dangerous." Racism assumes the innate superiority of one group over another and uses this to justify using violence for the purpose of maintaining this superiority. Totalitarian ideologies like apartheid imposed definitions of which groups were better and which were inferior—definitions that might be changed from one day to another. Culture pessimists wonder whether human societies can exist without enemies.

Europe, except in parts of former Yugoslavia, seems to have reached a stage in its development in which countries that within human memory still fought each other have now voluntarily joined a supranational union. Africa, on the other hand, has become the scene of large-scale war and genocide that some have compared to the World Wars of its former colonizers.[3] A functioning supra-national African union seems still far away.

Whereas cultural processes have a lot to do with issues of war and peace, war and peace will not be a main issue in this chapter. They represent "intended conflict" between human groups, and this is an issue too big for this book. The purpose of the present chapter is to look at the *unintended conflicts* that often arise during intercultural encounters and that happen although nobody wants them and all suffer from them. They have at times contributed to the outbreak of wars. It would be naive, however, to assume that all wars could be avoided by developing intercultural communication skills.

Owing to modern travel and communication technology, intercultural encounters in the modern world have multiplied at a prodigious rate. Embarrassments, such as those between Morier's English Elchi and the courtiers of the Shah, today occur between ordinary tourists and locals, between schoolteachers and the immigrant parents of their students, and between businesspeople trying to set up international ventures. More subtle misunderstandings than those pictured by Morier but with similar roots still play an important role in negotiations between modern diplomats and/or political leaders. Intercultural communication skills can contribute to the success of negotiations, on the results of which depend the solutions for crucial global problems. Avoiding unintended cultural conflicts will be the theme of this chapter.

Countries and regions differ in more than their cultures. Figure 9.1 distinguishes three kinds of differences between countries: identity, values, and institutions, all three rooted in history. Identity answers the question "To which group do I belong?" It is often rooted in language and/or religious affiliation, and it is perceived and felt both by the holders of the identity and by the environment that does not share it. Identity, however, is not a core part of national cultures; in the terminology of Figure 1.2, identity differences are rooted in practices (shared symbols, heroes, and rituals), not necessarily in values. Groups within or across countries that fight each other on the basis of their different identities may very well share basic values; this was or is the case for the Serbs and Croats in the former Yugoslavia and for the Catholics and Protestants in Northern Ireland. Identities can shift over a person's lifetime, as happens to many successful migrants.

Contrary to identity differences, value differences do form the core of cultures, as pictured in the "onion" of Figure 1.2. Identities are visible, values are invisible. Cultural values affect the consequences of identity differences. Collectivism rather than individualism means that identity groups isolate themselves from others; strong rather than weak uncertainty avoidance means that one group considers the other(s) as dangerous. Figure 5.2 plotted countries on the individualism-collectivism and uncertainty avoidance dimensions; in Chapter 5 we argued that the combined position of a country in this diagram clarified the different ways in which societies deal with intergroup conflict.

Countries also obviously differ in their historically grown institutions, the rules, laws, and organizations dealing with family life, schools, health care, business, government, sports, media, art, and sciences. The structure and functioning of a country's institutions is less related to differences in identity than to differences in values; therefore in Figure 9.1 the horizontal arrows have only been drawn between the "Values" and the "Institutions" blocks.

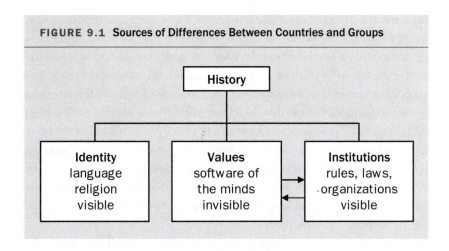

FIGURE 9.1 Sources of Differences Between Countries and Groups

Culture Shock and Acculturation

Intercultural encounters are often accompanied by similar psychological and social processes. The simplest form of intercultural encounter is between one foreign individual and a new cultural environment.

The foreigner usually experiences some form of *culture shock*. As illustrated over and over again in earlier chapters, our mental software contains basic values. These have been acquired early in our lives, and they have become so natural as to be unconscious. Based on them are our conscious and more superficial manifestations of culture: rituals, heroes, and symbols (see Figure 1.2). The inexperienced foreigner can make an effort to learn some of the symbols and rituals of the new environment (words to use, how to greet, when to bring presents), but it is unlikely that she or he can recognize, let alone feel, the underlying values. In a way, the visitor in a foreign culture returns to the mental state of an infant, in which she or he has to learn the simplest things over again. This usually leads to feelings of distress, of helplessness, and of hostility toward the new environment. Often one's physical functioning is affected. Expatriates and migrants have more need for medical help shortly after their displacement than before or later.[4]

People residing in a foreign cultural environment have reported shifts of feelings over time following more or less the *acculturation curve* pictured in Figure 9.2. Feelings (positive or negative) are plotted on the vertical axis and time on the horizontal one. Phase 1 is a, usually short, period of *euphoria*: the honeymoon, the excitement of traveling and of seeing new lands. Phase 2 is the period of *culture shock* when real life starts in the new environment, as described earlier. Phase 3, *acculturation*, sets in when the visitor has slowly learned to function under the new conditions, has adopted some of the local values, finds increased self-confidence, and becomes integrated into a new social network. Phase 4 is the *stable state* of mind eventually reached. It may remain negative compared to home (4a)— for example, if the visitor continues feeling alien and discriminated against. It may be just as good as before (4b), in which case the visitor can be considered to be biculturally adapted, or it may even be better (4c). In the last case the visitor has "gone native"—she or he has become more Roman than the Romans.

The length of the time scale in Figure 9.2 is arbitrary; it seems to adapt to the length of the expatriation period. People on short assignments of up to three months have reported euphoria, culture shock, and acculturation phases within this period; people on long assignments of several years have reported culture shock phases of a year or more before acculturation set in.

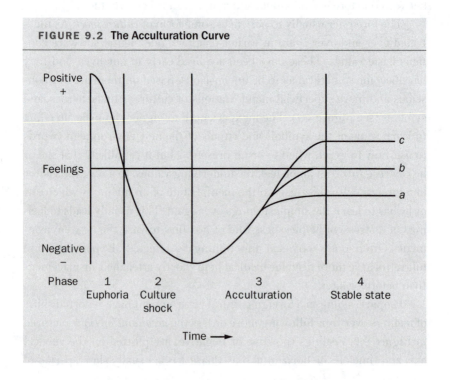

FIGURE 9.2 The Acculturation Curve

Culture shocks and the corresponding physical symptoms may be so severe that assignments have to be terminated prematurely. Most international business companies have experiences of this kind with some of their expatriates. There have been cases of expatriate employees' suicides. Culture shock problems of accompanying spouses, more often than those of the expatriated employees themselves, seem to be the reason for early return. The expatriate, after all, has the work environment that offers a cultural continuity with home. There is the story of an American wife, assigned with her husband to Nice, France, a tourist's heaven, who locked herself up inside their apartment and never dared to go out.

Articles in the management literature often cite high premature return rates for expatriates. Dutch-Australian researcher Anne-Wil Harzing critically reviewed more than thirty articles on the subject and found statements like this: "Empirical studies over a considerable period suggest that expatriate failure is a significant and persistent problem with rates ranging between 25 and 40 percent in the developed countries and as high as 70 percent in the case of developing countries." Trying to check the sources of these figures, Harzing discovered little evidence. The only reliable multicountry, multinationality study was by Professor Rosalie Tung from Canada, who had shown that in the late 1970s, before intercultural training became really common, mean levels of premature recall of expatriates for Japanese and European companies were under 10 percent; for U.S. companies the mean was somewhere in the lower teens, with exceptional companies reporting recall rates at the 20 to 40 percent level. And this situation probably improved in the years afterward, if we assume that human resources managers worked on solving their problems. The message of dramatically high expatriate failure rates sounds good to intercultural consultants trying to sell expatriate training and to convince themselves and others of the importance of their work, but it is a myth.[5] A better sales argument for the trainers is that premature return may be low, but it doesn't really measure the problem of expatriation: the damage caused by an incompetent or insensitive expatriate who stays is much larger.

Among refugees and migrants there is a percentage that fall seriously physically or mentally ill, commit suicide, or remain so homesick that they return, especially within the first year.

Expatriates and migrants who successfully complete their acculturation process and then return home will experience a reverse culture shock in readjusting to their old cultural environment. Migrants who have returned home sometimes find they do not fit in anymore and emigrate again, this time for good. Expatriates who successively move to new foreign environments report that the culture shock process starts all over again. Evidently, culture shocks are environment-specific. For every new cultural environment there is a new shock.

Ethnocentrism and Xenophilia

There are also standard types of reactions within host environments exposed to foreign visitors. The people in the host culture receiving a foreign culture visitor usually go through another psychological reaction cycle. The first phase is *curiosity*—somewhat like the euphoria on the side of the visitor. If the visitor stays and tries to function in the host culture, a second phase sets in: *ethnocentrism*. The hosts will evaluate the visitor by the standards of their culture, and this evaluation tends to be unfavorable. The visitor will show bad manners, like the English Elchi; he or she will appear rude, naive, and/or stupid. Ethnocentrism is to a people what egocentrism is to an individual: considering one's own little world the center of the universe. If foreign visitors arrive only rarely, the hosts will probably stick to their ethnocentrism. If regularly exposed to foreign visitors, the hosts may move into a third phase: *polycentrism*, the recognition that different kinds of people should be measured by different standards. Some will develop the ability to understand foreigners according to these foreigners' own standards. This is the beginning of bi- or multiculturality.[6]

As we saw in Chapter 5, uncertainty avoiding cultures will resist polycentrism more than uncertainty accepting cultures. Individuals within a culture vary around the cultural average, however, so in intolerant cultures one may meet tolerant hosts, and vice versa. The tendency to apply different standards to different kinds of people may also turn into *xenophilia*, the belief that in the foreigner's culture, everything is better. Some foreigners will be pleased to confirm this belief. There is a tendency among expatriates to idealize what one remembers from home. Neither ethnocentrism nor xenophilia is a healthy basis for intercultural cooperation.

Group Encounters: Auto- and Heterostereotypes

Intercultural encounters among groups rather than with single foreign visitors provoke group feelings. Contrary to popular belief, intercultural contact among groups does *not* automatically breed mutual understanding. It usually confirms each group in its own identity. Members of the other group are not perceived as individuals but in a stereotyped fashion— for example, all Chinese look alike; all Scots are stingy. As compared to the *heterostereotypes* about members of the other group, *autostereotypes* are fostered about members of one's own group. Such stereotypes will even affect the perception of actual events: if a member of one's own group attacks a member of the other group, one may be convinced ("I saw it with my own eyes") that it was the other way around.

As we saw in Chapter 3, the majority of people in the world live in collectivist societies, in which people remain throughout their lives members of tight in-groups that provide them with protection in exchange for loyalty. In such a society groups with different cultural backgrounds are out-groups to an even greater extent than out-groups from their own culture. Integration across cultural dividing lines in collectivist societies is even more difficult to obtain than in individualist societies. This is *the* major problem of many decolonized nations, like those of Africa where national borders were inherited from the colonial period that in no way respect ethnic and cultural dividing lines.

Establishing true integration among members of culturally different groups requires environments in which these people can meet and mix as equals. Sports clubs, universities, work organizations, and armies can assume this role. Some ethnic group cultures produce people with specific skills, like sailors or traders, and such skills can become the basis for their integration in a larger society.

Language and Humor

In most intercultural encounters the parties also speak different native languages. Throughout history this problem has been resolved by the use of trade languages, like Malay, Swahili, or, more and more, derivations of English. *Trade languages* are pidgin forms of original languages, and the trade language of the modern world can be considered a form of business pidgin English. Language differences contribute to cultural misperceptions. In an international training program within IBM, trainers used to rate participants' future career potential. A follow-up study of actual careers during a period of up to eight years afterward showed that the trainers had consistently overestimated participants whose native language was English (the course language) and underestimated those whose languages were French or Italian, with native German speakers taking a middle position.[7]

Communication in trade languages or pidgin limits exchanges to those issues for which these simplified languages have words. To establish a more fundamental intercultural understanding, the foreign partner must acquire the host culture language. Having to express oneself in another language means learning to adopt someone else's reference frame. It is doubtful whether one can be bicultural without also being bilingual.[8] Although the words a language consists of are symbols in terms of the onion diagram (Figure 1.2), which means that they belong to the surface level of a culture, they are also the vehicles of culture transfer. Moreover, words are obstinate vehicles: our thinking is affected by the categories for which words are available in our language.[9] Many words have migrated from their language of origin into others because they express something unique: *management, computer, apartheid, machismo, perestroika, geisha, sauna, Weltanschauung, Weltschmerz, mafia, savoir vivre.*

The skill of expressing oneself in more than one language is unevenly distributed across countries. People from smaller, affluent countries, like the Swiss, Belgians, Scandinavians, Singaporeans, and Dutch, benefit from both frequent contact with foreigners and good educational systems, and therefore they tend to be polyglot. Their organizations possess a strategic advantage in intercultural contacts in that they nearly always have people available who speak several foreign languages, and whoever speaks more than one language will more easily pick up additional ones.

Paradoxically, having English, the world trade language, as one's native tongue is a liability, not an asset, for truly communicating with other cultures. Native English speakers do not always realize this. They are like the proverbial farmer from Kansas, United States, who is supposed to have said, "If English was good enough for Jesus Christ, it is good enough for me."[10] Geert once met an Englishman working near the Welsh border who said he turned down an offer of a beautiful home across the border, in Wales, because in there his young son would have had to learn Welsh as a second language at school. In our view he missed a unique contribution to his son's education as a world citizen.

Language and culture are not so closely linked that sharing a language implies sharing a culture; nor should a difference in language always impose a difference in cultural values. In Belgium, where Dutch and French are the two dominant national languages (there is a small German-speaking area, too), the scores of the Flemish (Dutch-speaking) and Walloon (French-speaking) regions on the four dimensions of the IBM studies were fairly similar, and both regions scored rather like France and different from the Netherlands. This reflects Belgian history: the middle and upper classes used to speak French, whatever the language of their ancestors, and to adopt the French culture; the lower classes in the Flemish part spoke Dutch, whatever the language of their ancestors, but when up-classed they conformed to the culture of the middle classes. The IBM studies included a similar comparison between the German- and French-speaking regions of Switzerland. In this case the picture was different: the German-speaking part scored similar to Germany, and the French-speaking part scored similar to France. Switzerland's historical development was different from Belgium's: in Switzerland the language distribution followed the cantons (independent provinces) rather than the social class structure. This also helps to understand why language is a hot political issue in Belgium but not in Switzerland.[11]

Without knowing the language one will miss a lot of the subtleties of a culture and be forced to remain a relative outsider. One of these subtleties is humor. What is considered funny is highly culture-specific. Many Europeans consider that Germans have no sense of humor, but this simply means they have a different sense of humor. In intercultural encounters the experienced traveler knows that jokes and irony are taboo until one is absolutely sure of the other culture's conception of what represents humor.

Raden Mas Hadjiwibowo, the Indonesian businessman whose description of Javanese family visits was quoted in Chapter 3, has written an insightful analysis of the difference between the Indonesian and the Dutch sense of humor. One of his case studies runs as follows:

It was an ordinary morning with a routine informal office meeting. They all sat around the meeting table, and found themselves short of one chair. Markus, one of the Indonesian managers, looked in the connecting office next door for a spare chair.

The next door office belonged to a Dutch manager, Frans. He was out, but he would not mind lending a chair; all furniture belonged to the firm anyway. Markus was just moving one of Frans' chairs through the connecting door when Frans came in from the other side.

Frans was in a cheerful mood. He walked over to his desk to pick up some papers, and prepared for leaving the room again. In the process he threw Markus a friendly grin and as an afterthought he called over his

shoulder: "You're on a nice stealing spree, Markus?" Then he left, await-
ing no answer.

When Frans returned to his office after lunch, Markus was waiting for
him. Frans noticed Markus had put on a tie, which was unusual. "Markus,
my good friend, what can I do for you?" Frans asked. Markus watched him
gloomily, sat straight in his chair and said firmly and solemnly: "Frans, I
hereby declare that I am not a thief."

Dumbfounded, Frans asked what the hell he was talking about. It took
them another forty-five minutes to resolve the misunderstanding.[12]

In the Dutch culture in which the maintenance of face and status is not a big issue, the "friendly insult" is a common way of joking among friends. "You scoundrel" or "you fool," if pronounced with the right intonation, expresses warm sympathy. In Indonesia where status is sacred, an insult is always taken at its face value. Frans should have known this.

The Influence of Communication Technologies

Popular media often suggest that communication technologies, such as television, e-mail, Internet, and mobile telephones, will bring people around the world together in a global village where cultural differences cease to matter. But this perceived dominance of technology over culture is an illusion. The software of the machines may be globalized, but the software of the minds that use them is not.

Electronic communication enormously increases the amount of information accessible to its users, but it does not increase their capacity to absorb this information, nor does it change their value systems. As users we selectively process information according to our values. Like our parents we read newspapers and watch TV programs that we expect to present our preferred points of view, and confronted with the almost unlimited offer of electronic information, we again pick whatever reinforces our pre-existing ideas. The experience with the Internet has shown that people use it mostly to do things they would have done anyway, only maybe now with the Internet they do these things more often and faster.

Communication technologies increase our consciousness of differences between and within countries. Some disadvantaged peoples, watching TV programs showing how people live elsewhere in the world, will want their share of the world's wealth. Some privileged peoples, informed about suffering and strife elsewhere, will want to close their borders. Dividing the world into good and bad guys is more likely than increased tolerance.

In summary, communication technologies will not by themselves reduce the need for intercultural understanding. When wisely used they may be among the tools for intercultural learning.

Intercultural Encounters in Tourism

Tourism represents the most superficial form of intercultural encounter. Tourists in mass tourism may spend two weeks in Morocco, Bali, or Cancun without finding out anything about the local culture at all. Host country personnel working for tourism will learn something more about the culture of the tourists, but their picture of the way the tourists live at home will be highly distorted. What one picks up from the other group is on the level of symbols (see Figure 1.2): words, fashion articles, music, and so on.

The economic effects of mass tourism on the host countries may or may not be favorable. Traditional sources of income are often destroyed, and the revenues of tourism go to governments and foreign investors, so that the local population may suffer more than it benefits. The environmental effects can be disastrous. Tourism is, from many points of view, a mixed blessing.

Tourism can nevertheless be the starting point for more fundamental intercultural encounters. It breaks the isolation of cultural groups and creates an awareness that there exist other people who have other ways. The seed planted in some minds may ripen later. Some tourists start learning the language and history of the country they have visited and where they want to return. Hosts start learning the tourists' languages to promote their business. Personal friendships develop between the most unlikely people in the most unlikely ways. From an intercultural encounter point of view, the possibilities of tourism probably outweigh the disadvantages.

Intercultural Encounters in Schools

An American teacher at a foreign-language institute in Beijing exclaimed in class, "You lovely girls, I love you." Her students, according to a Chinese observer, were terrified. An Italian professor teaching in the United States complained bitterly about the fact that students were asked to formally evaluate his course. He did not think that students should be the judges of the quality of a professor. An Indian lecturer at an African university saw a student arrive six weeks late for the curriculum, but he had to admit him because he was from the same village as the dean. Intercultural encounters in schools can lead to much perplexity.[13]

Most intercultural encounters in schools are of one of two types: between local teachers and foreign, migrant, or refugee students or between expatriate teachers, hired as foreign experts or sent as missionaries, and local students. Different value patterns in the cultures from which the teacher and the student have come are one source of problems. In Chapters 2 through 6 consequences for the school situation of differences in values related to power distance, individualism, masculinity, uncertainty avoidance, and long- or short-term orientation have been described. They often affect the relationships between teacher and students, among students, and between teacher and parents.

As language is the vehicle of teaching, what was mentioned earlier about the role of language in intercultural encounters applies in its entirety to the teaching situation. The chances for successful cultural adaptation are better if the teacher is to teach in the student's language than if the student has to learn in the teacher's language, because the teacher has more power over the learning situation than any single student.

The course language affects the learning process. At INSEAD, an international business school in France, Geert taught the same executive course in French to one group and in English to another; both groups were composed of people from several nationalities. Discussing a case study in French led to highly stimulating intellectual discussions but few practical conclusions. When the same case was discussed in English, it would not be long before someone asked, "So what?" and the class tried to become pragmatic. Both groups used the same readings, partly from French authors translated into English, partly vice versa. Both groups liked the readings originally written in the class language and condemned the translated ones as "unnecessarily verbose, with a rather meager message which could have been expressed on one or two pages." The comments of the French-language class on the readings translated from English therefore were identical to the comments of the English-language class on the readings translated from French. What is felt to be a message in one language does not necessarily survive the translation process. Information is more than words: it is words that fit into a cultural framework. Culturally adequate translation is an undervalued art.

Beyond differences in language, students and teachers in intercultural encounters run into differences in cognitive abilities. "Our African engineers do not think like engineers; they tend to tackle symptoms, rather than view the equipment as a system" is a quote from a British training manager, unconscious of his own ethnocentrism. Fundamental studies by development psychologists have shown that the things we have learned are determined by the demands of the environment in which we grew up. A person will become good at doing the things that are important to him or her and that he or she has occasion to do often. Being from a generation that predates the introduction of pocket calculators in schools, Geert will perform by heart calculations for which his grandchildren use a machine. Learning abilities, including the development of memory, are rooted in the total pattern of a society. In China the nature of the script (for a moderately literate person, at least three thousand complex characters of up to twenty-four strokes) develops children's ability at pattern recognition, but it also imposes a need for rote learning.

Intercultural problems arise also because expatriate teachers bring irrelevant materials with them. A Congolese friend, studying in Brussels, recalled how at primary school in Lubumbashi her teacher, a Belgian nun, made the children recite in her history lesson *"Nos ancêtres, les Gaulois"* ("Our ancestors, the Gauls"). During a visiting teaching assignment to China, a British lecturer repeated word for word his British organizational behavior course. Much of what students from poor countries learn at universities in rich countries is hardly relevant in their home country situation. What is the interest for a future manager in an Indian company of mathematical modeling of the U.S. stock market? The know-how supposed to make a person succeed in an industrial country is not necessarily the same as what will help the development of a country presently poor.

Finally, intercultural problems can be based on institutional differences in the societies from which the teachers and students have come, differences that generate different expectations as to the educational process and the role of various parties in it. From what types of families are students and teachers recruited? Are educational systems elitist or antielitist? A visiting U.S. professor in a Latin American country may think she contributes to the economic development of the country, while in actual fact she only contributes to the continuation of elite privileges. What role do employers play in the educational system? In Switzerland and Germany, traineeships in industry or business are a respected alternative to a university education, allowing people to reach the highest positions, but this is not the case in most other countries. What role do the state and/or religious bodies play? In some countries (France, Russia) the government prescribes the curriculum in great detail; in others the teachers are free to define their own. In countries where both private and public schools exist, the private sector may be for the elites (United States) or for the dropouts (the Netherlands, Switzerland). Where does the money for the schools come from? How well are teachers paid and what is their social status? In China teachers are traditionally highly respected but poorly paid. In Britain the status of teachers has traditionally been low; in Germany and Japan, high.

Minorities, Migrants, and Refugees

What is considered minorities in a country is a matter of definition. It depends on hard facts like the distribution of the population, the economic situation of population groups, and the intensity of their interrelations. It also depends on cultural values (especially uncertainty avoidance and collectivism) and on cultural practices (languages, felt and attributed identities, interpretations of history). These affect the ideology of the majority and sometimes also of the minority and their level of mutual prejudice and discrimination. Minority problems are always also, and often primarily, majority problems.

Minorities in the world include a great variety of groups, of widely varying status, from underclass to entrepreneurial and/or academic elite, including:

- Original populations overrun by immigrants (like Native Americans, Australian Aborigines)
- Descendants of economic, political, or ethnic migrants or refugees (now the majorities in countries like the United States and Australia)
- Descendants of imported labor (like American blacks, Mediterraneans in northwestern Europe)

- Natives of former colonies (like Indians and Pakistanis in Britain, North Africans in France)
- International nomads (Sinti and Roma people—Gypsies—in most of Europe and partly even overseas)

In many countries the minority picture is highly volatile because of ongoing migration. The number of people in the second half of the twentieth century who left their native country and moved to a completely different environment is larger than ever before in human history. The effect in all cases is that persons and entire families are parachuted into cultural environments vastly different from the ones in which they were mentally programmed, often without any preparation. They have to learn a new language, but a much larger problem is that they have to function in a new culture:

Hassan Bel Ghazi, a Moroccan immigrant to the Netherlands, wrote:

Imagine: One day you get up, you look around but you can't believe your eyes. . . . Everything is upside down, inside as well as outside. . . . You try to put things back in their old place but alas—they are upside down forever. You take your time, you look again, and then you have an idea: "I'll put myself upside down too, just like everything else, to be able to handle things." It doesn't work. . . . And the world doesn't understand why you stand right.[14]

Political ideologies about majority-minority relations vary strongly. Racists and ultrarightists want to close borders and expel present minorities—or worse. Civilized governments' policies aim somewhere between two poles on a continuum. One pole is *assimilation*, which means that minority citizens should become like everybody else and lose their distinctiveness as quickly as possible. The other pole is *integration*, which implies that minority citizens, while accepted as full members of the host society, are at the same time encouraged to retain a link with their roots and their collective identity. Paradoxically, policies aiming at integration have led to better and faster adaptation of minorities than policies enforcing assimilation.

Migrants and refugees often came in as presumed temporary expatriates but turned out to be stayers. In nearly all cases they moved from a more traditional, collectivist to a more individualist society. For their adaptation it is important that they find support in a community of compatriots in the country of migration, especially if they are single, but even when they come with their families, which anyway represent a much narrower group than they were accustomed to in their home country. Maintaining migrant communities fits into the integration philosophy previously described. Unfortunately host country politicians from their individualist value position often fear the forming of migrant ghettos and try to disperse the foreigners, falsely assuming this will speed up their adaptation.

Migrants and refugees usually also experience differences in power distance. Host societies tend to be more egalitarian than the places the migrants have come from. Migrants experience this negatively and positively—lack of respect for elders but better accessibility of authorities and teachers, although they tend to distrust authorities at first. Differences on masculinity-femininity and on uncertainty avoidance between migrants and hosts may go either way, and the corresponding adaptation problems are specific to the pairs of cultures involved.

First-generation migrant families experience standard dilemmas. At work, in shops and public offices, and usually also at school, they interact with locals, learn some local practices, and are confronted with local values. At home they try to maintain the practices, values, and relationship patterns from their country of origin. They are marginal people between two worlds, and they alternate daily between one and the other.

The effect of this marginality is different for the different generations and genders. The immigrating adults are unlikely to trade their home country values for those of the host country; at best they make small adaptations. The *father* tries to maintain his traditional authority in the home, but at work his status is often low. Migrants start in jobs nobody else wants. The family knows this, and he loses face with his relatives. If he is unemployed this makes him lose face even more. He frequently has problems with the local language, which makes him feel a fool. Sometimes he is illiterate even in his own language. He has to call for the help of his children or of social workers in filling out forms and dealing with the authorities. He is often discriminated against by employers, police, authorities, and neighbors. The *mother* in some migrant cultures is virtually a prisoner in the home, locked up when the father has gone to work. In these cases she has no contact with the host society, does not learn the language, and remains completely dependent on her husband and children. In other cases the mother has a job, too. She may be the main breadwinner of the family, a severe blow to the father's self-respect. She meets other men, and her husband may suspect her of unfaithfulness. The marriage sometimes breaks up. Yet there is no way back. Migrants who have returned home often find they do not fit anymore and remigrate, this time for good.

The second generation, children born in or brought early to the new country, acquires conflicting mental programs from the family side and from the local school and community side. Their values reflect partly their parents' culture and partly their new country's, with wide variations between individuals, groups, and host countries.[15] The *sons* suffer most from their marginality. Some succeed miraculously well, and benefiting from the better educational opportunities, they enter skilled and professional occupations. Others, escaping parental authority at home, drop out of school and find collectivist protection in street gangs; they risk becoming a new underclass in the host society. The *daughters* often adapt better, although their parents worry more about them. At school they are exposed to an equality between the genders unknown in the society from which they have come. Sometimes parents hurry them into the safety of an arranged marriage with a compatriot.[16]

Yet many of these problems are transitional; third-generation migrants are mostly absorbed into the host country population, with host country values, and are only distinguishable by a foreign family name and maybe by specific religious and family traditions. This three-generation adaptation process has also operated in past generations; an increasing share of the population of modern societies descends partly from foreign migrants.

Whether migrant groups are thus integrated or fail to adapt and turn into permanent minorities depends as much on the majority as on the migrants themselves. Agents of the host society who interact frequently with minorities, migrants, and refugees can do a lot to facilitate their integration. They are the police, social workers, doctors, nurses, personnel officers, counter clerks in government offices, and teachers. Migrants coming from large-power-distance, collectivist cultures may distrust such authorities more than locals do, for cultural reasons. Yet teachers, for example, can benefit from the respect their status earns them from the parents of their migrant students. They will have to *invite* those parents (especially fathers) for discussion; the social distance perceived by the migrant parents is much larger than most teachers are accustomed to. Unfortunately in any host society, a share of the locals (politicians, police, journalists, teachers, neighbors) fall victim to ethnocentric and racist philosophies, compounding the felony of the migrants' in-adaptation through primitive manifestations of uncertainty avoidance: "What is different is dangerous."

Particular expertise is demanded from mental health professionals dealing with migrants and refugees. Ways of dealing with health and disability differ considerably between collectivist and individualist societies. The high level of acculturative stress in migrants puts them at risk for mental health disorders, and methods of psychiatric treatment developed for host country patients may not work for migrants, for cultural reasons. Countries with a large migrant population like Australia recognize transcultural psychiatry (and transcultural clinical psychology) as a special field. Some psychiatrists and psychologists specialize in the treatment of political refugees suffering from the aftereffects of war or torture.

Not only host country citizens can be blamed for racism and ethnocentrism; migrants themselves sometimes behave in racist and ethnocentric ways, toward other migrants and toward hosts. Living in an unfamiliar and often hostile environment, the migrants can be said to have a better excuse. Some resort to religious fundamentalisms, while at home they were hardly religious at all. Fundamentalism is often found among marginal groups in society, and these migrants are the new marginals.

Intercultural Negotiations

Negotiations, whether in politics or in business and whether international or not, share some universal characteristics:

- Two or more parties with (partly) conflicting interests
- A common need for agreement because of an expected gain from such agreement
- An initially undefined outcome
- A means of communication between parties
- A control and decision-making structure on either side by which negotiators are linked to their superiors or to their constituency

Books have been published on the art of negotiation; it is a popular theme for training courses. Negotiations have even been simulated on computers. The theories and computer models, however, nearly always use assumptions about the values and objectives of the negotiators taken from

Western societies, in particular from the United States. In international negotiations different players may hold different values and objectives.[17]

National cultures will affect negotiation processes in the following several ways:

- Power distance will affect the degree of centralization of the control and decision-making structure and the importance of the status of the negotiators.
- Collectivism will affect the need for stable relationships between (opposing) negotiators. In a collectivist culture replacement of a person means that a new relationship will have to be built, which takes time. Mediators (go-betweens) have an important role in maintaining a viable pattern of relationships that allows progress.
- Masculinity will affect the need for ego-boosting behavior and the sympathy for the strong on the part of negotiators and their superiors, as well as the tendency to resolve conflicts by a show of force. Feminine cultures are more likely to resolve conflicts by compromise and to strive for consensus.
- Uncertainty avoidance will affect the (in)tolerance of ambiguity and (dis)trust in opponents who show unfamiliar behaviors, as well as the need for structure and ritual in the negotiation procedures.
- Long-term orientation affects the perseverance to achieve desired ends even at the cost of sacrifices.

Effective intercultural negotiations demand an insight into the range of cultural values to be expected among partners from other countries, in comparison with the negotiator's own culturally determined values. They also demand language and communication skills to guarantee that the messages sent to the other party or parties will be understood in the way they were meant by the sender. They finally demand organization skills for planning and arranging meetings and facilities, involving mediators and interpreters, and handling external communications.

Experienced diplomats from whatever country have usually acquired a professional savoir faire that enables them to negotiate successfully with other diplomats on issues on which they are empowered to decide themselves. The problem, however, is that in issues of real importance diplomats are usually directed by politicians who have the power but not the diplomatic savoir faire. Politicians often make statements intended for domestic use, which the diplomats are supposed to explain to foreign negotiation partners. The amount of discretion left to diplomats is in itself a cultural characteristic that varies from one society and political system to another. Modern communication possibilities contribute to limiting the discretion of diplomats; Morier's English Elchi did have a lot of discretionary power by the simple fact that communicating with England in those days took at least three months. Yet there is no doubt that the quality of intercultural encounters in international negotiations can contribute to avoiding unintended conflict *if* the actors are of the proper hierarchical level for the decisions at stake. This is why summit conferences are so important—here are the people who do have the power to negotiate. Unfortunately they usually rose to their present position because they hold strong convictions in harmony with the national values of their country, and for this same reason they have difficulty recognizing that others function according to different mental programs. A trusted foreign minister or ambassador who has both the ear of the top leader *and* diplomatic sensitivity is a great asset to a country.

Permanent international organizations, such as the various United Nations agencies, the European Commission, and the North Atlantic Treaty Organisation, have developed their own organizational cultures, which affect their internal international negotiations. Even more so than in the case of the diplomats' occupational culture, these organizational cultures reside at the more superficial level of practices, common symbols, and rituals rather than of shared values. Exceptions are "missionary" international nongovernmental organizations (NGOs), such as the International Committee of the Red Cross, Amnesty International, or Greenpeace.

Thus the behavior of international negotiators is influenced by culture at three levels: national, occupational, and organizational.

Business negotiations differ from political negotiations in that the actors are more often amateurs in the negotiation field. Specialists can prepare negotiations, but especially if one partner is from a large-power-distance culture, persons with appropriate power and status have to be brought in for the formal agreement. International negotiations have become a special topic in business education, so hopefully future generations of business persons will be better prepared. In the following we will argue for the need for corporate diplomats in multinationals.

Multinational Business Organizations

If intercultural encounters are as old as humanity, multinational business is as old as organized states. Business professor Karl Moore and historian David Lewis have described four cases of multinational business in the Mediterranean area between 1900 and 100 B.C., run by Assyrians, Phoenicians, Greeks, and Romans. History does not justify claims that one particular type of capitalism is inevitably and forever superior to everything else.[18]

The functioning of multinational business organizations hinges on intercultural communication and cooperation. Chapter 8 related shared values to *national* cultures and shared practices to *organizational* (corporate) cultures. Multinationals abroad meet alien value patterns, but their shared practices (symbols, heroes, and rituals) keep the organization together.

The basic values of a multinational business organization are determined by the nationality and personality of its founder(s) and later significant leaders. Multinationals with a dominant home culture have a clearer set of basic values and therefore are easier to run than international organizations that lack such a common frame of reference. In multinational business organizations the values and beliefs of the home culture are taken for granted and serve as a frame of reference at the head office. Persons in linchpin roles between foreign subsidiaries and the head office need to be bicultural, because they need a double trust relationship, on the one side with their home culture superiors and colleagues and on the other side with their host culture subordinates. Two roles are particularly crucial:

1. **The country business unit manager:** he or she reports to an international head office.
2. **The corporate diplomat:** he or she is a home country or other national impregnated with the corporate culture, whose occupational background may vary but who is experienced in living and functioning in various foreign cultures. Corporate diplomats are essential to make multinational structures work, as liaisons in the national or regional head offices or as temporary managers for new ventures.[19]

Other managers and members of foreign national subsidiaries do not have to be bicultural. Even if the foreign subsidiaries formally adopt home culture ideas and policies, they will internally function according to the value systems and beliefs of the host culture.

As mentioned earlier in this chapter, biculturality implies bilingualism. There is a difference in coordination strategy between most U.S. and most non-U.S. multinational organizations. Most American multinationals put the burden of biculturality on the foreign nationals. It is the latter who are bi- or multilingual (most American executives in multinationals are monolingual). This goes together with a relatively short stay of American executives abroad; two to five years per foreign country is fairly typical. These executives often live in ghettos. The main tool of coordination consists of unified worldwide policies that can be maintained with a regularly changing composition of the international staff because they are highly formalized. Most non-American multinationals put the burden of biculturality on their own home country nationals. They are almost always multilingual (with the possible exception of the British, although even these are usually more skilled in other languages than the Americans). The typical period of stay in another country tends to be longer, between five and fifteen years or more, so that expatriate executives of non-American multinationals may "go native" in the host country; they mix more with the local population, have their children in local schools, and live less frequently in ghettos. The main tool of coordination is these expatriate home country nationals, rather than formal procedures.[20]

Biculturality is difficult to acquire after childhood, and the number of failures would be larger, were it not that what is necessary for the proper functioning of multinational organizations is only *task-related biculturality*. With regard to other aspects of life—tastes, hobbies, religious feelings, and private relations—expatriate multinational executives can afford to, and usually do, remain monocultural.

Chapter 7 argued that implicit models of organizations in people's minds depend primarily on the combination of power distance and uncertainty avoidance. Differences in power distance are more manageable than differences in uncertainty avoidance. In particular, organizations headquartered in smaller-power-distance cultures usually adapt successfully in larger-power-distance countries. Local managers in high-PDI subsidiaries can learn to use an authoritative style even if their international bosses behave in a more participative fashion.

Chapter 2 opened with the story of the French general Bernadotte's culture shock after he became king of Sweden. A Frenchman sent as a regional sales manager to Copenhagen by a French cosmetics company told Geert about his first day in the Copenhagen office. He called his secretary and gave her an order in the same way as he would do in Paris. But instead of saying, "Oui, Monsieur," as he expected her to do, the Danish woman looked at him, smiled, and said, "Why do you want this to be done?"

Countries with large-power-distance cultures have rarely produced large multinationals; multinational operations demand a higher level of trust than is normal in these countries, and they do not permit the centralization of authority that managers at headquarters in these countries need in order to feel comfortable.

Differences in uncertainty avoidance represent a serious problem for the functioning of multinationals, whichever way they go. This is because if rules mean different things in different countries, it is difficult to keep the organization together. In weak uncertainty avoidance cultures like the United States and even more in Britain and, for example, Sweden, managers and nonmanagers alike feel definitely uncomfortable with systems of rigid rules, especially if it is evident that many of these are never followed. In strong uncertainty avoidance cultures like most of the Latin world, people feel equally uncomfortable without the structure of a system of rules, even if many of these are impractical and impracticable. At either pole of the uncertainty avoidance dimension, people's feelings are fed by deep psychological needs, related to the control of aggression and to basic security in the face of the unknown (see Chapter 5).

Organizations moving to unfamiliar cultural environments are often badly surprised by unexpected *reactions of the public or the authorities* to what they do or want to do. Perhaps the effect of the collective values of a society is nowhere as clear as in this case. These values have been institutionalized partly in the form of legislation (and in the way in which legislation is applied, which may differ considerably from what is actually written in the law); in labor union structures, programs, and power positions; and in the existence of organizations of stakeholders, such as consumers or environmentalists. The values are partly invisible to the newcomer, but they become all too visible in press reactions, government decisions, or organized actions by uninvited interest groups. A few infer-ences from the value differences exposed in Chapters 2 through 6 with regard to the reactions of the local environment are:

- Civic action groups are more likely to be formed in low-PDI, low-UAI cultures than elsewhere.
- Business corporations will have to be more concerned with informing the public in low-PDI, low-UAI cultures than elsewhere.
- Public sympathy and legislation on behalf of economically and socially weak members of society are more likely in low-MAS countries.
- Public sympathy and both government and private funding for aid to economically weak countries and in the case of disasters anywhere in the world will be stronger in affluent low-MAS countries than in affluent high-MAS countries.
- Public sympathy and legislation on behalf of environmental conservation and maintaining the quality of life are more likely in low-PDI, low-MAS countries.

In world business there is a growing tendency for tariff and technological advantages to wear off, which automatically shifts competition, besides toward economic factors, toward cultural advantages or disadvantages. On the five dimensions of national culture, any position of a country offers potential competitive advantages as well as disadvantages; these are summarized in Table 9.1.

Table 9.1 shows that no country can be good at everything; cultural strengths imply cultural weaknesses. Chapter 8 arrived at a similar conclusion with regard to organizational cultures. This is a strong argument for making cultural considerations part of strategic planning and locating activities in countries, in regions, and in organizational units that possess the cultural characteristics necessary for competing in these activities.

Coordinating Multinationals: Structure Should Follow Culture

Most multinational corporations cover a range of different businesses and/or product or market divisions, in a range of countries. They have to bridge both national and business cultures.

TABLE 9.1 Competitive Advantages of Different Cultural Profiles in International Competition

Power Distance (small) Acceptance of responsibility	**Power Distance (large)** Discipline
Uncertainty Avoidance (weak) Basic innovations	**Uncertainty Avoidance (strong)** Precision
Collectivism Employee commitment	**Individualism** Management mobility
Femininity Personal service Custom-made products Agriculture Food Biochemistry	**Masculinity** Mass production Efficiency Heavy industry Chemistry Bulk chemistry
Short-Term Orientation Fast adaptation	**Long-Term Orientation** Developing new markets

The purpose of any organizational structure is the coordination of activities. These activities are carried out in business units, each involved in one type of business in one country. The design of a corporate structure is based on three choices, whether explicit or implicit, for each business unit:

1. Which of the unit's in- and outputs should be coordinated from elsewhere in the corporation?
2. Where should the coordination take place?
3. How tight or loose should the coordination be?

Multinational, multibusiness corporations face the choice between coordination along type-of-business lines or along geographic lines. The key question is whether business know-how or cultural know-how is more crucial for the success of the operation. The classic solution is a *matrix* structure. This means that every manager of a business unit has two bosses, one who coordinates the particular type of business across all countries, and one who coordinates all business units in the particular country. Matrix structures are costly, often requiring a doubling of the management ranks, and their functioning may raise more problems than it resolves. Yet a single structural principle is unlikely to fit for an entire corporation. In some cases the business structure should dominate; in others geographic coordination should have priority. The result is a patchwork structure that may lack beauty but that does follow the needs of markets and business unit cultures. Its justification is that variety within the environment in which a company operates should be matched with appropriate internal variety. The diversity in structural solutions advocated is one not only of place but also of time: optimal solutions will very likely change over time, so periodic reshufflings make sense.

Expanding Multinationals: International Mergers and Other Ventures

Mergers, acquisitions, joint ventures, and alliances across national borders have become quite frequent,[21] but they remain a regular source of cross-cultural clashes. Cross-national ventures have often turned out to be dramatic failures. Leyland-Innocenti, Vereinigte Flugzeugwerke–Fokker and later DASA-Fokker, Hoogovens-Hoesch and later Hoogovens–British Steel, Citroen-Fiat, Renault-Volvo, Daimler-Chrysler, and Alitalia-KLM are just a few of the more notorious ones. There is little doubt that the list will continue growing as long as management decisions about international ventures are based solely on financial considerations. They are part of a big money and power game and seen as a defense against (real or imaginary) threats by competitors. Those making the decisions rarely imagine the operating problems that arise inside the newly formed hybrid organizations. Within countries such ventures have a dubious success record, but across borders they are even less likely to succeed. If cultural conditions do look favorable, the cultural integration of the new cooperative structure should still be managed—it does not happen by itself. Cultural integration takes a great deal of time, energy, and money unforeseen by the financial experts who designed the venture.

Five ways of international expansion can be distinguished, in increasing order of cultural risk: (1) the greenfield start, (2) the international strategic alliance, (3) the joint venture with a foreign partner, (4) the foreign acquisition, and (5) the cross-national merger.

The *greenfield start* means that the corporation sets up a foreign subsidiary from scratch, usually sending over one expatriate or a small team who hires locals and gradually builds a local branch. Greenfield starts are by their very nature slow, but their cultural risk is limited. The founders of the subsidiary can carefully select host country employees who fit the corporation's culture. The culture of the subsidiary becomes a combination of national elements (mainly values; see Chapter 8) and corporate elements (mainly practices; see again Chapter 8). Greenfield starts have a high success rate. The IBM Corporation, many other older multinationals, and international accounting firms until the 1980s almost exclusively grew through greenfield starts.

The *international strategic alliance* is a prudent way of cooperation between existing partners. Without creating a new venture, the partners agree to collaborate on specific products and/or markets for mutual benefit. As the risks are limited to the project at hand, this is a safe way of learning to know each other; neither party's existence is at stake. The acquaintance could develop into a joint venture or merger, but in this case the partners should know each other's culture sufficiently to recognize the cultural pitfalls.

The *joint venture with a foreign partner* creates a new business by pooling resources from two or more founding parties. The venture can be started greenfield, or the local partner can transfer part of its people wholesale to the venture. In the latter case it, of course, transfers part of its culture as well. The cultural risk of joint ventures can be controlled by clear agreements about which partner supplies which resources, including what part of management. Joint ventures in which one partner provides the entire management have a higher success rate than those in which management responsibility is shared. Foreign joint ventures can develop new and creative cultural characteristics, based on synergy of elements from the founding partners. They are a limited-risk way of entering an unknown country and market. Not infrequently, eventually one of the partners buys the other(s) out.

In the *foreign acquisition* a local company is purchased wholesale by a foreign buyer. The acquired company has its own history and its own organizational culture; on top of this it represents a national culture differing from the acquiring corporation's national culture. Foreign acquisitions are a fast way of expanding, but their cultural risk is considerable. To use an analogy from family life (such analogies are popular for describing the relationships between parts of corporations), foreign acquisitions are to green-field starts as the bringing up of a foster child, adopted in puberty, is to the bringing up of one's own child. In order to overcome the problems of integrating the new member, one solution is to keep it at arm's length—that is, not to integrate it but to treat it as a portfolio investment. But usually this is not why the foreign company has been purchased. When integration is imperative, the cultural clashes are often resolved by brute power: key people are replaced by the corporation's own men and women. In other cases key people have not waited for this to happen and have left on their own account. Foreign acquisitions often lead to a destruction of human capital, which is eventually a destruction of financial capital as well. The same applies for acquisitions in the home country, but abroad the cultural risk is even larger. It is advisable to let foreign (and domestic) acquisitions be preceded by an analysis of the cultures of the corporation and of the acquisition candidate. If the decision is still to go ahead, such a match analysis can be used as the basis for a culture management plan.

The *cross-national merger* poses all the problems of the foreign acquisition, plus the complication that power has to be shared. Cultural problems can no longer be resolved by unilateral decisions. Cross-national mergers are therefore extremely risky.[22] Even more than in the case of the foreign acquisition, an analysis of the corporate and national cultures of the potential partners should be part of the process of deciding to merge. If the merger is concluded, this analysis can again be the basis of a culture integration plan that needs the active and permanent support of a *Machtpromotor* (see Chapter 8), probably the chief executive.

Two classic products of successful cross-national mergers are Royal Dutch Shell (dating from 1907) and Unilever (dating from 1930), both the result of Dutch-British mergers. They show a few common characteristics: the smaller country holds the majority of shares, *two* head offices have been maintained so as to avoid the impression that the corporation is run from one of the two countries only, there has been strong and charismatic leadership during the integration phase, there has been an external threat that kept the partners together for survival, and governments have stayed out of the business.

A highly visible international project that is a combination of a strategic alliance and a joint venture is the Airbus consortium in Toulouse, France. Airbus has become one of the two largest aircraft manufacturers in the world. Parts of the planes are manufactured by the participating companies in Britain, Germany, and Spain and then flown over to Toulouse, where the planes are assembled.

International Marketing, Advertising, and Consumer Behavior

Culture is present in the design and quality of many products and in the presentation of many services. An example is the difference in passenger aircraft cockpit design between Airbus (European, primarily French or German) and Boeing (U.S.). The Airbus has been designed to fly itself with minimum interference from the pilot, while the Boeing expects more discretion from and interaction with the pilot.[23] The Airbus is the product of an uncertainty avoiding design culture; the Boeing respects the pilot's supposed need to feel in command.

In 1983 Harvard University Professor Theodore Levitt published an article, "The Globalization of Markets," in which he predicted that technology and modernity would lead to a worldwide convergence of consumers' needs and desires. This should enable global companies to develop standard brands with universal marketing and advertising programs. In the 1990s more and more voices in the marketing literature expressed doubts about this convergence and referred to our culture indices to explain persistent cultural differences.[24] Chapters 3 through 7 provided ample evidence of significant correlations of consumer behavior data with the five indices, mainly based on research by Professor Marieke de Mooij. Analyzing national consumer behavior data over time, de Mooij showed that contrary to Levitt's prediction, buying and consumption patterns in affluent countries in the 1980s and '90s diverged as much as they converged. Affluence implies more possibilities to choose among products and services, and consumers' choices reflected psychological and social influences. De Mooij wrote:

> *Consumption decisions can be driven by functional or social needs. Clothes satisfy a functional need, fashion satisfies a social need. Some personal care products serve functional needs, others serve social needs. A house serves a functional, a home a social need. Culture influences what type of house people live in, how they relate to their homes and how they tend to their homes. A car may satisfy a functional need, but the type of car for most people satisfies a social need. Social needs are culture-bound.[25]*

De Mooij's analysis of the development of the market for private cars across fifteen European countries shows that the number of cars per one thousand inhabitants depended less and less on income: it was strongly related to national wealth in 1969 but no longer in 1994. This could be read as a sign of *convergence*. However, the preference for new over secondhand cars in both periods did not depend on wealth but only on uncertainty avoidance: uncertainty-tolerant cultures continued buying more used cars, without any convergence between countries. Owning two cars in one family in 1970 related to national wealth, but in 1997 it only related to masculinity. In masculine cultures husband and wife each wanted their own car; in equally wealthy feminine cultures they more often shared a car. In this respect there has been a *divergence* between countries.

From the cultural indices, UAI and MAS resist convergence most: UAI is mostly, and MAS entirely, independent of wealth, and therefore unaffected by it. Uncertainty avoidance stands for differences in the need for purity and for expert knowledge; masculinity versus femininity "explains differences in the need for success as a component of status, resulting in a varying appeal of status products across countries. It also explains the roles of males and females in buying and in family decision making."[26] Such differences are often overlooked by globally oriented marketeers who assume their own cultural choices on these dimensions to be universal.

The literature on *advertising* in the 1990s has increasingly stressed the need for cultural differentiation. On the basis of more than 3,400 TV commercials from eleven countries, de Mooij identified specific advertising styles for countries, linked to cultural themes. For example, single-person pictures are rare in collectivist cultures (if nobody wants to join this person, the product must be bad!). Discussions between mothers and daughters are a theme in both large- and small-power-distance cultures, but where PDI is high mothers advise daughters, and where it is low daughters advise mothers.

The same global brand may appeal to different cultural themes in different countries. Advertising, and television advertising in particular, is directed at the inner motivation of prospective buyers. TV commercials can be seen as modern equivalents of the myths and fairytales of previous generations, told and retold because they harmonize with the software in people's minds—and in spite of Professor Levitt's prediction, these minds have not been and will not be globalized.[27]

Further cultural differentiation, even in firms with globalized marketing approaches, is provided by the intermediate role of local sales forces who translate (sometimes literally) the marketing message to the local customers.[28] For example, the degree of directness a salesperson can use is highly culturally dependent. Ways of management and compensation of sales forces should be based on cultural values (theirs and the customers') and on characteristics of the industry. Conceptions of business ethics for salespersons vary strongly from one culture to another; they are a direct operationalization of some of the values involved in the culture indices.

Even less than the markets for goods, markets for services support globalization. Services are by their very nature personalized toward the customer. International companies in the service field tend to leave considerable marketing discretion to local management.

Any traveler in a new country knows the insecurity about how to relate to personal service personnel: when to give tips, in what way, and how much. Tipping customs differ by country; they reflect the mutual roles of client and service person (uncertainty avoidance) and stress their inequality (power distance).

Chances for globalization are relatively better for *industrial marketing*, the business-to-business area where international purchasers and international salespersons meet. Technical standards are crucial and participation in their establishment is a major industrial marketing instrument, in which negotiation processes, as described in a previous section, become very important.

International Politics and International Organizations

Glen Fisher, a retired U.S. foreign service officer, has written a perceptive book called *Mindsets* on the role of culture in international relations. In the introduction to the chapter titled "The Cultural Lens," he states:

> *Working in international relations is a special endeavor because one has to deal with entirely new patterns of mindsets. To the extent that they can be identified and anticipated for particular groups or even nations, some of the mystery inherent in the conduct of "foreign" affairs will diminish.*[29]

Different mind-sets must have played a role in the history of nations as long as there have been nations. Dutch sociologist Cornelis Lammers has demonstrated this on a case study from the early eighteenth century in the Spanish Netherlands (present-day Belgium). After the departure of the

Spanish overlords, during a period of some ten years (1706–16), the territory was occupied partly by French troops, partly by British, and partly by
Dutch. From the available records, Lammers has compared the different
regimes established by the three different occupying nations. The French
tried to reform obsolete institutions and to establish a French style of centralized, rationalized authority. The English and Dutch kept the old order
intact, but from these the Dutch tried to convince the local authorities to
modernize in the name of efficiency; the English kept at arm's length and
tried to get as little involved in civil affairs as possible.[30] We recognize
stronger power distance plus uncertainty avoidance in the French approach
as opposed to both the English and the Dutch, and from the latter two the
Dutch showed their femininity in attempts at governing by consensus.

Each of Chapters 2 through 6 has related a cultural values dimension
to national political *processes* and/or political *issues*. The former are the ways
the political game is played; the latter are the problems to which country
politicians attach priority, and which they tend to defend on the international scene. These chapters showed that relationships between values and
politics should always be seen against the backdrop of a country's national
wealth or poverty; the implication of values is moderated by the level of
economic prosperity.

Differences in power distance and uncertainty avoidance affect primarily the political processes. Larger power distance implies political centralization, lack of cooperation between citizens and authorities, and more
political violence. Stronger uncertainty avoidance implies more rules and
laws, more government intervention in the economy, and perceived incom-
petence of citizens versus authorities; both larger power distance and
stronger uncertainty avoidance imply more perceived corruption, after
elimination of the effect of national poverty.

Individualism-collectivism and masculinity-femininity affect primarily the issues countries will defend. Individualism implies concern with
human rights, political democracy, and market capitalism; collectivism with
group interests. Masculinity implies a focus on economic growth and competition and a belief in technology; femininity on supporting the needy in
the country (welfare) and in the world (development cooperation) and on
preservation of the global environment. Masculinity versus femininity
relates to political processes in that in masculine cultures the political discourse is more adversarial, in feminine cultures more consensus oriented.

Long- versus short-term orientation relates to pragmatism in politics versus fundamentalism: the latter means a focus on principles, even ineffective ones, and vested rights.

The influences of values and of economic prosperity imply that a number of Western political axioms cannot be applied to non-Western countries and are not very helpful as global guidelines:

1. The solution of pressing global problems does not presuppose worldwide democracy. The rest of the world is not going Western. Authoritarian governments will continue to prevail in most of the world. Elections are not a universal solution to political problems. In poor, collectivist, high-PDI and strong UAI cultures, elections may generate more problems than they resolve. One example is Algeria, where the first general elections in 1990 were won by fundamentalists committed to end political freedoms, after which the military declared the results invalid, and a wave of terrorism set in, which lasted for eight years and made tens of thousands of victims. Another example is Russia, where the disappearance of communism and of the Soviet Union in 1991 left a power vacuum; institutions necessary to execute democratically taken decisions were missing, and the local mafia established a kleptocracy (government by thieves).

2. Free market capitalism cannot be universal; it presumes an individualist mentality that is missing in most of the world. Chapter 3 showed a statistical relationship between individualism and national wealth, but with the arrow of causality from wealth to individualism: countries became more individualist after they increased in wealth, not wealthier by becoming more individualist. Free market capitalism suits countries already wealthy and is unlikely to turn poor countries into wealthy ones. The "dragon" economies of East Asia that grew rapidly in the mid-1960s to mid-1990s had a variety of economic systems with often strong involvement of government.

3. An additional problem that economists seldom address is the ecological cost of economic development. The Western democracies' standard of living implies a degree of environmental pollution and depletion of resources that precludes extending this standard of living to the entire world population. Whoever seeks development for everybody should find a new way of handling our ecosystem: sustaining the

rich countries' quality of life but drastically reducing its ecological cost. The concept of economic growth may in this respect already be obsolete; another measure for the quality and survival power of economic and ecological systems will have to be found.

4. Concepts of human rights cannot be universal. The Universal Declaration of Human Rights, adopted in 1948, was based on individualist Western values that were not and are not shared by the political leaders nor by the populations of the collectivist majority of the world population. Without losing the benefits of the present declaration, which in an imperfect way presents at least a norm used to appeal against gross violations, the international community should revise the declaration to include, for example, the rights of groups and minorities. On the basis of such a revised declaration, victims of political and religious fundamentalisms can be protected; this protection should prevail over national sovereignty.

Public and nongovernmental organizations that span national boundaries depend, for their functioning, entirely on intercultural communication and cooperation. Most international organizations are not supposed to have a home national culture; key decision makers usually have to come from different countries. Examples are the United Nations with its subsidiaries like UNESCO and UNIDO, the European Union, the International Labour Organization, or the World Council of Churches. Others have an implicit home culture related to their past: religious organizations like the Roman Catholic Church (Italian) and the Mormon Church (American) and humanitarian organizations like the Red Cross (Swiss) and Amnesty International (British).

Confederations like the United Nations or the European Union by definition should not have a dominant national culture. This is less a problem for the political part of such organizations, in which people are supposed to act as representatives of their own countries and to settle their differences by negotiation. It is, however, a considerable problem in daily operations where people are not supposed to represent their countries but the organization as such. Organizations can function only if their members share some kind of culture—if together they can take certain things for granted. In the daily operations of the UN and the EU, few things can be taken for granted. Personnel selection, nomination, and promotion procedures have to take account of arguments other than suitability for the job. Key persons may be transferred before they have learned their jobs; objectives are often unclear and where they are clear, means-ends relations are nebulous. Such organizations can escape from ineffectiveness and waste only by the development of a strong organizational culture at the level of shared practices (see Chapter 8). A good system of performance evaluation is critical. Differences in nationality within these organizations again affect both the *process* and the *content* of the organization's work: the way the organization's bureaucracy functions and the projects the organization decides to undertake. Like in the case of national politics, process is primarily linked with power distance and uncertainty avoidance, and content relates to individualism and masculinity.

Ad hoc international actions, such as joint military interventions and peacekeeping missions, are fraught with cultural conflict potential, not only between foreign military personnel and local populations, but also between nationalities within the foreign forces. The success of such actions calls for expert culture management skills.[31]

Economic Development, Nondevelopment, and Development Cooperation

The nineteenth and the first half of the twentieth century was the age of Europe; Europeans and their offspring overseas were the "lords of humankind,"[32] who colonized most of the outside world while wealth flowed from outside to inside. World War II was the breaking point that completely changed the relationships between continents and between rich and poor countries. In the thirty years after the war, nearly all former colonies became independent. Freedom from want became recognized as a fundamental human right, and around 1950 programs of development aid were gradually started, financed by the rich countries and with the poor ones as receivers. Between 1950 and 2000 the equivalent of more than a trillion U.S. dollars of public money from the rich countries was spent on the development of the poor ones.

In Chapter 4 it was shown that the percentage of their gross national products that governments of rich countries have allocated to development cooperation varies considerably (Denmark in 2000 spending more than ten times as much as the United States) and that this percentage was strongly correlated with the rich countries' femininity scores. Development assistance money is allocated according to the (psychological) needs of the donor countries more than according to the material needs of the receivers.

Looking back to half a century of development assistance, most observers agree that the effectiveness of much of the spending has been dismal. A number of countries did cross the line from poor to rich, especially in East Asia, but this was because of their populations' own values and efforts, not the amount of aid money received. In spite of the flow of aid money, the income gap between rich and poor countries has not been reduced. Development of poor countries is an uphill struggle because population growth often swallows any increase in resources. Cultural and religious traditions (in poor and in rich countries) that resist population control, besides threatening regional and global peace, are development's worst enemies.

Nobody can develop a country but its own population. Development is in the minds, not in the goods. Foreign money and foreign expertise are only effective to the extent they can be integrated into local knowledge. Success stories in the development literature always stress the emancipation of the locals from foreign expertise. The World Bank in 1992 launched a research program on "best practices" in Africa that in a number of case studies shows how quickly results could be obtained by building on indigenous institutions that had a strong hold on people's commitment, dedication, and sense of identity, while at the same time implementing essential modernizations like strengthening the rule of law.[33]

The dominant philosophy of development cooperation has too rarely recognized this need for local integration. Economic models dictated policies. Developing a country has for decades been considered a matter of transferring money and introducing new technology. Decisions about spending were made by politicians advised by technocrats at the giving and often also at the receiving end. The existence of cultural mental programs on either side received lip service at best, and the only mental programs used in development planning were those of the donors. The very real fact of corruption, for example, was hardly ever addressed in the literature.[34] Very little money was spent on studying the mutual relationship between culture and technological change, although anthropologists for decades had shown culture's crucial impact on getting successful results.

Intercultural encounters in the context of development cooperation have an institutional and an interpersonal side. On the institutional level many receiving countries, but also many donor countries, lack the organizational framework to make the cooperation a success. Usually the primitive institutional structures in the receiving countries are blamed. On the donor side, however, the situation is not always better. Many development agencies have grown out of the foreign service, the main objective of which is the promotion of the donor country's interests abroad. Diplomats lack both the skills and the organizational culture to act as successful entrepreneurs for development consulting activities. Development aid money often has political strings attached to it: it has to be spent in a way that satisfies the values, if not the interests, of the donor country citizens and politicians, regardless of whether such values are shared by citizens and politicians at the receiving end. Projects funded by *international* agencies like the World Bank in theory do not have this constraint, but they have to satisfy the agency's objectives that often also conflict with the receivers'.[35]

The institutional problem at the receiving end is the most serious for countries in which traditional institutional frameworks did not survive colonization and decolonization. Most of these lie in sub-Saharan Africa. Even when local wars do not destroy the products of peaceful development, forces in society make it difficult to attain. Without institutional traditions, personal interests can prevail unchecked. Politicians are out to enrich themselves and their families without being controlled by traditional norms. Institutions cannot be created from scratch: they are living arrangements, rooted in values and history, which have to grow. The economic success of certain countries of East Asia owes much to the fact that centuries-old institutional frameworks existed that were adapted to modern times.

Development cooperation has suffered from different implicit models of how organizations should function (see Chapter 7) between donor and host country technicians.

Take the story of a German engineering firm installing an irrigation system in an African country. Overcoming great technical difficulties, the engineers constructed an effective and easy-to-operate system. They provided all the necessary documentation for later use and repairs, translated into English and Swahili. Then they left. Four months later the system broke down and was never repaired. The local authority structure had not had an opportunity to adopt the project as its family property; it had no local "master."[36]

A classic study sponsored by the Canadian International Development Agency looked at factors determining the effectiveness of donor country personnel overseas. It covered 250 Canadian expatriates in six host countries, as well as 90 of their host country counterparts. It identified three components:

1. Intercultural interaction and training, related to involvement with the local culture and people, and with transfer of skills
2. Professional effectiveness, related to the performance of daily tasks, duties, and responsibilities on the job
3. Personal and family adjustment and satisfaction, related to the capacity for basic satisfaction while living abroad, as an individual and as a family unit

From these three, the expatriates were found to be generally competent on components 2 and 3 but lacking on component 1. Local counterparts stressed the transfer of job skills through intercultural interaction and training as the most crucial dimension of expatriate success.[37]

A study by the development cooperation agencies of the Nordic countries Denmark, Finland, Norway, and Sweden focused on the effectiveness of Nordic technical assistance personnel in East Africa. It criticized the priorities set by the donors: from nine hundred Nordic expatriates, two-thirds were implementers (carrying out projects themselves) while only one-fifth were trainers of local personnel or consultants in local institution building. According to the researchers, the ratio between the two categories should have been reversed. This would have sharply reduced the number of expatriates needed and changed the profile of skills required from them.[38]

In summary, assuming sufficient institutional support, intercultural encounters in the context of development cooperation will be productive if there is a two-way flow of know-how: technical know-how from the donor to the receiver, and cultural know-how about the context in which the technical know-how should be applied, from the receiver to the donor. A technical expert meets a cultural expert, and their mutual expertise is the basis for their mutual respect.

Learning Intercultural Communication

The acquisition of intercultural communication abilities passes through three phases: awareness, knowledge, and skills. *Awareness* is where it all starts: the recognition that I carry a particular mental software because of the way I was brought up, and that others brought up in a different environment carry a different mental software for equally good reasons. Max Pagès, a French social psychologist who came to the United States in the 1950s to study group training, described a situation where such awareness was lacking:

> *[T]t became very clear to me that it was I, Max, but not my culture which was accepted. I was treated as just another American who had this exotic peculiarity of being a Frenchman, which was something like, say, a particular style of shirt. In general no curiosity existed about the intellectual world I was living in, the kinds of books I had written or read, the differences between what is being done in France or Europe and in the United States.*[39]

Strong cultural awareness was ascribed to the author James Morier. The quote about him at the beginning of this chapter pictured Morier as:

> *. . . gifted with a humorous sympathy that enabled him to appreciate the motives actuating persons entirely dissimilar to himself.*

Knowledge should follow awareness. If we have to interact with particular other cultures, we have to learn about these cultures. We should learn about their symbols, their heroes, and their rituals; while we may never share their values, we may at least get an intellectual grasp of where their values differ from ours.

Skills are based on awareness and knowledge, plus practice. We have to recognize and apply the symbols of the other culture, recognize their heroes, practice their rituals, and experience the satisfaction of getting along in the new environment, being able to resolve first the simpler and later some of the more complicated problems of life among the others.

Intercultural communication can be taught. Some students are more gifted at learning it than others. Persons with unduly inflated egos, a low personal tolerance for uncertainty, a history of emotional instability, or known racist or extreme left- or right-wing political sympathies should be considered bad risks for a training that, after all, assumes people's ability to distance themselves from their own cherished beliefs. Such persons are probably unfit for expatriation anyway; if a family will be expatriated, it is wise to make sure that the spouse and children, too, have the necessary emotional stability.

There are two types of intercultural communication training courses. The more traditional ones focus on specific knowledge of the other culture; they are sometimes called *expatriate briefings*. They inform the future expatriates, and preferably their spouses, too, as well as sometimes their children, about the new country, its geography, some history, customs, hygiene, do's and don'ts, what to bring—in short, how to live. They do not provide much introspection into the expatriates' own culture. They are extremely useful, but the strongly motivated expatriate-to-be can also get this information from books and videos. In fact, the institutes offering this type of training usually maintain good book and video libraries for urgent individual preparation.

An even better preparation for a specific assignment is, of course, learning the local language. There is a big offer of crash courses, but unless the learner is exceptionally gifted, learning a new language at business level will take several months full-time—a bit less if the course takes place in the foreign country so that the learner is fully immersed. Most employers do not plan far enough ahead to allow their expatriates such an amount of time for language learning, to their own detriment. If the expatriate gets this chance, it is important to involve the spouse as well. Women, on average, are faster learners of languages than men. They are also better at picking up nonverbal cultural clues.

The other type of intercultural communication course focuses on awareness of and on general knowledge about cultural differences. *Awareness training* focuses on one's own mental software and where it may differ from others. It is not specific to any given country of expatriation; the knowledge and skills taught apply in any foreign cultural environment. They deal not so much with the question of how to live in the other culture but more with how to work, how to get a job done. Besides the (future) expatriate, the course may be attended by the spouse, too, because an understanding spouse is a major asset during the culture shock period.[40] It should, however, definitely be attended by the expatriate's boss at the head office and by staff specialists who communicate with the expatriates. Experience has taught that a chief problem of expatriates is to get the understanding and support of the persons who are not expatriated themselves, but who act as their contacts in the home country organization. The home front should acquire the same cultural sensitivity demanded of the expatriate. Conditions for success of this type of course are the commitment of top management, the investment of a sufficient share of the trainees' time, and the participation in the same type of program of a critical mass of company personnel.

In the design of intercultural competence courses, *process* is as important as *content*. The learning process itself is culturally constrained, and trainers who are not aware of this communicate something other than what they try to teach. Writing from extensive experience in Hong Kong, Michael Bond has warned against using Western procedures with Asian audiences.[41] The occupational culture of the emerging profession of intercultural trainers and consultants is built on the use of Western, mainly U.S., practices.

Using ideas from U.S. counseling expert Paul Pedersen and from Geert's five-dimensional model, Gert Jan has developed a method of group training in exploring cultural variety that can be used with a wide variety of participants and for an equally wide variety of practical applications. It asks participants to identify with a choice of ten *synthetic cultures*, "pure" culture types derived from the extremes of the five dimensions. Participants then play their culture in a simulated problem-solving situation. They learn from their experience and develop intercultural skills in a "safe" environment.[42]

Self-instruction is also possible. A classic instrument for this purpose is the *Culture Assimilator*. This is a programmed learning tool consisting of a number of short case descriptions, each picturing an intercultural encounter in which a person from the foreign culture behaves in a particular way. Usually four explanations are offered of this behavior. One of these is the insider explanation by informants from the foreign culture. The three others are naive choices by outsiders. The student picks one answer and receives a comment explaining why the answer chosen was correct (corresponding to the insiders' view) or incorrect (naive). Early culture assimilators were culture-specific toward both the home and the host culture. They therefore were costly to make and had relatively limited distribution, but an evaluation study showed their long-term effects to be quite positive. Later on, a General Culture Assimilator was published, incorporating the main common themes from the earlier specific ones.[43]

Cultural sensitivity is subtle, and bias is always looming around the corner. When in 1976 children of Vietnamese refugees attended regular schools in small towns in the United States, the U.S. Office of Education issued an instruction for teachers, *On Teaching the Vietnamese*. Part of it runs:

> *Student participation was discouraged in Vietnamese schools by liberal doses of corporal punishment, and students were conditioned to sit rigidly and to speak only when spoken to. This background . . . makes speaking freely in class hard for a Vietnamese. Therefore, don't mistake shyness for apathy.*[44]

To most western European and North American readers, this instruction looks OK at first. It becomes more problematic, however, when we look for all the clues about U.S. culture that the quote supplies, which are as many sources of bias. In fact, the U.S. Office of Education ascribes to the Vietnamese all the motivations of young Americans—like a supposed desire to participate—and explains their submission by corporal punishment rather than, for example, respect. At a doctoral seminar Geert taught in Sweden, one of the participants[45] opened the eyes of the others by reversing the statement—supposing American students would have to attend Vietnamese schools:

> *Students' proper respect for teachers was discouraged by a loose order and students were conditioned to behave disorderly and to chat all the time. This background makes proper and respectful behavior in class hard for an American student. Therefore, don't mistake rudeness for lack of reverence.*

Surviving in a Multicultural World

... the English, of any people in the universe, have the least of a national character; unless this very singularity may pass for such.

—DAVID HUME, *The Philosophical Works*, Essay XXI, 1742[1]

The Germans live in Germany, the Romans live in Rome, the Turkeys live in Turkey; but the English live at home.

—from a nursery rhyme by J. H. GORING, 1909[2]

The Message of This Book

In terms of the preceding quotes, the message of this book has been that everybody is like Hume's or Goring's English. Everybody looks at the world from behind the windows of a cultural home, and everybody prefers to act as if people from other countries have something special about them (a national character) but home is normal. Unfortunately there is no normal position in cultural matters. This is an uncomfortable message, as uncomfortable as Galileo Galilei's claim in the seventeenth century that the Earth is not the center of the universe.

Culture has been described in Chapter 1 through the metaphor of *mental software*—a usually unconscious conditioning that leaves individuals considerable freedom to think, feel, and act but within the constraints of what his or her social environment offers in terms of possible thoughts, feelings, and actions. These constraints are present in all spheres of life, and in order to understand them, human life should be seen as an integrated whole.

Cultural programming starts in the environment in which a young child grows up—usually a family of some kind. It continues at school, and what happens in schools can only be understood if one knows what happens before and after school. It continues at work. Workers' behavior is an extension of behavior acquired at school and in the family. Managers' behavior is an extension of the managers' school and family experiences, as well as a mirror image of the behavior of the managed. Politics and the relationships between citizens and authorities are extensions of relationships in the family, at school, and at work, and in their turn they affect these other spheres of life. Religious beliefs, secular ideologies, and scientific theories are extensions of mental software demonstrated in the family, at school, at work, and in government relations, and they reinforce the dominant patterns of thinking, feeling, and acting in the other spheres.

Cultural programs differ from one group or category of people to another in ways that are rarely acknowledged and often misunderstood. The cultural category to which most of the book has been devoted is the nation-state; some attention has been given to differences according to social class, gender, generation, work organization, and occupation. Every nation has a considerable moral investment in its own dominant mental software, which explains the common hesitation to make cultural differences discussable. The origins of the differences from one nation to another, and sometimes between ethnic, religious, or linguistic subgroups within nations, are hidden in history. In some cases causal explanations are possible; in many other cases one should assume that a small difference arose many centuries ago, and that in being transferred from generation to generation, this small difference grew into the large difference it is today.

The main cultural differences between nations lie in values. Systematic differences exist (and have been described in Chapters 2 through 6) with regard to values about power and inequality, with regard to the relationship between the individual and the group, with regard to the emotional and social roles expected from men or women, with respect to ways of dealing with the uncertainties in life, and with respect to whether one is mainly preoccupied with the future or with the past and present.

Chapters 7 and 8 have been devoted to the consequences of national culture differences for the functioning of organizations and to the supposed phenomenon of *organizational cultures*: differences in mental software between those employed by different corporations or other bodies. The national culture impact on organizations is profound and affects both businesses and governments. The organizational culture component is much less profound than is often claimed, to the extent that the use of the same term *culture* for both nations and organizations is slightly misleading. Organizational cultures are mainly expressed not in members' values but in more superficial manifestations, such as common symbols, heroes, and rituals.

The various chapters analyzing and describing cultural differences allow the reader to locate his or her own cultural value framework versus those in other countries and groups. Chapter 9, "Intercultural Encounters," represents the culmination of the message: if we think, feel, and act so differently, how can we manage one world together? An increased consciousness of the constraints of our mental programs versus those of others is essential for our common survival. The message of this book is that such a consciousness can be developed and that while we should not expect to become all alike, we can at least aspire at becoming more cosmopolitan in our thinking.

The Moral Issue

Some people wonder whether the advocated consciousness of the limits of one's own value system does not lead to moral laxity. Chapter 1 contains a call for *cultural relativism*: the recognition that, as a famous French anthropologist expressed it, "one culture has no absolute criteria for judging the activities of another culture as 'low' or 'noble.'" But this is no call for dropping values altogether. As a matter of fact, this entire book shows that no human being can escape from using value standards all the time. Successful intercultural encounters presuppose that the partners believe in their own values. If not, they have become alienated persons, lacking a sense of identity. A sense of identity provides the feeling of security from which one can encounter other cultures with an open mind.

The principle of surviving in a multicultural world is that one does not need to think, feel, and act in the same way in order to agree on practical issues and to cooperate. The IBM research discussed in Chapters 2 through 5 has illustrated this. The value differences among employees in different countries working for this multinational have been shown to be quite considerable. Nevertheless, IBM employees the world over have cooperated in reasonable harmony toward practical goals. There is nothing unique about IBM employees in this respect; other people can and do cooperate across national borders, too. The fact that organizational cultures are relatively superficial and value-free phenomena, as was demonstrated in the IRIC research reported in Chapter 8, is precisely the reason why international organizations can exist and be composed of different nationals, each with its own different national values.

People from cultures very dissimilar on the national culture dimensions of power distance, individualism, masculinity, uncertainty avoidance, and long-term orientation as described in the various chapters of this book can cooperate fruitfully. Yet people from some cultures will cooperate more easily than others with foreigners. The most problematic are nations and groups within nations that score very high on uncertainty avoidance and thus feel that what is different is dangerous. Also problematic is the cooperation with nations and groups scoring very high on power distance, because such cooperation depends on the whims of powerful individuals. In a world kept together by intercultural cooperation, such cultural groups will certainly not be forerunners. They may have to be left alone for some time until they discover they have no other choice but to join.

Cultural Convergence and Divergence

Research about the development of cultural values has shown repeatedly that there is little evidence of international convergence over time, except an increase of individualism for countries having become wealthier. Value differences between nations described by authors centuries ago are still present today, in spite of continued close contacts. For the next few hundred years at least, countries will remain culturally diverse.

Not only will cultural diversity between countries remain with us, but it even looks like differences within countries are increasing. Ethnic groups arrive at a new consciousness of their identity and ask for a political recognition of this fact. Of course, these ethnic differences have always been there. What has changed is the intensity of contact between groups, which has confirmed group members in their own identities. Also, the spread of information (by international media) on how people live elsewhere in the world has affected minorities, who compare their situation to the lives of others whom they suppose to be better off. World news media also spread information of suffering and strife much wider than ever before. Pogroms, uprisings, and violent repression are no new inventions, but in the past relatively few people beyond those directly involved would know about them; now they are visible on TV screens around the world. This has the effect of increasing anxiety, particularly in uncertainty avoiding cultures.

Educating for Intercultural Understanding: Suggestions for Parents

In this and the three following sections, some of the conclusions from this book will be translated into practical advice. Such advice is unavoidably subjective, for which we beg the reader's tolerance.

The basic skill for surviving in a multicultural world, as this book has argued, is understanding first one's own cultural values (and that is why one needs a cultural identity of one's own) and next the cultural values of the others with whom one has to cooperate. As parents, we have more influence on creating multicultural understanding in future world citizens than in any other role. Values are mainly acquired during the first ten years of a child's life. They are absorbed by observation and imitation of adults and older children rather than by indoctrination. The way parents live their own culture provides the child with his or her cultural identity. The way parents talk about and behave toward persons and groups from other cultures determines the degree to which the child's mind will be opened or closed for cross-cultural understanding.

Growing up in a bicultural environment (for example, having parents from different nationalities, living abroad during childhood, or going to a foreign school) can be an asset to a child. Whether such biculturality really is an asset or instead becomes a liability depends on the parents' ability to cope with the bicultural situation themselves. Having foreign friends, hearing different languages spoken, traveling with parents who awake the children's interests in things foreign are definite assets. Learning at least one other language—whatever other language—is a unique ingredient of education for multicultural understanding. This supposes, of course, that the teaching of the other language is effective: a lot of language classes in schools are a waste of time. The stress should be on full immersion, whereby using the foreign language becomes indispensable for practical purposes. Becoming really bi- or multilingual is one of the advantages of children belonging to a minority or to a small nation. It is more difficult for those belonging to a big nation.

Coping with Cultural Differences: Suggestions for Managers

The past chapters have offered many examples of the ways in which cultural values affect the practices and theories of organizations. Culturally a manager is the follower of his or her followers: she or he has to meet the subordinates on these subordinates' cultural ground. There is some free choice in managerial behavior, but the cultural constraints are much tighter than most of the management literature admits.

The work situation is basically a highly suitable laboratory for intercultural cooperation, as the problems are practical and results are visible to everybody. Yet managers, workers, and worker representatives are rarely in the front ranks for promoting intercultural understanding. Narrow economic interest viewpoints tend to prevail on all sides. An exception is maybe the increasing use of expatriate manager training. When managers are sent abroad, their organizations more and more offer opportunities for some cross-cultural training or briefing. Managers chronically underestimate cultural factors in the case of mergers and acquisitions, as was argued in Chapter 9.

Experiments with intercultural diversity in the workplace are easier to start in public than in private organizations, as the former by definition have a greater responsibility to society. They are also easier in service organizations than in manufacturing, especially in those service organizations having a culturally diverse clientele. The ideal organization from an intercultural point of view, in our opinion, is one in which members can fully use their skills, even those deriving from their cultural identity—be these artistic, social, linguistic, temperamental, or other.

Spreading Multicultural Understanding: Suggestions for the Media

Media people—journalists, reporters, and radio and TV producers—play a uniquely important role in creating multicultural understanding, or misunderstanding. The battle for survival in a multicultural world will to a large extent be fought in the media. Media people are human: they have cultural values of their own. With regard to other cultures, their position is ambiguous. On the one hand, they cater to a public and their success depends on the extent to which they write or speak what the public wants to read or hear. On the other hand, they are in a position to direct people's attention—to create an image of reality that to many people becomes reality itself. A member of the public has to be pretty sophisticated to critically scrutinize the beliefs about other cultures reflected in television shows, radio programs, and newspapers.

The consciousness that people in other parts of one's society, and people in other societies, think, feel, and act on the basis of other but not necessarily evil value assumptions may or may not be recognized by media people and reflected in their productions. Simple information of the public can avoid big misunderstandings. There undoubtedly exist reporters who only want simple black-and-white messages or even have a vested interest in showing who are the good guys and who are the bad ones. For those with a greater sense of responsibility, there still is a big untapped potential for spreading understanding about differences in cultural values and practices. For example, using the television eye to compare similar aspects of daily behavior in different countries can be extremely powerful and is still too seldom done.[3]

A problem particular to small countries like our own, the Netherlands, is that both TV and newspapers buy materials from larger countries without stressing the different cultural contexts in which these materials were produced. An example is newspaper articles reporting on survey research about trends in society. The material used is most frequently from the United States, and the implicit assumption of the editor responsible is that the conclusions are valid for the Netherlands as well. If one realizes the large distance between the two societies on the masculinity-femininity dimension (Chapter 4), which affects many societal phenomena, Dutch readers should at least be cautioned when interpreting U.S. data. The funny thing is that no Dutch journalist would dream of producing Japanese or German statistics with the tacit assumption that these apply in the Netherlands.

Reading Mental Programs: Suggestions for Researchers

The manner in which animals learn has been much studied in recent years, with a great deal of patient observation and experiment. Certain results have been obtained as regards the kinds of problems that have been investigated, but on general principles there is still much controversy. One may say broadly that all the animals that have been carefully observed have behaved so as to confirm the philosophy in which the observer believed before his observations began. Nay, more, they have all displayed the national characteristics of the observer. Animals studied by Americans rush about frantically, with an incredible display of hustle and pep, and at last achieve the desired result by chance. Animals observed by Germans sit still and think, and at last evolve the solution out of their inner consciousness. To the plain man, such as the present writer, this situation is discouraging. I observe, however, that the type of problem which a man naturally sets to an animal depends upon his own philosophy, and that this probably accounts for the differences in the results. The animal responds to one type of problem in one way and to another in another; therefore the results obtained by different investigators, though different, are not incompatible. But it remains necessary to remember that no one investigator is to be trusted to give a survey of the whole field.

—Bertrand Russell, *An Outline of Philosophy*, 1927, Chapter 3[4]

This quote, written three generations ago by a great British philosopher, is a warning that results of scientific research depend on the researcher in ways that may not even be conscious to him or her. The same theme returns in a different way in the work of the American Thomas Kuhn, who in 1962 published a famous little book titled *The Structure of Scientific Revolutions*,[5] in which he illustrates, with examples from various sciences, how scientific innovation is brought about. In a given period certain common assumptions called paradigms dominate a scientific field and constrain the thinking of the scientists in this field. Kuhn labeled the work done within these paradigms "normal" science. Every now and then, normal science runs into limits: it is unable to explain new facts or unable to meet new challenges. Then a paradigm change is initiated, but those who start the change are, at first, rejected and ridiculed by those involved in normal science. The new paradigm is seen as a threat. Gradually, however, more and more people move to the new paradigm, which then becomes part of a new type of normal science.

Intercultural comparative studies often belong to such a new normal science. A common approach is for a master's or doctoral student to take an instrument (mostly a paper-and-pencil questionnaire) developed in one country, usually in the United States by a U.S. scholar who tested it on U.S. respondents, and to have it administered to respondents in one or more other countries. Unfortunately such instruments cover only issues considered relevant in the society in which they were developed, and they exclude questions unrecognized by the designer because they do not occur in his or her society. Such questions are precisely the ones most interesting from a cultural point of view. The hidden ethnocentrism in this type of research leads to trivial results.

Prospective cross-cultural researchers who feel inspired by this book and who want to use parts of its approach in their own project are referred to the 2001 edition of Geert's scholarly volume *Culture's Consequences*, especially its Chapter 10. This will caution them against many pitfalls that continue to trap novice and even experienced researchers.

Global Challenges Call for Intercultural Cooperation

The word *surviving* in the title of this chapter is no exaggeration. Humankind today is threatened by a number of disasters that have all been manmade: they are disasters of culture rather than the disasters of nature to which our ancestors were regularly exposed.

Their common cause is that man has become both too numerous and too clever for the limited size of our globe. But while we are clever about technology and getting more so each day, we are still naive about ourselves. Our mental software is not adapted to the environment we created in recent centuries. The only way toward survival is getting to understand ourselves better as social beings, so that we may control our technological cleverness and not use it in destructive ways. This demands concerted action on issues for which, unfortunately, different cultural values make people disagree rather than agree. In these circumstances intercultural cooperation has become a prime condition for the survival of humankind.

A number of value-laden world problems have been signaled in this book. There are the economic problems: international economic cooperation versus competition and the distribution of wealth and poverty across and within countries. There are the technology-induced problems. In the past, whenever a new technology had been invented, it could also be applied. This is no longer the case, and decisions have to be made whether some of the things humans can make should be made and, if so, subject to which precautions. Such decisions should be agreed upon on a world scale, and if countries, groups, or persons do not respect the decisions or the precautions, they should be forced to do so. Examples are certain uses of nuclear energy both for peaceful and aggressive purposes, certain chemical processes and products, certain applications of informatics, and certain applications of genetic manipulation. An example of the latter is influencing whether a baby to be born will be a boy or a girl. In some cultures the desirability of having boys over girls is very strong (see Chapter 4). In view of both ethical and demographic considerations, should this technology be allowed to spread? If so, where and under what conditions, and if not, can one stop it?

The combination of world population growth, economic development, and technological developments affects the world ecosystem in ways that are only very partly known. Uncontrolled tree cutting in many parts of the world destroys forests; acid rain threatens other forests. The problem of the reduction of the ozone layer is known, but its seriousness is not. Long-term climate changes resulting from the greenhouse effect of increased emission of CO_2 and other gases are evident; they have a built-in delay of decades, so that even if we were to stop emitting now, the greenhouse effect will increase for a long time. Coping with these problems requires worldwide research and political decision making in areas in which both perceived national interests and cultural values are in conflict. Decisions about sacrifices made today for benefits to be reaped by the next generation have to be made by politicians whose main concern is with being reelected next year or surviving a power struggle tomorrow. In addition, the sacrifices may lie in other parts of the world than the main benefactors. The greenhouse effect can be reduced if the tropical countries preserve their rain forests. These countries are mainly poor, and their governments want the revenue of selling their hardwoods. Can they be compensated for leaving intact what remains of their rain forests?

The trends depicted are threats to humankind as a whole. They represent the common enemy of the future. A common enemy has always been the most effective way of making leaders and groups with conflicting values and interests cooperate. Maybe these threats will become so imminent as to force us to achieve a global intercultural cooperation that has never existed.

Much will depend on the acquisition of intercultural cooperation skills as part of the mental software of politicians. Former U.S. diplomat Glen Fisher in his book *Mindsets* has written about the relationship between economics, culture, and politics:

> *An interdisciplinary approach to international economic processes hardly exists. Most important, routine applications of conventional economic analysis cannot tolerate "irrational" behavior. But, from a cross-national and cross-cultural perspective, there is a real question as to what is rational and what irrational; both are very relative terms and very much culture bound; one person's irrationality might turn out to be another's orderly and predictable behavior. . . . Despite the frequent assertion that sentimentality and the pursuit of economic interests don't mix, economic systems are in fact ethical systems. Whether by law and regulation or by custom, some economic activities are sanctioned while others are not. And what is sanctioned differs from culture to culture.*[6]

Both what is "rational" and what is "ethical" depend on cultural value positions. In politics value positions are further confounded by perceived interests. There is a strong tendency in international politics to use different ethical standards toward other countries than toward one's own.

A case study that should encourage modesty about ethics in politics is the international drug trade. Western countries for decades have been involved in a virtual war to prevent the importation of drugs. Not so long ago, from 1839 to 1842, a Western country (Britain) fought an opium war with Imperial China. The Chinese emperor took the position Western governments are taking now, trying to keep drugs out of his country. The British, however, had strong economic interests in a Chinese market for the opium they imported from India, and through an active sales promotion they got large numbers of Chinese addicted. The British won the war, and in the peace treaty they not only got the right to continue importing opium but they also acquired Hong Kong Island as a permanent foothold on the Chinese coast. The return of Hong Kong to China in 1997 in a way was a belated victory of the Chinese in their war against drugs.[7]

From a values point of view it is difficult to defend the position that the trade in arms is less unethical than the trade in drugs. One difference is that in the drugs traffic the poor countries tend to be the sellers, in the arms traffic the rich countries. The latter have made more money on selling arms to Third World countries than they spent on development assistance to these countries. Of course, in this case the buyers and the sellers are both to blame, but the rich countries are in a better position to break the vicious circle.

Reducing the trade in arms would reduce civil wars, terrorism, and murder. It would improve the chances of respect for human rights in the world, as these arms are often used to crush human rights. While it is unrealistic to expect all countries of the world to become Western-style democracies, a more feasible goal is to strive for more respect for human rights even in autocratically led states.

As we argued in Chapter 9, the Universal Declaration of Human Rights adopted in 1948 is based on universalist, individualist Western values that clearly are not shared by the political leaders nor by the populations of all other parts of the world. On the other hand, the Declaration is a fact, and international organizations as well as individuals will undoubtedly continue to signal infringements, regardless of the country in which these take place. No government is powerful enough to silence, for example, Amnesty International. All but the most ruthless governments try to maintain an appearance of international respectability. The fact that the world has become one scene leads to the public being informed about more suffering than ever before, but it also offers more opportunities to act against this suffering.

On the global scene, many of us see the same plays in terms of world news, sports events, and marketing messages. But we do not get together to discuss the play. If we inhabit a global village,[8] it only consists of a theater and a marketplace. We need houses, sanctuaries, and other places to meet and talk in our global village.

In London in the fall of 2003, Gert Jan sat in a pub with four students from four continents. An Indian and a man from Ghana were arguing whether and how they could help their respective countries. The Indian pressed the other to admit that if he could only spare one pound a day for educating children in his home country, that would make a difference. But the Ghanaian said that giving money only made things worse and that, for the time being, educating himself was the only thing he could do. They got pretty heated and did not agree, but they did listen to one another, and they left as friends. In the global village we need many more pubs like that one.

Endnotes

Chapter 1

1. British sociologist Anthony Giddens (born 1938) defines sociology as "the study of human life, groups and societies" (Giddens, 2001, p. 2), which would incorporate social anthropology. The practical division of labor between sociologists and anthropologists is for the former to focus on social processes within societies and for the latter on societies as wholes.

2. A *group* means a number of people in contact with each other. A *category* consists of people who, without necessarily having contact, have something in common (e.g., all women managers, or all people born before 1940).

3. The concept of a "collective programming of the mind" resembles the concept of habitus proposed by the French sociologist Pierre Bourdieu (1930–2002): "Certain conditions of existence produce a *habitus*, a system of permanent and transferable dispositions. A habitus . . . functions as the basis for practices and images . . . which can be collectively orchestrated without an actual conductor" (Bourdieu, 1980, pp. 88–89; translation by GH).

4. Results obtained with the same personality test (the *NEO-PI-R*, measuring the "Big Five" personality dimensions) in different countries show that average or "normal" personality varies with culture (Hofstede & McCrae, 2004). These differences will be discussed in Chapters 3, 4, and 5.

5. For a critical discussion of this genetic inferiority thesis, see Gould, 1996.

6. Translation by GH from Lévi-Strauss & Eribon, 1988, p. 229.

7. Discourse is an area of study uniting linguists, psychologists, and other social scientists. For a broad introduction, see van Dijk, 1997a, 1997b.

8. de Tocqueville, 1956 [1835], p. 155.

9. de Waal, 2001. Other higher social animals, like whales and dolphins, have also been shown to hold distinct group cultures (Rendell & Whitehead, 2001).

10. Cavalli-Sforza, 2000.

11. Mithen, 2003.

12. Moore & Lewis, 1999; see also Chapter 9.

13. For example, in a 1998 U.S. bestseller by Samuel Huntington, *The Clash of Civilizations and the Remaking of the World Order.*

14. Some nations are less culturally integrated than others. Examples are some of the former colonies and multilingual, multiethnic countries such as Belgium, Malaysia, or the former Yugoslavia. Yet even in these cases, ethnic and/or linguistic groups that consider themselves as very different from each other may have common traits in comparison with the populations of other countries. We have shown this to be the case for Belgium and the former Yugoslavia (*Culture's Consequences*, 2001, p. 501).

15. Montesquieu, 1989 [1742], p. 310.

16. Harris, 1981, p. 8.

17. In popular parlance, the words *norm* and *value* are often used indiscriminately, or the twin expression "values and norms" is handled as an inseparable pair, such as Laurel and Hardy. In this latter case, one of the two words is redundant.

18. *Culture's Consequences*, 2001, p. 91.

19. Inkeles & Levinson, 1969 [1954], pp. 447ff.

20. This analysis is extensively described in *Culture's Consequences*, 2001, Chapter 2.

21. *Culture's Consequences*, 2001, p. 64.

22. IMEDE (now IMD), Lausanne, see *Culture's Consequences*, 2001, pp. 91 and 219.

23. Søndergaard, 1994.

24. *Culture's Consequences* uses both *product moment* (Pearson) correlation coefficients and *rank order* (Spearman) correlation coefficients; the first are based on the absolute values of measurements, the second on their relative ranks.

25. For readability reasons, this book generally does not show correlation coefficients, except in endnotes; the text only refers to the conclusions drawn from them. Readers interested in statistical proof are referred to *Culture's Consequences*, 2001.

26. Ng et al., 1982.

27. Hofstede & Bond, 1984.

28. Besides, they changed the scoring from ranking values relative to each other to rating each value by itself.

29. Published in an article authored by the Chinese Culture Connection, 1987, the name chosen by Michael Bond for his team of twenty-four researchers. See Chapters 2, 3, and 6 and Hofstede & Bond, 1988.

30. *Culture's Consequences*, 2001, pp. 503–20.

31. The role of paradigms in science was first described by U.S. philosopher Thomas S. Kuhn (1922–96) in his famous little book *The Structure of Scientific Revolutions* (1970).

32. The number of countries is still growing. The numbers fifty-four groups of students and fifty-six of teachers are mentioned in Schwartz & Bardi, 2001. As some countries are only represented by students and others only by teachers, the total number of countries is even larger: sixty-three.

33. Based on data from teachers in twenty-three countries: individualism correlated significantly with hierarchy and with egalitarian commitment. Masculinity correlated significantly with mastery. Uncertainty avoidance correlated significantly with harmony. Intellectual autonomy, affective autonomy, and conservatism (negatively) correlated more with wealth (1990 GNP per capita) than with any of the IBM indices. See Schwartz, 1994; Sagiv & Schwartz, 2000; *Culture's Consequences*, 2001, p. 265. Smith, Peterson, & Schwartz, 2002, show correlations of our indices with three summary dimensions computed from Schwartz's data; all three are most strongly correlated with individualism-collectivism.

34. Trompenaars, 1993.

35. The first five from Parsons & Shils, 1951, the latter two from Kluckhohn & Strodtbeck, 1961.

36. Smith, Trompenaars, & Dugan, 1995; Smith, Dugan, & Trompenaars, 1996; Smith, Peterson, & Schwartz, 2002. As far as we know, these are the only academic publications about Trompenaars's database. The numbers and categories of respondents reported differ from those claimed by Trompenaars in his book. See *Culture's Consequences*, 2001, p. 274, notes 26 and 27.

37. Javidan & House, 2001, 2002; House, Javidan, Hanges, & Dorfman, 2002.

38. Smith, 2004, has included GLOBE data in a comparison of response patterns (acquiescence) across six major cross-national studies. His findings are described in Chapters 3 and 5.

39. A summary of WVS data has been published in Inglehart, Basañez, & Moreno, 1998.

40. Inglehart, 1997, pp. 81–98.

41. Halman, 2001. Van Haaf, Vonk, & van de Vijver, 2002, analyzed a subset of the WVS questionnaire, the Social Norms scale: whether each of twenty-four trespasses (like "avoiding a fare on public transport") could be justified. They focused on the statistical properties of the scale and found that its meaning to respondents differed between European Union countries and Latin countries. For the latter, they found an answer bias correlated with our uncertainty avoidance dimension.

Chapter 2

1. Mulder, 1976, 1977.

2. The matrix on which the factor analysis was carried out consisted of thirty-two questions (variables) and forty countries (cases). Handbooks on factor analysis do not recommend using the technique for matrices with few cases, because the factors become unstable: they can be too much affected by a single deviant case. This limitation does not apply, however, for *ecological* factor analyses, in which the score for each case is the mean of a large number of independent observations. In this situation the stability of the factor structure is determined by the number of individuals whose answers went into the mean scores. Therefore ecological factor analyses give stable results even with fewer cases than variables.

3. In statistical terms: items with high loadings on the factor.

4. For details, see *Culture's Consequences*, 2001, pp. 501–2 and Kolman, Noorderhaven, Hofstede, & Dienes, 2003.

5. Pierre Bourdieu (see Chapter 1, note 3) sees this as one of the key characteristics of a habitus. It represents necessity turned into virtue (*nécessité faite vertu*). See Bourdieu, 1980, p. 90.

6. Sadler & Hofstede, 1976.

7. The correlation coefficients with PDI measured for the populations listed in Table 1.1 were 0.67 for the elites (0.80 with the newer VSM formulas), 0.59 for the employees of six other organizations, 0.76 for the airline pilots, 0.71 for the heads of municipal organizations, and 0.59 for the bank employees. All of these are significant at the 0.01-level or better.

8. The correlations between the various replications were weaker than the correlations of each of them with the original IBM set (e.g., in van Nimwegen, 2002, p. 153).

9. de Mooij, 2004.

10. Chinese Culture Connection, 1987. Across the twenty countries in both studies, moral discipline correlated 0.55 with power distance and −0.54 with individualism, both significant at the 0.01-level.

11. The term *working class* is, of course, curiously archaic. If anything, in many countries it covers more people who are *out of* work than does the middle class.

12. *Culture's Consequences*, 2001, p. 89.

13. The samples of IBM employees upon which the cross-national comparison was based included all categories of Table 2.1 except unskilled workers. The mean score of the cross-national samples for Great Britain, France, and Germany was 46.

14. Kohn, 1969.

15. *Four Families*, a classic motion picture produced by the National Film Board of Canada in 1959, with expert advice from anthropologist Margaret Mead, shows the relationships between parents and small children in more or less matched farmer families in India, France, Japan, and Canada. Audiences to whom we showed the film, before giving them the PDI scores, were able to rank the four countries correctly on the power distance dimension just on the basis of the parent-child relationships pictured in the film.

16. *Transcultural psychiatry* has become a special subdiscipline for mental health professionals dealing with immigrants.

17. d'Iribarne, 1989, p. 77. Translation by GH.

18. Management by objectives is a system of periodic meetings between superior and subordinate in which the latter commits him- or herself to the achievement of certain objectives. In the next meeting this achievement is assessed and new objectives for the coming period are agreed upon.

19. Smith, Peterson, & Schwartz, 2002. The correlation of the verticality index with PDI across forty overlapping countries was 0.60, significant at the 0.001-level. It was the strongest correlation with external data found in the event management research project.

20. Except for the Basque country, where a violent minority has continued to strive for independence.

21. The correlation with PDI is weaker for the exporters than for their customers. Some lower-PDI-exporting countries scored cleaner internally than in an exporter

role. The clearest example was the United States, which scored 7.7 out of 10 for itself, but only 5.3 out of 10 as an exporter. The United States has strict rules for its government deals but is reluctant to impose these on its private companies.

22. More about Confucianism in Chapter 6.

23. "Store up no treasures for yourselves on earth, where moth and rust corrode, where thieves break in and steal: store up treasures for yourself in heaven, where neither moth nor rust corrode, where thieves do not break in and steal. For where your treasure lies, your heart will lie there too" (St. Matthew 6:19–21, Moffatt translation).

24. Machiavelli, 1955 [1517], p. 91.

25. Triandis, 1973, pp. 55–68.

26. *Culture's Consequences*, 2001, pp. 115–117.

27. *Culture's Consequences*, 2001, p. 136.

28. *Culture's Consequences*, 2001, p. 118.

29. The data were from Harding & Phillips, 1986; Inglehart, Basañez, & Moreno, 1998; Halman, 2001. The countries were Belgium, Denmark, France, Germany, Great Britain, Ireland, Italy, Netherlands, Northern Ireland, and Spain.

30. Translation by GH from the Dutch newspaper *NRC/Handelsblad*, December 23, 1988.

Chapter 3

1. See the scoring guides for the 1982 and 1994 Values Survey Modules issued by the Institute for Research on Intercultural Cooperation (IRIC).

2. The correlation coefficients with IDV measured for the populations listed in Table 1.1 were 0.69 for the elites, 0.63 for the employees of six other organizations, 0.60 for the consumers, 0.70 for the airline pilots, and 0.61 for the bank employees. All of these are significant at the 0.01-level or better.

3. Chinese Culture Connection, 1987. Across the twenty countries in both studies, integration correlated 0.65 with individualism, significant at the 0.001-level, and −0.58 with power distance, significant at the 0.01-level.

4. On the basis of data from teachers in twenty-three countries: Schwartz, 1994, pp. 112–15, and *Culture's Consequences*, 2001, pp. 220–21 and 265. Three of Schwartz's categories correlated with IDV: conservation, affective autonomy, and intellectual autonomy, were even more strongly correlated with GNP per capita. The remaining two were hierarchy, which was negatively correlated with IDV, and egalitarian commitment, which was positively correlated with IDV. When Schwartz's seven categories were simplified into three clusters, two of these were highly significantly correlated with IDV (Smith, Peterson, & Schwartz, 2002).

5. Smith, Peterson, & Schwartz, 2002. They called one dimension *egalitarian commitment versus conservatism*, and it correlated with IDV with 0.61, significant at the 0.001-level. Their second dimension was labeled *loyal involvement versus utilitarian involvement*; it correlated with PDI with 0.74, significant at the 0.001-level, and with IDV with −0.59, significant at the 0.01-level.

6. Both factors were also strongly correlated with GNP per capita. Well-being versus survival correlated 0.74 with GNP per capita and also with IDV (0.001-level). In a

regression analysis on the four IBM dimensions, well-being versus survival related to (1) IDV, (2) MAS (negatively, see Chapter 4), and (3) PDI (also negatively). See Chapter 4; Inglehart, 1997, p. 93; and *Culture's Consequences*, 2001, pp. 222–23 and 266.

7. Smith, 2004. Acquiescence in questions dealing not with values but with descriptions of the actual situation was correlated with uncertainty avoidance; see Chapter 5.

8. An extensive review of measurements of individualism and collectivism at the individual level was published by Oyserman, Coon, & Kemmelmeier, 2002.

9. The correlation between PDI and IDV across the seventy-four countries or regions from Tables 2.1 and 3.1 was −0.55; across the fifty-three cultures in the IBM database it was −0.68.

10. Crozier, 1964, p. 222.

11. d'Iribarne, 1989, p. 59. Translation by GH.

12. Harrison, 1985, pp. 55–56.

13. Keeping national wealth (GNP per capita) constant, the correlation between PDI and IDV across sixty-nine countries from Tables 2.1 and 3.1 was −0.36; across fifty countries from the IBM database, it was −0.32.

14. Triandis (1995, pp. 44–52) has introduced a distinction between *horizontal* and *vertical* individualism and collectivism. He applies this distinction mostly at the level of individuals. At the level of societies, the horizontal versus vertical distinction is identical to small versus large power distance.

15. A distinction between occupations in which some demand more individual initiative and some more group loyalty is conceivable, but the questions in the IBM database were not suitable for measuring it.

16. Herzberg, Mausner, & Snyderman, 1959.

17. St. Matthew 21:28–31, Moffatt translation.

18. From a speech by R. M. Hadjiwibowo to Semafor Senior Management College, the Netherlands, September 1983. Translation from the Dutch by GH with suggestions from the author.

19. Hall, 1976.

20. Ho, 1976, p. 867.

21. Triandis, 1972, p. 38.

22. Buss, 1989; Buss et al., 1990; *Culture's Consequences*, 2001, pp. 230–31.

23. Yelsma & Athappilly, 1988; Dion & Dion, 1993; *Culture's Consequences*, 2001, p. 230.

24. Levine, Sato, Hashimoto, & Verma, 1995; *Culture's Consequences*, 2001, p. 230.

25. The correlations were −0.75 across sixty countries and −0.64 across thirty languages, both significant way beyond the 0.001-level. From Kashima & Kashima, 1998; *Culture's Consequences*, 2001, p. 233. In a follow-up study, Kashima & Kashima, 2003, showed that for countries with pronoun drop, the relationship of IDV with wealth was weaker, but the relationship of IDV with geographic latitude (climate) was stronger.

26. Habib, 1995, p. 102.

27. Hsu, 1971, pp. 23–44. In the title of his article, the concept was labeled *jen*, which is an older transcription of the same Chinese sound.

28. Markus & Kitayama, 1991.

29. R. Bond & Smith, 1996; *Culture's Consequences*, 2001, p. 232. R. Bond & Smith also did a longitudinal analysis of the U.S. data, which showed that conformity had declined since the 1950s.

30. The correlation was 0.64 (0.001-level). The relationship between personality scores and culture dimensions is analyzed in Hofstede & McCrae, 2004.

31. Matsumoto, 1989; *Culture's Consequences*, 2001, p. 232.

32. Levine & Norenzayan, 1999; *Culture's Consequences*, 2001, p. 233.

33. de Mooij, 2004; *Culture's Consequences*, 2001, pp. 241–42.

34. Humana, 1992; OECD, 1995; *Culture's Consequences*, 2001, pp. 242–43.

35. Westbrook & Legge, 1993; Westbrook, Legge, & Pennay, 1993.

36. *Culture's Consequences*, 2001, p. 240.

37. Earley, 1989, pp. 565–81.

38. See Chapter 2, note 18.

39. From a paper by Alfred J. Kraemer, "Cultural Aspects of Intercultural Training," presented at the International Congress of Applied Psychology, Munich, August 1978.

40. This was shown empirically by Pedersen & Thomsen, 1997.

41. *Culture's Consequences*, 2001, p. 247.

42. Humana, 1992; *Culture's Consequences*, 2001, pp. 247–48.

43. English version of the text from Harding & Phillips, 1986, p. 86.

44. Stoetzel, 1983, p. 78; *Culture's Consequences*, 2001, p. 275, note 31. The rank correlation between the freedom/equality ratio and IDV was 0.84 (0.01-level); between the freedom/equality ratio and PDI it was about 0.

45. Maslow, 1970.

46. Anchored to the level of the IBM scores for the white Australians, the Aboriginals' scores were a PDI of 80, an IDV of 89, an MAS of 22, a UAI of 128, and an LTO of −10. See *Culture's Consequences*, 2001, p. 501. About the Aboriginals' LTO score, see Chapter 6.

47. For the countries from the IBM sample, the correlation of IDV with GNP per capita was 0.85 in 1970, 0.79 in 1980, 0.74 in 1990, and 0.72 in 2000—all way beyond the 0.001-limit. For the total set of countries in Table 3.1 it was 0.64 in 2000.

Chapter 4

1. For example, Mead, 1962 [1950].

2. Costa, Terraciano, & McCrae (2001) compared mean scores on the NEO-PI-R Big Five personality test for women and men in twenty-six cultures. They found consistent gender differences across cultures. Women scored themselves higher on all facets of N (neuroticism) and A (agreeableness), and from the other dimensions of personality women scored higher on some facets: warmth, gregariousness, positive emotions, and openness to aesthetics. Men scored themselves higher on the facets assertiveness, excitement seeking, and openness to ideas.

3. *Culture's Consequences*, 2001, p. 280, following Broverman, Vogel, Broverman, Clarkson, & Rosenkrantz, 1972.

4. Several of these validations were combined into a separate volume: Hofstede with Arrindell, Best, de Mooij, Hoppe, Van de Vliert, Van Rossum, Verweij, Vunderink, & Williams, 1998.

5. According to the Sign Test, this provides significant support for the dimension at the 0.05-level (one-tailed).

6. *Culture's Consequences*, 2001, p. 265. The correlation across twenty-three countries was 0.53 (0.01-level).

7. Bond's Chinese Value Survey across twenty-three countries produced a human-heartedness dimension correlated with MAS. Students in countries scoring high on masculinity stressed patience, courtesy, and kindness; those in feminine countries stressed patriotism and righteousness. These associations are surprising—one would have expected the poles to be reversed. Geert has always retained a suspicion that in the data processing a minus sign was lost. If the analysis was right, we have to interpret this result as an example of the difference between the desired and the desirable, described in Chapter 1.

8. *Culture's Consequences*, 2001, p. 266. The multiple correlation with IDV and MAS was 0.86 (0.001-level).

9. Bem, 1975, p. 636.

10. The percentage of women in the IBM survey population varied from 4.0 in Pakistan to 16.2 in Finland. In *Culture's Consequences*, 2001, p. 286, the MAS scores have been recalculated keeping the percentage of women constant for all countries. The effect on the scores was minimal, as the percentages of women in themselves were correlated with femininity.

11. Gray, 1993. We owe this observation to Marieke de Mooij.

12. Lynn, 1991; van de Vliert, 1998, Table 7.2; *Culture's Consequences*, 2001, p. 308.

13. Based on *Culture's Consequences*, 2001, pp. 289–91.

14. Stevens, 1973; Gonzalez, 1982; *Culture's Consequences*, 2001, p. 309.

15. van Rossum, 1998; *Culture's Consequences*, 2001, p. 300.

16. *Culture's Consequences*, 2001, p. 302.

17. Hofstede, 1996b; *Culture's Consequences*, 2001, p. 302.

18. Mead, 1962 [1950], pp. 271ff.

19. *Culture's Consequences*, 2001, p. 309.

20. From a description in a KLM in-flight magazine on a transatlantic flight where the movie was shown.

21. This section draws heavily on Hofstede et al., 1998, Chapter 10 ("Comparative Studies of Sexual Behavior").

22. Hofstede, Neuijen, Ohayv, & Sanders, 1990. See also Chapter 8.

23. Pryor, DeSouza, Fitness, Hutz, Kumpf, Lubbert, Pesonen, & Erber, 1997, p. 526.

24. *Culture's Consequences*, 2001, p. 325; Ross, 1989.

25. Dr. Jan A. C. de Kock van Leeuwen, personal communication.

26. As was the case in the one-time U.S. bestseller *In Search of Excellence* (Peters & Waterman, 1982).

27. The difference between the two types of ethos is not a recent phenomenon. Lord Robert Baden-Powell (1857–1941), the founder of the international Boy Scouts move-

ment, wrote a book for Rover Scouts (boys over age sixteen) called *Rovering to Success*. Its translation into Dutch, dating from the 1920s, is called *Zwervend op de weg naar levensgeluk* (*Roving on the Road to Happiness*). To the Dutch translators *success* was not a goal likely to appeal to young men. The word in Dutch has a flavor of superficiality. No youth leader would defend it as a purpose in life.

28. Sandemose, 1938. Translation by GH with thanks to Denise Daval Ohayv.

29. Cohen, 1973.

30. Lasch, 1980, p. 117, attributed this dictum to George Allen. Others claim it to have come from Vince Lombardi.

31. Hastings & Hastings, 1980; *Culture's Consequences*, 2001, p. 303. The samples were quite large: about 1,500 per country. Hastings & Hastings provided no information about the gender distribution of the respondents, but we assume fifty-fifty for all five countries. In the picture of the fighters, the actors were clearly boys.

32. Correlation was 0.97 (0.01-level).

33. Ryback, Sanders, Lorentz, & Koestenblatt, 1980; *Culture's Consequences*, 2001, p. 301.

34. Cooper & Cooper, 1982, p. 80.

35. Verhulst, Achenbach, Ferdinand, & Kasius, 1993; *Culture's Consequences*, 2001, pp. 303–4.

36. U.S. author Christopher Lasch called this *The Culture of Narcissism* (Lasch, 1980).

37. OECD, 1995; Hofstede et al., 1998, Table 5.2; *Culture's Consequences*, 2001, p. 304. Across seven countries and language groups the percentages of those rating themselves "excellent" were rank correlated with MAS 0.71 (0.05-level).

38. *Culture's Consequences*, 2001, p. 304.

39. Witkin, 1977, p. 85; Witkin & Goodenough, 1977, p. 682.

40. A recent study comparing two masculine and two less masculine countries is Kühnen, Hannover, Roeder, Shah, Schubert, Upmeyer, & Zakaria (2001). The authors attribute the differences found erroneously to individualism-collectivism.

41. *Culture's Consequences*, 2001, pp 310–11; de Mooij & Hofstede, 2002; de Mooij, 2004.

42. Tannen, 1992.

43. Fleishman, Harris, & Burtt, 1955; Blake & Mouton, 1964.

44. Philippe d'Iribarne considers the need for consensus the key characteristic of management in the Dutch manufacturing plant he studied. See d'Iribarne, 1989, p. 234ff.

45. Especially in the United States, the relationships between labor unions and enterprises are governed by extensive contracts serving as peace treaties between both parties. Philippe d'Iribarne describes these contracts as a unique feature of the U.S. industrial relations scene (d'Iribarne, 1989, p. 144).

46. About this sense of moderation in France, see d'Iribarne, 1989, pp. 31 and 60–61.

47. *Culture's Consequences*, 2001, pp. 290 and 317.

48. Quoted by William F. Whyte in Webber (ed.), 1969, p. 31.

49. *Culture's Consequences*, 2001, p. 317.

50. Statham, 1987.

51. *Culture's Consequences*, 2001, pp. 307–8.

52. Herzberg, 1966.

53. *Culture's Consequences*, 2001, pp. 315–16.

54. *Human Development Report 2002*, Table 4.

55. The correlations were 0.93 (0.001-level) for the percentage of functional illiterates, 0.72 (0.01-level) for the percentage of poor, and 0.64 (0.01-level) for the percentage of earning less than half the median income.

56. Diderot, 1982 [1780], pp. 124–25. Translation by GH.

57. Eurobarometer, 1990; *Culture's Consequences*, 2001, pp. 318–19. The correlation with MAS across eleven countries (excluding Luxembourg) was −0.63 (0.05-level).

58. European Values Study: Stoetzel, 1983, p. 37. The rank correlation coefficient between permissiveness index and MAS was −0.83 (0.01-level).

59. Eurobarometer, 1997. The correlation with MAS was −0.72 (0.01-level).

60. *Human Development Report 2002*, Table 15.

61. Across twenty donor countries the correlation between MAS and aid in 2000 in percent of GNP was −0.75 (0.001-level).

62. Across twenty-one donor countries the correlation between MAS and CDI was −0.46 (0.05-level). Data from *Foreign Policy*, 2003.

63. *Culture's Consequences*, 2001, p. 271.

64. An eloquent defense of the need to limit growth is Schumacher, 1973.

65. *Culture's Consequences*, 2001, p. 321. Rank correlations across twenty-six countries of MAS were with "center," 0.59 (0.01-level), and with "left," −0.36 (0.05-level).

66. Lammers, 1989, p. 43.

67. *Human Development Report 2002*, Tables 23 and 27.

68. The first correlation of the Catholic/Protestant ratio is with uncertainty avoidance; see Chapter 5 and *Culture's Consequences*, 2001, p. 200.

69. Cooper & Cooper, 1982, p. 97.

70. Verweij, 1998; Verweij, Ester, & Nauta, 1997; *Culture's Consequences*, 2001, p. 327.

71. St. Matthew 22:37–40, Moffatt translation.

72. Stoetzel, 1983, pp. 98–101.

73. Halman & Petterson, 1996.

74. Reported in *The Economist*, June 22, 1996. The correlation with MAS was −0.60 (0.01-level). Low MAS explains 36 percent of the variance; low MAS plus low PDI together explain 57 percent.

75. Levine, Norenzayan, & Philbrick, 2001; Hofstede, 2001b. The rank correlation with MAS −was 0.36 (0.05-level).

76. Walter, 1990, p. 87.

77. Stoetzel, 1983, p. 92.

78. The quotations are from the Authorized Version of the British and Foreign Bible Society (1954).

79. From H. Samsonowicz, "Die Bedeutung des Grosshandels für die Entwicklung der polnischen Kultur bis zum Beginn des 16. Jahrhunderts," in *Studia Historiae Economica*, 5, 1970, pp. 92ff., cited in Schildhauer, 1985, p. 107.

80. Erasmus, 2001 [1524], pp. 174–81.

81. Haley, 1988, pp. 39 and 110–11.

82. Schama, 1987, pp. 404, 541, and 240.

83. A French reader on collective identities edited by Michaud (1978, p. 75) referred to the "feminine image of France."

84. *Culture's Consequences*, 2001, p. 331.

85. Levinson, 1977, p. 763.

86. Adebayo, 1988; UNICEF, 1995, p. 29.

87. The data were from Harding & Phillips, 1986; Inglehart, Basañez, & Moreno, 1998; Halman, 2001. The countries were Belgium, Denmark, France, Germany, Great Britain, Ireland, Italy, Netherlands, Northern Ireland, and Spain.

88. From 2000 to 2015 the population of the high-income countries in the world is expected to grow by an average of 0.4 percent per year, of the low-income countries by 1.7 percent per year (*Human Development Report 2002*, Table 5).

Chapter 5

1. Personal communication.

2. Lawrence, 1980, p. 133.

3. The term first appeared in Cyert & March, 1963, pp. 118ff.

4. *Webster's New World Dictionary of the American Language*, College Edition, 1964.

5. *Culture's Consequences*, 2001, pp. 155–56 and 188.

6. Costa & McCrae's *NEO-PI-R*. Correlation coefficients were UAI with "neuroticism" 0.58, significant at the 0.01-level; UAI plus MAS 0.74 (0.001-level); UAI with "agreeableness" −0.55 (0.01-level). Source: Hofstede & McCrae, 2004.

7. A check was done in which UAI scores per country were computed *controlling for age*. It showed that assuming a constant average age, the country differences remained very similar to those in Table 5.1. See *Culture's Consequences*, 2001, pp. 184–85.

8. Personal communication.

9. Douglas, 1966.

10. Kashima & Kashima, 1998. Across fifty-two countries the correlation between UAI and having more than one second-person pronoun was 0.43 (0.01-level).

11. *Culture's Consequences*, 2001, pp. 157 and 191. Rank correlation across nineteen wealthier countries was −0.71 (0.001-level).

12. For fifteen European Union countries plus Australia, Canada, New Zealand, Norway, Switzerland, and the United States. Data from *Human Development Report 2002*, Table 5. In 1970–75 these countries had fertility rates between 1.6 and 3.8, and these were only rank correlated −0.56 (0.01-level) with 1970 GNP per capita, not with any of the culture dimensions. In 1995–2000 the same countries had fertility rates between 1.2 and 2.0, and these were no longer related to national income: rank correlation with 2000 GNP per capita −0.25 (not significant). The main rank correlation was with UAI: −0.59 (0.01-level).

13. *Culture's Consequences*, 2001, p. 157. Rank correlation coefficient across twenty-six countries was −0.55 (0.01-level).

14. Based on Veenhoven, 1993. See *Culture's Consequences*, 2001, p. 158. Correlation across twenty-one countries was −0.64 (0.01-level).

15. Correlation of UAI with dispersion of happiness across twenty-six countries was 0.50 (0.01-level). *Culture's Consequences*, 2001, on p. 158 erroneously refers to a negative correlation but interprets it correctly.

16. Smith, 2004. The data were from the "As is" section of the GLOBE study. The correlation between overall level of scores and UAI was −0.68 (0.01-level).

17. Hastings & Hastings, 1981; *Culture's Consequences*, 2001, pp. 158 and 189–90.

18. Rank correlation across twenty-six countries was −0.75 (0.001-level).

19. Payer, 1989.

20. *Human Development Report 1999*, Table 9. Rank correlation of nurses per doctor with UAI was −0.54 (0.001-level).

21. Stroebe, 1976, pp. 509–11.

22. For example, the works of Pierre Bourdieu cited in previous chapters.

23. *Culture's Consequences*, 2001, p. 163. The studies were done by Chandler, Shama, Wolf, & Planchard (1981) and by Yan & Gaier (1994) and used an American scale, the Multidimensional-Multiattributional Causality Scale (MMCS). Attributions could be made to ability and effort (internal locus of control), to context (or task), and to luck (external). In spite of the small numbers of countries, the relative tendency to attribute achievement to ability was significantly negatively correlated with UAI (with Chandler et al.'s data −0.87, with Yan & Gaier's data −0.91, both significant at the 0.05-level).

24. de Mooij, 1998a, 2004; *Culture's Consequences*, 2001, p. 170; de Mooij & Hofstede, 2002.

25. de Mooij, 2004, p. 154.

26. d'Iribarne, 1989, pp. 26 and 76.

27. *Culture's Consequences*, 2001, pp. 190 and 192.

28. Horovitz, 1980.

29. *Culture's Consequences*, 2001, p. 167; Shane, 1993.

30. *Culture's Consequences*, 2001, p. 166; Shane, Venkataraman, & Macmillan, 1995.

31. d'Iribarne, 1998.

32. Wildeman, Hofstede, Noorderhaven, Thurik, Verhoeven, & Wennekers, 1999; *Culture's Consequences*, 2001, p. 165. For one country, Great Britain, a longitudinal study proved that people who started businesses for themselves did become more satisfied with their lives than similar people employed by others. For these people at least the flight from dissatisfaction into self-employment paid off (Blanchflower & Oswald, 1998).

33. *Culture's Consequences*, 2001, pp. 163–65 and 192. The rank correlation coefficient between UAI and McClelland's "need for achievement" scores for 1925 was −0.64, significant at the 0.001-level; the multiple correlation coefficient of "need for achievement" with UAI and MAS was 0.73. The 1950 ranking of countries does not show any correlation with any of the IBM indices *nor* with the 1925 ranking of the same countries. A plausible explanation is that only the 1925 stories were like the anthropologists' folktales that McClelland sought to match. In 1950 (after World War II) international communication had increased dramatically, and children's books from this period were more likely to reveal the ideas of innovative educators and less the old traditions.

34. McClelland's "need for affiliation" scores for 1925 were rank correlated positively with IDV (0.48, significant at the 0.01-level), showing that affiliation is more

important if relationships are not predetermined by the social structure. "Need for power" scores for 1925 and scores for all three needs for 1950 did not produce any significant correlations with either IBM indices or GNP per capita. See *Culture's Consequences*, 2001, p. 192.

35. The data are from Djankov, La Porta, Lopez-de-Silanes, & Shleifer, 2003, and were obtained with the kind help of Professor Erhard Blankenburg of the Free University of Amsterdam. We found across the sixty-seven countries a Spearman rank correlation of 0.42 for the duration of check collection, 0.40 for tenant eviction, and 0.47 for the mean duration of the two procedures (all beyond the 0.001-level).

36. Almond & Verba, 1963.

37. *Culture's Consequences*, 2001, p. 172.

38. Aberbach & Putnam, 1977; *Culture's Consequences*, 2001, p. 173.

39. Based on data from the 1990–93 World Values Survey and the 1994 Eurobarometer; see *Culture's Consequences*, 2001, pp. 171 and 174.

40. Personal communication.

41. Levine, Norenzayan, & Philbrick, 2001; Hofstede, 2001b. Rank correlation with UAI was 0.59 (0.01-level).

42. *Culture's Consequences*, 2001, p. 172; *NRC Handelsblad*, September 28, 2001. Contrary to what was mentioned in *Culture's Consequences*, there is no identity card obligation in Austria. This reduces the rank correlation to 0.81, still significant at the 0.001-level. In the Netherlands a proposal has been submitted to Parliament to (re)introduce identity cards, as a consequence of the September 2001 terrorist attacks on the United States. If this will be adopted, the correlation is lowered to 0.75 (0.01-level).

43. *Culture's Consequences*, 2001, p. 129.

44. Personal communication from "Anneke" and her parents.

45. One of the exceptions was Bruno Kreisky (1911–90), the leader of the socialist majority party who for many years was the chancellor (prime minister). Paradoxically, Kreisky was enormously popular among large groups of the Austrian population.

46. *Culture's Consequences*, 2001, pp. 175 and 196.

47. *Culture's Consequences*, 2001, p. 200.

48. Paul Schnabel in *NRC Handelsblad*, December 23, 1989.

49. According to Joseph Campbell, U.S. author on mythology, religion is rooted in science. The present world religions reflect the state of science at the time they were founded, thousands of years ago. Campbell, 1988 [1972], p. 90.

50. *Deduction*: reasoning from a known principle to a logical conclusion. *Induction*: reaching a general conclusion by inference from particular facts.

51. Observations from Marieke de Mooij in an unpublished conference paper, *The Reflection of Values of National Culture in Literature*, September 2000.

52. *Culture's Consequences*, 2001, p. 201.

53. *Culture's Consequences*, 2001, p. 182.

Chapter 6

1. Cao, 1980 [1760], vol. 3, p. 69.

2. The CVS question added " . . . and observing this order."

3. See *Culture's Consequences*, 2001, Appendix 5.

4. In 1988 private savings as a share of GNP were 12 percent for Japan, 8 percent for Germany, 4 percent for Britain, and 3 percent for the United States.

5. Ben Knapen in *NRC Handelsblad*, February 9, 1989. Back-translated from the Dutch by GH.

6. Zürcher, 1993.

7. Elias, 1969, pp. 336–41.

8. Schneider & Lysgaard (1953) in a survey of U.S. high school students showed that deferment of gratification increased with the occupational class of the parents.

9. Levine, Sato, Hashimoto, & Verma, 1995; *Culture's Consequences*, 2001, p. 360.

10. *Culture's Consequences*, 2001, pp. 360–61.

11. Best & Williams, 1996; *Culture's Consequences*, 2001, p. 361.

12. *Culture's Consequences*, 2001, p. 359; Hill & Romm, 1996. Their study also included mothers from Israel whose answers were somewhere in between those from the two Australian groups.

13. Argyle, Henderson, Bond, Iizuka, & Contarello, 1986; *Culture's Consequences*, 2001, pp. 359–60.

14. Bond & Wang, 1983, p. 60.

15. Redding, 1990, p. 187.

16. From Alitto, 1986, p. 131.

17. Yan & Gaier, 1994; Stevenson & Lee, 1996, p. 136; *Culture's Consequences*, 2001, p. 365.

18. National Center for Education Statistics, 1999.

19. The correlations between math scores and LTO were 0.58 (0.05-level) for fourth grade and 0.72 (0.01-level) for eighth grade. Science scores and math scores were correlated for the two age groups with 0.81 and 0.87, respectively (both 0.001-level). The correlations of science scores with LTO were not significant: 0.06 for fourth grade, 0.18 for eighth grade. The correlations of math and science with wealth (GNP per capita, eighth grade) were both 0.38, just significant at the 0.05-level. See *Culture's Consequences*, 2001, p. 365.

20. Hofstede, 1986; Biggs, 1996.

21. G. J. Hofstede, 1995.

22. Redding, 1980, pp. 196–97.

23. Wu, 1980.

24. Chew-Lim, 1997, p. 98.

25. From the *Li Chi*, a collection of writings of the disciples of Confucius codified around 100 B.C.; in Watts, 1979, p. 83.

26. Wirthlin Worldwide, 1996.

27. *Culture's Consequences*, 2001, p. 356. The correlation across eleven countries was −0.51 (0.05-level). Leisure time was rated "very important" by 68 percent of respondents in Nigeria and by 14 percent in China.

28. Peterson, Dibrell, & Pett (2002) compared western European, Japanese, and U.S. firms in the chemical and transportation industries in the period 1986–95. They took return on investment and return on assets as measures of short-term orientation and, as measures of long-term orientation, market share as well as research and development

expenditures in percents of sales. None of these measures followed the supposed LTO order: Japan, Europe, United States. The authors suggested their findings may be too specific to the time period and to the particular industries for these measures to be valid operationalizations of LTO.

29. Mamman & Saffu, 1998.

30. Hofstede, Van Deusen, Mueller, Charles, & the Business Goals Network, 2002, p. 800. The multiple correlation across twelve overlapping countries was 0.62 (0.05-level).

31. Redding, 1990, p. 209.

32. Hastings & Hastings, 1981. Correlation across eleven countries was 0.69 (0.01-level).

33. Yeung & Tung, 1996.

34. Across the nineteen countries for which 2002 data were available, CIEC and LTO were correlated with −0.67 (0.01-level; high-LTO countries more often paying bribes).

35. Chenery & Strout, 1966.

36. Colombia's GNP per capita was $340 in 1970 and $2,080 in 2000. In South Korea the figures were $250 in 1970 and $8,910 in 2000 (World Bank, 1972; World Development Report, 2002).

37. Kahn, 1979.

38. The correlation between LTO and the thirty-year ratio of GNP per capita is 0.57 across the twenty-three countries in the CVS (0.01-level), 0.76 (0.001-level) if mainland China is excluded, and 0.45 (0.01-level) across all thirty-eight countries in Table 6.1.

39. Read, 1993. The correlation between LTO and MPS across the twenty-three CVS countries was 0.58 (0.01-level).

40. de Mooij, 2004. The rank correlations across fifteen countries were 0.43 for real estate (nearly significant, 0.054-level) and −0.66 for mutual funds (0.01-level).

41. *Human Development Report 2002*, Table 5.

42. Stiglitz, 2002.

43. Data from an article by Rob Schoof in *NRC Handelsblad*, January 18, 2003, based on information from the International Center for Prison Studies, King's College, London.

44. The twenty-four countries were Australia, Austria, Belgium, Canada, the Czech Republic, Denmark, Finland, France, Germany, Great Britain, Hungary, Ireland, Italy, Japan, the Netherlands, New Zealand, Norway, Poland, Portugal, Slovakia, Spain, Sweden, Switzerland, and the United States. Because of the extreme value of the rate of imprisonment in the United States, the analysis was based on rank correlations. Zero-order rank correlations with the rate of imprisonment were 2000 GNP per capita −0.67 (0.001-level); LTO −0.61 (0.01-level). The multiple rank correlation with both was 0.79. Adding IDV increased this to 0.84, although the zero-order rank correlation of IDV with imprisonment was insignificant (0.12).

45. Herman Vuijsje, "Twee koffie, twee koekjes," in *NRC Handelsblad*, April 16, 1988. Quotes translated by GH.

46. *Culture's Consequences*, 2001, p. 363.

47. Campbell, 1988 [1972], pp. 71–75.

48. Hastings & Hastings, 1981; *Culture's Consequences*, 2001, p. 361.

49. Worm, 1997, p. 52, citing a 1936 book, *My Country and My People,* by the Chinese author Lin Yutang.

50. Carr, Munro, & Bishop, 1996.

51. Gao, Ting-Toomey, & Gudykunst, 1996, p. 293.

52. Kim, 1995, p. 663.

53. Dr. Yukawa Hideki, in Moore, 1967, p. 290.

54. Russell, 1976 [1952], p. 101.

55. Lewis, 1982, pp. 297, 229, 224, 168, and 302.

56. Burundi, Ethiopia, Sierra Leone, Malawi, Niger, Eritrea, Chad, Burkina Faso, Mali, Mozambique, and Rwanda, in this order from poorest to least poor. Non-African Tajikistan came in fifth position.

57. van der Veen, 2002, pp. 171–75.

58. Institute for Research on Intercultural Cooperation, established successively in Arnhem, Maastricht, and Tilburg. IRIC was closed in 2004.

59. Noorderhaven & Tidjani, 2001.

60. The article by Noorderhaven & Tidjani refers to eight factors, but they split the first and strongest factor again into three subfactors. Our interpretation of factors 3 through 6 differs slightly from theirs, but it is based on the same data.

61. *Culture's Consequences,* 2001, pp. 369–70. The correlation across the ten countries for which LTO scores were available was −0.95 (0.001-level).

62. Stiglitz, 2002.

63. Research by Ray Simonsen. See *Culture's Consequences,* 2001, p. 501.

64. Kelen, 1983 [1971], p. 44.

65. Helgesen & Kim, 2002, pp. 28–29.

66. Helgesen & Kim, 2002, pp. 8–9.

Chapter 7

1. Pugh & Hickson, 1976.

2. Negandhi & Prasad, 1971, p. 128.

3. van Oudenhoven, 2001. The countries were Belgium, Canada, Denmark, France, Germany, Greece, the Netherlands, Spain, the United Kingdom, and the United States.

4. *Culture's Consequences,* 2001, p. 378. The correlations were bureaucracy with PDI 0.66 and with UAI 0.63, both 0.05-level; individual work with IDV 0.47; hostile work ambiance with MAS 0.49, both 0.10-level.

5. Mouritzen and Svara, 2002, pp. 55–56 and 75.

6. Fayol, 1970 [1916], p. 21. Translation by GH.

7. Weber, 1976 [1930], p. 224.

8. Weber, 1970 [1948], p. 196. Translated from *Wirtschaft und Gesellschaft,* 1921, Part III, Chapter 6, p. 650.

9. Fayol, 1970 [1916], p. 85.

10. Laurent, 1981, pp. 101–14.

11. From a paper presented in 1925, in Metcalf & Urwick, 1940, pp. 58–59.

12. Confucian values were also evident in Sun Yat-sen's extension of the *trias politica:* the examination and control branches had to guarantee the virtue of the civil servants.

13. Williamson, 1975.

14. Ouchi, 1980, pp. 129–41.

15. Kieser & Kubicek, 1983.

16. Crozier & Friedberg, 1977; Pagès, Bonetti, de Gaulejac. & Descendre, 1979.

17. Mintzberg, 1983. Later on (Mintzberg, 1989), the author added a "missionary configuration" with "standardization of norms." To us, this is an aspect of the other types rather than a type by itself. It deals with the strength of an organization's culture, which will be discussed in Chapter 8.

18. Mintzberg, 1983, pp. 34–35.

19. As described in a French classic: organization sociologist Michel Crozier's *The Bureaucratic Phenomenon* (Crozier, 1964).

20. Mintzberg, 1993.

21. *Culture's Consequences*, 2001, p. 382.

22. Harzing & Sorge, 2003, based on nearly three hundred foreign subsidiaries in twenty-two countries, from more than one hundred multinationals originating from nine countries in eight industries. Their article does not describe in what way the home cultures affect the control process, but an obvious hypothesis is that home-country uncertainty avoidance affects impersonal control by systems and home-country power distance affects personal control by expatriates.

23. Hypotheses for research on the subject have been formulated by Gray, 1988, pp. 1–15.

24. Gambling, 1977, pp. 141–51.

25. Cleverley, 1971.

26. Hofstede, 1967.

27. Morakul & Wu, 2001.

28. Baker, 1976, pp. 886–93.

29. Hofstede, 1978.

30. Pedersen & Thomsen, 1997. The countries were Austria, Belgium, Denmark, Finland, France, Germany, Italy, the Netherlands, Norway, Spain, Sweden, and the United Kingdom.

31. Product moment correlation was 0.65 (0.05-level).

32. The correlation was 0.52 (0.05-level). See *Culture's Consequences*, 2001, p. 384.

33. In spite of the Austrian score, the correlation was −0.77 (0.01-level).

34. Semenov, 2000. The countries were the same as in the study by Pedersen & Thomsen plus Australia, Canada, Ireland, New Zealand, and the United States.

35. Weimer, 1995, p. 336; *Culture's Consequences*, 2001, p. 385.

36. Hofstede, van Deusen, Mueller, Charles, & the Business Goals Network, 2002.

37. An exception is our compatriot Manfred Kets de Vries, who analyzed the behavior of managers in Freudian terms (e.g., Kets de Vries, 2001).

38. Herzberg, Mausner, & Snyderman, 1959.

39. McGregor, 1960. The following part is based on Hofstede, 1988, and *Culture's Consequences*, 2001, p. 387.

40. Schuler & Rogovsky, 1998; *Culture's Consequences*, 2001, pp. 387–88.

41. *The Ruler*, Machiavelli, 1955 [1517].

42. *Culture's Consequences*, 2001, p. 388.

43. Schramm-Nielsen, 2001, pp. 410–12.

44. Jackofsky & Slocum, 1988; *Culture's Consequences*, 2001, p. 388.

45. Tollgerdt-Andersson, 1996. The countries were Denmark, France, Germany, Italy, Norway, Spain, Sweden, and the United Kingdom. The percentages were correlated with UAI: −0.86 (0.01-level); and with UAI plus MAS: −0.95 (0.001-level).

46. *Culture's Consequences*, 2001, pp. 388–89.

47. Triandis, 1973, p. 165.

48. *Culture's Consequences*, 2001, p. 389.

49. Klidas, 2001.

50. McGregor, 1960; Blake & Mouton, 1964; Likert, 1967.

51. Jenkins, 1973, p. 258; the lecturer was Frederick Herzberg.

52. Triandis, 1973, pp. 55–68.

53. Hoppe & Bhagat, forthcoming.

54. Laaksonen, 1977.

55. *Culture's Consequences*, 2001, p. 391.

56. Drucker, 1955, Chapter 11.

57. *Führung durch Zielvereinbarung*; Ferguson, 1973, p. 15.

58. Franck, 1973. Translation by GH.

59. *Culture's Consequences*, 2001, p. 390.

60. Inspired by Magalhaes, 1984, and by discussions with Anne-Marie Bouvy and Giorgio Inzerilli.

61. Hofstede, 1980b; comments by Goodstein, 1981, and by Hunt, 1981, and a reply by Hofstede, 1981. An amusing detail is that in the final version of the article, a number of changes had been made at the request of the editor, but by an administrative error the original, unchanged version got published.

62. Pascal, *Pensées*, 60, 294: "Vérité en-deça des Pyrénées, erreur au-delà." Montaigne, *Essais* II, XII, 34: "Quelle vérité que ces montagnes bornent, qui est mensonge au monde qui se tient au delà?" ("What kind of a truth is this that is bounded by a chain of mountains and is falsehood to the people living on the other side?" Translation by GH.)

63. "There is nothing as practical as a good theory," attributed to Kurt Lewin.

64. Peterson & Hunt, 1997, p. 214.

65. Stewart, 1985, p. 209.

66. Locke, 1996.

67. Generally felt in Europe but proven by Baruch, 2001, based on an analysis of the location of almost two thousand authors in more than one thousand articles in seven top management journals.

68. Pugh & Hickson, 1993; Hickson & Pugh, 2001, p. 8.

69. Porter, 1990. For critiques of Porter's ethnocentrism, see van den Bosch & van Prooijen, 1992, with an answer by Porter, 1992; Davies & Ellis, 2000; Barney, 2002, p. 54.

70. The most cited psychologists in the Social Science Citation Index are all Americans; the most cited sociologists are nearly all Europeans, in spite of the fact that the SSCI is mainly based on U.S. journals.

71. Bourdieu & Wacquant, 1992, pp. 45 and 115.

72. Hofstede, 1996a; *Culture's Consequences*, 2001, p. 381.

Chapter 8

1. This case is derived from Hofstede, Neuijen, Ohayv, & Sanders, 1990. The remainder of this chapter also draws heavily upon this paper.

2. Deal & Kennedy, 1982; Peters & Waterman, 1982.

3. Peters & Waterman, 1982, pp. 75–76.

4. See, for example, the critiques of Wilkins & Ouchi, 1983, p. 477; Schein, 1985, p. 315; Weick, 1985, p. 385; Saffold, 1988.

5. Pagès, Bonetti, de Gaulejac, & Descendre, 1979.

6. This is also noticeable in French organization sociology, such as in the work of Crozier, 1964, and Crozier and Friedberg, 1977.

7. Soeters, 1986; Lammers, 1988.

8. For example, in Westerlund & Sjöstrand, 1975; March & Olsen, 1976; Broms & Gahmberg, 1983; Brunsson, 1985.

9. Alvesson, 2002, pp. 38–39.

10. Smircich, 1983.

11. What we call *practices* can also be labeled *conventions, customs, habits, mores, traditions, usages*. They were recognized as part of culture already by the British pioneer anthropologist Edward Tylor (1924 [1871]): "Culture is that complex whole which includes knowledge, beliefs, art, morals, law, customs and any other capabilities and habits acquired by man as a member of society."

12. For example, Inglehart, Basañez, & Moreno, 1998; Halman, 2001.

13. Harzing & Sorge, 2003.

14. Soeters & Schreuder, 1986.

15. Carlzon, 1987.

16. A *Hawthorne effect* means that employees selected for an experiment are so motivated by their being selected that this alone guarantees the experiment's success. It is named after the Hawthorne plant of Western Electric Corporation in the United States, where Professor Elton Mayo in the 1920s and '30s conducted a series of classic experiments in work organization.

17. In a factor analysis of only these $6 \times 3 = 18$ questions for the twenty units, they accounted for 86 percent of the variance in mean scores between units.

18. Culture strength was statistically operationalized as the mean standard deviation, across the individuals within a unit, of scores on the eighteen key practices questions (three per dimension): a low standard deviation meant a strong culture. Actual mean standard deviations varied from 0.87 to 1.08, and the Spearman rank order correlation between these mean standard deviations and the twenty units' scores on results orientation was −0.71 (0.001-level).

19. Blake & Mouton, 1964.

20. Merton, 1968 [1949].

21. Crossing forty characteristics with six dimensions, one can expect by chance two or three correlations significant at the 0.01-level and twelve at the 0.05-level. In fact,

there were fifteen correlations at the 0.01-level and beyond and twenty-eight at the 0.05-level. Chance therefore could only account for a minor part of the relationships found.

22. Pugh & Hickson, 1976.

23. A correlation coefficient of 0.78, significant at the 0.001-level.

24. *Culture's Consequences*, 2001, pp. 405–8.

25. Hofstede, Bond, & Luk, 1993, and *Culture's Consequences*, 2001, pp. 411–13.

26. McCrae & John, 1992.

27. *Culture's Consequences*, 2001, pp. 413–14; Hofstede, 1995, p. 216.

28. *Culture's Consequences*, 2001, pp. 414–15.

29. Soeters, 2000, pp. 465–66, found common occupational cultures in uniformed occupations: police, armed forces, and fire brigade, all of whom are relatively isolated from their societies.

30. Sanders & van der Veen, 1998, reported on the reuse of the IRIC questionnaire in intensive care units in hospitals in twelve countries. Unit cultures varied along four dimensions: the numbers 1, 2, and 4 from the IRIC study, plus a dimension of high versus low need for security. A custom-designed questionnaire, based on interviews within the units, would undoubtedly have produced additional, maybe new, dimensions.

31. Swiss management consultant Cuno Pümpin has described a model with seven dimensions, of which five are similar to those found in the IRIC project (results orientation, employee orientation, company orientation, cost orientation, and customer orientation); his publications do not explain how these dimensions were found (Pümpin, 1984; Pümpin, Kobi, & Wüthrich, 1985). In India, Professor Pradip Khandwalla, 1985, in a study of managers across seventy-five organizations, using five-point survey questions similar to our "Where I work . . . " questions, found a first factor closely resembling our process versus results orientation.

32. The article by Hofstede, Neuijen, Ohayv, & Sanders, 1990, lists the content of the questions used to compute the indices in the IRIC study.

33. This is simpler than the McKinsey consultants' "7-S" framework: Structure, Strategy, Systems, Shared values, Skills, Style, and Staff (Peters & Waterman, 1982, p. 10).

34. Witte, 1973. A summary in English appeared in Witte, 1977.

Chapter 9

1. Morier, 1923 [1824]. The quote from the text is from pp. 434–35; the quote from the editor is from p. vi.

2. This paragraph has been inspired by Campbell, 1988 [1972], pp. 174–206.

3. van der Veen, 2002.

4. For a review of studies with regard to culture shock, see Ward, Bochner, & Furnham, 2001.

5. Harzing, 1995, 2001; Tung, 1982, pp. 57–71.

6. U.S. Professor Howard V. Perlmutter developed the sequence *ethnocentric, polycentric, geocentric* as three phases in the development of a multinational business corporation. In the case of a host population, it is unlikely that they will ever become geocentric—abolishing all nation-specific standards.

7. Hofstede, 1994, Chapter 15.

8. Peterson & Pike, 2002.

9. In cultural anthropology the phenomenon that our thinking is influenced by our language is known as the Sapir-Whorf theorem, after Edward Sapir and Benjamin Lee Whorf, who formulated it.

10. Attributed to Henry Louis Mencken (1880–1956), U.S. critic and satirist.

11. *Culture's Consequences*, 2001, pp. 63–65.

12. From a speech by R. M. Hadjiwibowo, September 1983. Translation from the Dutch by GH with suggestions by the author.

13. This section uses extracts from Hofstede, 1986.

14. Bel Ghazi, 1982, p. 82. Translation from the Dutch by GH.

15. For a review of relevant research, see *Culture's Consequences*, 2001, pp. 430–31 plus notes.

16. Many Muslim cultures are endogamous (they allow marriage between first cousins), and girls are conveniently married to relatives back home.

17. For some examples, see Sebenius, 2002.

18. Moore & Lewis, 1999, p. 278.

19. Saner & Yiu, 2000.

20. This leads to different criteria in the selection of candidates for expatriation. See Caligiuri, 2000, and Franke & Nicholson, 2002.

21. World Investment Report, 2000.

22. Schenk, 2001; Apfelthaler, Muller, & Rehder, 2002.

23. Sherman, Helmreich, & Merritt, 1997.

24. For example, Lord & Ranft, 2000; Lynch & Beck, 2001. For a review, see *Culture's Consequences*, 2001, p. 448 and notes.

25. de Mooij, 1998b, pp. 58–59.

26. de Mooij, 1998b, p. 57.

27. Another area of sustained and sometimes increasing cultural differentiation is packaging design. The same products, in order to be sold in different cultures, need different packaging (van den Berg-Weitzel & van de Laar, 2000).

28. The rest of this section is a summary of research reported in *Culture's Consequences*, 2001, pp. 450–51 and notes.

29. Fisher, 1988, p. 41. Without being aware of Geert's work, Fisher has used a very similar approach to culture. For example, he also used the computer analogy for the human mind.

30. Lammers, 2003.

31. Groterath, 2000; Soeters & Recht, 2001.

32. From the title of a book by Kiernan (1969) about the British imperial age.

33. Dia, 1996.

34. For example, Professor Michael Porter's 1990 book *The Competitive Advantage of Nations* does not mention corruption.

35. The World Bank is perceived by many as serving U.S. interests (Stiglitz, 2002).

36. A group of authors committed to the development of Africa stresses fulfilling social rather than individual achievement needs (Afro-Centric Alliance, 2001). See also d'Iribarne, 2002.

37. Hawes & Kealey, 1979.

38. Forss, Carlsen, Frøyland, Sitari, & Vilby, 1988. This study continued a pilot study by the Institute for Research on Intercultural Cooperation in the Netherlands. IRIC's design had been to combine development agencies *and* multinationals in the same study about factors leading to the effectiveness of expatriates. See Andersson & Hofstede, 1984. After the proposed public and private cooperation fell through, the Nordic development agencies went ahead on their own.

39. Pagès, 1971, p. 281.

40. Professor Nancy Adler from Canada has focused on the role of the executive spouse and produced videos of interviews with spouses. See also Adler, 1991.

41. Bond, 1992.

42. Hofstede, Pedersen, & Hofstede, 2002.

43. Cushner & Brislin, 1996. The differences it covers are mainly those between the United States and Third World cultures: most deal with individualism–collectivism and power distance.

44. Taken from an unpublished conference paper by Alfred J. Kraemer, Munich, 1978.

45. Åke Phillips.

Chapter 10

1. Hume, 1882 [1742], p. 252.

2. "The Ballad of Lake Laloo and Other Rhymes," quoted by Renier, 1931.

3. A classic example was Margaret Mead's film *Four Families*, showing the relationship between parents and small children in India, France, Japan, and Canada, produced in 1959 by the National Film Board of Canada. A more recent example is a video produced along with a book by Tobin, Wu, & Danielson (1989) about classroom behavior of four-year-old preschool children in Japan, China, and Hawaii.

4. Russell, 1979 [1927], pp. 23–24.

5. Kuhn, 1970.

6. Fisher, 1988, pp. 144 and 153.

7. The war of 1839–42 was only the First Opium War. After the Second Opium War, which ended in 1860, the British also got Kowloon, on the Chinese mainland opposite Hong Kong Island, and in 1898 they leased the New Territories, adjacent to Kowloon. This lease was concluded for ninety-nine years and expired in 1997, at which point the entire colony was returned to China.

8. The term *global village* was coined by the Canadian media philosopher Marshall McLuhan. See de Mooij, 2004, p. 1.

Glossary

For TERMS not mentioned in this Glossary, see the Subject Index.

AGENCY: the way in which persons, empowered to act on behalf of an organization, fulfill this task.

ANTHROPOLOGY: the science of man in his physical, social, and cultural variation. In this book *anthropology* always stands for social or cultural anthropology, which is the integrated study of human societies, in particular (although not only) traditional or preliterate ones.

ANXIETY: a diffuse state of being uneasy or worried about what may happen.

BUREAUCRACY: a form of organization based on strict rules and competences attached to positions.

COLLECTIVISM: the opposite of *individualism*; together, they form one of the dimensions of national cultures. *Collectivism* stands for a society in which people from birth onward are integrated into strong, cohesive in-groups, which throughout people's lifetime continue to protect them in exchange for unquestioning loyalty.

CONFUCIAN DYNAMISM (ORIGINALLY CONFUCIAN WORK DYNAMISM): a dimension of national cultures found through research among student samples using the Chinese Value Survey. Rebaptized in this book *long-term versus short-term orientation* (see under these catchwords).

CORRELATION: a term from mathematical statistics expressing the degree of common variation of two sets of numbers. The coefficient of correlation can vary from a maximum of 1.00 (perfect agreement) via the value 0 (no relationship) to a minimum of −1.00 (perfect disagreement).

CULTURE: (1) the training or refining of the mind; civilization; (2) the collective programming of the mind that distinguishes the members of one group or category of people from another—this meaning corresponds to the use of the term *culture* in anthropology and is used throughout this book.

CULTURE ASSIMILATOR: a programmed learning tool for developing intercultural communication skills.

CULTURE SHOCK: a state of distress following the transfer of a person to an unfamiliar cultural environment. It may be accompanied by symptoms of physical illness.

DIMENSION: an aspect of a phenomenon that can be measured (expressed in a number).

DIMENSIONAL MODEL: a set of dimensions used in combination in order to describe a phenomenon.

EMPOWERMENT: the process of increasing employees' influence on their work situation.

ETHNOCENTRISM: applying the standards of one's own society to people outside that society.

EXTENDED FAMILY: a family group including relatives in the second and third degree (or beyond), such as grandparents, uncles, aunts, and cousins.

FACE: in collectivist societies, a quality attributed to someone who meets the essential requirements related to his or her social position.

FACTOR ANALYSIS: a technique from mathematical statistics designed to assist the researcher in explaining the variety in a set of observed phenomena by a minimum number of underlying common factors.

FEMININITY: the opposite of *masculinity*; together, they form one of the dimensions of national cultures. *Femininity* stands for a society in which emotional gender roles overlap: both men and women are supposed to be modest, tender, and concerned with the quality of life.

FUNDAMENTALISM: the belief that there is only one Truth and that one's own group is in possession of this Truth, which is usually defined in great detail.

GESTALT: an integrated whole that should be studied as such and loses its meaning when divided into parts; from a German word meaning "form."

GROSS NATIONAL PRODUCT (GNP): a measure of the total flow of goods and services produced by the economy of a country over a year, including income from foreign investments by domestic residents, but excluding income from domestic investments by foreign residents.

HEROES: persons, alive or dead, real or imaginary, assumed to possess characteristics highly prized in a culture and thus serving as models for behavior.

HOMEOSTASIS: the tendency in an organism or a social system to maintain internal stability by compensating for external changes.

INDIVIDUALISM: the opposite of *collectivism*; together, they form one of the dimensions of national cultures. *Individualism* stands for a society in which the ties between individuals are loose: everyone is expected to look after himself or herself and his or her immediate family only.

INDIVIDUALISM INDEX (IDV): a measure for the degree of individualism in a country's culture, based on the IBM research project.

IN-GROUP: a cohesive group that offers protection in exchange for loyalty and provides its members with a sense of identity.

LONG-TERM ORIENTATION: the opposite of *short-term orientation*; together, they form a dimension of national cultures originally labeled *Confucian work dynamism*. *Long-term orientation* stands for the fostering of virtues oriented toward future rewards, in particular perseverance and thrift.

LONG-TERM ORIENTATION INDEX (LTO): a measure for the degree of long-term orientation in a country culture, based on the Chinese Value Survey research project among student samples.

MASCULINITY: the opposite of *femininity*; together, they form one of the dimensions of national cultures. *Masculinity* stands for a society in which emotional gender roles are clearly distinct: men are supposed to be assertive, tough, and focused on material success; women are supposed to be more modest, tender, and concerned with the quality of life.

MASCULINITY INDEX (MAS): a measure for the degree of masculinity in a country's culture, based on the IBM research project.

MATRIX ORGANIZATION: an organization structure in which a person can report to two or three superiors for different aspects of his or her work—for example, one for the task and one for the professional aspects, or one for the business line and one for the country.

MOTIVATION: an assumed force operating inside an individual inducing him or her to choose one action over another.

NATIONAL CHARACTER: a term used in the past to describe what is called in this book *national culture*. A disadvantage of the term *character* is that it stresses the individual aspects at the expense of the social system.

NATIONAL CULTURE: the collective programming of the mind acquired by growing up in a particular country.

NUCLEAR FAMILY: a family group including only relatives in the first degree (parents and children).

ORGANIZATIONAL CULTURE: the collective programming of the mind that distinguishes the members of one organization from another.

PARADIGM: set of common assumptions that dominate a scientific field and constrain the thinking of the scientists in this field.

PARTICULARISM: a way of thinking prevailing in collectivist societies, in which the standards for the way a person should be treated depend on the group to which this person belongs.

POWER DISTANCE: the extent to which the less powerful members of institutions and organizations within a country expect and accept that power is distributed unequally. One of the dimensions of national cultures (from small to large).

POWER DISTANCE INDEX (PDI): a measure for the degree of power distance in a country's culture, based on the IBM research project.

RELATIVISM: a willingness to consider other persons' or groups' theories and values as equally reasonable as one's own.

RISK: the chance that an action will have an undesirable but known outcome.

RITUALS: collective activities, technically superfluous to reach desired ends, but that within a culture are considered as socially essential: they are therefore carried out for their own sake.

SHORT-TERM ORIENTATION: the opposite of *long-term orientation* (see there); together, they form a dimension of national cultures. *Short-term orientation* stands for the fostering of virtues related to the past and present—in particular, respect for tradition, preservation of "face," and fulfilling social obligations.

SIGNIFICANT: see *statistically significant.*

SOCIALIZATION: the acquisition of the values and practices belonging to a culture, by participating in that culture.

STATISTICALLY SIGNIFICANT: a term indicating that the relationship between two measures is sufficiently strong to rule out the possibility that it is because of pure chance. The significance level, usually 0.05, 0.01, or 0.001, is the remaining risk that the relationship could still be accidental.

SYMBOLS: words, pictures, gestures, or objects that carry a particular meaning only recognized as such by those who share a culture.

TYPOLOGY: a set of ideal types used to describe a phenomenon.

UNCERTAINTY AVOIDANCE: the extent to which the members of a culture feel threatened by ambiguous or unknown situations. One of the dimensions of national cultures (from weak to strong).

UNCERTAINTY AVOIDANCE INDEX (UAI): a measure for the degree of uncertainty avoidance in a country's culture, based on the IBM research project.

UNIVERSALISM: a way of thinking prevailing in individualist societies, in which the standards for the way a person should be treated are the same for everybody.

VALIDATION: testing the conclusions from one piece of research against data from independent other sources.

VALUES: broad tendencies to prefer certain states of affairs over others.

XENOPHILIA: the feeling that persons and things from abroad must be superior.

XENOPHOBIA: the feeling that foreign persons or things are dangerous.

Bibliography

NEWSPAPER CUTTINGS and unpublished documents other than theses have not been listed.

Aberbach, J. D., and R. D. Putnam. 1977. *Paths to the top: The origins and careers of political and administrative elites.* Ann Arbor: University of Michigan Press.

Adebayo, A. 1988. The masculine side of planned parenthood: An explanatory analysis. *Journal of Comparative Family Studies* 19: 55–67.

Adler, N. J. 1991. *International dimensions of organizational behavior.* 2nd ed. Boston: Kent Publishing Company.

Afro-Centric Alliance. 2001. Indigenising organisational change: Localisation in Tanzania and Malawi. *Journal of Managerial Psychology* 16: 59–78.

Alitto, G. S. 1986. *The last Confucian: Liang Shu-ming and the Chinese dilemma of modernity.* 2nd ed. Berkeley: University of California Press.

Almond, G. A., and S. Verba. 1963. *The civic culture: Political attitudes and democracy in five nations.* Princeton, NJ: Princeton University Press.

Alvesson, M. 2002. *Understanding organizational culture.* London: Sage.

Andersson, L., and G. Hofstede. 1984. *The effectiveness of expatriates: Report on a feasibility study.* Tilburg, Neth.: IRIC.

Apfelthaler, G., H. J. Muller, and R. R. Rehder. 2002. Corporate global culture as competitive advantage: Learning from Germany and Japan in Alabama and Austria? *Journal of World Business* 37: 108–18.

Argyle, M., M. Henderson, M. Bond, Y. Iizuka, and A. Contarello. 1986. Cross-cultural variations in relationship rules. *International Journal of Psychology* 21: 287–315.

Baker, C. R. 1976. An investigation of differences in values: Accounting majors versus non-accounting majors. *The Accounting Review* 51 (4): 886–93.

Barney, J. B. 2002. Strategic management: From informed conversation to academic discipline. *Academy of Management Executive* 16: 53–57.

Baruch, J. 2001. Global or North American? A geographical based comparative analysis of publications in top management journals. *International Journal of Cross Cultural Management* 1: 109–26.

Bel Ghazi, H. 1982. *Over twee culturen: Uitbuiting en opportunisme.* Rotterdam: Futile.

Bem, S. L. 1975. Sex role adaptability: One consequence of psychological androgyny. *Journal of Personality and Social Psychology* 31: 634–43.

Best, D. L., and J. E. Williams. 1996. Anticipation of aging: A cross-cultural examination of young adults' views of growing old. In *Asian contributions to cross-cultural psychology,* ed. J. Pandey, D. Sinha, and D. P. S. Bhawuk, 274–88. New Delhi: Sage.

Biggs, J. B. 1996. Approaches to learning of Asian students: A multiple paradox. In *Asian contributions to cross-cultural psychology,* ed. J. Pandey, D. Sinha, and D. P. S. Bhawuk, 180–99. New Delhi: Sage.

Blake, Robert R., and J. S. Mouton. 1964. *The managerial grid.* Houston: Gulf Publishing Co.

Blanchflower, D. G., and A. J. Oswald. 1998. What makes an entrepreneur? *Journal of Labour Economics* 16 (1): 26–60.

Bond, M. H. 1992. The process of enhancing cross-cultural competence in Hong-Kong organizations. *International Journal of Intercultural Relations* 16: 395–412.

Bond, M. H., and S. H. Wang. 1983. Aggressive behavior and the problem of maintaining order and harmony. In *Global perspectives on aggression,* ed. A. P. Goldstein and M. H. Segall, 58–73. New York: Pergamon.

Bond, R., and P. B. Smith. 1996. Culture and conformity: A meta-analysis of studies using Asch's (1952, 1956) line judgment task. *Psychological Bulletin* 119: 111–37.

Bourdieu, P. 1980. *Le sens pratique.* Paris: Editions de Minuit.

Bourdieu, P., and L. J. D. Wacquant. 1992. *Réponses: Pour une anthropologie réflexive.* Paris: Seuil.

Broms, H., and H. Gahmberg. 1983. Communication to self in organizations and cultures. *Administrative Science Quarterly* 28: 482–95.

Broverman, I. K., S. R. Vogel, D. M. Broverman, F. E. Clarkson, and P. S. Rosenkrantz. 1972. Sex-role stereotypes: A current appraisal. *Journal of Social Issues* 28 (2): 59–78.

Brunsson, N. 1985. *The irrational organization.* Chichester, UK: Wiley.

Buss, D. M. 1989. Sex differences in human mate preferences: Evolutionary hypotheses tested in 37 cultures. *Behavioral and Brain Sciences* 12: 1–49.

Buss, D. M., et al. 1990. International preferences in selecting mates. *Journal of Cross-Cultural Psychology* 21: 5–47.

Caligiuri, P. M. 2000. The Big Five personality characteristics as predictors of expatriate's desire to terminate the assignment and supervisor rated performance. *Personnel Psychology* 53: 67–88.

Campbell, J. 1988. *Myths to live by.* New York: Bantam Books. [Original work published 1972.]

Cao Xueqin. 1980. *The story of the stone, also known as The dream of the red chamber.* Vol. 3: *The Warning Voice.* Translated by David Hawkes. Harmondsworth, Mddx., UK: Penguin Books. [Original Chinese version published c. 1760.]

Carlzon, J. 1987. *Moments of truth.* Cambridge, MA: Ballinger Publishing Company.

Carr, S. C., D. Munro, and G. D. Bishop. 1996. Attitude assessment in non-Western countries: Critical modifications to Likert scaling. *Psychologia* 39: 55–59.

Castells, M. 2001. *The Internet galaxy.* Oxford: Oxford University Press.

Cavalli-Sforza, L. L. 2000. *Genes, peoples and languages.* Berkeley: University of California Press.

Chandler, T. A., D. D. Shama, F. M. Wolf, and S. K. Planchard. 1981. Multiattributional causality: A five cross-national samples study. *Journal of Cross-Cultural Psychology* 12: 207–21.

Chenery, H. B., and A. M. Strout. 1966. Foreign assistance and economic development. *American Economic Review* 56 (4): 679–733.

Chew-Lim, F. Y. 1997. Evolution of organisational culture: A Singaporean experience. Doctoral dissertation, University of Hong Kong, School of Business.

Chinese Culture Connection. 1987. Chinese values and the search for culture-free dimensions of culture. *Journal of Cross-Cultural Psychology* 18 (2): 143–64.

Cleverley, G. 1971. *Managers and magic.* London: Longman.

Cohen, P. 1973. *The gospel according to the Harvard Business School: The education of America's managerial elite.* Garden City, NY: Doubleday.

Cooper, R., and N. Cooper. 1982. *Culture shock! Thailand . . . , and how to survive it.* Singapore: Times Books International.

Costa, J. T. Jr., A. Terraciano, and R. R. McCrae. 2001. Gender differences in personality traits across cultures: Robust and surprising findings. *Journal of Personality and Social Psychology* 81: 322–31.

Crozier, M. 1964. *The bureaucratic phenomenon.* Chicago: University of Chicago Press.

Crozier, M., and E. Friedberg. 1977. *L'acteur et le système: Les contraintes de l'action collective.* Paris: Seuil.

Cushner, K., and R. W. Brislin. 1996. *Intercultural interactions: A practical guide.* 2nd ed. Thousand Oaks, CA: Sage.

Cyert, R. M., and J. G. March. 1963. *A behavioral theory of the firm.* Englewood Cliffs, NJ: Prentice-Hall.

Davies, H., and P. Ellis. 2000. Porter's competitive advantage of nations: Time for the final judgement? *Journal of Management Studies* 37 (December 8): 1189–1213.

Deal, T. E., and A. A. Kennedy. 1982. *Corporate cultures: The rites and rituals of corporate life.* Reading, MA: Addison-Wesley.

de Mooij, M. 1998a. *Global marketing and advertising: Understanding cultural paradoxes.* Thousand Oaks, CA: Sage.

de Mooij, M. 1998b. Masculinity/femininity and consumer behavior. In G. Hofstede et al., *Masculinity and femininity: The taboo dimension of national cultures,* 55–73. Thousand Oaks, CA: Sage.

de Mooij, M. 2004. *Consumer behavior and culture: Consequences for global marketing and advertising.* Thousand Oaks, CA: Sage.

de Mooij, M., and G. Hofstede. 2002. Convergence and divergence in consumer behavior: Implications for international retailing. *Journal of Retailing* 78: 61–69.

de Tocqueville, A. 1956. *Democracy in America.* Edited and abridged by R. D. Heffner. New York: Mentor Books. [Original work published 1835.]

de Waal, F. 2001. *The ape and the sushi master: Cultural reflections of a primatologist.* New York: Basic Books.

Dia, M. 1996. *Africa's management in the 1990s and beyond: Reconciling indigenous and transplanted institutions.* Washington, DC: World Bank.

Diderot, D. 1982. *Voyage en Hollande.* Paris: François Maspéro. [Original work published 1780.]

Dion, K. K., and K. L. Dion. 1993. Individualistic and collectivistic perspectives on gender and the cultural context of love and intimacy. *Journal of Social Issues* 49 (3): 53–69.

d'Iribarne, P. 1989. *La logique de l'honneur: Gestion des entreprises et traditions nationales.* Paris: Seuil, 1989.

d'Iribarne, P. 1998. Comment s'accorder: Une rencontre franco-suédoise. In *Cultures et mondialisation: Gérer par-delà des frontières,* ed. P. d'Iribarne, A. Henry, J. P. Segal, S. Chevrier, and T. Globokar, 89–115. Paris: Seuil.

d'Iribarne, P. 2002. Motivating workers in emerging countries: Universal tools and local adaptations. *Journal of Organizational Behaviour* 23 (3): 243–56.

Djankov, S., R. La Porta, F. Lopez-de-Silanes, and A. Shleifer. 2003. *The practice of justice.* Report by the World Bank. worldbank.org/publicsector/legal/index.cfm.

Douglas, M. 1966. *Purity and danger.* London: Routledge and Kegan Paul.

Drucker, P. F. 1955. *The practice of management.* London: Mercury.

Earley, P. C. 1989. Social loafing and collectivism: A comparison of the United States and the People's Republic of China. *Administrative Science Quarterly* 34: 565–81.

Elias, N. 1969. *Ueber den Prozess der Zivilisation.* Frankfurt (Main): Suhrkamp.

Erasmus, D. 2001. *Gesprekken Colloquia.* Amsterdam: Athenaeum–Polak & van Gennep.

Eurobarometer. 1980. *Public opinion in the European Community.* Brussels: European Commission.

Eurobarometer. 1990. *The perception of poverty in Europe.* Brussels: European Commission, March.

Eurobarometer. 1994. *Trends 1974–1994: Public opinion in the European Union.* Brussels: European Commission.

Eurobarometer. 1997. *Racism and xenophobia in Europe.* Brussels: European Commission.

Fayol, H. 1970. *Administration industrielle et générale.* Paris: Dunod. [Original work published 1916.]

Ferguson, I. R. G. 1973. *Management by objectives in Deutschland.* Frankfurt: Herder und Herder.

Fisher, G. 1988. *Mindsets: The role of culture and perception in international relations.* Yarmouth, ME: Intercultural Press.

Fleishman, E. A., E. F. Harris, and H. E. Burtt. 1955. *Leadership and supervision in industry.* Columbus: Ohio State University, Bureau of Educational Research.

Foreign Policy magazine and the Center for Global Development. 2003. Ranking the rich: Which country really helps the poor? foreignpolicy.com, May 9.

Forss, K., J. Carlsen, E. Frøyland, T. Sitari, and K. Vilby. 1988. *Evaluation of the effectiveness of technical assistance personnel financed by the Nordic countries*. Stockholm: Swedish International Development Authority.

Franck, G. 1973. Épitaphe pour la D.P.O. *Le Management* 3: 8–14.

Franke, J., and N. Nicholson. 2002. Who shall we send? Cultural and other influences on the rating of selection criteria for expatriate assignments. *International Journal of Cross-Cultural Management* 1: 21–36.

Gambling, T. 1977. Magic, accounting and morale. *Accounting, Organizations and Society* 2: 141–51.

Gao, G., S. Ting-Toomey, and W. B. Gudykunst. 1996. Chinese communication processes. In *The handbook of Chinese psychology*, ed. M. H. Bond, 280–93. Hong Kong: Oxford University Press.

Giddens, A. 2001. *Sociology*. 4th ed. Cambridge, UK: Polity Press.

Gonzalez, A. 1982. Sex roles of the traditional Mexican family: A comparison of Chicano and Anglo students' attitudes. *Journal of Cross-Cultural Psychology* 13: 330–39.

Goodstein, L. D. 1981. Commentary: Do American theories apply abroad? *Organizational Dynamics* 10 (1): 49–54.

Gould, S. J. 1996. *The mismeasure of man*. New York: Norton & Company.

Gray, J. 1993. *Men are from Mars, women are from Venus*. London: HarperCollins.

Gray, S. J. 1988. Towards a theory of cultural influence on the development of accounting systems internationally. *Abacus* 24 (1): 1–15.

Groterath, A. 2000. *Operatione Babele: La comunicazione interculturale nelle missioni di pace*. Thesis Peacekeeping and Security Course, Rome University.

Habib, S. 1995. Concepts fondamentaux et fragments de psychosociologie dans l'oeuvre d'Ibn-Khaldoun: Al-Muqaddima (1375–1377). *Les Cahiers Internationaux de Psychologie Sociale* 27: 101–21.

Haley, K. H. D. 1988. *The British and the Dutch: Political and cultural relations through the ages*. London: George Philip.

Hall, E. T. 1976. *Beyond culture*. Garden City, NY: Doubleday Anchor Books.

Halman, L. 2001. *The European values study: A third wave*. Tilburg, Neth.: ESC, WORC, Tilburg University.

Halman, L., and T. Petterson. 1996. The shifting sources of morality: From religion to post-materialism? In *Political value change in Western democracies: Integration, values, identification, and participation*, ed. L. Halman and N. Nevitte, 261–84. Tilburg, Neth.: Tilburg University Press.

Harding, S., and D. Phillips, with M. Fogarty. 1986. *Contrasting values in Western Europe*. London: Macmillan.

Harris, M. 1981. *America now: The anthropology of a changing culture*. New York: Simon & Schuster.

Harrison, L. E. 1985. *Underdevelopment is a state of mind*. Lanham, MD: Madison Books.

Harzing, A. W. 1995. The persistent myth of high expatriate failure rates. *International Journal of Human Resource Management* 6: 457–74.

Harzing, A. W. 2001. Are our referencing errors undermining our scholarship and credibility? The case of expatriate failure rates. *Journal of Organizational Behavior* 23: 127–48.

Harzing, A. W., and A. Sorge. 2003. The relative impact of country of origin and universal contingencies on internationalization strategies and corporate control in multinational enterprises: Worldwide and European perspectives. *Organization Studies* 24 (2): 187–214.

Hastings, H. E., and P. K. Hastings. 1980. *Index to international public opinion 1979–1980.* Oxford: Clio.

Hastings, H. E., and P. K. Hastings. 1981. *Index to international public opinion 1980–1981.* Oxford: Clio.

Hawes, F., and D. J. Kealey. 1979. *Canadians in development: An empirical study of adaptation and effectiveness on overseas assignment.* Ottawa: Canadian International Development Agency.

Helgesen, G., and U. Kim. 2002. *Good government: Nordic and East Asian perspectives.* Copenhagen: NIAS Press in collaboration with DUPI (Dansk Udenrigspolitisk Institut–Danish Institute of International Affairs).

Helmreich, R. L., and A. C. Merritt. 1998. *Culture at work in aviation and medicine: National, organizational and professional influences.* Aldershot, Hants., UK: Ashgate.

Herzberg, F. 1966. *Work and the nature of man.* Boston: World Publishing Co.

Herzberg, F., B. Mausner, and B. B. Snyderman. 1959. *The motivation to work.* New York: John Wiley & Sons.

Hickson, D. J., and D. S. Pugh. 2001. *Management worldwide: Distinctive styles amid globalization.* New enhanced ed. Harmondsworth, Mddx., UK: Penguin Books.

Hill, C., and C. T. Romm. 1996. The role of mothers as gift givers: A comparison across 3 cultures. *Advances in Consumer Research* 23: 21–27.

Ho, D. Y. F. 1976. On the concept of face. *American Journal of Sociology* 81: 867–84.

Hofstede, G. 1967. *The game of budget control: How to live with budgetary standards and yet be motivated by them.* Assen, Neth.: Van Gorcum.

Hofstede, G. 1978. The poverty of management control philosophy. *Academy of Management Review* 3: 450–61.

Hofstede, G. 1980a. *Culture's consequences: International differences in work-related values.* Beverly Hills, CA: Sage.

Hofstede, G. 1980b. Motivation, leadership, and organization: Do American theories apply abroad? *Organizational Dynamics* 9 (1): 42–63.

Hofstede, G. 1981a. Do American theories apply abroad? A reply to Goodstein and Hunt. *Organizational Dynamics* 10 (1): 63–68.

Hofstede, G. 1981b. Management control of public and not-for-profit activities. *Accounting, Organizations and Society* 6 (3): 193–221.

Hofstede, G. 1984. *Culture's consequences: International differences in work-related values.* Abridged ed. Beverly Hills, CA: Sage.

Hofstede, G. 1986. Cultural differences in teaching and learning. *International Journal of Intercultural Relations* 10 (3): 301–20.

Hofstede, G. 1988. McGregor in Southeast Asia? In *Social values and development: Asian perspectives*, ed. D. Sinha and H. S. R. Kao, 304–14. New Delhi: Sage.

Hofstede, G. 1994. *Uncommon sense about organizations: Cases, studies, and field observations*. Thousand Oaks, CA: Sage.

Hofstede, G. 1995. Multilevel research of human systems: Flowers, bouquets, and gardens. *Human Systems Research* 14: 207–17.

Hofstede, G. 1996a. An American in Paris: The influence of nationality on organization theories. *Organization Studies* 17: 525–37.

Hofstede, G. 1996b. Gender stereotypes and partner preferences of Asian women in masculine and feminine cultures. *Journal of Cross-Cultural Psychology* 27: 533–46.

Hofstede, G. 2001a. *Culture's consequences: Comparing values, behaviors, institutions, and organizations across nations*. Thousand Oaks, CA: Sage.

Hofstede, G. 2001b. Comparing behaviors across nations: Some suggestions to Levine and Norenzayan. *Cross Cultural Psychology Bulletin* 35 (3): 27–29.

Hofstede, G., et al. 1998. *Masculinity and femininity: The taboo dimension of national cultures*. Thousand Oaks, CA: Sage.

Hofstede, G., and M. H. Bond. 1984. Hofstede's culture dimensions: An independent validation using Rokeach's Value Survey. *Journal of Cross-Cultural Psychology* 15 (4): 417–33.

Hofstede, G., and M. H. Bond. 1988. The Confucius connection: From cultural roots to economic growth. *Organizational Dynamics* 16 (4): 4–21.

Hofstede, G., and R. R. McCrae. 2004. Personality and culture revisited: Linking traits and dimensions of culture. *Cross-Cultural Research* 38 (1): 52–88.

Hofstede, G., M. H. Bond, and C. L. Luk. 1993. Individual perceptions of organizational cultures: A methodological treatise on levels of analysis. *Organizational Studies* 14: 483–503.

Hofstede, G., B. Neuijen, D. D. Ohayv, and G. Sanders. 1990. Measuring organizational cultures. *Administrative Science Quarterly* 35: 286–316.

Hofstede, G., C. A. van Deusen, C. B. Mueller, T. A. Charles, and the Business Goals Network. 2002. What goals do business leaders pursue? A study in fifteen countries. *Journal of International Business Studies* 33 (4): 785–803.

Hofstede, G. J. 1995. Open problems, formal problems. *Revue des Systèmes de Décision* 4 (2): 155–65.

Hofstede, G. J., P. B. Pedersen, and G. Hofstede. 2002. *Exploring culture: Exercises, stories and synthetic cultures*. Yarmouth, ME: Intercultural Press.

Hoppe, M. H. 1990. *A comparative study of country elites: International differences in work-related values and learning and their implications for management training and development*. Ph.D. dissertation, University of North Carolina at Chapel Hill.

Hoppe, M. H. 1998. Validating the masculinity/femininity dimensions on elites from nineteen countries. In G. Hofstede et al., *Masculinity and femininity: The taboo dimension of national cultures*, 29–43. Thousand Oaks, CA: Sage.

Hoppe, M. H., and R. Bhagat. Forthcoming. Leadership in the U.S.: The leader as a cultural hero. In *Managerial cultures of the world: A project GLOBE anthology*, ed. J. Chhokar, F. Brodbeck, and R. J. House. Thousand Oaks, CA: Sage.

Horovitz, J. H. 1980. *Top management control in Europe.* London: Macmillan.

House, R. J., M. Javidan, P. Hanges, and P. Dorfman. 2002. Understanding cultures and implicit leadership theories across the globe: An introduction to project GLOBE. *Journal of World Business* 37: 3–10.

Hsu, F. L. K. 1971. Psychological homeostasis and jen: Conceptual tools for advancing psychological anthropology. *American Anthropologist* 73: 23–44.

Humana, C. 1992. *World human rights guide.* 3rd ed. New York: Oxford University Press.

Human Development Report 1999. New York: Oxford University Press.

Human Development Report 2002. New York: Oxford University Press.

Hume, D. 1882. *The philosophical works,* 3 vol. Edited by T. H. Green and T. H. Grose. London; reprinted in facsimile, 1964, by Scientia Verlag, Aalen, Ger FRG. [Original text published 1742.]

Hunt, J. W. 1981. Commentary: Do American theories apply abroad? *Organizational Dynamics* 10 (1): 55–62.

Huntington, S. P. 1998. *The clash of civilizations and the remaking of the world order.* New York: Simon & Schuster.

Inglehart, R. 1997. *Modernization and postmodernization: Cultural, economic, and political change in 43 societies.* Princeton, NJ: Princeton University Press.

Inglehart, R., M. Basañez, and A. Moreno. 1998. *Human values and beliefs: A cross-cultural sourcebook.* Ann Arbor: University of Michigan Press.

Inkeles, A., and D. J. Levinson. 1969. National character: The study of modal personality and sociocultural systems. In *The handbook of social psychology,* ed. G. Lindzey and E. Aronson. 2nd ed., vol. 4. Reading, MA: Addison-Wesley. [Original work published 1954.]

Jackofsky, E. F., and J. W. Slocum. 1988. CEO roles across cultures. In *The executive effect: Concepts and methods for studying top managers,* ed. D. C. Hambrick, 76–99. Greenwich, CT: JAI.

Javidan, M., and R. J. House. 2001. Cultural acumen for the global manager: Lessons from project GLOBE. *Organizational Dynamics* 29 (4): 289–305.

Javidan, M., and R. J. House. 2002. Leadership and cultures around the world: Findings from GLOBE: An introduction to the special issue. *Journal of World Business* 37: 1–2.

Jenkins, D. 1973. *Blue and white collar democracy.* Garden City, NY: Doubleday.

Kahn, H. 1979. *World economic development: 1979 and beyond.* London: Croom Helm.

Kashima, E. S., and Y. Kashima. 1998. Culture and language: The case of cultural dimensions and personal pronoun use. *Journal of Cross-Cultural Psychology* 29: 461–86.

Kashima, Y., and E. S. Kashima. 2003. Individualism, GNP, climate, and pronoun drop: Is individualism determined by affluence and climate, or does language use play a role? *Journal of Cross-Cultural Psychology* 34 (1): 125–34.

Kelen, B. 1983. *Confucius in life and legend.* Singapore: Graham Brash (Pte.) Ltd. [Original work published 1971.]

Kets de Vries, M. F. R. 2001. *The leadership mystique: A user's manual for the human enterprise.* London: Financial Times/Prentice-Hall.

Khandwalla, P. N. 1985. Pioneering innovative management: An Indian excellence. *Organization Studies* 6: 161–83.

Kiernan, V. G. 1969. *The lords of humankind: European attitudes towards the outside world in the imperial age.* Harmondsworth, Mddx., UK: Pelican.

Kieser, A., and H. Kubicek. 1983. *Organisation.* Berlin: Walter de Gruyter.

Kim, U. 1995. Psychology, science, and culture: Cross-cultural analysis of national psychologies. *International Journal of Psychology* 30: 663–79.

Klidas, A. K. 2001. *Employee empowerment in the European hotel industry: Meaning, process and cultural relativity.* Ph.D. dissertation, University of Tilburg. Amsterdam: Thela Thesis.

Kluckhohn, F. R., and F. L. Strodtbeck. 1961. *Variations in value orientations.* Westport, CT: Greenwood.

Kohn, M. L. 1969. *Class and conformity: A study in values.* Homewood, IL: Dorsey Press.

Kolman, L., N. G. Noorderhaven, G. Hofstede, and E. Dienes. 2003. Cross-cultural differences in central Europe. *Journal of Managerial Psychology* 18: 76–88.

Kuhn, T. S. 1970. *The structure of scientific revolutions.* 2nd enlarged ed. Chicago: University of Chicago Press.

Kühnen, U., B. Hannover, U. Roeder, A. A. Shah, B. Schubert, A. Upmeyer, and S. Zakaria. 2001. Cross-cultural variations in identifying embedded figures: Comparisons from the United States, Germany, Russia, and Malaysia. *Journal of Cross-Cultural Psychology* 32 (3): 365–71.

Laaksonen, O. J. 1977. The power of Chinese enterprises. *International Studies of Management and Organization* 7 (1): 71–90.

Lammers, A. 1989. *Uncle Sam en Jan Salie: Hoe Nederland Amerika ontdekte.* Amsterdam: Balans.

Lammers, C. J. 1988. Transience and persistence of ideal types in organization theory. *Research in the Sociology of Organizations* 6: 203–24.

Lammers, C. J. 2003. Occupational regimes alike and unlike: British, Dutch and French patterns of inter-organizational control of foreign territories. *Organization Studies* 9: 1379–1403.

Lasch, C. 1980. *The culture of narcissism: American life in an age of diminishing expectations.* New York: Warner.

Laurent, A. 1981. Matrix organizations and Latin culture. *International Studies of Management and Organization* 10 (4): 101–14.

Lawrence, P. 1980. *Managers and management in West Germany.* London: Croom Helm.

Levine, R. V., and A. Norenzayan. 1999. The pace of life in 31 countries. *Journal of Cross-Cultural Psychology* 30: 178–205.

Levine, R. V., A. Norenzayan, and K. Philbrick. 2001. Cross-cultural differences in helping strangers. *Journal of Cross-Cultural Psychology* 32 (5): 543–60.

Levine, R., S. Sato, T. Hashimoto, and J. Verma. 1995. Love and marriage in 11 cultures. *Journal of Cross-Cultural Psychology* 30: 178–205.

Levinson, D. 1977. What have we learned from cross-cultural surveys? *American Behavioral Scientist* 20: 757–92.

Lévi-Strauss, C., and D. Eribon. 1988. *De près et de loin.* Paris: Editions Odile Jacob.

Lewis, B. 1982. *The Muslim discovery of Europe.* London: Weidenfeld & Nicholson.

Locke, R. R. 1996. *The collapse of the American management mystique.* Oxford: Oxford University Press.

Lord, M. D., and A. L. Ranft. 2000. Organizational learning about new international markets: Exploring the internal transfer of local market knowledge. *Journal of International Business Studies* 31 (4): 573–89.

Lynch, P. D., and J. C. Beck. 2001. Profiles of Internet buyers in 20 countries: Evidence for region-specific strategies. *Journal of International Business Studies* 32 (4): 725–48.

Lynn, R. 1991. *The secret of the miracle economy: Different national attitudes to competitiveness and money.* London: Social Affairs Unit.

Machiavelli, N. 1955. *The ruler.* Translated by P. Rodd. Los Angeles: Gateway Editions. [Originally published in Italian, 1517.]

Magalhaes, R. 1984. Organisation development in Latin countries: Fact or fiction. *Leadership and Organization Development Journal* 5 (5): 17–21.

Mamman, A., and K. Saffu. 1998. Short-termism, control, quick-fix and bottom line. *Journal of Managerial Psychology* 13: 291–308.

March, J. G., and J. P. Olsen. 1976. *Ambiguity and choice in organizations.* Bergen, Norway: Universitetsforlaget.

Markus, H. R., and S. Kitayama. 1991. Culture and the self: Implications for cognition, emotion, and motivation. *Psychological Review* 98: 224–53.

Maslow, A. H. 1970. *Motivation and personality.* 2nd ed. New York: Harper & Row.

Matsumoto, D. 1989. Cultural influences on the perception of emotion. *Journal of Cross-Cultural Psychology* 20: 92–105.

McClelland, D. 1961. *The achieving society.* Princeton, NJ: Van Nostrand.

McCrae, R. R., and O. P. John. 1992. An introduction to the five-factor model and its applications. *Journal of Personality and Social Psychology* 60: 175–215.

Mead, M. 1962. *Male and female.* London: Penguin Books. [Original work published 1950.]

Merritt, A. 2000. Culture in the cockpit: Do Hofstede's dimensions replicate? *Journal of Cross-Cultural Psychology* 31 (3): 283–301.

Merton, R. K. 1968. *Social theory and social structure.* Enlarged ed. New York: Free Press. [Original work published 1949.]

Metcalf, H. C., and L. Urwick. 1940. *Dynamic administration: The collected papers of Mary Parker Follett.* New York: Harper & Row.

Michaud, G., ed. 1978. *Identités collectives et relations inter-culturelles.* Paris: Presses Universitaires de France.

Mintzberg, H. 1983. *Structure in fives: Designing effective organizations.* Englewood Cliffs, NJ: Prentice-Hall.

Mintzberg, H. 1989. *Mintzberg on management: Inside our strange world of organizations.* New York: The Free Press.

Mintzberg, H. 1993. The pitfalls of strategic planning. *California Management Review* 36 (1): 32–47.

Mithen, S. 2003. *After the ice: A global human history 20,000–5,000 B.C.* London: Weidenfeld & Nicolson.

ntesquieu, C.-L. de. 1979. *De l'esprit des lois,* vol. 1. Paris: GF-Flammarion. [Original ork published 1742.]

Moore, C. A. 1967. Editor's supplement: The enigmatic Japanese mind. In *The Japanese mind: Essentials of Japanese philosophy and culture*, ed. C. A. Moore, 288–313. Tokyo: C. E. Tuttle.

Moore, K., and D. Lewis. 1999. *Birth of the multinational: Two thousand years of ancient business history, from Ashur to Augustus*. Copenhagen: Copenhagen Business School Press.

Morakul, S., and F. H. Wu. 2001. Cultural influences on the ABC implementation in Thailand's environment. *Journal of Managerial Psychology* 16: 142–58.

Morier, J. J. 1923. *The adventures of Hajji Baba of Ispahan*. Edited with an introduction and notes by C. W. Stewart. London: Oxford University Press. [Original work published 1824.]

Mouritzen, P. E., and J. H. Svara. 2002. *Leadership at the Apex: Politicians and administrators in Western local governments*. Pittsburgh, PA: University of Pittsburgh Press.

Mulder, M. 1976. Reduction of power differences in practice: The power distance reduction theory and its applications. In *European Contributions to Organization Theory*, ed. G. Hofstede and M. S. Kassem, 79–94. Assen, Neth.: Van Gorcum.

Mulder, M. 1977. *The daily power game*. Leiden, Neth.: Martinus Nijhoff.

National Center for Education Statistics. 1999. *TIMSS (Third International Mathematics and Science Study)*. http://nces.ed.gov/timss.

Negandhi, A. R., and S. B. Prasad. 1971. *Comparative management*. New York: Appleton-Century-Crofts.

Ng, S. H., et al. 1982. Human values in nine countries . In *Diversity and unity in cross-cultural psychology*, ed. R. Rath et al., 196–205. Lisse, Neth.: Swets & Zeitlinger.

Noorderhaven, N. G., and B. Tidjani. 2001. Culture, governance, and economic performance: An explorative study with a special focus on Africa. *International Journal of Cross-Cultural Management* 1: 31–52.

OECD (Organisation for Economic Co-operation and Development). 1995. *Literacy, economy and society: Results of the first international adult literacy survey*. Paris: OECD and Development Statistics Canada.

Ouchi, W. G. 1980. Markets, bureaucracies and clans. *Administrative Science Quarterly* 25: 129–41.

Oyserman, D., H. M. Coon, and M. Kemmelmeier. 2002. Rethinking individualism and collectivism: Evaluations of theoretical assumptions and meta-analyses. *Psychological Bulletin* 128: 3–72.

Page, M. 1972. *The company savage: Life in the corporate jungle*. London: Coronet.

Pagès, M. 1971. Bethel culture, 1969: Impressions of an immigrant. *Journal of Applied Behavioral Science* 7: 267–84.

Pagès, M., M. Bonetti, V. de Gaulejac, and D. Descendre. 1979. *l'Emprise de l'organisation*. Paris: Presses Universitaires de France.

Pascal, B. 1972. *Pensées*. Preface and introduction by Léon Brunschvicg. Paris: Le Livre de Poche. [Original work published 1667.]

Parsons, T., and E. A. Shils. 1951. *Toward a general theory of action*. Cambridge, MA: Harvard University Press.

Payer, L. 1989. *Medicine and culture: Notions of health and sickness in Britain, the U.S., France and West Germany*. London: Victor Gollancz.

Pedersen, T., and S. Thomsen. 1997. European patterns of corporate ownership: A twelve-country study. *Journal of International Business Studies* 28: 759–78.

Peters, T. J., and R. H. Waterman. 1982. *In search of excellence: Lessons from America's best-run companies.* New York: Harper & Row.

Peterson, M. F., and J. G. Hunt. 1997. International perspectives on international leadership. *Leadership Quarterly* 8 (3): 203–31.

Peterson, M. F., and K. L. Pike. 2002. Emics and ethics for organizational studies: A lesson in contrast from linguistics. *International Journal of Cross-Cultural Management* 2: 5–19.

Peterson, R. M., C. C. Dibrell, and T. L. Pett. 2002. Long- vs. short-term performance perspectives of Western European, Japanese, and U.S. countries: Where do they lie? *Journal of World Business* 37: 245–55.

Porter, M. E. 1990. *The competitive advantage of nations.* London: Macmillan.

Porter, M. E. 1992. A note on culture and competitive advantage: Response to van den Bosch and van Prooijen. *European Management Journal* 10: 178.

Pryor, J. B., E. R. DeSouza, J. Fitness, C. Hutz, M. Kumpf, K. Lubbert, O. Pesonen, and M. W. Erber. 1997. Gender differences in the interpretation of social-sexual behavior: A cross-cultural perspective on sexual harassment. *Journal of Cross-Cultural Psychology* 28: 509–34.

Pugh, D. S., and D. J. Hickson. 1976. *Organizational structure in its context: The Aston Programme I.* Westmead, Farnborough, Hants., UK: Saxon House.

Pugh, D. S., and D. J. Hickson. 1993. *Great writers on organizations.* Omnibus ed. Aldershot: Dartmouth.

Pümpin, C. 1984. Unternehmenskultur, Unternehmensstrategie und Unternehmenserfolg. *GDI Impuls* 2: 19–30, Bern, Switz.: Gottlieb Duttweiler Institut.

Pümpin, C., J. M. Kobi, and H. A. Wüthrich. 1985. *La culture de l'entreprise: Le profil stratégique qui conduit au succès.* Bern, Switz.: Banque Populaire Suisse.

Read, R. 1993. *Politics and policies of national economic growth.* Ph.D. dissertation, Stanford University.

Redding, S. G. 1980. Management education for Orientals. In *Breaking down barriers: Practice and priorities for international management education,* ed. B. Garratt and J. Stopford. Westmead, Farnborough, Hants., UK: Gower, 193–214.

Redding, S. G. 1990. *The spirit of Chinese capitalism.* Berlin: Walter de Gruyter.

Rendell, L., and H. Whitehead. 2001. Culture in whales and dolphins. *Behavioral and Brain Sciences* 24 (2): 309–30.

Renier, G. J. 1931. *The English: Are they human?* London: William & Norgate.

Rose, R. 1955. *Twelve angry men: A play in two acts.* London: Samuel French.

Ross, M. W. 1989. Gay youth in four cultures: A comparative study. *Journal of Homosexuality* 17: 299–314.

Russell, B. 1976. *The impact of science on society.* London: Unwin Paperbacks. [Original work published 1952.]

Russell, B. 1979. *An outline of philosophy.* London: Unwin Paperbacks. [Original work published 1927.]

Ryback, D., A. L. Sanders, J. Lorentz, and M. Koestenblatt. 1980. Child-rearing practices reported by students in six cultures. *Journal of Psychology* 110: 153–62.

Sadler, P. J., and G. Hofstede. 1976. Leadership styles: Preferences and perceptions of employees of an international company in different countries. *International Studies of Management and Organization* 6 (3): 87–113.

Saffold, G. S. 1988. Culture traits, strength, and organizational performance: Moving beyond "strong" culture. *Academy of Management Review* 13: 546–58.

Sagiv, L., and S. H. Schwartz. 2000. A new look at national culture: Illustrative applications to role stress and managerial behavior. In *Handbook of organizational culture and climate*, ed. N. M. Ashkanasy, C. P. M. Wilderom, and M. F. Peterson, 417–35. Thousand Oaks, CA: Sage.

Sandemose, A. 1938. *En flygtling krydser sit spor* [A fugitive crosses his own track]. Copenhagen: Gyldendals Bogklub. [Danish translation. Originally published in Norwegian, 1933.]

Sanders, G., and J. van der Veen. 1998. Culture in ICUs. In *Organisation and management of intensive care*, ed. D. Reis Miranda, D. W. Ryan, W. B. Schaufeli, and V. Fidler, 208–19. Berlin: Springer-Verlag.

Saner, R., and L. Yiu. 2000. Developing sustainable trans-border regions: The need for business diplomats, entrepreneurial politicians and cultural ambassadors. *Social Strategies* 23 (October): 411–28.

Schama, S. 1987. *The embarrassment of riches: An interpretation of Dutch culture in the golden age.* New York: Alfred A. Knopf.

Schein, E. H. 1985. *Organizational culture and leadership: A dynamic view.* San Francisco: Jossey-Bass.

Schenk, E. J. J. 2001. *Economie en strategie van de megafusie.* The Hague: Elsevier Wetenschappelijke Publicaties.

Schildhauer, J. 1985. *The Hansa: History and culture.* Leipzig, Ger.: Edition Leipzig.

Schneider, L., and S. Lysgaard. 1953. The deferred gratification pattern: A preliminary study. *American Sociological Review* 18: 142–49.

Schramm-Nielsen, J. 2001. Cultural dimensions of decision making: Denmark and France compared. *Journal of Managerial Psychology* 16: 404–23.

Schuler, R. S., and N. Rogovsky. 1998. Understanding compensation practice variation across firms: the impact of national culture. *Journal of International Business Studies,* 29 (1): 159–77.

Schumacher, E. F. 1973. *Small is beautiful: A study of economics as if people mattered.* London: Sphere.

Schwartz, S. H. 1994. Beyond individualism/collectivism—new cultural dimensions of values. In *Individualism and collectivism: Theory, method and applications,* ed. U. Kim, et al., 85–119. Thousand Oaks, CA: Sage.

Schwartz, S. H., and A. Bardi. 2001. Value hierarchies across cultures: Taking a similarities perspective. *Journal of Cross-Cultural Psychology* 32 (3): 268–90.

Sebenius, J. K. 2002. The hidden challenge of cross-border negotiations. *Harvard Business Review* (March): 76–85.

Semenov, R. 2000. *Cross-country differences in economic governance: Culture as a major explanatory factor.* Ph.D. dissertation, Tilburg: Tilburg University.

Shane, S. A. 1993. Cultural influences on national rates of innovation. *Journal of Business Venturing* 8: 59–73.

Shane, S. A. 1995. Uncertainty avoidance and the preference for innovation championing roles. *Journal of International Business Studies* 26: 47–68.

Shane, S. A., and S. Venkataraman. 1996. Renegade and rational championing strategies. *Organization Studies* 17: 751–72.

Shane, S. A., S. Venkataraman, and I. C. Macmillan. 1995. Cultural differences in innovation championing strategies. *Journal of Management* 21: 931–52.

Sherman, P. J., R. L. Helmreich, and A. C. Merritt. 1997. National culture and flight deck automation: Results of a multination survey. *International Journal of Aviation Psychology* 7 (4): 311–29.

Smircich, L. 1983. Concepts of culture and organizational analysis. *Administrative Science Quarterly* 28: 339–58.

Smith, P. B. 2004. Acquiescent response bias as an aspect of cultural communication style. *Journal of Cross-Cultural Psychology.* 35 (1): 50–61.

Smith, P. B., F. Trompenaars, and S. Dugan. 1995. The Rotter Locus of Control Scale in 43 countries: A test of cultural relativity. *International Journal of Psychology* 30: 377–400.

Smith, P. B., S. Dugan, and F. Trompenaars. 1996. National culture and the values of organizational employees: A dimensional analysis across 43 nations. *Journal of Cross-Cultural Psychology* 27: 231–64.

Smith, P. B., M. F. Peterson, and S. H. Schwartz. 2002. Cultural values, sources of guidance, and their relevance to managerial behavior: A 47-nation study. *Journal of Cross-Cultural Psychology* 33 (2): 188–208.

Soeters, J. 1986. Excellent companies as social movements. *Journal of Management Studies* 23: 299–313.

Soeters, J. 2000. Culture in uniformed organizations. In *Handbook of organizational culture and climate*, ed. N. M. Ashkanasy, C. P. M. Wilderom, and M. F. Peterson, 465–81. Thousand Oaks, CA: Sage.

Soeters, J., and R. Recht. 2001. Convergence or divergence in the multinational classroom? Experiences from the military. *International Journal of Intercultural Relations* 25: 423–40.

Soeters, J., and H. Schreuder. 1986. Nationale en organisatieculturen in accountantskantoren. *Sociologische Gids* 33 (2): 100–21.

Søndergaard, M. 1994. Hofstede's consequences: A study of reviews, citations and replications. *Organization Studies* 15: 447–56.

Søndergaard, M. 2002. Values of local government CEOs in job motivation: How do CEOs see the ideal job? In *Social Bonds to City Hall*, ed. P. Dahler-Larsen, 57–75. Odense, Den.: Odense University Press.

Statham, A. 1987. The gender model revisited: Differences in the management styles of men and women. *Sex Roles* 16: 409–29.

Stevens, E. P. 1973. Marianismo: The other face of machismo in Latin America. In *Female and male in Latin America*, ed. A. Pescatello, 90–101. Pittsburgh, PA: University of Pittsburgh Press.

Stevenson, H. W., and S. Y. Lee. 1996. The academic achievement of Chinese students. In *The handbook of Chinese psychology*, ed. M. H. Bond. Hong Kong: Oxford University Press.

Stewart, E. C. 1985. Culture and decision-making. In *Communication, culture, and organizational processes*, ed. W. B. Gudykunst, L. P. Stewart, and S. Ting-Toomey, 177–211. Beverly Hills, CA: Sage.

Stiglitz, J. E. 2002. *Globalization and its discontents*. New York: W. W. Norton & Company.

Stoetzel, J. 1983. *Les valeurs du temps présent*. Paris: Presses Universitaires de France.

Stroebe, W. 1976. Is social psychology really that complicated? A review of Martin Irle's Lehrbuch der Sozialpsychologie. *European Journal of Social Psychology* 6 (4): 509–11.

Tannen, D. 1992. *You just don't understand: Women and men in conversation*. London: Virago.

Tobin, J. J., D. Y. H. Wu, and D. H. Danielson. 1989. *Pre-school in three cultures: Japan, China, and the United States*. New Haven, CT: Yale University Press.

Tollgerdt-Andersson, I. 1996. Attitudes, values and demands on leadership: A cultural comparison among some European countries. In *Managing across cultures: Issues and perspectives*, ed. P. Joynt and M. Warner, 166–78. London: Thomson.

Triandis, H. C. 1972. *The analysis of subjective culture*. New York: Wiley-Interscience.

Triandis, H. C. 1973. Culture training, cognitive complexity and interpersonal attitudes. In *Readings in intercultural communication*, ed. D. S. Hoopes. Pittsburgh, PA: Regional Council for International Education, 55–68.

Triandis, H. C. 1995. *Individualism and collectivism*. Boulder, CO: Westmore.

Trompenaars, F. 1993. *Riding the waves of culture: Understanding cultural diversity in business*. London: Economist Books.

Tung, R. L. 1982. Selection and training procedures of U.S., European and Japanese multinationals. *California Management Review* 25 (1): 57–71.

Tylor, E. B. 1924. *Primitive culture*. Gloucester, MA: Smith. [Original work published 1871.]

UNICEF. 1995. *The state of the world's children 1995*. New York: UNICEF/Oxford University Press.

van den Berg-Weitzel, L., and G. van de Laar. 2000. Relation between culture and communication in packaging design. *Brand Management* 8 (3): 171–84.

van den Bosch, F. A. J., and A. A. van Prooijen. 1992. The competitive advantage of European nations: The impact of national culture, a missing element in Porter's analysis. *European Management Journal* 10: 173–78.

van der Veen, R. 2002. *Afrika: van de Koude Oorlog naar de 21e Eeuw*. Amsterdam: KIT Publishers.

van de Vliert, E. 1998. Gender role gaps, competitiveness, and masculinity. In G. Hofstede et al., *Masculinity and femininity: The taboo dimension of national cultures*, 117–29. Thousand Oaks, CA: Sage.

van Dijk, T., ed. 1997a. *Discourse as structure and process*. London: Sage.

van Dijk, T., ed. 1997b. *Discourse as social interaction*. London: Sage.

van Haaf, J., M. C. C. Vonk, and F. J. R. van de Vijver. 2002. Structural equivalence of the social norms scale of the world values survey. In *New directions in cross-cultural psychology*, ed. P. Boski, F. J. R. van de Vijver, and A. M. Chodynicka, 165–82. Warsaw: Wydawnictwo Instytutu Psychologii PAN.

van Nimwegen, T. 2002. *Global banking, global values: The in-house reception of the corporate values of ABN AMRO.* Ph.D. dissertation, Nyenrode University, Delft: Eburon.

van Oudenhoven, J. P. 2001. Do organizations reflect national cultures? A 10-nation study. *International Journal of Intercultural Relations* 25: 89–107.

van Rossum, J. H. A. 1998. Why children play: American versus Dutch boys and girls. In G. Hofstede et al., *Masculinity and femininity: The taboo dimension of national cultures,* 130–38. Thousand Oaks, CA: Sage.

Veenhoven, R. 1993. *Happiness in nations: Subjective appreciation of life in 56 nations, 1946–1992.* Rotterdam: Erasmus University, Department of Social Sciences.

Verhulst, F. C., T. M. Achenbach, R. F. Ferdinand, and M. C. Kasius. 1993. Epidemiological comparisons of American and Dutch adolescents' self-reports. *Journal of the American Academy of Child and Adolescent Psychiatry* 32: 1135–44.

Verweij, J. 1998. The importance of femininity in explaining cross-national differences in secularization. In G. Hofstede et al., *Masculinity and femininity: The taboo dimension of national cultures,* 179–91. Thousand Oaks, CA: Sage.

Verweij, J., P. Ester, and R. Nauta. 1997. Secularization as an economic and cultural phenomenon: A cross-national analysis. *Journal for the Scientific Study of Religion* 36: 309–24.

Walter, T. 1990. Why are most churchgoers women? In *Vox Angelica XX: Biblical and other essays from London Bible College,* ed. H. Rowdon. London: Paternoster.

Ward, C., S. Bochner, and A. Furnham. 2001. *The psychology of culture shock.* 2nd ed. London: Routledge.

Watts, A. 1979. *Tao: The watercourse way.* Harmondsworth, Mddx., UK: Pelican.

Webber, R. A., ed. 1969. *Culture and management.* Homewood, IL: Irwin.

Weber, M. 1970. *Essays in sociology.* Edited by H. H. Gerth and C. W. Mills. London: Routledge & Kegan Paul. [Original work published 1948.]

Weber, M. 1976. *The Protestant ethic and the spirit of capitalism.* London: George Allen & Unwin. [Original work published 1930.]

Weick, K. E. 1985. The significance of corporate culture. In *Organizational culture,* ed. P. J. Frost, L. F. Moore, M. R. Louis, C. C. Lundberg, and J. Martin, 381–89. Beverly Hills, CA: Sage.

Weimer, J. 1995. *Corporate financial goals: A multiple constituency approach to a comparative study of Dutch, U.S., and German Firms.* Ph.D. dissertation. Enschede, Neth.: Twente University.

Westbrook, M. T., and V. Legge. 1993. Health practitioners' perceptions of family attitudes towards children with disabilities: A comparison of six communities in a multicultural society. *Rehabilitation Psychology* 38 (3): 177–85.

Westbrook, M. T., V. Legge, and M. Pennay. 1993. Men's reactions to becoming disabled: A comparison of six communities in a multicultural society. *Journal of Applied Rehabilitation Counseling* 24 (3): 35–41.

Westerlund, G., and S. E. Sjöstrand. 1975. *Organizational myths.* London: Harper & Row.

Wildeman, R. E., G. Hofstede, N. G. Noorderhaven, A. R. Thurik, W. H. J. Verhoeven, and A. R. M. Wennekers. 1999. *Culture's role in entrepreneurship: Self-employment out of dissatisfaction.* Rotterdam: Rotterdam Institute for Business Economic Studies.

Wilkins, A. L., and W. G. Ouchi. 1983. Efficient cultures: Exploring the relationship between culture and organizational performance. *Administrative Science Quarterly* 28: 468–81.

Williamson, O. E. 1975. *Markets and hierarchies: Analysis and antitrust implications.* New York: Free Press.

Wirthlin Worldwide. 1996. *Asian values and commercial success.* wirthlin.com

Witkin, H. A. 1977. Theory in cross-cultural research: Its uses and risks. In *Basic problems in cross-cultural psychology,* ed. Y. H. Poortinga, 82–91. Amsterdam: Swets & Zeitlinger.

Witkin, H. A., and D. R. Goodenough. 1977. Field dependence and interpersonal behavior. *Psychological Bulletin* 84: 661–89.

Witte, E. 1973. *Organisation für Innovationsentscheidungen: Das Promotoren-Modell.* Göttingen, FRG: Verlag Otto Schwarz & Co.

Witte, E. 1977. Power and innovation: A two-center theory. *International Studies of Management and Organization* 7 (1): 47–70.

World Bank. 1972. *World Bank atlas.* Washington, DC: World Bank.

World Development Report. 2002. *Building institutions for markets.* New York: Oxford University Press.

World Investment Report. 2000. *Cross-border mergers and acquisitions and development.* New York: United Nations.

Worm, V. 1997. *Vikings and Mandarins: Sino-Scandinavian business cooperation in cross-cultural settings.* Copenhagen: Handelshøjskolens Forlag.

Wu, T. Y. 1980. *Roots of Chinese culture.* Singapore: Federal Publications.

Yan, W. F., and E. L. Gaier. 1994. Causal attributions for college success and failure: An Asian-American comparison. *Journal of Cross-Cultural Psychology* 25: 146–58.

Yelsma, P., and K. Athappilly. 1988. Marital satisfaction and communication practices: Comparisons among Indian and American couples. *Journal of Comparative Family Studies* 19: 37–54.

Yeung, I. Y. M., and R. L. Tung. 1996. *Achieving business success in Confucian societies: The importance of guanxi (connections).* New York: American Management Association.

Zürcher, E. 1993. Confucianism for development? Valedictory lecture, Leiden University.

Name Index

Kelen, B., 392*n*64
Kemmelmeier, M., 382*n*8
Kennedy, A. A., 282, 395*n*2
Kets de Vries, M., 393*n*37
Kettering, C. F., 144
Khandwalla, P. N., 396*n*31
Khomeini, A., 199
Kiernan, V. G., 397*n*32
Kieser, A., 393*n*15
Kim, U., 231, 392*n*52, 392*n*65, 392*n*66
Kitayama, S., 93, 382*n*28
Klidas, A. K., 394*n*49
Kluckhohn, F. R., 379*n*35
Knapen, B., 390*n*5
Kobi, J. M., 396*n*31
Koestenblatt, M., 385*n*33
Kohn, M. L., 380*n*14
Kolman, L., 379*n*4
Korotich, V., 103
Kraemer, A., 103, 383*n*39, 398*n*44
Kreisky, B., 389*n*45
Kubicek, H., 393*n*15
Kuhn, T. S., 370, 378*n*31, 398*n*5
Kühnen, U., 385*n*40
Kumpf, M., 384*n*23
Kuznets, S., 204

La Porta, R., 389*n*35
Laaksonen, O. J., 394*n*54
Lammers, C. J., 283, 351, 352, 386*n*66, 395*n*7, 397*n*30
Lasch, C., 385*n*30, 385*n*35
Laurel, S., 378*n*17
Laurent, A., 183, 249, 250, 392*n*10
Lawrence, P., 164, 387*n*2
Lazega, E., 278
Lee, S. Y., 390*n*17
Legge, V., 383*n*35
Levine, R., 154, 193, 382*n*24, 383*n*32, 386*n*75, 389*n*41, 390*n*9
Levinson, D. J., 22, 23, 160, 378*n*16, m387*n*85
Lévi-Strauss, C., 6, 377*n*6
Levitt, T., 349, 350
Lewin, K., 201, 394*n*63
Lewis, B., 233, 234, 392*n*55
Lewis, D., 341, 378*n*12, 397*n*18
Liang, S. M., 214, 215
Likert, R., 394*n*50
Lin, Y. T., 392*n*49
Linnaeus, C., 201
Locke, R., 277, 394*n*66
Lombardi, V., 385*n*30
Lopez-de-Silanes, F., 389*n*35
Lord, M. D., 397*n*24
Lorentz, J., 385*n*33
Lubbert, K., 384*n*23
Luk, C. L., 304, 396*n*25
Lynch, P. D., 397*n*24
Lynn, R., 125, 170, 171, 204, 205, 384*n*12
Lysgaard, S., 390*n*8

Machiavelli, N., 65, 266, 381*n*24, 393*n*41
Macmillan, I. C., 388*n*30
Magalhaes, R., 394*n*60
Mamman, A., 391*n*29
Mao, Z. D., 64, 106, 251, 252
March, J. G., 165, 387*n*3, 395*n*8
Marcuse, H., 201–2
Markus, H. R., 93, 382*n*28
Marx, K., 40, 65, 201
Maslow, A. H., 108, 188, 264, 383*n*45

Matsumoto, D., 94, 383*n*31
Mausner, B., 382*n*16, 393*n*38
Mayo, E., 395*n*16
Mbeki, T., 236
McClelland, D. C., 186–88, 264, 388*n*33, 388*n*34
McCrae, R. R., 94, 377*n*4, 383*n*30, 383*n*2, 387*n*6, 396*n*26
McGregor, D., 266, 271, 393*n*39, 394*n*50
McLuhan, M., 398*n*8
Mead, M., 22, 131, 158, 380*n*15, 383*n*1, 384*n*18, 398*n*3
Mencken, H. L., 397*n*10
Merritt, A. C., 26, 397*n*23
Merton, R. K., 295, 306, 395*n*20
Metcalf, H. C., 392*n*11
Mintzberg, H., 252–55, 393*n*17, 393*n*18, 393*n*20
Mithen, S., 378*n*11
Montaigne, M., 276, 394*n*62
Montesquieu, C. L., 19, 378*n*15
Moore, C. A., 392*n*53
Moore, K., 341, 378*n*12, 397*n*18
Morakul, S., 393*n*27
Moreno, A., 379*n*39, 381*n*29, 387*n*87, 395*n*12
Morier, J. J., 320, 321, 340, 359, 396*n*1
Mouritzen, P. E., 246, 392*n*5
Mouton, J. S., 271, 294, 385*n*43, 394*n*50, 395*n*19
Mueller, C. B., 391*n*30, 393*n*36
Mulder, M., 41, 379*n*1
Muller, H. J., 397*n*22
Munro, D., 392*n*50

Nauta, R., 386*n*70
Negandhi, A. R., 246, 392*n*2
Neuijen, B., 384*n*22, 395*n*1, 396*n*32
Newton, I., 201
Ng, S. H., 378*n*26
Nicholson, N., 397*n*20
Nietzsche, 201
Noorderhaven, N. G., 235, 236, 379*n*4, 388*n*32, 392*n*59, 392*n*60
Norenzayan, A., 383*n*32, 386*n*75, 389*n*41

Ohayv, D. D., 384*n*22, 384*n*28, 395*n*1, 396*n*32
Olsen, J. P., 395*n*8
Orwell, G., 64
Oswald, A. J., 388*n*32
Ouchi, W. G., 251, 252, 393*n*14, 395*n*4
Oyserman, D., 382*n*8

Pagès, M., 283, 359, 393*n*16, 395*n*5, 398*n*39
Parsons, T., 379*n*35
Pascal, B., 249, 276, 394*n*62
Payer, L., 178, 388*n*19
Pearson, K., 378*n*24
Pedersen, P., 361, 383*n*40, 393*n*30, 398*n*42
Pennay, M., 383*n*35
Perlmutter, H. V., 396*n*6
Pesonen, O., 384*n*23
Peters, T. J., 282, 283, 286, 293, 294, 299, 308, 395*n*2, 395*n*3, 396*n*33
Peterson, M. F., 276, 379*n*33, 379*n*36, 380*n*19, 381*n*4, 381*n*5, 384*n*64, 397*n*8
Peterson, R. M., 390*n*28
Pett, T. L., 390*n*28
Petterson, T., 386*n*73
Philbrick, K., 386*n*75, 389*n*41
Phillips, Å., 398*n*45
Phillips, D., 381*n*29, 383*n*43, 387*n*87
Piepers, J., 283
Pike, K. L., 397*n*8
Planchard, S. K., 388*n*23

Subject Index

(page numbers in **bold** refer to definitions)

About the Authors

 GEERT HOFSTEDE (born 1928) graduated from Delft Technical University as a mechanical engineer and spent ten years in Dutch industry in technical and management jobs. Studying part-time, he completed a doctorate in social psychology at Groningen University; his thesis was called *The Game of Budget Control.* He subsequently joined IBM Europe, where he founded and managed the Personnel Research department. His academic career started at IMD (Lausanne) and continued at INSEAD (Fontainebleau), the European Institute for Advanced Studies in Management (Brussels), the International Institute for Applied Systems Analysis (Laxenburg Castle, Austria), and Maastricht University, where he taught organizational anthropology and international management until his retirement in 1993. From 1980 to 1983 he made a brief return to industry as a director of human resources of Fasson Europe at Leiden. He was the cofounder and first director of the Institute for Research on Intercultural Cooperation (IRIC), which moved with him to Maastricht University and after his retirement moved again, to Tilburg University; it was closed in 2004. Geert is an extramural fellow of the CentER for Economic Research at Tilburg University. From 1993 to 2000 he was an honorary professor at the University of Hong Kong.

Geert's books have appeared in eighteen languages, and his articles have been published in social science and management journals around the world. For years he has been among the top one hundred most cited authors in the Social Science Citation Index, and from these one of few non-Americans. He is a fellow of the Academy of Management in the United States and holds honorary doctorates from universities in four European countries. He has lectured in Dutch, English, French, and German at universities, training institutes, and in-company programs worldwide and has served as a consultant or guest speaker to national and international business and government organizations, including the World Bank, the Organisation for Economic Co-operation and Development, the Asian Productivity Organization, and the Commission of the European Union.

 GERT JAN HOFSTEDE (born 1956), eldest son of Geert, went to school in the Netherlands and Switzerland and acquired French as his second language. He holds a degree in population biology from Wageningen University in the Netherlands. In 1984 he became a computer programmer. In 1986 he joined Wageningen University as an assistant professor. In 1992 he completed a Ph.D. in production planning from the same university; his thesis was called *Modesty in Modelling*. Currently he is an associate professor of information technology at the Social Sciences Group of Wageningen University.

In the 1980s and '90s Gert Jan mainly taught, wrote, and consulted in the area of data modeling. As the Web brought society closer to computer users and ideas of the virtual "international office of the future" circulated in his profession, he started using Geert's work for creating simulation games about cross-cultural communication. This resulted in the book *Exploring Culture: Exercises, Stories and Synthetic Cultures* (2002).

Currently Gert Jan publishes papers on transparency in international supply chains and organization networks. He is also involved in research on leadership in multinational settings and on using simulation gaming to study communication in interorganizational networks.

Gert Jan lectures and conducts simulation games in a variety of places and contexts. These include the "Afternoon Tea Game" at the London School of Economics, keynotes at conferences, and invited lectures at universities and for multinational companies.